Chicken Soup for the Soul Cookbook

101 Stories with Recipes from the Heart

Jack Canfield
Mark Victor Hansen
and
Diana von Welanetz Wentworth

Health Communications, Inc.
Deerfield Beach, Florida

We would like to acknowledge the following publishers and individuals for permission to reprint the following material. (Note: The stories that were penned anonymously, that are public domain or were written by Jack Canfield or Mark Victor Hansen are not included in this listing.

Mimi's Kitchen by Diana von Welanetz Wentworth. Reprinted by permission of Diana von Welanetz Wentworth. ©1995 Diana von Welanetz Wentworth.

Lauretta's "Down-Home" Chicken Noodles by Thea Alexander. Reprinted by permission of Thea Alexander. ©1995 Thea Alexander.

Memories of a Swedish Kitchen by Norma Brandel Gibbs. Reprinted by permission of Norma Brandel Gibbs. ©1995 Norma Brandel Gibbs.

A Mother's Advice by Chris Cavert. Reprinted by permission of Chris Cavert. ©1995 Chris Cavert.

Doomsday Cookies by Barbara Curtis. Reprinted by permission of Barbara Curtis. ©1995 Barbara Curtis.

(Continued on page 448)

Library of Congress Cataloging-in-Publication Data

Chicken soup for the soul cookbook: 101 stories with recipes from the
    heart /(compiled by) Jack Canfield, Mark Victor Hansen, and Diana von Welanetz
    Wentworth.
        p.   cm.
    Rev. ed. of: Chicken soup for the soul. ©1993.
    Includes index.
    ISBN 1-55874-354-5 (trade paper). — ISBN 1-55874-363-4 (hard cover)
    1. Parables. 2. Cookery. I. Canfield, Jack, 1944–
II. Hansen, Mark Victor. III. Von Welanetz Wentworth, Diana, 1941–. IV. Title: Chicken
soup for the soul.
BL624.C457   1995b   95-32259
158'.12—dc20   CIP

©1995 Jack Canfield, Mark Victor Hansen and Diana von Welanetz Wentworth
ISBN 1-55874-363-4 (hard cover) — ISBN 1-55874-354-5 (trade paper)

Publisher: Health Communications, Inc.
                3201 S.W. 15th Street
                Deerfield Beach, Florida 33442-8190

Cover re-design by Linda Golden; concept and cover illustration by Diana von Welanetz Wentworth

*To the great nurturing energy
that mothers are . . .
we dedicate this book to all mothers and
in particular our three mothers:*

Ellen Taylor Angelis (Jack Canfield)

Una Petersen Hansen (Mark Victor Hansen)

*Marguerite Rufi Schneider
(Diana von Welanetz Wentworth)*

*Our moms embodied the love of the kitchen
and food that lingers fondly in our
memories and on our tastebuds.*

Contents

Acknowledgments

Writing this cookbook was a labor of love and celebration from its beginning. We had a good deal of loving support and would like to thank the following people for their contributions.

Our spouses, Georgia, Patty and Ted.

Peter Vegso and Gary Seidler at Health Communications, for talking us into it in the first place. Thank you, too, for continuing to share the dream of a world full of love that works for everyone.

The Reading Is Fun program, for distributing *Chicken Soup* to teachers and thus their students nationwide. Our appreciation also for encouraging us in this unique endeavor.

Christine Belleris, Matthew Diener, and Marcia Ledwith, our brilliant editors at HCI for continually improving upon our manuscript. Marsha Donohoe, Mim Harrison, Erica Orloff and Christine Winter, for their superb proofreading. Ileana Wainwright for her splendid design, and to Lawna Oldfield for typesetting this book into the wee hours of the morning.

Patty Aubery, who took Diana's computer discs with all the separate stories and recipes and spun the manuscript into its final form.

Nancy Mitchell, who handled the multitude of permissions and authors' biographies that had to be obtained.

Wanda Pate, who typed many of the stories, poems and graces.

Kerrie Callaham, who tested many of the recipes and happily cleaned up around us.

Mary and Don Kelly, who enthusiastically read and listened to a reading of the manuscript in each stage of its development, encouraging us and applauding throughout. Bobbie Probstein, who gave valuable input on editing and kept us smiling with her silly faxes.

Julia Cameron, author of *The Artist's Way* (J. P. Tarcher) for a writing assignment that became Diana's stories in this book.

Susie Gross, Pat Rypinski, Kiki Leusebrink, Jodi Olsen, Louise Carrter, Marilyn Poliquin and the other ladies in Diana's painting class for their enthusiasm and ceaseless celebration.

Lexi von Welanetz and Christy and Kathy Wentworth for all the hugs provided to "Mom" and their "wicked step-monster." And to Mimi, Jack Schneider and Alice Wentworth, for just being.

Jack and Mark's Introduction

❧

When *Chicken Soup for the Soul: 101 Stories to Open the Heart and Rekindle the Spirit* was first published, it was often mistakenly placed in the cookbook section of bookstores. A lot of people (including many bookstore owners) thought it must be a book of chicken soup recipes.

Since we are both professional speakers, we give more than 100 presentations a year at hotels and conference centers. We usually forward our books and audio tapes to the presentation site a week before the actual event. Once we had to look for 33 boxes of *Chicken Soup for the Soul* that had been sent to the hotel prior to our arrival. When we arrived and checked with the concierge to pick up our books, the hotel staff was unable to find them. We looked in the luggage storage room, the receiving room, the head of catering's office and the conference services office, but the books were nowhere to be found. After checking with UPS, they confirmed that the books had indeed been delivered to the hotel and signed for by someone named George. Since no one named George worked in the catering office or receiving department, the hotel was at a loss to explain where the books went.

Because we knew the books had to be somewhere, we arranged to walk the entire hotel with a security person to look. After two hours of searching, we finally found them—in the kitchen in storage with all of the other boxes of canned soup. Since the boxes had CHICKEN SOUP stenciled on them, they had been carted to the kitchen by the uninformed delivery person!

After this happened a few more times, we wondered if the heavens were trying to tell us something. Our publisher then suggested that we put together a book of chicken soup recipes. After all, cookbooks were perennial bestsellers. *In the Kitchen with Rosie* was on the bestseller lists for over a year! With more than 2 million copies of *Chicken Soup for the Soul* in print it had commercial success written all over it. Our publisher said he had a distributor that could sell 200,000 copies of a *Chicken Soup for the Soul* cookbook. Still, the idea of compiling a recipe book didn't really appeal to either of us. We had not written and compiled *Chicken Soup for the Soul* for the purpose of making money. We had followed a heartfelt impulse to collect our most moving stories in a book so that they could be shared with more people than we could ever reach through our speeches.

Then our publisher suggested the possibility of a chicken soup recipe book by famous people—a celebrity cookbook with chicken as the main theme. That idea didn't inspire us, either. What do we know about cookbooks, recipes or food? For all we know, someone could submit a recipe that would taste awful, or worse. How would we know?

Luckily for you, Mark's wife Patty suggested we write a book with Diana von Welanetz Wentworth, a longtime friend who has coauthored six very successful cookbooks. We knew Diana through her work with the Inside Edge, a consciousness-raising breakfast group she founded 10 years ago in Beverly Hills, California. She had asked us to be on her advisory board with many other leaders of the human potential movement such as Norman Cousins, Barbara DeAngelis, Ken Blanchard, Susan Jeffers, Nathaniel Branden, Louise Hay and Dennis Weaver.

So we called Diana and invited her to a meeting, and then the fun began. Diana suggested that maybe a book of deeply touching and humorous stories centered around food and accompanied by a related recipe from the story's author would be worthwhile. We immediately agreed. After all, we reasoned, we ate three meals a day. Lots of life—good and bad, painful and joyful, life-affirming and life-negating—occurred around the family dinner table.

Over meals stories were told, days reviewed, wisdom imparted, lessons learned, traditions passed down, dreams discussed, grief shared and differences resolved. Boyfriends came home to meet the parents, engagements were announced, family reunions held, holidays celebrated and many deep memories created. In the family kitchen, three generations often shared cooking a single meal. Secret recipes were imparted with care, and complex feelings were discussed and explored. Cookies and milk consumed after school helped children and parents reconnect at the end of what may have been a day of painful experiences or wondrous discoveries. One's favorite food was often prepared as an act of love, special soups like only Grandma made were eaten in the safety of home and many bruised spirits were consoled with a cup of Mama's hot chocolate. And we can all relate to the memories evoked by the smell of baking bread, a roasting Thanksgiving turkey or a steaming apple pie.

Suddenly, the book had a focus we could get excited about. Once again we could create a book that would speak to and from the heart, deeply touching people of all ages, from all walks of life, to make them laugh at themselves and at life and inspire them to reach a little higher and express themselves more fully in the pursuit of happiness and self-fulfillment.

In addition to authors from *Chicken Soup for the Soul* and *A 2nd Helping of Chicken Soup for the Soul,* we compiled a list of famous cookbook authors, chefs and celebrities that we mutually knew, and sent them all letters requesting a story and a recipe for the book.

A month later the stories and recipes began to pour in. We were delightfully surprised by the depth of feeling, range of topics and wonderful recipes submitted. We received many more than we were able to use. At Diana's house we spent days reading these wonderful narratives from the heart and hearth and were treated to lunches prepared by Diana from the recipes that had been sent.

Diana committed to test all the recipes in the book and we were willing, satiated, guinea pigs.

Having read and edited all of these stories ourselves and having feasted on much of the food described herein, we know you are in for a real treat as you read this book and share both the stories and the meals with family and friends.

We are excited to share these stories and special foods with you; however, we must caution you. Just as you could not possibly eat or prepare all of the wonderful foods described in this book in one sitting, you should not try to read all of the stories in one sitting either. There is a great deal to digest in this book—both literally and figuratively. Take your time and savor each story as you would each meal. Don't hurry. Let this book be a constant companion and friend. Turn to it when you need a warm hug, some comfort, strength or inspiration.

Our hope is that after reading this book, you will be inspired to share your favorite stories about food and eating accompanied by a relevant recipe for our next book. All of us have experienced special moments in our lives that have affected us deeply. Each of us connects at the deepest level of our humanity when we share our stories. We look forward to hearing yours.

Much as any cook expectantly waits for reactions to his or her creation, we also look forward to hearing from you about your reaction to this book. We hope you love reading it as much as we have enjoyed cooking it up. Let us know what you think. And until then . . . *bon appétit!*

Diana's Introduction

*What you love is a sign from your higher
self of what you are to do.*

—Sanyana Roman

I have felt an urge to share food with others all my life. As a child,
I loved to dine in restaurants with my family. Not knowing my father
paid for the food, I thought waitresses were angels who, out of
loving kindness, took joy in bringing us anything we wanted. Once,
when someone asked what I wanted to be when I grew up, I said,
"Either a movie star or a waitress!" The two vocations had equal
glamour and prestige in my eyes. As the saying goes, be careful
what you wish for!

My favorite restaurant was Little Joe's, a large Italian restaurant in
downtown Los Angeles across from Chinatown. The real Little Joe,
a portly and kindly man, would stand near the kitchen door and
inspect the room. His quiet aura of satisfaction stirred within me an
indefinable sense of purpose which, combined with my mother's
love of cooking, seemed to propel me toward a career in food service. Much later in life, however, I discovered that my deep-seated
calling was never really toward the food itself.

In my early twenties I began five years of cooking classes with a
well-known French chef in Beverly Hills. Then, as a young mother
seeking diversion and self-expression, I taught classes in cooking
and entertaining in my own kitchen. There was such camaraderie

and celebration in those early classes that my late husband Paul and I created a career of teaching, writing cookbooks and hosting a television series. In that 20-year period, I did, indeed, become a combination waitress/movie star.

As so often happens when play becomes work, our original passion dimmed. Eventually, through soul-searching, Paul and I realized that our true passion over the years had been hosting—it was the communal feeling of gathering people together that we loved.

One of the intriguing results of Paul and my years of hosting activities is that two spiritual and high-minded men, Jack Canfield and Mark Victor Hansen, met, joined forces to write *Chicken Soup for the Soul* and made publishing history. When they telephoned one morning to tell me their publisher thought there should be a cookbook, and that I was the person they wanted to work with, my heart smiled and I said, "YES!"

The writing of this book has been an absolute joy. My six previous books have served as dress rehearsals for this one. In the deeply pleasurable process of my work herein, the soul-hunger of the five-year-old standing next to Little Joe has been immeasurably satisfied.

Grace

❧

Before you taste anything, recite a blessing.
—Rabbi Akiva

Saying grace at a meal blesses you, the meal and, most importantly, God. Grace provides that moment of remembrance, that isolated second of quiet and faithful thankfulness for our many gifts. The more we are thankful, the more we'll have to be thankful for . . .

Privately expressed grace is as good as windy, loud, pontificating orations. Regardless of whether anyone else says grace over their meal, it's a good habit to quietly close your eyes, however briefly, and commune openly with the Infinite.

A wise man taught me that after saying grace, one should rub one's hands together to generate what is called "healing energy," and then, with open hands at the outside perimeter of the food, energize the food. It is also good to ask your inner knowledge if your food is safe to eat. Your higher self will tell you what to avoid. Since learning this little process, I have never suffered from food poisoning. Whether it's intuition or superstition, it seems to work for me and I wholeheartedly recommend it to you. The more you train yourself and your higher self with questions about what is or isn't good for you to eat, the healthier, happier and better nourished you will become.

Throughout the book we have included graces and blessings from many different cultural and spiritual traditions. We invite you to use them to deepen your awareness of and appreciation for the abundance of food, friendship and love that flows into your life.

—*Mark Victor Hansen*

A Note About the Recipes

~

The recipes you'll find here are intertwined with cherished memories, and are from a time long before today's more enlightened approach to fat in the diet. We implore critics to embrace the notion that some foods may be so soulful that their love content outweighs their fat content! All the recipes herein have been tested, but none have been adjusted to make them more nutritionally correct.

1
Mom's
Kitchen

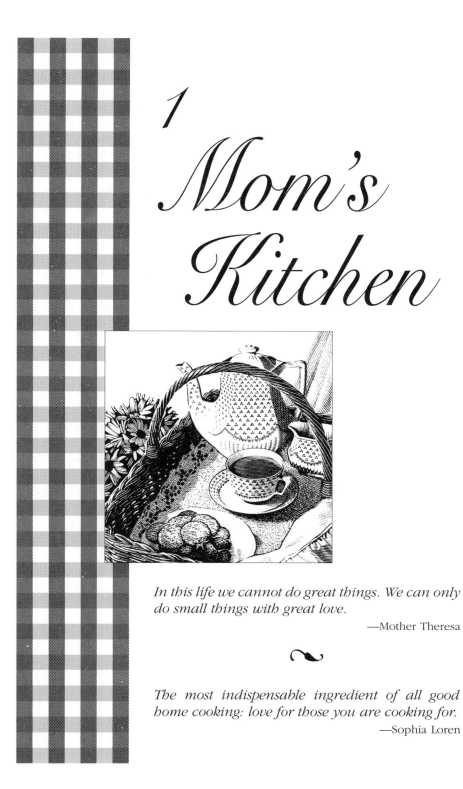

In this life we cannot do great things. We can only do small things with great love.

—Mother Theresa

The most indispensable ingredient of all good home cooking: love for those you are cooking for.

—Sophia Loren

Prayer
for Our Home

God of mercy,
God of Grace,
Be pleased to bless
This dwelling place.
May peace and kindly deeds
Be found;
May gratitude and love abound.

—Norma Woolbridge

Mimi's Kitchen

Diana von Welanetz Wentworth

One word frees us of all the weight and pain of life: that word is love.

—Sophocles

My mother loved being in the kitchen—it was her sanctuary. Like most families of the time, we ate the same foods over and over on a semi-regular rotation: spaghetti with tomato sauce, pot roast with mashed potatoes and gravy, tamale pie, fried chicken with mashed potatoes and gravy, roast leg of lamb with mint sauce and pan-roasted potatoes (lamb curry was for leftovers the next day), chicken-fried steak, pork chops with homemade apple sauce and potato pancakes, and Polynesian spare ribs with pineapple, garlic and soy sauce. But we didn't mind the repetition, for along with the spices and seasoning, Mimi added that one special ingredient that only a mother could add—love.

Our shared moments in Mimi's kitchen and the flavors and aromas of her repertoire of menus stay with me to this day. Mimi would tie an apron around me and ask me to shell and chop the walnuts for her fudge (still the best), which we packed in tins and kept in the antique French bombé chest in the dining room. My brother and I had permission to help ourselves.

But I was happiest when my mother made her spaghetti sauce for dinner. While the tangy tomato sauce simmered and splattered all over the white enamel stove-top, I would spoon a little into a saucer, open the freezer right next to the stove and place it on top of the frozen vegetables (lima beans—yuck!), close the door and wait restlessly until it was cool enough to taste. We still smile about the time I ate so much sauce there wasn't enough left for dinner! I was surprised I didn't get in trouble for it.

It was my job to hold the bundle of dried spaghetti and insert it into the huge kettle of boiling water (with a thin film of butter on top to prevent boiling over); I liked to watch the thin strands fall against the sides of the pot like a burst of the sun's rays.

A few years ago, Mimi gave me the greatest gift I can imagine. The family was gathered in the living room, but she and I were alone in the kitchen. She took my arm and said, "Come with me, I need to tell you something." She led me to her pantry where we could speak privately. Mimi took both my hands and looked into my eyes. "Listen to me carefully, darling girl. You have been the most wonderful daughter any mother could ask for. I am more proud of you than I can ever say. When I'm gone, I want you to promise me you won't spend one moment feeling guilty about me! I've spent years feeling guilty about my mother—about things I didn't think to do for her . . . words I didn't say. I always wished I had done more for her—I just didn't know how.

"I've decided I don't want you to *ever* feel guilty about me for even one moment. You have been perfect and you have nothing to feel guilty for. Promise me!"

I promised. That moment became one of the great treasures of my life—absolved by my mother of all my failings!

Mimi, my dear mother—her presence has permeated every moment of my life. She is 89 now. I dread losing her, not having her nearby or physically available. But her spirit will live on in all I do. And so will her Spaghetti Sauce and the very best Fudge in the world.

Mimi's Spaghetti Sauce

Makes 4 servings

❧

A humble sauce by today's standards. It is from a time before fresh herbs were available everywhere. Fresh herbs may be substituted throughout these recipes at a ratio of three parts fresh to one part dried.

1 large onion, chopped
¼ cup olive oil
4 cloves garlic, cut in
  thin slivers
1 (6-ounce) can tomato paste
1 (1-pound, 14-ounce) can
  crushed tomatoes
1½ teaspoons chili powder
½ teaspoon crumbled dried
  basil

¼ teaspoon crumbled dried
  thyme
1 whole bay leaf
Salt and pepper
Hot buttered spaghetti
  (prepared from 16 ounces
  dried), or other pasta of
  your choice
Freshly grated Parmesan
  for serving

1. In a large stainless steel or enamel skillet, sauté onion in olive oil until it is just beginning to brown. Add garlic and sauté briefly. Stir in remaining ingredients except pasta and Parmesan.

2. Simmer sauce slowly for 30 to 45 minutes or until it is the thickness you prefer. Season to taste with salt and pepper. Serve over hot buttered spaghetti and pass the Parmesan.

Mimi's Old-Fashioned Fudge

Makes 1 pound

Mimi was so talented that she could quadruple the recipe in a large pot at one time. We suggest you practice by making the recipe first as it is presented here. It gets easier once you know how.

Butter, for the pan
¾ cup milk
2 squares (2 ounces) Baker's
   unsweetened chocolate
1 cup sugar

1 tablespoon corn syrup
⅛ teaspoon salt
2 tablespoons butter
1½ teaspoons vanilla
½ cup broken walnuts

1. Grease an 8- or 9-inch square cake pan with butter. Combine milk and chocolate in a heavy 4-quart saucepan; stir over low heat until the chocolate is melted. Add sugar, corn syrup and salt; stir constantly over medium-high heat until all the sugar is dissolved. As soon as the mixture comes to a boil, stop stirring. Use a wet towel to remove any of the grains of sugar adhered to the inside of the pan. Lower the heat, insert a candy thermometer, and boil gently, without stirring, until the thermometer reaches 234°F (soft-ball stage).

2. Remove the pan from the heat and place it, without stirring, on a rack. Gently place the butter and vanilla on top of the mixture and let the fudge cool undisturbed until the thermometer registers 110°F. Remove the thermometer, add the broken walnuts, and begin beating the mixture with a wooden spoon. At the point when the fudge is just beginning to lose its gloss and thicken, quickly spread it into the prepared pan. Using a spatula, spread the mixture quickly into the corners, then leave it alone—if you fuss with it too much, the fudge will not be creamy.

3. Using a large knife dipped in hot water, score the fudge into 36 or more squares. Let cool completely, then cut again. Store in an airtight container. For best flavor and texture, store the fudge at room temperature for 24 hours before serving.

Lauretta's "Down-Home" Chicken Noodles

Thea Alexander

In my earliest memories of my mother, I see her in a cotton house dress—they were all flowered—and a bibbed apron, standing at the stove holding a baby in her left arm while her right arm stirred a huge pot of chicken with what I felt sure was the world's longest wooden spoon. She was always singing to the baby. I usually sang along.

As the rich aroma of boiling chicken broth filled the air, I curled my fingertips over the edge of the table, stood on my toes, and peeked over the top, hoping to find a soft piece or two of freshly cut noodle that hadn't made it to the pot. Reaching as far as my tiny arm would go, I stretched across the table, knowing that my hand sometimes found things that my body couldn't stretch tall enough for my eyes to see. My hand searched the floured table top where Mother had mixed (she never used a bowl), rolled out and cut the homemade noodles. Somehow a scrap or two was always left behind for each child in the room. She lived for children—her's and anybody else's.

Noodles must have been bigger in those days because as my tiny fingers clasped the soft scrap of uncooked noodle, it seemed to fill my whole hand. The first thing I saw as I looked up to view this, as yet unseen, treasure, was always my arm, covered elbow to wrist, with the flour that dusted off the table into my face. Unwilling to let go of the noodle, I brushed my face with my left hand to get the flour off my eyelashes. Finally, there was my prize! A plump, flour-dredged noodle left there especially for me.

In my 20s, when I left my home in California to visit Mom in LaPorte, Indiana, I could smell those delectable chicken noodles before I reached her door. In my 30s, when my husband, children, and I left our Pennsylvania home to visit Mom, there was fresh pie, homemade candy for the kids, and, of course, a pot of delicious chicken noodles and gravy waiting for me.

Now, there's a right and a wrong way to enjoy "Down-Home" Chicken Noodles. I, of course, passed on to my children the fine art of shaping a huge deep well in a generous size mound of mashed potatoes, then filling that well to overflowing with Mom's chicken noodles and gravy.

This is a good place to address formalities, so I'll confess that I know my sister is technically right. It's three words, chicken *and* noodles, not two words, chicken noodles. I, however, feel that I came half-way when I moved from the *one* word I used for this dish since I was old enough to claim a portion by saying, "Chickenoodles, please!"

In my 40s, when I called Mom to say I'd be visiting soon from my home in Arizona, the words had not left my mouth before she laughed, "I suppose you'll want some chicken noodles, right?" In my 50s, either Mom or my sister, Laura, still had homemade chicken noodles waiting for me when I traveled east. For 30 years, those noodles were always awaiting me at the homes of my sisters Marion and Emily in California when my travels carried me westward. They all knew!

When I was 55, I rushed to my mother's side. She had been paralyzed by a stroke that left her unable to speak, unable to swallow, and unable to move any part of her body except her lower left arm. The first thing I did was improvise a board containing commonly used words and phrases along with the alphabet. With her arm propped up, she could, then, point to or spell out a few words at a time before running out of energy.

Her first message was spelled out to my sister, Wilma, who is a bookkeeper. Dramatically demonstrating that imprisoned deep within this rapidly fading, almost totally incapable body, was our mother's exceptionally sharp, witty, capable mind, the message emerged letter by letter, "Quarterly taxes due. Please pay!"

Her first, and essentially last, message to me, "Love the kids for me. Sorry, no chicken noodles this time."

Lauretta's "Down-Home" Noodles (with or without chicken)
For 8 generous servings with leftovers

∾

NOODLES:
4 or 5 cups of flour   *1 teaspoon baking powder*
4 large (or 5 medium or small) eggs   *1 teaspoon salt*

1. On a large counter top, or in a big bowl, make a mound of the flour with a well in the center. Break the eggs into the flour well. Combine baking powder and salt, and mix into the eggs. Hand mix from the center outward, gradually incorporating, little by little, just enough of the flour to form a soft ball of dough. (Sift remaining flour to use when kneading the dough.)

2. On a lightly floured surface, knead dough until smooth and elastic in the following manner: Fold dough in half by bringing the far edge toward you. Press with the heels of your hands to push the top layer of dough away from you in a rolling motion. Give dough a quarter turn, and repeat for about 10 minutes or until smooth and elastic. Cover the dough and set it aside for 30 minutes to an hour.

3. At this point you can either run the dough through a pasta machine (or the pasta-forming attachment of your food processor) or, if you would like to roll it out, like Mom did, cut the dough in two equal pieces. On a large, flat surface dusted with flour, use a rolling pin to roll each dough ball into a 25-inch diameter circle until it is at least as thin as a dime, turning frequently to prevent

holes or sticking. Let dry on a lightly floured surface for 1 to 3 hours, depending on the dough's thickness and the outside humidity. (These circles can also be hung, like pants, across a clothes hanger lined with paper or foil.)

4. While the circles are still pliable, cut each in half. Lay one half on top of the other, dusting lightly with flour between each layer to prevent sticking. Cut in half across the middle, and lay one on top of the other, matching straight edges. Repeat this process until you have strips about 12 inches long by 1 to 1¼ inches wide. This will result in stacks of strips about 20 inches long by about 1 inch wide. Cut strips in half to create 10-inch strips for ease of handling. (For long noodles, roll sheets rather than making stacks for cutting.)

5. Cut strips into noodles ¼-inch wide. Every 5 to 6 cuts, separate noodles and toss gently, dusting lightly with flour if needed. (For freezing, use a little extra flour after cutting into noodles, and spread on a floured surface until still pliable but close to dry. Put in freezer bags, squeeze air out, and freeze. Will keep several months.)

Noodles may be cooked in vegetarian broth, broth made with 3 bouillon cubes per quart of water, or, like Mom did, in this homemade broth with chicken.

Chicken with Broth

~

2 whole chicken breasts plus 5 backs and necks with a little fat on them, for flavor (other chicken parts can be used instead of these, if desired)	*1 teaspoon salt* *Flour to thicken, if desired* *Salt and pepper to taste*

1. Place chicken in an 8-quart pot. Add salt and enough water to cover the chicken by an inch or two (about 6 quarts). Bring to a simmer, skim the foam from the top, and simmer again for 30

minutes, or until chicken is tender when pierced with a knife. Lift chicken into colander, using cake pan to catch the drippings, and let stand until cool enough to handle. Strip the meat from the bones, shredding into bite-size pieces, eliminating all fat, skin, gristle and bone. Pour drippings back into the soup pot.

2. Strain the broth into another container. Wash the pot, and return the broth to it. (If you like a more yellow broth, add just a drop or two of yellow food coloring.)

3. Bring broth to a full boil. Add a few noodles at a time, stirring constantly so they don't stick together. After noodles, add the chicken pieces. Boil just until the noodles are tender (10 to 15 minutes), tasting often for doneness. Season with salt and pepper to taste. (For a thicker gravy, shake 2 tablespoons flour with 4 tablespoons water in a jar to blend thoroughly. Stir the broth while gradually adding just enough of this flour mixture to reach the desired thickness.)

Memories of a Swedish Kitchen

Norma Brandel Gibbs

Let no one ever come to you without leaving better and happier.

— Mother Theresa

The earliest memory I have of my mother is in the kitchen with me hugging her around her knees. As a child it seemed to me she was always there. A Swedish immigrant, her kitchen was filled with the wonderful aromas of food from her homeland—delicious Swedish coffeecake and rolls scented with cardamom and sprinkled with sugar, and Swedish *limpa*, a coarse rye bread baked in a circle and cut in pie-shaped wedges, which was my father's favorite.

The aroma of bread fresh from the oven greeted my father each evening after his hard day of work as a carpenter. Daddy's face would light up as he came up the basement stairs. He'd head straight for the kitchen, give Mother a kiss and hug, and praise her for her baking. My brother and I would then run into the kitchen to be included in Daddy's big hug. He'd sweep us up in his arms and rub our cheeks with his beard. In the kitchen with my parents there was a warm, safe feeling that made me feel somehow that everything was all right, and perhaps that is why, to this day, the kitchen is where I feel most secure.

Nowadays, my happiest moments are spent concocting dishes to feed my family and friends. Even though I love to travel, when I've been gone awhile, I'm eager to invite people over and get back in the kitchen and cook. My freezer must be full and my pantry over-flowing—a carryover from the Depression that is essential to my sense of well-being. I take joy in serving unexpected guests at a moment's notice.

During the Depression, when we barely had enough to eat our-selves, I remember Mother serving sandwiches to a homeless man on our back stairs. She taught me that no matter how little we had, we could still share—and I have never forgotten that lesson. There is an old Swedish saying, "Five people were invited, ten showed up. Put more water in the soup and everybody enjoy!"

Here is a wonderful Old European recipe I would love to share with you. This is delicious served with a lemon gelatin salad con-taining grated cabbage, carrots and crushed pineapple.

Old European Casserole

Makes 8 servings

8 ounces wide egg noodles
2 tablespoons butter
1½ pounds ground chuck
3 (8-ounce) cans tomato sauce
¾ cup condensed beef
  bouillon
½ teaspoon crumbled dried
  oregano
½ teaspoon black pepper

1 cup cottage cheese
8 ounces cream cheese,
  softened
¼ cup sour cream
½ cup green onions, very
  finely sliced
1 tablespoon minced green
  pepper

1. Early in the day, cook the noodles as package directs; drain. Meanwhile, melt butter in a skillet and sauté the meat, mashing it with the back of a spoon, until browned. Stir in the tomato sauce, beef bouillon, oregano and black pepper. Remove from heat.

2. In a mixing bowl, combine cottage cheese, cream cheese, sour cream, green onions and green pepper.

3. In a buttered 3-quart casserole, spread half the noodles. Cover with the cheese mixture, the rest of the noodles, and top with the meat. Chill.

4. About an hour before serving, preheat oven to 375°F. Bake the casserole for 45 minutes or until bubbly.

A Mother's Advice

Chris Cavert

A food is not necessarily essential just because your child hates it.

—Katherine Whitehorn

It was just Mom and me from day one. At the time, some might have said I was unfortunate. Others may have said, "The boy needs a father." I don't remember feeling bad about the situation, and if I did, my mother must have helped me through it unharmed. Looking back on it now, I have come to realize how much she taught me and how much I have used her advice with the many youth I have worked with.

I recall one of the first episodes when I came to know the most important piece of advice she ever gave me. We had moved 30 miles north out of a big city to, at what that time was, "the country." I remember getting our first refrigerator that had a freezer. We could hardly wait to make ice cubes. Mom and I put the water in early and waited around, with a few progress checks, until the frigid change had occurred. What a treat it was for us. Mom never took for granted the simple things in life.

Once, I came home famished on a day my mom was trying her hand with new recipes. I smelled something different in the kitchen. But Mom wouldn't reveal the contents of the pot just yet. I could see her wonderful Date Bran Muffins rising in the oven, the kind she often made to accompany main dishes. (I think she made them as a backup just in case the main dish didn't turn out, because the muffins were always great.) I stood beside the stove for the moment of unveiling. Then when I saw it I thought, "What in the world?" while I said out loud, "What is it?" in a voice I'm sure my mother didn't appreciate. "Cauliflower Soup," she answered.

I was not going to have any part of that. "Is there anything else?" I asked.

"No," she replied calmly, "I want you to try it. If you don't like it, you don't have to eat it. But you're not going to say you don't like something if you've never tried it."

I remember crying and carrying on quite foolishly for what seemed to be a long time, but my mother never surrendered. My stomach must have won the battle over my brain because I slowly picked up the spoon, dipped it in the white lumpy substance, and took a sip. It was wonderful. (If any of my friends had been around, however, I would have said I hated it after all my fuss!)

To this day, my mother's Cauliflower Soup and Date Bran Muffins make up my favorite meal. Mom's advice about not liking something without trying it first is a rule I follow not only with food, but with job experiences, travel, friends, and my plans and dreams for the future. I'm not afraid to try new things because I know that, more often than not, I will enjoy them. Besides, there are always the Date Bran Muffins to back me up.

Cauliflower Soup

Makes 6 servings, or 8 cups

1 medium head cauliflower, broken into small pieces
½ stick (4 tablespoons) butter
⅔ cup finely chopped onions
2 tablespoons flour
2 cups chicken broth

2 cups light cream (half and half)
Salt to taste
½ teaspoon Worcestershire sauce
Grated Cheddar cheese
Fresh cut chives, for garnish

1. Cook cauliflower in boiling salted water to cover until just tender; drain and save the liquid. In a large pot, melt butter over low heat. Add onions and sauté until soft and transparent.

2. Stir in flour, cook for a minute or two, then blend in chicken broth. Cook over medium-high heat, stirring constantly, until the mixture comes to a boil. Add 1 cup of the reserved cauliflower liquid, the light cream, salt and Worcestershire sauce, then add reserved cauliflower.

3. Just before serving, heat soup to boiling; remove from heat and stir in grated Cheddar cheese to taste. Ladle into bowls, sprinkling more grated cheese and some fresh cut chives over the top of each serving.

Date Bran Muffins

Makes 18 muffins

1 cup bran	*2½ teaspoons baking soda*
1 stick (½ cup) butter	*2 cups All Bran cereal*
1½ cups sugar	*1 to 2 cups chopped,*
2 eggs	*pitted dates (depending*
2 cups buttermilk	*on how much you like dates)*
2½ cups flour	

1. Preheat oven to 400°F. In a small bowl, pour 1 cup boiling water over bran. In a large bowl, cream butter with sugar. Add eggs and blend well. Add buttermilk, the cooled bran mixture, the flour and baking soda, stirring until well blended. Fold in the All Bran cereal. Add chopped, pitted dates to the batter.

2. Line muffin tins with paper-lined foil cups; fill cups ⅔ full. Bake 15 to 20 minutes. Extra batter may be stored, covered, in the refrigerator for up to three weeks—use it to make only the number of muffins you need for each meal.

Doomsday Cookies

Barbara Curtis

One of my earliest memories is standing in the little yellow kitchen in our house in Pleasant Hill, watching my mom make cookies. Of course, she didn't make just regular old sugar cookies like our friends' moms. My mom made special oatmeal, walnut and chocolate chip cookies—and she made a lot of them.

My mom never believed in doing a little of something that took a lot of work. She would double or triple most recipes so that we would have plenty of leftovers. As a child of the Depression, Mom always liked lots of food around. There were generally cases of Spam, Vienna sausages and oil-packed tuna stacked in the garage, and the freezer was always jammed with carefully dated packages of leftovers. I used to think we could live forever just on the stuff stored in our garage.

I grew up in the 50s, during the height of the Cold War, a time defined by the threat of another world war and "the bomb." In those days, grade schools would show movies describing the ways one could save oneself during and after a nuclear bomb attack. We all practiced hiding under our desks during simulated bombing raids and heeded very seriously the practice of stockpiling food against a wartime shortage.

I remember seeing a movie during school that showed how to open a plastic-wrapped loaf of Wonder Bread that had been dusted with radiation fallout. You were supposed to carefully cut the bread wrapper with scissors and take the bread out without touching the wrapper. Somehow this would keep the bread uncontaminated. It's amazing to look back on those days and realize how ignorant we all were about the long-term effects of nuclear radiation.

So, my sister and I would "help" Mom make dozens of cookies. We must have asked her at some time how long the cookies would last. I remember clearly Mom saying, "Oh, we're making so many— they should last until Doomsday!" From that time on these cookies have been called Doomsdays. I didn't know what she meant (being too little to go to school yet) and asked when Doomsday was. I thought it was some kind of holiday you could plan for, like Christmas. Mom said that Doomsday was the time when our enemies would drop a bomb on us. Scary! But Mom never believed in lying to children. I remember feeling so confused. How could something as good as these cookies be related to a terrible scenario like Doomsday?

My life had been very simple up to this point—things were either good or bad, pleasant or uncomfortable, tasty or nasty. For me, Doomsday Cookies will always be associated with the first time I ever questioned my version of reality.

I took over the Doomsday Cookie baking chore early. Mom was always thrilled when my sister or I helped in the kitchen. I loved to bake, mainly because my family would heap so much praise on the baker. I think the original recipe for Doomsdays came from the box of Old-fashioned Quaker Oats, but over the years the recipe has been molded to meet my particular cravings at the time. During the 60s I switched from solid shortening to oil and added granola and various interesting flours and grains to the mix. There were a few years where nothing but whole wheat flour with rice polish and wheat germ would do. I experimented with carob chips, but you just can't beat the taste of chocolate.

Various people have wanted to commercialize the recipe, but the recipe is constantly changing—I don't think I have ever made them the same way twice. What each version has in common, however, is that so far none of them have lasted until Doomsday. Let's hope they never will.

Doomsday Cookies
Makes 2 dozen or so large cookies
❧

You can freeze this dough (which is unbelievably good as is!) for months if wrapped tightly. I generally make 8 times this recipe—you can never have too many Doomsdays!

1¼ cups canola oil
1¾ cups light or dark brown
  sugar (firmly packed)
1 egg
1 teaspoon vanilla extract
1 cup whole wheat flour
  (or ½ cup white flour and
  ½ cup whole wheat flour,
  if you prefer a lighter cookie)
½ teaspoon salt

½ teaspoon baking soda
½ teaspoon baking powder
6 ounces chocolate chips
½ cup coarsely chopped
  walnuts or pecans
½ cup unsweetened shredded
  coconut (optional)
3 cups old-fashioned oatmeal
  (see Note)

Note: *You may substitute 1½ cups granola for the oatmeal if desired, but reduce sugar and oil each by ¼ cup if using granola.*

1. Preheat oven to 350°F. In a large bowl, cream together canola (or other vegetable) oil, brown sugar and egg. Add vanilla extract, then flour, salt, baking soda and baking powder, and mix well. Then add chocolate chips, nuts, coconut and oatmeal. Combine these ingredients by hand or with a large wooden spoon—the mixture will feel very stiff. If necessary, add ¼ cup of warm water to moisten all ingredients.

2. Generously grease a baking sheet (or spray with no-stick cooking spray). Use a ⅓-cup measure to drop batter in mounds, leaving 1 to 2 inches between the mounds. Bake for 10 to 13 minutes until cookies feel done when pressed with a finger—do not overcook or try to brown them. Cool briefly, then use a metal spatula to remove from baking sheet. Serve warm or cool completely.

No Depression Cake

Dottie Walters

*You may be dead broke and that's a reality, but in spirit
you may be brimming over with optimism, joy and energy. The reality of your life may result from many outside
factors, none of which you can control. Your attitudes,
however, reflect the ways in which you evaluate what is
happening.*

—H. Stanley Judd

It was the depths of the Great Depression. Several families on our
block were receiving baskets of food from the welfare people. The
grownups kept talking about it—Depression. Hard times for everyone. But it was my birthday, and I was just a little girl.

My mother said there was no money for a gift or a cake. I sat for-
lornly on the front stoop and felt sorry for myself. Then Mama came
out and sat beside me, "Remember, there is always hope. Come and
see. I have a surprise inside for your birthday today!" I ran in to find
a cardboard box with a little bit of old blanket in it and snuggled
inside was the most adorable kitten with huge blue eyes. I immediately fell in love with it and called it "Fluffy."

Then I noticed a cake on the table with a candle on the top. "How
did you do it Mama?" I asked, my eyes all aglow. "The kitten came
from nice Mrs. Jones down the street. She gave us the recipe for this
No Depression Cake. When you bake it you can't be sad! Mrs. Jones
said we must think of what we have on hand, not what we don't
have. We can always create something new and useful if we think
positively. That is why it is called the No Depression Cake!"

Mama was right, I will never forget the happiness of that day. I took a piece of my birthday cake to Mrs. Jones to thank her.

I remembered the No Depression Cake when my own babies were little and my husband's dry cleaning business failed. To help him, I began a tiny advertising business on foot, pushing our children ahead of me on a broken-down baby stroller in the rural town of Baldwin Park, California.

Because there were no jobs, I asked the weekly newspaper to sell me space at a wholesale rate. Then I went out and resold the space in the form of a shopper's column to merchants. When the rocks in the road wore out my shoes, I cut cardboard and stuck it in, carrying extra pieces in my purse. Soon I had the house payment covered.

Then I spoke to service club luncheons to promote my advertising column. I had no car or baby sitter, so I made a deal with my neighbor: I traded baby sitting for the use of her car. Another helping of No Depression Cake! All of the businesses I run today, worldwide, began with that No Depression system.

As the children grew up we had many ups and downs. I especially remember one time when we had no money for groceries. I sat down with them and said, "Let's make a No Depression Cake! Let's see what we have on hand." My son said, "Mom, the avocado tree is full of fruit. I'll sell them today by the curb."

"There aren't enough oranges on our tree to sell," my daughter said. "I'll pick them, keep some for us, and take a bag to our neighbor to see if they'll trade for some of their great tasting plums!"

We all got busy. With the first avocado sales, I ran to the grocery store and bought day-old bread, a big bag of pinto beans, some brown sugar and powdered milk. Then I baked a No Depression Cake. We had a grand lunch, counting all of our blessings and thinking of all the good things we could do together.

By the end of the afternoon, our son had sold many more of the avocados, and I had a big bowl of beans bubbling and baking in the oven. Then the phone rang. It was one of my advertisers asking me to come over and pick up a big ad and a check.

Next time you're feeling low, try counting the good things you have on hand. Do with what you have. Bake up a positive-thinking No Depression Cake!

Here is the recipe. It is milkless, eggless and butterless. You can substitute other ingredients for any you don't have. The one thing this cake is *full* of, however, is memories of cheerfully creating with what is at hand and on hand—and never giving up hope.

No Depression Cake

Makes 12 to 15 servings and lots of smiles!

1 cup white sugar
2 cups firmly packed brown
  sugar
2 cups water
1 cup shortening
4 cups seedless raisins
  (if you have any)
1 teaspoon cinnamon
1 teaspoon nutmeg

½ teaspoon cloves
2 teaspoons salt
4 cups flour
2½ teaspoons baking powder
2 teaspoons baking soda
2 cups chopped nuts
  (if you have any)
Powdered sugar, to decorate

1. Preheat oven to 350°F. Grease a 13 x 9-inch baking pan. In a large saucepan, combine sugars, water, shortening, raisins, spices and salt. Boil together 3 minutes; cool.

2. Sift together flour, baking powder and baking soda; add to saucepan, along with nuts. Mix well and pour into prepared pan. Bake for 45 minutes.

3. Remove from oven. Let cool for 10 minutes, then turn onto a cake plate. When thoroughly cool sprinkle with a little powdered sugar, or mix lemon juice and grated lemon rind into powdered sugar for frosting.

> *Give us, O Lord, thankful hearts which never forget Your goodness to us. Give us, O Lord, grateful hearts, which do not waste time complaining.*
>
> —Saint Thomas Aquinas

The Fruitcake Recipe

Gino Sky

Happy and successful cooking doesn't rely only on know-how; it comes from the heart, makes great demands on the palate and needs enthusiasm and a deep love of food to bring it to life.

—Georges Blanc
from *Ma Cuisine des Saisons*

After my mother's 80th birthday, I decided that her famous fruitcake recipe should not be lost. I knew that she kept it in her head, or, as she explained, she "knew it by heart." She had a photographic memory, which allowed her to take a great deal of liberty with her baking and cooking. I realized that it wasn't going to be easy to extricate this recipe from her, but I had to try.

I took a few days off from work and drove from San Francisco to Pocatello, Idaho. It was a 12-hour trip, mostly through the high, semi-arid Nevada desert, but I had a mission and time passed quickly as I tried to remember as much as I could about my mother, a woman who had left home when she was six because she didn't like the way her own mother kept house.

It was nine in the evening when I arrived at our family home on the banks of the Porneuf River. As always, I found her in the kitchen. She had just finished baking six dozen cinnamon rolls for friends who were away in nursing homes. I hesitated about asking her, but pressed on with my mission. Paper and pencil ready, I asked for the fruitcake recipe. She looked at the wall clock. "That takes too long," she replied.

"I don't want the cake, Mom, just the recipe."

"It doesn't work unless I'm making the cake," she confessed, proudly.

"Just pretend you're making it," I suggested.

She looked at me as though my IQ had dropped 50 points on the way through Nevada. "By the time I figure it out, we could have them made." She looked at the clock. "You're always trying to take the easy way out, that's your problem."

"My problem," I said, "is that I really love your fruitcake, and I would like to have the recipe before you go off to your celestial fandango."

"It's called Heaven," she corrected.

"Well, a cattle ranch in Tahiti would be good enough for me," I replied.

"And cleaning up the heavenly stalls will be your reward if you don't change your ways," she countered, not missing a beat. She loved the challenge—it was a gauge of her mental acumen—or, as she preferred saying, *acuperson.*

The next thing I knew, she had two large mixing bowls on the counter, plus flour and sugar. "Hey, wait up," I yelled.

She opened a 15-ounce can of pineapple. "One of the secrets," she began, "is to candy your own pineapple."

"With canned pineapple?" I challenged, picking up the can after she had emptied its contents into a stainless steel pot.

"This is Idaho, not California," she replied, putting a hard bite on my adopted state. "We don't have fresh pineapple at the all-night liquor store."

"Nor do you have much of a liquor store."

"Praise the Lord . . ."

"Okay," I said, as I wrote down *canned pineapple,* "that's the first secret to your prize-winning fruitcake."

"Now, put one and one-half cups of sugar in with the pineapple and slowly cook off most of the juice. What's left you pour over the dried fruit."

The phone rang, and my mother told the caller that she had been commandeered by her son into making fruitcake. Therefore, she would probably be up most of the night. As soon as she hung up, she asked, "When was the last time you went to church?"

Playfully, I crossed two wooden spoons and held them in front of me. "I'm always in church," I answered, quoting Thoreau.

"You've been using that same excuse for years."

"It worked for him . . ."

"That's your problem," she answered, as she dumped four sticks of butter onto the counter, "you think God is everywhere so you don't have to look for Him." She shook her head. "You're going to end up in the lowest degree of heaven along with your Henry David and the Unitarians. They can't figure out whether God is a tree frog or a car muffler." Pleased with her analogy, she handed me the empty butter carton. "Stuff these really good dates into the box and that's how many I use."

Filling the box, I tried not to laugh. "What kind are they?" I asked.

"Oh, you know . . . those expensive kind . . . from California, that's the secret." That was the first lapse of word retrieval that I had experienced with her.

"*Medjool*," I mumbled, which I wrote down with *expensive* in parentheses.

"I was just testing you," she quickly added, as if she were covering for herself. She handed me a knife that resembled a small machete. "You can chop up the dates."

She then placed a medium pot of water on the stove and poured in a bag of shelled almonds. "These aren't necessary, I'm just trying to clean out the fridge." She shrugged. "Therefore, it's not important for you to know how many almonds to put in."

"Oh, the fridge needs cleaning?"

She nodded her head. "Everything needs cleaning."

I jotted down blanched almonds with question marks spread across the page. She dumped about two cups of walnuts onto the cutting board. As I chopped the nuts, I thought about how my mother had left home at six. I tried to imagine this little girl with her bags packed, standing among the hollyhocks as my grandmother tried to figure out what planet her daughter had come from. Even then my mother knew how she wanted the world to be—peaceful, serene, not one weed in sight, with every house painted at least once a year. That was for starters.

"You can look for the flour sifter," she said as the young girl dissolved into a beautiful 80-year-old woman. She had a trim figure, and her short, wavy hair was just beginning to turn gray. She talked about her last suitor, who had recently died from liver cancer.

"Was that the Fruit Man?" I questioned. She referred to her suitors by what they did or how they looked or behaved. There was the Train Man, the Lumbering Goose, Mahatma Gandhi, the Cadillac Man, the Fruit Man. She liked the Fruit Man more than the others, and sometimes she even called him her Peach Man.

"Oh, he had such wonderful fruit, and he would always bring me lots of everything." She paused, looked at me as though she were inspecting my appearance, and continued. "But he was way too old."

"How old was that?"

She hesitated and then gave me her best smile. "Eighty-one." She leaned closer. "But you know, there's a big difference between an 81-year-old man and an 80-year-old woman."

"It's obvious to me . . ."

She continued her story. "When he insisted that we get married, I prayed and prayed that something would make him change his mind. One month later he died from liver cancer."

She didn't even look up. Not even a smile. Her prayers had been answered. Just like that. *So there!* I moved to the other side of the kitchen. "Please Ms. . . . Sky, stop praying for me."

"Oh, you're too far gone," she replied, as she wiped up some spilled flour. She glanced at the clock. "Oh, my gracious! Look at the time. I'm beat. You're always starting projects like this when we should be in bed." She poured the candied pineapple into a copper pot of dried fruits that had been steaming on the stove. "Now, here's the real secret," she said, as she took out a jar of homemade orange marmalade. "This drives them wild."

"How many tricks do you need?" I questioned.

She emptied the contents of the jar into the fruit and then waved a wooden spoon as though it were a magic wand. "At my age, as many as possible." She began to sift the flour.

"What kind of flour is this?" I asked. Growing up, white flour was forbidden in our house.

She held up the package. "See, it's just flour."

"I can remember when you wouldn't even let us make paper paste from white flour."

"You never missed a day of school, either." Again, she waved the spoon as though I were being blessed by the Health Wizard. "Don't forget the yogurt we made."

"Right," I replied, "when all of my friends were eating ice cream, we could only have plain yogurt." I thumped my chest.

A finger was wagged, stopping on the third beat. "And they're all dying from mucous buildup and hardening of the arteries."

"Right on, Mom!"

She set the oven to 300 degrees and started mixing the soft butter into the brown sugar. I separated the egg yolks from the whites.

"As soon as we get these cakes in the oven, I'm going to trim your beard."

"I did that before I left."

"I'm wide awake," she continued.

"Perhaps you should go outside and trim your trees."

She laughed at the family joke. During an earlier visit, I mentioned that her trees looked as if they had been pruned by a professional. Proudly, she replied, "I did them, and you know, I had to get up at four in the morning because if the neighbors saw me on that rickety old ladder they'd want to help, and you know they don't know how to prune trees worth a darn."

Many a time I would catch her mowing the neighbors' lawns. She wouldn't even bother to ask for permission. With power mower, rakes and trimmers, she would move in like an invading Hun. "Here she comes!" they would joke. "It's like living in Poland." Her excuse was that she had to keep the neighborhood from going to ruin.

She started mixing the butter, brown sugar and egg yolks into the flour. "Just a little flour at a time," she instructed, and then she spun around and opened the fridge. "Oh, I forgot the cherries. Where are they?" She got down on her knees and looked into the refrigerator. "Look at this mess." The fridge was full. She kept another equally loaded one in the basement. I called them the Dueling Refrigerators.

"What about all those starving people in China?" I asked smugly.

"You just wait. When the millennium comes you'll be begging me to let you in."

"Kind of like Aesop's fable of the grasshopper and the ants, right?"

"It won't be like the Disney version, that's for darn sure," she replied. Once again came the wagging finger. You *do* know the difference."

"Yes, Mom," I answered. "With Disney the grasshopper plays first violin for the Boston Pops, saves his money, and ends up as a sex slave for a herd of African Ant Goddesses. But in Aesop's fable, he's a lazy bum who gets busted for being a street musician and winds up in prison marrying Leona Helmsley."

She nodded her head in approval. "Now that's punishment!"

She located the cherries in the back of the fridge and threw them to me. Still on her knees, she took a swipe at the vinyl floor. "Look at this floor!"

The linoleum was more than 25 years old and looked brand-new. "Right," I said, "it's frightful."

From the cupboard, she took out a bottle of lemon extract and held it in the palm of her hand. "Now this is the real secret," she said. "It drives them wild." She emptied the contents into the batter. "And the more the better." She turned the mixing bowl over to me and started lining the bread pans with waxed paper. "I've never liked fruitcake," she confessed, "but everyone seems to love mine."

I stared in amazement. My mother the Venusian. She had grown up in southern Utah with hardly enough to eat, a father who drank too much, and only God knows what else. The youngest of seven children, she left home when she was six years old, and at 27 married my father, the traveling salesman—a fly-fishing junkie who left for good when I was eight. If she missed him, she never let on. It was sort of like, "Well, where did he go this time?" She had her kids, and it was time to get on with her life. It was just like the fruit-cakes—she made them for some higher purpose, and only she and the fruitcake gods knew what that was about. I thought of Bob

Dylan's line, *"She's an artist, she don't look back."*

With everything mixed together, I poured the batter into the pans, put them in the oven, and started licking the bowl. It was past midnight and in six hours she would be working at the temple in Idaho Falls, 50 miles away. I was almost envious. Not about where she was going but the way she did everything. It was her special way, and it always made me feel as if I were partaking from a sacred bowl filled with life's real ingredients.

After we cleaned the kitchen, she asked if I would take the cakes out at 1:30 A.M. She admitted that she was tired. So was I, but I was also feeling victorious. She tugged at my beard. "Not only do you have the fruitcake recipe, but you have four cakes to take back with you."

I squeezed her hands and kissed her forehead. "I feel like I've been to the sacred mountain."

"I hope you pulled some weeds on the way up." Again, the finger wagged.

"I weeded on the way up and planted flowers on the way down. Just like you said."

"Now, that's my son . . ."

I sat with the cakes as though they were my children—the fruitcake kids with 80 years of life in them. I was determined to protect them, no matter what. Someday my daughters might ask for the recipe and perhaps, just like Grandma Linda, I could do it from the heart.

That was the secret.

Grandma Linda's Fruitcake

Makes 2 loaves

1 (20-ounce) can pineapple
  chunks and juice
1½ cups white sugar
1 pound dates, cut up
1 pound candied fruit mix
2 cups walnuts, cut medium-fine
1 (15-ounce) box golden raisins
13 ounces candied cherries
1 pound (4 sticks) butter (or 2
  sticks butter, 2 sticks margarine)

2 cups white sugar
6 eggs
5 cups white flour
1 teaspoon salt
1 teaspoon baking soda
1 teaspoon baking powder
1 ounce lemon extract
8 ounces orange marmalade
  (optional—see Note)

Note: *Mother has left this out of the new recipe, although, two years ago, it was "one of the secrets." If candied fruit mix isn't available, use fresh, finely cut apples or use two cans of pineapple instead of one.*

1. Preheat oven to 300° F. Line two 9 x 5-inch loaf pans with wax paper. Place pineapple chunks and juice in a 1½-quart saucepan. Cook slowly with 1½ cups of white sugar. When the pineapple syrup thickens, pour it over the dates, candied fruit, walnuts, raisins and candied cherries. (Save some cherries and walnuts to place on top of the cakes before baking.)

2. Sift together flour, baking soda, baking powder and salt. Cream together the butter and 2 cups sugar. Separate the eggs (placing the whites in a grease-free bowl to be beaten later) and add the beaten egg yolks, the flour and the lemon extract (as well as the orange marmalade if desired).

3. Combine the batter and the fruit mixture and mix well. Beat the egg whites just until they hold stiff peaks when the beater is lifted and fold them into the mixture.

4. Pour the batter into the prepared pans. Decorate the tops with the reserved walnuts and cherries. Place in the oven with a shallow pan of water under the loaves on the lower rack. Bake for 1½ hours. (Check after 1 hour, as ovens and climate vary.)

Mary Ann's Maryland Crab

Anne Cooper Ready

Some of my favorite memories of home are of how I spent my summer vacations on the Maryland shore in a coastal town called Easton. My family moved often. Where we didn't live, we visited . . . and tasted. My father's philosophy was, "Try it, you might like it."

Crabs are to Maryland's Eastern Shore what clams are to New England, conch is to the Bahamas, oysters are to New Orleans, and prime rib is to Kansas City. We liked Maryland and Blue Crab the best! They call it that for the color of the male crab claws before you steam 'em. And crabbing is a local pastime—done in a most unconventional way.

You can crab barefoot from a dock, and all it takes is a raw chicken neck tied on the end of a string lowered into the local waters. When the crabs swim up to it, grab on and begin to nibble, you gently pull the string up out of the water so you can scoop them into your fish net before they let go. Then you drop them into a bucket of water or a bushel basket to clamor and claw till it's time to steam them.

Beginning at daybreak on those long, lazy summer vacation days, a couple of chicken necks would last a whole morning and I could catch a mess of crabs by lunchtime. My mother would steam them in a pot of boiling, seasoned water, and when you couldn't hear them complaining anymore, they were ready. When the lid came off, the crabs were bright red and steaming, ready to crack open and eat on a newspaper-covered picnic table and then wash down with mugs of beer. Everyone had a favorite way of eating those fresh steamed crabs. Some would shell a whole pile of crab meat and dip a fork-full in melted butter. Others would dip every bite with their fingers as soon as they pulled it, warm and succulent, from the shell.

What we couldn't eat we saved for Mom's best recipes, culled from the locals and tested in her kitchen. The Crab Claw, a local restaurant with a dock for boats (even for carry-out), couldn't beat Mary Ann Cooper's Crab Imperial or Crab Dip.

But a mother's work is never done. Early on the summer days, when I worked the breakfast shift, she woke me up, made me breakfast, and before the first customer arrived got me to the Crab Claw in an apron she'd freshly laundered, bleached, starched and ironed the day before. Sometimes, she'd even bring my little brothers and sisters for lunch. They were my best customers.

When I left for California, she sent along a decoupage recipe box filled with her favorite recipes. Here are two of the best.

Mothering for her is a labor of love. She taught us the meaning of the old saying, "Give them fish and they'll eat once, teach them to fish (or cook) and they'll eat for a lifetime." To this day, Mary Ann is still taste-testing recipes on Papa Joe. From her kitchen to yours, with love. Try it, you might like it!

Mary Ann's Crab Dip

Makes 6 to 8 servings

❧

16 ounces cream cheese
1 cup sour cream
1 cup grated Cheddar cheese,
  divided
¼ cup mayonnaise
2 to 3 teaspoons Worcestershire
  sauce
1 teaspoon Dijon mustard

½ teaspoon lemon juice
2 to 3 shakes garlic salt
Salt and pepper to taste
1 pound fresh or canned crab
  meat, picked over to remove
  any cartilage or shell (see Note)
Crackers or potato chips
  for dipping

Note: *If fresh crab is unavailable, use expensive canned crab and it will still taste almost as good.*

1. Preheat oven to 350°F. In the bowl of an electric mixer, combine cream cheese, sour cream, ½ cup of the grated Cheddar, mayonnaise, Worcestershire sauce, mustard, lemon juice and garlic salt. Salt and pepper to taste. Mix well. Stir in crab meat and transfer to a baking dish.

2. Sprinkle the remaining ½ cup grated Cheddar over the top. Bake for 30 to 40 minutes, until hot and bubbly. Serve with sturdy crackers or potato chips for dipping.

Mary Ann's Crab Imperial

Makes 6 servings

༄

*1 pound fresh or canned
crab meat*
½ cup mayonnaise
*3 to 4 tablespoons Worcestershire
sauce, or to taste*
*½ jar (2 ounces) chopped
pimento*

⅛ teaspoon dry mustard
*¼ to ½ cup light cream
(half and half)*
Salt and pepper to taste
Paprika

1. Preheat oven to 400°F. In a mixing bowl, combine crab meat, mayonnaise, Worcestershire sauce, pimento and dry mustard. Mix well. Stir in enough light cream for a sauce consistency. Season to taste with salt and pepper.

2. Spoon the crab and sauce into individual dishes or shells and sprinkle the tops lightly with paprika. Bake for 10 to 15 minutes until bubbly. Serve as a first course.

The Butcher's Chicken and Mom's Irish Potatoes

Kathy Fellows

Growing up in the 1940s, one of my favorite "chores" was walking to the local butcher shop to pick up wrapped packages for our family's evening meal. I was 10 years old, and it wasn't until later that I realized just how important the butcher's package was to my mother. We were very poor at the time because my father had died and my mother's meager salary had to stretch for six people. The butcher would save the chicken wings, second joints and gizzards for us—parts his customers usually had him remove from their meat order. I've never forgotten the butcher's kindness.

My mother invented creative ways to cook the giblets to make broth, and cook the wings and second joints for our dinners. Sometimes the broth served as a base for a chicken stew dish served over rice, and sometimes the wings and second joints were served on a platter. In any case, it was one of my favorite meals growing up.

I never noticed at the time that when mother served the meal at the dinner table, she hardly ever ate any of the food. Dinner was the time she asked each of us how our day went, so we were too busy talking about ourselves to notice how little Mom was eating. It was only when I had a family of my own that I understood how by not eating the butcher's chicken she could stretch the contents of his small package to feed all five of her children.

I also began to understand why, at the end of grace before our meals, Mother would always add, "And, thank you, God, for the butcher's chicken. Amen."

Mom's Irish Potatoes became a family tradition when my three brothers entered their teen years. I watched them consume incredible amounts of food in record time. My brothers would come home from football practice, a track meet or their after-school jobs ravenously hungry. The bigger they got, the bigger their appetites, and the more potatoes Mom would add to the pot.

Eventually the recipe expanded into the one below. To this day this is our favorite dish and an absolute requirement at all family get-togethers. There isn't a Thanksgiving, Christmas, Easter, or family backyard barbecue planned without someone asking the question, "Who's cooking Grandma's Irish Potatoes?"

Chicken Giblets in Broth

Chicken gizzards, livers
and hearts
1 small onion, diced

Salt and pepper
Cooked rice for serving,
or 1 cup raw rice

1. In a medium saucepan, place chicken giblets in cold water to cover by 1 inch. Add onion, salt and pepper. Bring to a boil, skimming off any foam that rises to the surface. Cover and simmer slowly for 1 hour, removing the liver after 15 or 20 minutes when it is no longer pink.

2. Remove giblets, chop and return to the broth. Serve over cooked rice, or add 1 cup raw rice to broth and simmer until the rice is cooked.

The Butcher's Poached Chicken

Chicken wings and second
   joints
Salt and pepper
1 bay leaf

A sprig of parsley or a pinch
   of crumbled dried thyme
A strip of orange or lemon peel

1. In a large saucepan, cover wings and second joints with cold water. Add remaining ingredients.

2. Poach the chicken gently for about 40 minutes or until done, regulating the heat so that hardly a bubble breaks the surface. Serve with vegetables or your choice of sauce.

Mom's Irish Potatoes a.k.a. Grandma's Irish Potatoes

Makes 16 servings

18 to 20 potatoes, peeled
1 onion
3 stalks celery
1 green bell pepper
¼ pound butter or
   margarine
2 (10¾-ounce) cans cream
   of chicken soup

1 cup milk
½ to ¾ pound grated Tillamook
   Cheddar cheese
1 (4-ounce) jar diced pimento
Salt and pepper to taste

1. In a very large pot, boil the potatoes until tender; drain, cool, then dice. Place cubed potatoes in a casserole large enough to hold them below the rim.

2. Finely chop onion, celery and bell pepper. In a skillet, melt butter or margarine and sauté vegetables until the onion is transparent. Add cream of chicken soup and milk; bring to a boil, stirring occasionally. Add cheese and heat, stirring just until cheese is melted. Stir in diced pimento.

3. Pour sauce over diced potatoes. Sprinkle with salt and pepper to taste. Bake immediately at 350°F for 20 to 25 minutes, or prepare ahead and bake chilled casserole for 40 to 45 minutes.

Rhubarb Pie

Bettie B. Youngs

*"Who inu hell," I said to myself, "wants to try to make
pies like Mother makes when it's so much simpler to let
Mother make um inu first place?"*

—Hariette Arnow

Our sprawling 40-acre farm was ideal for a large family with six
children and the many pets who considered themselves one of us.
A half-acre garden grew to the east of our house; and to the right
of it, grew the rhubarb patch. The garden received mixed reviews.
It produced fresh vegetables, but it also needed constant attention
and occasionally we children had to "serve time" in the garden—for
an injustice committed or just to keep idle hands busy hoeing and
pulling weeds. The rhubarb patch, however, was another story.

First of all, the rhubarb patch never required weeding. So determined to dominate this little plot of soil, the rhubarb sprouted forth
each and every spring, and pushed aside and crowded out any
weed that dared get in its way. Second, with enormous rich green
leaves and tall, hearty stalks painted in various hues of pink, green
and purple, the rhubarb plants were quite a regal sight.

Aside from being willful and majestic, the plants were also mys-
terious and enchanting. From dusk to dawn, the heavily veined
leaves of mature plants drooped themselves over the tightly coiled
baby leaves as though to protect them and to allow the tiny leaves
to suckle droplets of dripping dew. But as planet earth made its
daily rotation to face the sun, the larger leaves abandoned their
caretaking roles and turned their long necks skyward to bask in the

glorious morning light. Now exposed, the smaller leaves were awakened—slowly they unfolded their palms and drank in the rays, nourishing the fruit below.

Beauty deceived their taste! Saying that a young, tender stalk of raw rhubarb tastes significantly better than a mature stalk, while true, isn't saying much. And as children we used to say, "Last one to the house (or barn, mailbox, shed, school bus, garden, you name it) has to eat an entire stalk of rhubarb!" With my brothers and sisters, being a "rotten egg" for finishing last wasn't bad enough; having to eat a stalk of tart, acidic rhubarb was far and away more of an incentive to join in the game and to cooperate competitively!

In the spring and summer my mother performed the seasonal ritual of harvesting the young tender stalks. The lovely vision of my mother gathering the rhubarb took second place only to how she transformed the tart stalk into scrumptious pies and puddings and other desserts for our family. Those that weren't immediately used were frozen in plastic bags for use in the late fall and winter months.

Our family loved Mother's rhubarb desserts—our favorite was rhubarb pie. This is not to say it was the only pie we enjoyed, goodness knows there were many—cherry, blueberry, mulberry, blackberry, strawberry, peach, apple and pecan pies—all made by Mother, yet none had the following of her rhubarb pie. Perhaps this was because the rhubarb pie as Mother made it was absolutely delicious—and because we knew and appreciated the time, toil and love involved.

Sometimes we helped her make rhubarb-strawberry pudding or rhubarb custard, but making the pastry for rhubarb pie and filling it was our most favorite thing to do. Mother showed us how to wash the long stalks and carefully cut them into cubes.

Meticulously, our mother taught us how to accurately measure out the flour and butter needed for the pie crust. Patiently, she helped us learn how to roll out the pastry larger than the pie dish, cut away the outer strip of pastry, and lay it on the dampened rim.

At this point the fruit mixture was packed into the pie dish, mounded high in the middle, and covered with a "pastry lid" and trimmed. As a finishing touch, Mother decorated the pie crust by pinching the dough on the rim into small, even scallops. She let each child use a knife to make one small slit in the pastry top to allow steam to escape during cooking.

Brrring! The timer announced the magical moment we'd all been waiting for and we all gathered around. The fruits of our labor were about to be realized. Breathlessly we watched as mother removed our masterpiece from the oven and placed it on the table. Seeing it in all it's golden majesty and inhaling its warm, sweet aroma gave each one of us a great sense of accomplishment. For small children, the feeling of mastery and satisfaction was nothing less than what Michelangelo must have experienced when at last he completed his paintings on the ceiling of the Sistine Chapel. Our pie was perfect. We need only look at our mother's smiling face for confirmation.

Perhaps because rhubarb pie was always present for holidays, birthdays and other special events, it became synonymous with joy and festivity. Whatever the reason, rhubarb pie was ever-popular, and grew in stature and importance as time went by. Soon we all left home and began lives of our own. But we returned to the family nest to share our joys, woes—and rhubarb pie. Later when we brought home spouses and children of our own, a rhubarb pie was always prepared for our homecoming. And when we were ready to leave, accompanying hugs, wet eyes and third-time goodbyes, nestled beside a care basket of homemade breads, jams and *kringlas*, sat a rhubarb pie.

It is hard, though not impossible, to find rhubarb in grocery stores. It can't be found in all restaurants, but in some it will be on the menu. Maybe you will want to remedy this as I have: I planted my own rhubarb patch. And every time I go out to pick from it, I wear my mother's flowered apron.

Though I can make a mean rhubarb pie, it just doesn't quite taste like the one that my mother serves. So when I make rhubarb pie, I call her just to tell her how much I enjoyed all those rhubarb pies and how wonderful it is to be her daughter.

Rhubarb Pie

PIE FILLING:
3 cups young rhubarb
Finely grated rind of 1 orange
1 tablespoon cornstarch
1 cup sugar

1 teaspoon ground cinnamon
  or 2 tablespoons chopped
  candied ginger
1 tablespoon butter
1 egg

PASTRY FOR A TWO-CRUST PIE:
1½ cups all-purpose flour
6 tablespoons unsalted butter
Ice water
½ teaspoon salt

Milk, to brush pastry
Sugar, to sprinkle over the
  crust

1. Wash and cut rhubarb into ½-inch cubes. In a large bowl, mix orange rind, corn starch, sugar, cinnamon (or ginger), butter and egg. Add the rhubarb and mix; set aside.

2. To make pastry, place flour with butter in a mixing bowl. Using 2 knives or a pastry cutter, cut the butter into the flour until it looks like coarse meal. Sprinkle ice water as needed over the mixture, while tossing the mixture with a fork until it is just damp enough to hold together. Gently shape into 2 balls, one slightly larger than the other, on a lightly floured pastry cloth, then flatten into circular patties about 1 inch thick. Refrigerate for at least 15 minutes.

3. Preheat oven to 450°F. Roll out the larger pastry patty to a size larger than the pie dish and fit it into the dish. Pack the rhubarb mixture into the pie dish, mounding it high in the middle. Roll out the smaller patty and lay it as a pastry lid on top, trim, and flute the rim into scallops. Make a small slit in the pastry top to allow steam to escape during cooking, and brush all over with milk.

4. Place the pie dish on a baking sheet and bake for 10 minutes at 450°F. Reduce heat to 375°F and bake for 30 minutes more. Sprinkle pie crust with a little sugar and allow it to cool slightly before serving.

The Seat at the Head of the Table

Florence Littauer

We all have hometown appetites. Every other person is a bundle of longing for the simplicities of good taste once enjoyed on the farm or in the hometown (he or she) left behind.

—Clementine Paddleford

I grew up in the Depression in three rooms behind my father's store in Haverhill, Massachusetts. Times were simple and our food even simpler. The word "gourmet" had not yet entered common parlance, and our total "pasta experience" was heating up a can of Franco-American Spaghetti.

My mother's favorite meal was what she called New England Boiled Dinner—throw everything in a pot and boil it. Our only seasonings were salt and pepper. We'd never heard of sage, let alone saffron.

When I married Fred, a restaurant manager in New York, I had much to learn. "I hope you don't cook like your mother," he said on our honeymoon. "How else?" I thought to myself. Fred put me on an instant training program. When I served him hot dogs and baked beans on our first Saturday night, as I'd been brought up to do, he exclaimed, "Hot dogs belong in Yankee Stadium. I don't ever want to be served these beans again."

I left my New England heritage behind and quickly moved from tapioca pudding to Grand Marnier soufflés. When my mother visited, I would prepare unusual gourmet treats, feeling it was my job to expand her culinary horizons.

During my mother's last years at a retirement hotel, she seemed to enjoy the bland food and simple surroundings. One day I asked her, "How do you like it here?" She replied, "This is the nicest place I have ever lived." I could hardly believe it! "Why?" I asked. "The first day I arrived," she said proudly, "they assigned me my seat in the dining room. They put me at the head of the table and gave me the only chair with arms on it."

Suddenly I realized that I had never put her at the head of the table or even cooked what she enjoyed. The next time I returned from a speaking trip I invited my mother over for the evening. I prepared a New England Boiled Dinner, seated her at the head of the table and gave her the only chair with arms on it.

While I was on my next trip, my mother passed away peacefully in the night and I realized I'd spent my life trying to train my mother instead of pleasing her. She had simple tastes and asked for so little, but it took me until the last month of her life to put her at the head of the table and give her the only chair with arms on it.

> *If you wish to be a blessing*
> *And do all that you are able,*
> *Find someone in need of a meal*
> *And seat them at the head of the table.*

Our Favorite New England Boiled Dinner

Makes 8 servings

❧

4 pounds corned beef brisket,
  flat cut
10 small red potatoes
6 medium carrots
2 turnips, 2 to 3 inches in
  diameter

1 large onion
1 medium green cabbage
8 small beets, about 1 inch
  in diameter
Butter
Mustard

1. Four hours before serving, bring a large pot of water to a boil over medium-high heat. Rinse corned beef. (In the package may be a separate packet of spices; add them to the water along with the corned beef.) Bring water to a boil, then lower heat and simmer, covered, for about three hours, or 45 minutes per pound.

2. While the meat is cooking, peel potatoes, carrots and turnips. Cut carrots into 2-inch-long pieces. If the top part of the carrot is especially thick, cut those pieces in half lengthwise so that their thickness is similar to the pieces from the thinner end. Cut the turnips into quarters. Peel 1 large onion, leaving enough of the root section to hold the onion together. Cut the onion in quarters. Forty-five minutes before serving add the vegetables to the corned beef. Continue to simmer.

3. Cut cabbage into quarters, starting at the root end and cutting straight through to the other side. Cut each piece in half lengthwise so that you have 8 even-sized wedge-shaped pieces. Fifteen minutes before serving, place the cabbage pieces on top of the vegetables and corned beef. Cover and continue to cook for 15 minutes.

4. Meanwhile, boil beets separately—their deep color would turn everything else red. Bring a medium pot of water to a boil. Add beets and continue to boil for 15 minutes. Remove from the heat and drain; add cool water. One by one remove the beets and squeeze them.

They will pop right out of their skins. Arrange them on the platter with the other vegetables and top with thin slices of butter.

5. To serve, remove cabbage and vegetables and arrange on a platter. Top with thin slices of butter. Remove corned beef and place on a cutting board. Cut into ¼-inch-thick slices and place on platter. Pass the platter at the table, and set out mustard for the corned beef.

Tapioca Cream Dessert
Makes 8 servings

2 eggs
1 quart milk
⅓ cup quick-cooking tapioca
½ cup sugar

¼ teaspoon salt
1 teaspoon vanilla
Cherries or strawberries,
  to garnish

1. Separate eggs, placing yolks in a medium saucepan and the whites in a medium mixing bowl. Lightly beat the yolks with 2 tablespoons of the milk. Add tapioca, sugar, salt and rest of milk. Bring the mixture just to a boil over medium heat, stirring constantly. When it begins to bubble, remove it from heat. (Mixture will be thin.) Stir in vanilla and set aside.

2. In a medium bowl, beat the whites until they form stiff peaks that just barely fold over at the top when you lift the beaters. Fold the hot mixture into the egg whites. Spoon into 8 individual dessert dishes and chill for several hours. To serve, top with a cherry or strawberry for garnish.

2
Childhood Memories

The great man is he who has not lost the heart of a child.

—Mencius

The richness of life lies in memories we have forgotten.

—Cesare Pavese

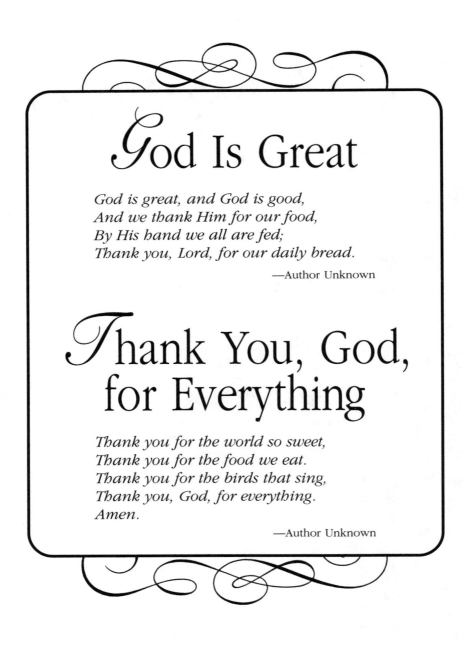

God Is Great

God is great, and God is good,
And we thank Him for our food,
By His hand we all are fed;
Thank you, Lord, for our daily bread.

—Author Unknown

Thank You, God, for Everything

Thank you for the world so sweet,
Thank you for the food we eat.
Thank you for the birds that sing,
Thank you, God, for everything.
Amen.

—Author Unknown

The Legend of Glass-Eyed Gus

Mike Buettell

Nothing in life is to be feared.
It is only to be understood.

—Marie Curie

It was July 1959, and my buddy John Latta and I were serving our fifth consecutive day of "KP" (kitchen police) duty at Wolverton Boy Scout Camp in California's High Sierras. We'd earned the first two days of KP duty by placing candy bars all around our counselor's tent and waiting until a bear showed up. Day three was earned by throwing firecrackers at an adjoining troop. On day four we were caught with a cigarette (we never did learn how to inhale). Day five literally took the cake—we served a huge vanilla cake to the other scouts with an old tennis shoe hidden in the middle. We were the bad boys of Troop 106!

"You little punks think you're pretty cute, don't you?" snarled Tommy, the camp cook—our newly appointed counselor who we now spent 24 hours a day with. "Little pranks and tricks—bah—Girl Scouts do those. You babies haven't got the nerve to pull off anything really big."

John and I knew a challenge when we heard one. Our prepubescent male egos salivated at the possibility of true campwide renown. "What are you talking about Tommy?" John asked.

"Give it up, ladies. You haven't got the nerve!" Tommy had hooks in our mouths and was reeling us in.

"Come on Tommy. Tell us. We're not afraid of anything."

"Well, if you really had guts, you'd go up to Pear Lake and try and steal Old Gus' glass eye."

"Pear Lake? Glass eye? Who's Gus?"

"Old Gus is the last of the mountain men. He camps all summer way out at Pear Lake. Has a glass eye, he does; lives off the land. Legend has it he can take the eye out, hold it in his hand and still see things with it. He hates Boy Scouts. You'd be the true camp heroes if you could bring the eye back to camp."

That evening John and I were the fastest kitchen helpers Camp Wolverton had ever seen. By seven o'clock our 12-year-old brains had formulated the following imbecilic plan:

1. Run all the way (six miles) to Pear Lake by nightfall.
2. Steal the glass eye while Gus slept.
3. Run back at daybreak in time for breakfast.
4. Become camp heroes.

We went for it.

At first everything ran smoothly. I had two blankets strapped to a pack frame and John had a bunch of paper sacks filled with pilfered food and mess gear. The trail was smooth, the evening cool, and the anticipation limitless. Nothing would stop us. Except, of course, it got dark long before we ever got near Pear Lake.

I vaguely remember both of us falling into a creek, losing all the mess gear, building a fire, and sitting huddled in a tiny blanket when the most enormous man I had ever seen appeared in front of us. It was Glass-Eyed Gus! I was so terrified, I thought my heart would jump out of my shirt.

"You boys eaten yet?" the giant whispered in a calm and gentle voice. We shook our heads. Then without a word he prepared one of the most amazing meals I have ever eaten.

He took a dry paper lunch sack and lined the inside with strips of bacon. Next he took three eggs, shook them, broke them open and poured the yolk and whites into the bag on top of the bacon. He then held the bag about a foot from the fire, watching the bottom of the bag carefully. In about three minutes I could hear the bacon sizzling inside the bag. Two or three minutes later he ripped the bag about half-way down revealing a perfect bacon and eggs meal which we ate using small sticks. After we had finished, Gus tossed the bag and sticks into the fire. "I hate washing dishes."

When our clothes had dried, Gus led us back to camp, telling stories to keep us awake. He became our friend and for the next few summers taught us more about the wilderness than any book ever could. Oh, could he really see things with his glass eye when he took it out? Well, let's just say, that's another story.

Editors' Note: We don't expect you to try the recipe for bacon and eggs in a paper sack, but we loved the story too much to leave it out.

Baking Recipe for Mothers

Author Unknown

Contributed by Bobbie Lippman

Preheat oven. Check to be certain that there are no rubber balls or plastic soldiers on the shelves. Remove blocks and toy autos from table. Grease pan. Crack nuts. Measure 2 cups flour; remove Johnny's hands from flour; wash flour off him. Remeasure flour. Crack more nuts to replace those Johnny ate.

Put flour, baking powder and salt in sifter. Get dustpan and brush up pieces of bowl Johnny knocked on floor. Get another bowl. Answer doorbell.

Return to kitchen. Remove Johnny's hands from bowl. Wash Johnny. Answer telephone. Return. Remove ¼ inch salt from greased pan. Look for Johnny. Grease another pan. Answer telephone.

Return to kitchen and find Johnny. Remove his hands from bowl. Take up greased pan and remove layer of nut shells in it. Head for Johnny, who runs, knocking bowl off table. Wash kitchen floor, table, walls, dishes. Call bakery, place order. Take two aspirin. Lie down!

Hot Pink Chocolate

Nancy Richard-Guilford

My baby brother, Orvin, had turned three only four days before going to the hospital to have his tonsils out. Although he could be quite an imp, I truly missed him and was looking forward to his return. I did, though, have a few ulterior motives. Being the youngest member of the family, and the only boy, Orvin was used to receiving and thriving on my parents' attention. This did not always sit well with me, but I figured I could now use this behavior to my advantage. I figured that my brother's recuperation would be the perfect time to convert him back to the former live doll status I had bestowed on him when he was a baby. Since he could now talk, but had not yet developed the skill to determine what one should and should not tell my father, I knew I could no longer get away with dressing him up in doll clothes, but I was betting that Orvin would let me rock him all I wanted and brush his hair. Back then, my own hair was as straight as a stick, and I was absolutely fascinated with my baby brother's curly hair. This was as great an opportunity to play beauty parlor as I'd ever seen.

The day my mom and brother came home from the hospital, my sister Dorine and I ran out to the yard and flung the car door open. All ready to lavish attention on him, we were startled to see Orvin, sitting on his knees and facing backwards, turn and absolutely glare at us! Marme (my name for my mom, taken from the book *Little Women*) said Orvin was cranky and to leave him alone.

A nap usually took care of my brother's crankiness so I was all set to get down to some serious hair brushing on those adorable curls when he woke up. Orvin, however, wanted absolutely nothing to do with hair brushing, and, in fact, wanted very little to do with any of us. He'd sit in the corner of the sofa, and if one of us got close, he would clench his little teeth and give us dirty looks.

Marme told us the doctor said that Orvin's tonsils were so huge when he took them out, he was amazed that he had been able to eat solid food the previous few months. The poor little guy was now in a lot of pain and had obviously chosen not to trust anyone. I don't know if he thought there might be something more down there for us to yank out, but he was determined to keep his mouth shut. And keep it shut, he did. He wouldn't talk, he wouldn't eat, he wouldn't even open his mouth to say his formerly favorite word, *no*. And he kept up the dirty looks.

My parents and oldest sister Linda, who had reached the worldly age of 13, finally decided that Orvin would eat when he got hungry enough. In the past, Dorine and I had often been able to get Orvin to do things the others couldn't. True, I had often done it through bribes, but I got the job done. My attitude was that the grown-ups should have stepped aside long ago and let us pros handle the situation. We tried pudding. We tried ice cream. I tried a really good bribe. But, Orvin kept his mouth clenched shut.

Dorine, motivated by genuine concern, and I, more by not wanting to be outsmarted by a three-year-old, set out on a full-scale mission to get baby brother to eat. We plotted; we planned; we held meetings. We had zero success.

Before too long, Orvin was feeling better and starting to enjoy all the attention. He still wouldn't open his mouth, but at least he stopped glaring! Spurred on by that small success, we kept up our vigil. I almost lost my resolve, though, when Orvin turned down Marme's homemade cocoa. Marme makes the best cocoa in the world, and I wasn't so sure I wanted to encourage him if his turning it down meant that *I* might get more.

The next morning, I found my sister in the kitchen, pouring some of Marme's cocoa into my brother's mug. "He wouldn't even *touch* it last night," I said. "How are we going to get him to *drink* it today?" Dorine smiled, opened up the kitchen cabinet and pulled out a small bottle. "I think," she said, "I've found a way." She then proceeded to put several drops of red food coloring into the cocoa, turning it pink. We looked at the cocoa; we looked at each other. By golly, *this* was going to work!

Even at age eight, I knew that one way to get a kid excited was to be truly excited yourself, so I literally bounded into the living room and excitedly yelled, "Orvin, Orvin, come quick! We've got a surprise for you!" Never one to miss out on a surprise, Orvin came dashing into the kitchen where Dorine and I announced with unbridled joy, "Look, Orvin look! *Pink* cocoa!" He looked down at the mug, surveying our latest offering. We could almost hear him thinking, *Well now, this* is *something new!* He picked up the mug, and for the first time in days, opened his mouth and drank.

The next day he asked for more of that new cocoa. We thought that was about the cutest thing we'd ever seen. Almost choking with laughter, we eagerly obliged. We were immensely proud of ourselves and our overwhelming success. But, our plan worked a little too well. For the next three years, our little brother would drink Marme's cocoa anytime—but *only* if we put red food coloring in it.

Marme's Hot Pink Cocoa

Makes six 6-ounce servings, or three 12-ounce servings

❧

3 tablespoons cocoa
¼ cup hot water (always use hot
water to turn cocoa powder
into a smooth paste, then use
milk for the remaining liquid)
¼ cup plus 2 tablespoons sugar
A dash of salt (to bring out the
flavor of the cocoa)

4½ cups milk
Red food coloring, if desired
Mini-marshmallows, for serving
(Although Marme insists that
marshmallows are mandatory,
my baby brother, at age 40,
still likes his without!)

1. Place cocoa in a medium saucepan. Pour in hot water and stir until smooth. Add sugar, salt and milk. Over medium heat, stirring constantly, bring just to a simmer—do not boil. Remove from heat.

2. Add red food coloring, if desired (the cocoa will turn pinkish, not a true pink). Top with mini-marshmallows and serve with love.

Country Roads

Theodore S. Wentworth

I thank You God for most this amazing
day; for the leaping greenly spirits of trees
and a blue true dream of sky: and for every thing
which is natural which is infinite which is yes.

—e.e. cummings

I was a lucky country kid. My job was to explore every pool and waterfall in the many little creeks around my house in northern New Jersey. We lived in the woods, two miles from a small town where I went to school. I wasn't 10 yet, so you can see why it was important that I spend my days climbing trees, turning over wet leaves to find yellow and black salamanders, catching frogs, turtles, and poison ivy, and nibbling on the fresh watercress I found in little brooks meandering from running springs on the hill.

The water in the brook by our house was crystal blue and icy cold! The large pond it fed was so frigid that a fast plunge into it, even in late summer, would loft me out of the water onto the bank like a golf ball from a sand trap. I'd stand there straight as a board for several seconds before I could move, my pinky-red body like a boiled lobster. I did it only on a dare.

In June, my chums and I made our annual pilgrimage to the swamp where we gathered punk (cattails to the uninitiated). We cut the longest, fattest ones we could find. If it was a good year, they were at least a foot long and an inch or more in diameter. After drying them on a huge flat boulder in the full sun for several weeks, we would light them with wooden matches found next to Mom's gas stove. The stems were 18 inches long, allowing us to wave the smoking punk around, sometimes clenching the stem between our teeth like a pipe. The smoke made our clothes smell great and kept the mosquitoes and gnats away after dusk as we walked down the white gravel path from our house to the lake.

Several evenings a week we would sit in lawn chairs watching the view down the four-mile lake to the trees on the other end. From our place we could see the largest of the two small islands in the lake and a few bass fishermen wishing away the sunset. No gasoline motors were allowed on the lake, so it was paddle, sail or rely on an electric motor. If no weather was coming in, the evening quiet of the lake set a peaceful mood.

The four of us spent such evenings talking about what young boys talk about, while alternating between blowing the red, hot ash on the end of the punk and trying to poke it at lingering mosquitoes. We found stars and planets, caught fireflies, watched the lights across the lake and the occasional victorious bass fisherman coming home late. All the captured fireflies were released shortly after they were caught—otherwise they stopped blinking. I understood that, because people are the same way.

As the summer progressed, the evenings grew warmer and more humid and the lake water more inviting. By August, we ended hot evenings with a skinny dip before going home to bed. The warm lake and evening just hung with a sultry stillness that time of year. From a hundred yards away in the stillness we could hear sounds of swimming and laughter—confirming that a good idea is contagious.

Hot, moonless nights were the best family events. Moonlight brought out the couples, but the moonless nights brought out my parents and grandparents to wade into the lake. After they were in, they took off their bathing suits and threw them on the edge, joined by the kids. It was a funny time. The moms talked and we fought Dad and Grandpa for standing room on the underwater rock. Grandma was deathly afraid of the harmless, black water snake that lived in the wall separating the lawn from the lake. Of course, there developed a family tradition of telling her the snake was behind her as she was busting the party by heading for shore. She knew we were kidding, but the picture of it in her mind made it real. Her hasty retreat always added great comedy to what would have otherwise been a dignified retrieval of her towel in the dark. After Grandma got out, the rest would, within a few minutes, end their conversations and slowly drift to the wall by the lawn where they, too, would retrieve their strategically placed towels to wear as they headed for their beds not 50 yards away.

I walked barefoot along dirt roads all summer, knowing that someday I'd have to leave my country heaven to work in a big city like my dad. I didn't want to be like my dad. He had a poor sense of humor and was an all-business, no-polliwog type of guy. I thought the city did that to people. That was the only fear I had . . . that, and the boy-eating black bear that followed me at night when I was walking home alone. That bear taught me to sprint the finish, a virtue I have carried with me all of my life. On those occasions, the screen door slamming behind me was the best sound in the world.

My Favorite Chicken Sandwich

Makes 4 sandwiches

∾

I am in my late 50s now but I am still seduced by the fresh watercress crowding the banks of a little creek. Shoes off, trousers up, wade in—and never pull it up by the roots!

*1 long loaf sourdough French
  bread (a brown-and-serve
  style works best)
Boursin (or other garlic and
  herb flavored spreadable cheese)
Mayonnaise (reduced-calorie
  is fine)*

*Lemon juice
Dijon mustard
Tabasco
Sliced roast chicken
Fresh watercress from a
  stream, or assorted tender
  lettuce*

1. Cut sourdough French bread into four 6- to 8-inch crosswise sections. Cut each section in half and pull some of the extra bread

from the middle of the top part to make room for the filling. Place in a 350°F oven (or toaster oven if making a smaller amount) and toast just until lightly brown and crisp.

2. Spread Boursin cheese and mayonnaise that you have seasoned with extra lemon juice, a bit of Dijon mustard and Tabasco, on the cut sides of the bread. Fill sandwiches with chicken and watercress or lettuce. Serve while the bread is still warm.

Aunt Minnie's Peanut Brittle

Zoie Kaye

Holiday time brings back many fond memories—the Christmas tree, hanging stockings, hot-mulled cider, my uncle pulling a sled for all the neighborhood kids behind his old beat-up Ford and, of course, the anticipation of Santa's arrival. And for me the Christmas season was even more special because it was the beginning of my birthday celebration. My birthday is exactly two weeks before Christmas.

For some, being a December baby has its disadvantages because Christmas and birthday blend into one celebration—friends and relatives tend to combine the occasions into one event and one present—but I was blessed with wonderful parents who were determined to see that I never felt cheated out of my special day.

One of my fondest memories at birthday time was a visit from Aunt Minnie. When she came, special things happened. She would pull up in a very shiny old black car that did not look anything like the cars my parents or other family members drove—a 20-year-old Buick that had only been driven to the store and back once a week. Her handyman kept that car sparkling.

Aunt Minnie was a pretty lady with soft, gray curls circling her round face. I don't know what color her hair was before it turned gray—that's the only color I ever saw. The only jewelry she ever wore was a single strand of pearls that her husband had given her at their wedding. I never saw her without her pearls on in the 37 years she was in my life. Aunt Minnie was always picture perfect—

the family says she never let her husband see her without makeup.

Aunt Minnie's arrival marked the beginning of Christmas candy-making. We made divinity, pralines and fudge, but the most special recipe was Aunt Minnie's Peanut Brittle. That was reserved for my birthday party. An invitation to my party was coveted by a lot of children in our neighborhood.

All of the ingredients would be sitting on the kitchen table when everyone arrived. Each child had an ingredient they were responsible for measuring and putting in the pan on the stove. We all stood around anticipating the first opportunity to test it with the cup of water we were given for that purpose. As soon as the mixture reached the soft-ball stage Aunt Minnie or Mom would give us each a drop of the mixture. We would swirl it around and check it with our fingers to see if it had formed a soft ball. No doubt, the mixture was overtested, but it gave all of us a chance to taste it.

As soon as the announcement was made that it had reached the hard-crack stage, we were given pats of butter to rub on our hands. We waited and chattered with excitement, the old candy-making hands explaining to the new ones about the next step.

When it had cooled enough to touch, we were given a large spoonful of the candy mixture and a tray to put it on, and were told to start pulling. The secret of success with Aunt Minnie's Peanut Brittle was the pulling that would make it very delicate and tender. The final stage was to see who could stretch their candy into the thinnest piece without breaking it.

Prizes were given to the child who had pulled the largest piece without a hole in it, the one who had the most peanuts in their piece, and the pieces that were pulled the thinnest. Even today, there are a lot of adults who still talk about Aunt Minnie's Peanut Brittle and the merriment around my birthday candy-making parties.

Aunt Minnie's Peanut Brittle

Makes about 2 pounds

3 cups sugar
1½ cups light corn syrup
1 cup water
1 stick butter, cut in half
1 pound (2½ cups) raw peanuts
* with skins (preferably Spanish*
* peanuts)*

2 tablespoons baking soda
½ teaspoon salt (if peanuts
* are unsalted)*

1. In a 4-quart heavy saucepan, combine the sugar, corn syrup and water. Bring the mixture to a boil over high heat, stirring until sugar dissolves. Insert a candy thermometer, and cook uncovered to the soft-ball stage (approximately 238°F), scraping the bottom of the pan from time to time with a wooden spoon to prevent scorching. Meanwhile, butter a slab, tray or other surface where the brittle will be poured with half the butter.

2. Add the peanuts, stir, and return to a boil. Cook until the mixture reaches the "hard-crack" stage (about 300°F). Remove from heat, add the remaining ½ stick butter, then add the baking soda.

3. Pour the mixture out onto the buttered surface at once, scraping out the bottom of the pan. Spread the mixture as thin as possible with a metal or wooden spatula. As soon as the mixture can be handled, use either rubber gloves or buttered fingers to stretch and pull the brittle as thin as possible. It should stretch to almost double the original size.

4. When cool, crack into bite-size pieces. Extra brittle may be stored in an air-tight container.

Moma's Scappa e Fuggi

Antoineta Baldwin

I was born in Redondo Beach, California, to Italian immigrant parents. My dad was from Naples, and my mom from Bari, Italy. We had many *paisanos* (fellow countrymen) who, after coming through Ellis Island in New York, headed for the West Coast for the weather and the type of work they were used to in the old country— farming, cheese-making, wine-making and brick-laying. They lived all over the Los Angeles area, but gathered each year to celebrate their Italian patron saint's day in Redondo Beach's Veteran's Park.

The celebration was always a time of great fun and festivity. The men would walk out at low tide, pant legs rolled up, laughing and yelling as they gathered the abundant sea urchins, whelks, crabs, rock scallops, abalone and sometimes a fish, off the rocks and in the tidepools. Back at the park, the women cooked on their stoves while telling stories, laughing and singing. And everyone was on duty to watch the children who were running, crying, eating and sleeping. There was no such thing as a baby-sitter.

The aroma from each pot was wonderful and blended together harmoniously into one glorious appetite-inspiring scent. Fresh vegetables, homemade pasta and the catch of the day were always available in large helpings. Sea urchins were opened, their eggs scooped out to be eaten with crusty bread and washed-down with homemade red wine. Shellfish were usually boiled, then dipped in olive oil and minced garlic.

My mom always made her *Scappa e Fuggi* (fast and hurry) sauce—a staple in most Italian kitchens—from home-canned tomatoes and home-grown basil and garlic.

Back then, Redondo Beach was a wonderful melting pot of different cultures. In the park people of many nationalities were doing just as we were, using the same foods, but preparing them differently. Though language barriers made verbal communication a problem, our facial expressions and hand motions seemed to do the job, and there was always good-natured camaraderie.

Moma's Scappa e Fuggi Sauce for Pasta

Makes 3 to 4 servings

This sauce has a lot of flavor and just lightly coats the pasta.

3 tablespoons good olive oil
8 large cloves garlic, smashed
1 (15-ounce) can crushed plum
  tomatoes and their liquid
1 teaspoon, or more, freshly
  ground black pepper
½ cup fresh, minced basil leaves
Salt to taste

Optional ingredients you may
  wish to add to the sauce: fresh
  fish, calamari, broccoli, cauli-
  flower or a can of drained
  clams (but only one addition
  at a time)
About ¾ pound (12 ounces)
  pasta of your choice

1. Heat olive oil in a large skillet, add garlic and cook until golden, but not brown. Stir in tomatoes and their liquid with black pepper. Add basil leaves and salt to taste. Cook at a fast simmer over high heat, stirring the sauce often for about 10 to 15 minutes

2. Put on a large pot of water in which to cook pasta. (When your pasta is done, so is the sauce.)

Memories from the Great Depression

Betty Fobair McDermott

My tongue is smiling.

—Abigail Trillin, age four, after eating chocolate ice cream.
From *Alice, Let's Eat*

I grew up in South Dakota in the 1930s, during the height of the Great Depression. My family of four lived on a large parcel of land at the edge of a small town where we grew most of our food: potatoes, carrots, cabbages, tomatoes, corn, green beans, pumpkins, onions, peas, radishes and many varieties of lettuce. Queen Anne cherries from our tree were canned to make delicious juicy pies in the winter. Grain-fed chickens, providing eggs and protein, were purchased as tiny chicks each spring at the local hatchery. Pheasants and wild ducks were often entrees on our table during hunting season.

All of our breads, cakes, pies and cookies were home-baked. Cream was purchased weekly from local farmers to churn into butter and to make luscious, smooth hand-cranked ice cream.

Social life centered around church events, school activities and 4-H classes, where we learned about the history, production and preservation of food.

In the summer our kitchen was steamy as Mother and I worked together for hours to can and preserve foods for the long, cold winter months. At social events, my mother and her friends delighted in sharing their seasonal canning count, such as 87 quarts of green beans, 62 quarts of peach halves, 10 pints of dill pickles and 50 quarts of tomato juice.

After my father died suddenly in 1937, my mother baked whole-wheat bread daily for a year to support my younger brother and me. I pulled my little red wagon through the streets, delivering 17-cent loaves of bread to welcoming customers. Looking back now, I'm sure that kneading the dough each day helped my mother work through her grief over my father's untimely death. After a year of punching the dough, she gave up baking and went into politics to experience a different kind of pummeling.

As a reward for our hard work, my mother, brother and I made a pilgrimage each Friday evening to Derby's, our town's only ice cream parlor and creamery. The peculiar smell of a creamery is indescribable, but unforgettable. Here butter was churned, the buttermilk was sold as a byproduct, and three flavors of ice cream were served: chocolate, strawberry and vanilla.

Our budget allowed for only one five-cent scoop each of ice cream served in a crackly cone. Licking our cones, savoring each bite of the smooth treat, we would walk happily and slowly up and down the small main street. Along the way we greeted other residents and farmers picking up their weekly provisions and satisfying their need for hand-cranked ice cream. With the memory of these joyful Friday evening strolls recalled in my mind, I created these two special updated hand-cranked ice cream recipes.

Fresh Lemon Ice Cream

Makes 1 gallon

❧

(*"Fresh Lemon Ice Cream" and "Ginger Ice Cream" by Bette Fobair McDermott. Reprinted from* California Cooks! *by permission of Betty Fobair McDermott. © 1995 Betty Fobair McDermott.*)

3 large eggs	*1 quart half and half*
2½ cups sugar	*1 quart heavy cream*
½ teaspoon salt	*½ teaspoon yellow food*
2 tablespoons grated fresh	*coloring*
lemon peel	*Chipped ice and ice cream*
1½ cups fresh lemon juice	*salt for freezing*

1. Beat eggs in the large bowl of an electric mixer for 1 minute. Add sugar, salt and lemon peel; beat until blended. Stir in fresh lemon juice. Add half and half, heavy cream and yellow food coloring. Stir well. Refrigerate 2 to 3 hours.

2. Pour into 1-gallon can of electric or hand-crank ice cream freezer. Use 6 to 10 parts chipped ice to 1 part ice cream salt for freezing. (The larger proportion of salt speeds freezing, but the smaller proportion produces a finer texture.)

3. After cranking or electric freezing, the ice cream should be packed into four 1-quart containers or a 1-gallon container and allowed to ripen for 2 hours in the freezer section of the refrigerator before serving.

Ginger Ice Cream

Makes 1 gallon

∾

2½ cups sugar
4 eggs
½ teaspoon salt
2 tablespoons ground ginger
1 teaspoon vanilla
1 quart homogenized milk

1 quart heavy cream
½ cup finely chopped
  crystallized ginger
Chipped ice and ice cream
  salt for freezing

1. In a mixing bowl, beat together sugar, eggs, salt, ground ginger and vanilla until well blended. Stir in milk and cream. Chill 2 to 3 hours. Stir in crystallized ginger.

2. Pour into 1-gallon can of electric or hand-crank ice cream freezer. Pack freezer with 4 to 6 parts chipped ice to 1 part ice cream salt. Freeze. Pack into 1-quart containers and allow to ripen in the freezer section of the refrigerator for 2 hours before serving.

Heavenly Spicy Chicken

Jean Brady

We do not remember days, we remember moments.

—Cesare Pavese

My boys grew up with a mother/cooking teacher; it was a package deal. Classes in those early years were held in our home, and the pitter-patter of little feet and the chatter of two small children were included in the class fee.

I clearly remember an important moral issue that arose during a class and needed to be resolved on the spot, as a roomful of patient students, many of them mothers themselves, sat and waited.

My older son David was selling 10-cent bouquets of watercress from the creek that runs through our garden; my younger son Scott, wanting profit for himself, lay down in the middle of the class kicking his feet and screaming, "I want a dime! I want a dime, too." I tried to explain quickly and calmly to Scott that David had earned the dimes by harvesting and bundling the watercress himself. Scott was not listening and continued, "I want a dime, too."

I became uncomfortable, then anxious, as the screaming and kicking continued, but I was determined not to give in to his unreasonable demands. Finally, after what seemed like an eternity, Scott stopped kicking, lifted his small, wet face, looked up at me with his gentle smile and meekly pleaded, "How about a nickel?"

Raising two boys, of course, meant refereeing a lot of knock-down drag-out tussles that left me feeling frazzled. Many of them, however, provided me with sweet memories. Perhaps the sweetest memory involved a day-long confrontation with Scott as he lumbered toward puberty at about age 12. As dinnertime approached, my husband and I were wondering why we'd become parents in the first place. Scott swallowed his pride that evening, slinked to the dinner table in tears, took one bite of Spicy Chicken with Black Bean Sauce, lifted his sad face and said, "This is heaven!"

Cooking classes, food and family were inexorably intertwined at 680 Brooktree, and memories of the preparation and sharing favorite recipes are woven through the essence of our lives. The boys are all grown-up now; David is soon to be a doctor, and Scott will be a lawyer. Hopefully, neither of them will need to sell watercress again, but the thoughts of cooking classes and those special dishes will linger with them forever.

Spicy Chicken with Black Bean Sauce

Makes 4 to 6 servings

FERMENTED BLACK BEAN SAUCE:

3 tablespoons peanut oil
2 tablespoons fermented Chinese black beans (see Note)
1 to 2 teaspoons dark (roasted) sesame oil (see Note)

5 cloves minced garlic
1 tablespoon minced fresh ginger
1 tablespoon water
1 teaspoon pale dry sherry
¼ to ½ teaspoon dried red pepper flakes

CHICKEN STIR-FRY:

2 teaspoons cornstarch	1 cup skinny green beans
2 teaspoons pale dry sherry	2 to 3 cloves garlic
½ teaspoon peanut oil	1 quarter-size slice of fresh,
A sprinkling of salt and pepper	peeled ginger
1¼ pounds boneless, skinless	Peanut oil
chicken breast, cut in	Finely chopped cilantro (fresh
1-inch pieces	coriander or Chinese parsley),
1 red bell pepper	to garnish

Note: *Both these ingredients are available in Asian markets.*

1. To make Fermented Black Bean Sauce (which can be used as a wonderful seasoning for many other stir-fry dishes), combine the ingredients in a small saucepan. Cover and cook over very low heat until garlic is soft. Set aside. (Store any you don't use in a covered jar in the refrigerator—it will keep indefinitely.)

2. For the Chicken Stir-Fry, stir together in a mixing bowl the cornstarch, dry sherry, peanut oil, salt and pepper. Mix chicken pieces into the cornstarch mixture; let stand 10 minutes. Meanwhile, prepare the vegetables: Cut bell pepper and carrots into attractive small chunks. Wash green beans and blanch them (drop into simmering water for 2 minutes, rinse under cold water and drain). Finely chop the garlic and ginger.

3. Heat a wok until very hot, and add a thin drizzle of peanut oil. Pour in the chicken mixture and stir-fry until brown, about 2 minutes. Add carrots, cook 1 minute, then peppers, green beans, garlic, ginger and desired amount of black bean sauce. When veggies are just tender, transfer to a warm platter. Sprinkle finely chopped cilantro over the top and serve immediately.

A Recipe for Laughter

Glenna Salsbury

Illinois winters meant trudging through the snow and carrying my lunch to school in a brown paper bag. When the noon bell rang, a group of freshman girls and I would grab our brown bags and head for a corner of the bleachers in the boys' gym to giggle and trade cookies and stories.

Part of the laughter always revolved around the "weird" things we each had buried in those bags. Peanut butter, banana and Miracle Whip sandwiches were Barb's mainstay. June preferred sweet pickles, bologna and mayonnaise with her peanut butter. Somebody always had Rainbo white bread with lumps of butter and sugar.

One November day it was my turn to create the most interesting lunch. As the sacks began to crackle open, I announced the prize for the day—real corn-fed beef sandwiches with lettuce and tomatoes! And, I offered to trade half a beef sandwich for half of anyone's sandwich that held the most appeal for me.

A bidding contest erupted! My friends were throwing in extras to gain the prize—cookies, candy, a piece of chocolate cake with butter icing. After savoring the excitement, I made my choice and the trade was complete. We then munched on our selections. I waited for the perfect moment to make my carefully planned announcement . . .

Immediately after Marj swallowed the last bite of the beef sandwich she bartered for, I asked if she wanted to know what kind of beef she had just eaten. Her eyebrows raised and I announced, "You just ate six big slices of cow's tongue!"

Marj gasped and, as the reality set in, she leapt over the bleachers, hand to her mouth, on a dead run for the girls' bathroom. We all watched and howled with laughter.

The truth remains. My mom made the greatest boiled tongue dinners in the state of Illinois. It was a family favorite, especially when it was fresh, warm and doused in vinegar! For the adventurous, this is a recipe that remains filled with fond memories—and a chorus of laughter.

The Best Boiled Beef Tongue in Town!

Makes 4 to 6 servings

1 fresh calf tongue (about 2 pounds)
20 whole black peppercorns
2 chopped white onions
1 teaspoon crumbled dried basil

4 whole, peeled cloves fresh garlic
Fresh horseradish and/or garlic vinegar, for serving

1. In a large stainless steel, enamel or non-stick pot, place tongue, peppercorns, onions, basil and garlic. Add cold water to cover tongue by 1 inch. Bring to a boil and skim off any foam that rises to the surface. Cover, and simmer slowly for approximately 2 to 2½ hours or until tender.

2. Remove tongue from juices and put in a bowl of cold water to loosen the skin. Pat dry, slit skin on underside of tongue from root to tip and peel it off; trim away fat and outer tissues.

3. Slice tongue in ¼-inch-thick slices. Serve with fresh horseradish and/or garlic vinegar with vegetables of choice. Or, create great tongue sandwiches with lettuce, tomatoes and a serving of laughter.

Slumgullion

Joe Batten

I grew up in the hill country of southern Iowa, 12 miles from the nearest town. It was the 1930s and we had no electricity and, of course, no central heating. In order to keep the house warm during the long, cold Midwestern winters, my older brother Hal, my Dad and I had to cut down trees and saw them into logs for firewood virtually every weekend. We then hauled the wood home in a horse-drawn wagon to fuel the waiting woodstove.

Many days during the winter, the temperature dropped well below zero. The frigid air chilled us to the bone. The only way to keep warm was to chop swiftly and steadily. Dad stressed the importance of always keeping my axe sharp and swinging it in a carefully focused, yet relaxed way that permitted the axe to bite deep and allowed me to swing it for literally hours on end. His instructions not only helped with the task at hand, but served as a philosophy of life. The axe was a metaphor for a sharp mind, and those long days in the woods, spent with my father and brother, taught me to keep my mental tools—my mind and vocabulary— acute and focused.

In the summer, with winter's chill a distant memory, we maintained a large garden which I worked in after my day spent in the fields. The garden was my mother's domain and, as my father had in the woods, her guidance and instructions provided me with many other important life lessons. A woman of the highest integrity, Mom taught me the importance of goal-setting, discipline and perseverance by telling me, "Joe, never quit before a job is done."

At the end of a hard day's work, whether winter or summer, I was always happy when Mom cooked Slumgullion. It was truly food for body and spirit. It was energizing and nourishing. Above all, it was delicious.

Slumgullion

Makes 4 servings

~

8 ounces elbow macaroni
1 tablespoon oil
1 cup minced onion
½ pound lean ground beef
2½ cups diced canned
  tomatoes
1 cup diced celery
¾ cup minced green pepper

1 teaspoon Worcestershire
  sauce
2 teaspoons salt
¼ to ½ teaspoon cayenne
  pepper to taste
½ to 1 cup grated sharp
  American cheese or ¼ cup
  grated Parmesan cheese

1. Cook macaroni according to package directions; drain and set aside.

2. Meanwhile make the sauce: In a skillet, sauté the onion in oil. Add ground beef and cook until brown, breaking it up with the back of a spoon. Add tomatoes, celery, green pepper, Worcestershire sauce, salt and cayenne. Cook 5 minutes or so, then stir in noodles. Just before serving, sprinkle cheese over the top (or mix it in if you prefer).

My Favorite Food

Bobbie Probstein

When I was a young girl our family lived in a small Nevada town of about 25,000 people that lured cowboys to gamble and soon-to-be-divorcees to get legally quick fixes for unhappy marriages. It was an unsophisticated place that offered my dad a chance to earn a living. Since this was during the Depression he had to take the job.

My mother, a wonderful cook, always complained that there wasn't even a decent restaurant to eat in, and she was probably right. At last a diner opened that had interesting dishes besides the usual steak and fries and iceberg lettuce salad with mayonnaise; it even featured the newest rage from Los Angeles: Caesar salad.

I had never eaten anything more wonderful. I loved it, craved it and begged to be taken to the diner as often as possible. I couldn't wait to visit my aunt and uncle in Los Angeles because I knew they would help me satisfy this insatiable craving. They loved eating out, and I had fun with them no matter what we did.

In Los Angeles at last, I was taken to Chasens, where I was the only child within view. The women wore fancy dresses, and I had on the new velvet dress my aunt had made me. I tried to act very grown up. My uncle even ordered me a Shirley Temple cocktail. I couldn't wait to order dinner because my aunt had told me the Caesar salad was especially wonderful at Chasens. When the waiter came around for our orders, he approached me first.

In a clear strong voice that left no doubt about my passion, I said (rather too loudly, I'm sure), "I'll have a caesarean, please!"

The waiter turned away quite suddenly, and all the people at our table quickly brought napkins to their mouths to stifle laughter. I kept asking, "Well, what did I say that was so funny?" but no one responded.

Caesar Salad

Makes 4 to 6 servings

❧

1 clove garlic
¼ cup olive oil or vegetable oil
Romaine lettuce, cut up to
 make 12 cups
3 or 4 canned anchovy fillets
 (or 2 teaspoons anchovy paste)
¼ cup freshly grated
 Parmesan cheese
3 tablespoons commercial
 mayonnaise (to replace the
 traditional coddled egg which
 is no longer considered safe)

1 tablespoon fresh lemon juice
1 tablespoon red wine vinegar
1 teaspoon Dijon mustard
 (optional, but very nice)
½ teaspoon Worcestershire
 sauce
Freshly ground black pepper

CROUTONS:
1 cup cubed day-old French bread 2 tablespoons olive oil

1. In a small bowl, place garlic with olive oil or vegetable oil. Set aside to develop flavor while you prepare the other ingredients.

2. Wash, pat dry and cut up romaine lettuce, wrap in a damp towel and place in the refrigerator until ready to serve.

3. To make croutons, toss cubed French bread with olive oil. Bake in a single layer in a 325°F oven or toaster oven until browned, stirring from time to time.

4. In a large salad bowl, mash anchovy fillets or anchovy paste with the reserved garlic oil. Mix in Parmesan cheese, mayonnaise, lemon juice, red wine vinegar, Dijon mustard, Worcestershire sauce and freshly ground black pepper to taste. Add the crisp romaine pieces and the croutons and toss well. Serve immediately.

Thunder Cake

Patty Hansen

Action conquers fear.

—Peter Nivio Zarlenga

When my oldest daughter was in kindergarten, she brought home a little book to read with me entitled *Thunder Cake*. It told the story of a young girl who was afraid of storms, and how her grandmother kept her so busy helping to make a cake that she forgot to be afraid of the approaching storm.

It wasn't long after this that we had one of the most earth-shaking thunder and lightning storms I have ever experienced. My two girls quivered and cried during the loud BOOMS that shook the house. I remembered that I had saved the recipe for Thunder Cake and when I suggested that we get busy, they both pitched in, glad to have a diversion. There we were, a five-year-old, a three-year-old and Mom crazily mixing and blending while the house shook, the landscape outside lit up with lightning, and torrents of rain poured from the eaves of the house.

We had great fun, even though my kids weren't too sure (Yuck, they said) about the addition of tomatoes to the cake batter. As it turned out, I didn't have enough cocoa to make frosting so we dusted the top with powdered sugar. It was great! We all sat down together in front of a cozy fire for tea and slices of our own Thunder Cake while we watched the storm outside together.

It has become a family tradition, even when it just looks like a storm could be on the way, for the three of us to get out the recipe for our own version of Thunder Cake. It is a time I look forward to because we share not only the baking of a cake, but our fears, questions, dreams and desires. We Hansens are convinced that a Thunder Cake only tastes good when all the ingredients—cake batter, thunder, lightning, fears, questions, dreams and desires—are included.

Thunder Cake

Makes a 9 × 13-inch cake

This recipe was adapted from Thunder Cake *by Patricia Polacco (Philomel Books, 1990).*

3 eggs
1¾ cup sugar
1 fresh tomato, peeled
  (see Note) and pureed
  in the blender
1 cup cold water
2 sticks (½ pound) butter

1 teaspoon vanilla
2½ cups cake flour
½ cup dry cocoa
1½ teaspoons baking soda
½ teaspoon salt
Powdered sugar, to decorate

Note: *To peel a tomato, dip in boiling water for several seconds, which loosens skin and makes it simple to remove. Cut tomato in half crosswise and squeeze out seeds.*

1. Preheat oven to 350°F. Grease and flour a 9 × 13-inch cake pan. Separate the eggs, placing the yolks in a small dish and the whites in a large, grease-free bowl.

2. In a large mixing bowl, cream together butter and sugar until fluffy. Beat in the yolks and vanilla, followed by the water and pureed tomato. Sift together the cake flour, cocoa, baking soda and salt into the mixing bowl and mix well.

3. Beat the whites until they hold stiff peaks. Fold them into the batter lightly—it won't matter if a few lumps of white still show. Pour into prepared pan and bake for 35 to 40 minutes, until firm when pressed in the center. Let cool and sprinkle with powdered sugar pressed through a kitchen strainer.

3

Grand-
parents

What comes from the heart, touches the heart.
—Don Sibet

_A_ Traditional Blessing

The Lord bless us and keep us, the Lord make his face to shine upon us, and be gracious unto us, the Lord lift up the light of his countenance upon us and give us peace.

—(Based on the opening verse of Psalm 67, this blessing has been repeated since at least the seventh century before Christ and has passed into use in Christian teachings.)

Arroz con Leche

Rosemarie Cortez

Love and skill together can create a miracle.

—Anonymous

I still remember the sweet aroma of cinnamon, sugar, rice and milk filling the rooms of her tiny house. As a small child there was nothing much better than eating a bowl of her hot rice pudding straight from the stove. My brother, sister and I would gobble our first servings then beg for seconds. Grandmother's laughter would fill the kitchen as she happily refilled our bowls.

Today, relatives on my father's side gather each December in her memory. We lay out a huge spread of traditional family foods, rolls, cheeses, hams, salads, olives and garlic butter. But none taste quite as good as they did when Grandma made them.

As dessert time approaches, everyone whispers, "Did Aunt Juanita make the Arroz con Leche?" Aunt Juanita is the oldest of my grandmother's five daughters and one son. She likes to keep whether or not she has made the rice pudding a mystery—when she feels ready, she ceremoniously brings out the Arroz con Leche. She carefully dishes out small portions—making sure everyone gets their fair share. Fortunately, her Arroz con Leche always tastes just the way "Grandma used to make it."

Over the years I have come to realize that the secret ingredients my grandmother, Maria Encarnacion Navarro Cortez, always included in everything she made were huge doses of laughter and love. Those are the elements none of us will ever forget.

My brother, sister and I figured out that in order to get bigger portions of Arroz con Leche we needed to learn to make it for ourselves. I know you will appreciate our passion for it as soon as you taste your first spoonful! Here is Aunt Juanita's recipe from Grandma Cortez. It takes time, patience and a lot of love.

Arroz con Leche
(Rice Pudding)
Makes approximately 8 servings

2 quarts whole milk
1 cup white rice
7 strips of lemon peel
7 to 10 cinnamon sticks

¾ to 1 cup sugar (according to taste)
Cinnamon and nutmeg, to sprinkle on top

1. In a large non-stick pot, heat the whole milk, white rice, lemon peel and cinnamon sticks. Bring to a boil over medium heat, stirring frequently. Turn down heat to low setting and cook for approximately 25 minutes, stirring occasionally. Test a grain of the rice to see if it is almost soft; if not, continue to cook until soft.

2. Stir in sugar and bring to a boil over medium heat, stirring frequently. Place over a low setting and cook very slowly for approximately 30 more minutes, stirring often. Cook until thick—not too soupy and not too dry.

3. Transfer to a 2-quart serving bowl. Sprinkle with cinnamon and nutmeg. Allow to cool—it will set like a pudding. Tastes delicious chilled or warm from the stove. *Enjoy!*

Nanny's Raisin Nut Cake

Barbara DeAngelis

My grandmother Esther was a powerful woman in a tiny body. Born in Russia at the turn of the century, she fled religious persecution and came to America as a young child. Like many Jewish immigrants, she grew up poor in material wealth, but rich in love and family. Fifty years later, when she had more than enough money to lead a comfortable life, she still valued a call from one of her grandchildren more than a trip around the world.

Nanny, as we called her, was a complicated person who led a sometimes-controversial life. Born way ahead of her time, she was independent, passionate, opinionated, outspoken and fiercely protective of those she loved. I often told her if she had been born in the 1950s, like me, she probably would have had a successful career. Instead, she was stuck in an era when a "woman's place was in the home," which I think inhibited her intensity and vivacity not to mention limiting her opportunities. She was like a racehorse confined to a tiny pasture, with no room to run. Her personality often expressed itself in ways that weren't considered by those around her to be particularly healthy. She poured all of her passion into loving her son and grandchildren—sometimes too much.

Nanny never conformed to society's standards. She chose colorful, exotic clothing when her friends sported grandmotherly suits; she wore low-cut blouses and Italian bikinis into her 60s. Best of all, she never cut her beautiful silver hair, leaving it long and shining, down to the middle of her back. I have wonderful memories of her brushing her hair, and then arranging it with pins and combs into a stylish bun. I know her sense of style influenced me—I've kept my hair long, and I have never been a conservative dresser.

One thing that was traditional about Nanny was that she loved to cook, and she was terrific at it! She spent many years in Italy, so we got the best of both worlds—great Jewish and Italian food. One of her specialties was her delicious Raisin Nut Cake. She would almost always have this waiting for us when we visited her as children.

When I left Philadelphia to go to college, and later to study in Europe, I regularly received packages from Nanny of carefully wrapped Raisin Nut Cake. She had stopped traveling and stayed pretty much confined to her apartment, so baking was one of her only joys. Therefore, I looked upon each cake as the sacred gift it was.

Nanny's Raisin Nut Cake

Makes about 12 servings

1 cup tightly packed dark raisins	2 cups sugar
1½ cups water	1 cup oil
3 cups flour	4 eggs
1 teaspoon baking powder	½ cup finely chopped walnuts
1 teaspoon baking soda	1 teaspoon vanilla

1. Preheat oven to 350°F. Grease and flour a 9 x 13-inch pan. Place raisins and water in a saucepan, bring to a simmer and cook for 10 minutes. Remove from heat and set aside without draining.

2. Sift together flour, baking powder and baking soda. In a large mixing bowl, beat together sugar and oil. Add eggs, one at a time, beating well after each addition. Gradually add the flour mixture, the raisins with their cooking liquid, the walnuts and vanilla.

3. Bake for 35 to 45 minutes, until firm when pressed in the center. Like Nanny said, "This is one of my mother's recipes, so I never had the exact timing. I usually check the cake when I begin smelling it!"

Grandma's Thick "Everything" Soup

Irene C. Kassorla

I remember how excited I felt when I was five years old and Sunday finally came around. That was the day when my parents, my sister Char and I would all pile in the car and go to Grandma and Grandpa's house.

When we arrived, I'd run into the kitchen. I knew Grandma would be there cooking Sunday dinner. After enjoying her hugs and kisses, I'd climb onto my favorite place on the high stool next to the cutting board table. When Grandma needed something she'd usually ask me by making up a song to the tune of "Twinkle, Twinkle, Little Star." Her songs were fun and they rhymed: "Irene, Irene, girl I love, get the salt please, high above." I was her helper, watching her every move. Grandma was happy as she sang and cooked—I was too!

Reassuring me that I was her *best* helper (even at four I could shell peas and nuts, mix the batter for the apple pies, roll out dough for cookies, measure the beans, rice and barley for soup—and run around fetching things), she'd often let me test her creations and ask how they tasted. I felt so important and loved every minute of those special times with her.

Everything Grandma made was a delicious treat, especially her breads, tarts and pies. In fact, her apple pies were so memorable that even now, in whatever country I'm working, I can't resist tasting the apple desserts. I keep hoping to find something that will match Grandma's. Of course, nothing ever compares.

Grandma was also famous for her thick "Everything" Soup. And it did have everything in it, including chicken, beans, barley, rice, vegetables—everything, all mixed up together! The family unanimously agreed that it was truly the healthiest, most deliciously magical concoction we had ever eaten. And Grandma would always tell us that two bowls of her soup were a sure cure for colds, headaches, backaches, sadness and depression. I believed her.

I'm sure my grandma would enjoy helping *you* to be healthy and happy now, too. So here's her recipe. Serve it following a cold, tossed salad topped with feta cheese. Warm garlic bread is a great accompaniment for both courses. Top off the meal with peach or raspberry sorbet drizzled with liqueur (Amaretto or Kahlúa is fine), and fresh berries. A small chocolate chip cookie on the side finishes the meal to perfection!

"Everything" Soup
Makes 10 servings

1½ cups dried beans (such as green and orange peas, lentils, black and/or white beans, garbanzo beans, kidney beans, etc.; see Note)
1 cup pearl barley
⅓ cup long-grain rice
¼ cup oat flakes, or raw oat meal
1 large yam, peeled and cut in chunks
1 head white cabbage, sliced
10 cloves garlic, chopped
3 large red onions, chopped
¼ cup olive oil
2 whole chickens, cut up, skinned and defatted
2 leeks, white part only, well-rinsed and chopped
12 stalks celery, chopped
5 or 6 carrots, finely chopped
Salt and pepper to taste
10 mushrooms, thinly sliced
Thinly sliced green onions, to sprinkle over each serving

Note: *You may want to cook dried garbanzo beans separately, as they may need more time to cook to proper softness.*

1. Place 3 quarts of water in a large soup pot and bring to a boil. Wash the beans thoroughly and add to the pot with barley, rice, oats, yam and cabbage. With the lid on, turn the heat down low, and cook approximately 1½ hours, stirring frequently. To maintain the thickness you prefer, add small amounts of boiling water as the beans and vegetables cook. (Cold water will cloud the soup.)

2. In another soup pot, lightly sauté garlic and onions in olive oil. Add 2 quarts of boiling water, cut-up chicken, leeks and celery. Cover and cook over low heat for approximately 1 hour. Add carrots during the last 5 minutes of cooking. Salt and pepper modestly to taste. (You won't need to use many seasonings—the vegetables and chicken give the soup a rich flavor.)

3. Remove lids and let the two pots of soup stand for 10 minutes before mixing together. Add the mushrooms and stir gently to allow all the flavors to mingle. Place one piece of chicken in the middle of each soup bowl, and ladle in the "everything" magical concoction. Garnish with thinly sliced green onions and enjoy.

How I Learned to Love Tomatoes

Jeanne Jones

When I was a little girl I didn't like to eat tomatoes. Instead of avoiding serving me food with them, grandmother cleverly decided that if I grew the tomatoes myself I might find them more appealing. She helped me prepare a little garden to plant some. We tended our tomato plants with care, defending them against all predators. They grew and flourished, producing an abundance of flavorful red and juicy tomatoes. With such a generous crop it was only right that they would find their way into our kitchen and our favorite family recipes.

It was in my grandmother's kitchen, full of my first and favorite memories and smells, that she and I made a Cream of Fresh Tomato Soup that her mother had taught her to make as a little girl. It was delicious, and I developed a true passion for tomatoes. To this day, my lighter version of her recipe still gives me that warm "fuzzy" feeling that familiar memories and fond recollections inspire. I can always count on my grandmother's Cream of Fresh Tomato Soup to "cure" whatever ails me!

Cream of Fresh Tomato Soup

Makes 6 cups, 12 ½-cup servings

6 large, ripe tomatoes
1 tablespoon corn oil
Margarine
1½ tablespoons minced
   onion

2 teaspoons arrowroot
3 cups non-fat milk
1 teaspoon salt

1. Peel tomatoes by dipping them in boiling water for several seconds, which loosens skin and makes it simple to remove. Cut tomatoes in half crosswise and squeeze out seeds, carefully removing any remaining seeds with a grapefruit spoon. Chop tomatoes into small pieces and set aside.

2. In a large saucepan over medium heat, melt margarine. Add minced onion and cook until soft and clear. Add reserved tomatoes, cover and cook, stirring occasionally, until tomatoes are very soft (about 30 minutes).

3. While tomatoes are cooking, dissolve arrowroot in ½ cup of water. Add 1 more cup of water, transfer mixture to a saucepan, and bring mixture to a slow boil over medium heat, stirring constantly until thickened; set aside.

4. Place cooked tomato mixture in a blender with 1 cup non-fat milk and blend to a smooth, creamy consistency. Pour back into saucepan and add reserved arrowroot mixture, 2 more cups non-fat milk, salt and a dash of white pepper, mixing thoroughly with a wire whisk. Place saucepan back on medium heat and bring to serving temperature. Do not boil.

Utah Pioneer Scones

Susie Gross

I grew up in California but my earliest, and perhaps my fondest food memories involve our vacations in Utah when we visited with both my parents' families. My mother and father were both born in Park City and when I went there as a child, it was a deserted mining town with just a few occupied Victorian-style homes, not the ski resort it is today. Many houses were boarded up—we thought they were haunted.

I remember climbing the front steps of Grandpa Raddon's home, which is still standing, and opening the kitchen door to the marvelous aroma of Aunt Mary's homemade bread. Aunt Mary was a superb breadmaker and although she had only an old wood-burning stove, her culinary talents were unsurpassed.

Aunt Mary always left a batch of bread dough in the icebox overnight so that the next morning we could enjoy deep-fried buttermilk scones. She served it with wild chokecherry syrup, an astringent type of cherry almost impossible to come by these days. My sister and I were sent on a wild chokecherry hunt to gather them for Aunt Mary's chokecherry syrup. I loved it, but my, it was tart.

I'd almost forgotten these memories until they were rekindled by my son Bill's marriage to a Utah girl. Bill and his wife DeAnn surprised me with breakfast in bed one morning: Utah Scones with chokecherry syrup. DeAnn said she'd made them from her old family recipes handed down from the pioneers who trekked across the plains to Salt Lake Valley.

When we compared notes, we discovered our recipes were exactly the same, and we further discovered that our great grand-mothers had been best friends in Park City. They probably gathered chokecherries together just as I had as a child.

Utah Pioneer Scones with Raspberry Sauce
Makes about 80 small fried scones

❧

I now serve these with a delicious tart Raspberry Sauce instead of chokecherry syrup.

SCONES:
4 cups (1 quart) buttermilk
2 packages active dry yeast
¼ cup sugar
2 eggs, beaten
2 tablespoons oil
1 teaspoon salt

1 tablespoon baking powder
½ teaspoon baking soda
8 cups all-purpose flour,
  divided
Oil or shortening, for frying

RASPBERRY SAUCE:
4 baskets raspberries or 2
  (10-ounce) packages frozen
  raspberries, thawed
¼ cup sugar

2 teaspoons arrowroot or
  1 tablespoon cornstarch
¼ cup cold water
¼ cup fresh lemon juice

1. To make the dough for the scones, heat buttermilk until warm. Sprinkle the yeast over ¼ cup lukewarm water and set aside.

2. In a large bowl combine buttermilk, sugar, eggs, oil, salt, baking powder, baking soda and 4 cups of the flour. Add the yeast and beat until smooth. Add the remaining 4 cups flour and mix to form a soft dough.

3. Cover with a towel and allow to rise in a warm place until doubled. Punch down dough, cover tightly with plastic wrap, and place in the refrigerator overnight (or up to 3 days, if you keep punching it down).

4. Meanwhile, make the Raspberry Sauce. Purée raspberries in a blender or food processor. Press through a sieve to remove seeds and reserve the juice in a heavy small saucepan. Stir together sugar and arrowroot or cornstarch, then add the water, mixing to form a paste; stir paste into the raspberries. Cook and stir over low heat until the sauce thickens slightly. Add the lemon juice. (If making ahead, refrigerate; serve cold or reheat gently.)

5. Heat about 1 inch oil or shortening in a wide saucepan or deep skillet to 375°F. Roll dough on a floured board to about ½-inch thickness. Cut into 2 x 2-inch squares.

6. Drop into hot oil, six or seven pieces at a time, taking care not to crowd them. Fry on one side until golden, then flip over and fry until golden on the second side. Drain on paper towels. Serve hot with Raspberry Sauce or honey butter.

Grammy Rufi's Country Cooking

Diana von Welanetz Wentworth

My maternal grandmother, Johanna Rufi, was the most loving and *real* person I knew as a child. Grammy, her husband Samuel, and their four children moved from a farm in Missouri to a large home next to the trolley tracks on Virgil Avenue in Los Angeles. Grampy, deaf since childhood, was a photographer, but he was not a very good one and he seldom worked.

Grammy, full of grace in taking charge of the family's finances, decided their surest route to security would be to run a boarding house. She loved to sew, and she set about making organdy curtains and chintz bedspreads for all the bedrooms and refinishing furniture from second-hand shops.

Her love of handcrafts and joy in making beautiful objects out of discarded fragments were contagious; by the time I was four I was after her constantly to teach me to knit and crochet and tat. Grammy never seemed too busy to stop what she was doing to make ruffled dresses for my dolls out of the scraps of flowered fabrics, laces and ribbons she kept in her lacquered ribbon box.

Mother used to be upset that Grammy's boarders would sometimes leave without paying their bills. "What a way for them to repay you for all your hard work!" she'd lament. But Grammy said she didn't really mind. "I'd rather lose a little money once in a while than stop trusting people."

I thrived in her unconditional generosity and wisdom. She taught me to keep my heart open even if life was not meeting my expectations;

to generate my own flame when the winds of fortune shifted, and, most of all, to love purely.

If we were staying for dinner, Grammy would go out to the hen-house for a chicken for a fried chicken dinner. Her kitchen was part of a large dining room with a big table, a sunny window overlooking her rose garden and an ice box that held the huge frozen blocks delivered by the ice man. For my favorite childhood meal she'd put an old cast iron chicken fryer with a domed glass lid on her small gas stove and brown the savory chicken while she shaped the dough for potato rolls, prepared the fixin's for country gravy, boiled and mashed potatoes, shelled fresh peas from her garden, and opened a jar of homemade boysenberry preserves from the cellar. That is how she made the chicken, gravy and rolls, and to this day, so do I.

Grammy's Old-Fashioned Fried Chicken

Makes 4 servings

Buy yourself a good, free-range chicken, the kind that are still allowed to run around gathering their own food from the ground. Most supermarket chickens today are cooped up in cages and given large doses of antibiotics to prevent disease, so you may have to search for a source for these. I assure you the wholesomeness and flavor of free-range chicken will be worth it.

1 (3-pound) chicken, cut into pieces	1 tablespoon salt
2 cups buttermilk	1 teaspoon ground black pepper
3 cups all-purpose flour	Peanut oil or vegetable shortening

1. Rinse and dry chicken; place in a glass dish with buttermilk and let soak for 10 to 30 minutes.

2. In a paper bag place the flour, salt and black pepper, close the

top and shake to mix well. Drain the chicken and drop it in the bag, two or three pieces at a time, shaking the bag until each piece is thoroughly coated. Set chicken on a piece of waxed paper.

3. Heat about ½ inch peanut oil or vegetable shortening in an electric frying pan set at 350° F, or a large skillet over medium heat. Dredge the chicken once more in the flour, shaking off any excess. Test the oil temperature by dropping in a sprinkle of water—it should sizzle. Add the chicken, taking care not to crowd it. Brown chicken well on both sides, then set the heat to low and cover the pan for 15 minutes.

4. Remove the lid and test for doneness—the juices from the thigh should run clear when prodded with a fork. (The chicken will look soggy, but don't worry.) Turn the heat back up to medium and cook until the chicken is brown and very crisp, top and bottom. Remove with tongs and drain well on paper towels. Serve immediately.

Country Gravy

½ cup of the drippings from
   cooking the fried chicken
½ cup flour

3 cups whole milk
Salt and lots of freshly ground
   black pepper

1. Pour out all but ½ cup of the fat from the chicken pan. Return the pan to the heat and stir in the flour, scraping up all the lovely, crispy brown bits from the bottom of the pan. Cook for a minute or two until the flour begins to turn golden, then slowly whisk in the whole milk.

2. Cook, stirring constantly, until the gravy is the desired thickness. Season to taste with salt and lots of freshly ground black pepper. Serve with mashed potatoes.

Grammy's Potato Rolls

Makes 2 to 3 dozen

*1 large potato peeled and cut
   into cubes
⅓ cup sugar
2 packages active dry yeast
4 to 5 cups unbleached flour,
   divided*

*3 eggs
1 stick (¼ pound) butter,
   melted
Butter and boysenberry jam,
   or other fruit jam for serving*

1. Boil the potato in water to cover until tender. Drain, reserving the cooking water, and mash the potato in a large mixing bowl. Add sugar and yeast. Stir in 1½ cups of the flour, beating until very smooth. Cover with a dish towel and let rise, at room temperature, until doubled in bulk, about an hour.

2. Beat the eggs into the mixture along with the melted butter. Gradually beat in 2½ cups flour, and when it is hard to mix, turn out onto a lightly floured surface, kneading for about 5 minutes, adding no more flour than necessary to keep the dough from sticking to your hands. The dough will be very soft.

3. Preheat oven to 350°F. Oil two 8×8- or 9×9-inch square or 7×11-inch baking pans. Sprinkle dough, work surface and rolling pin generously with flour, and roll dough out to less than 1-inch thickness. Cut into 2-inch squares and place, ½ inch apart, in the prepared pans. Cover with a damp towel and let rise at room temperature for an hour or two until almost double in bulk.

4. Bake in the center of the oven for about 12 minutes, until puffy and golden brown. Transfer to a rack to cool for a few minutes before serving. Serve with room-temperature butter and boysenberry (or other berry) jam.

Bukda, a Braided Bohemian Bread

Pat Wayne

Bread is the warmest, kindest of words. Write it always with a capital letter, like your own name.

—Russian cafe sign

My mother's parents, Lillian and Emil, were two of the special people who loved me during a challenging childhood due to the fact that I was born with one leg almost three inches shorter ꞌhan the other. I had to wear special shoes and endure four leg operations before I was ten. When other 12-year-olds were wearing penny loafers, I was restricted to clunky saddle shoes that made me feel ugly and conspicuous.

Nevertheless, my grandparents never failed to make me feel unconditionally loved and my memories of their home are special to me. When they moved to Marina City in downtown Chicago, I'd stroll arm-in-arm with my grandfather along State Street, imagining he was my boyfriend. He cried at my eighth grade graduation, and although I didn't fully understand why, his tears made me feel special.

I especially loved going to my grandmother's house for dinner. She seemed to effortlessly prepare wonderful meals served on her rosebud china while simultaneously providing tastes that would please me and my eight brothers and sisters.

We always pestered my grandfather to show us again, on a special painting of a German village, which house he had been born in.

With a flip of a switch, twinkling lights shone from each window. It was only as I grew older that I realized Grandpa changed which window he pointed to every time we went through this ritual.

The highlight of every dinner was my Grandma's Bukda. This delicious bread was presented with much fanfare because, visually, the golden-brown braided bread is a masterpiece. We all hoped she'd send the leftovers home with us—it made fantastic French toast the next morning.

After my grandfather died and we left home to start our own families, we each tried to coax the recipe from my grandmother. She did not have it written down though—she put it together from memory. No measurements were involved. So, my sister Kate, watching her one day, translated her handfuls and pinches into measurements.

Here it is. I know she'd be flattered to have her recipe passed along to so many. Just as she nourished a little girl's self-worth, I know this bread will please and nourish your family.

Bukda
(Bohemian Braided Bread)

Makes 1 loaf

❧

2 cups milk, divided	*½ cup sugar*
1½ packages instant dry yeast	*1 tablespoon salt*
1 teaspoon sugar	*3 eggs, beaten*
2 tablespoons softened butter	*8 to 10 cups flour, sifted*
or margarine	*Oil, to brush over the bread*

1. Heat ½ cup milk to lukewarm. Stir in yeast and sugar. Set aside for 30 minutes.

2. Meanwhile, in a large mixing bowl, combine softened butter or margarine with sugar and salt. Add beaten eggs. Warm 1½ more cups of milk and stir into the other ingredients. Set aside.

3. When the yeast mixture is ready, add it to the bowl along with 4 cups of the flour. Mix, and continue adding flour, 1 cup at a time, until the dough can be easily handled—it should pull away from the sides of the bowl and not be too sticky. Cover the bowl with a damp towel and put in a warm place (a turned-off oven with a pilot light works well). Let rise until nearly doubled, then punch down and turn out onto a floured surface. Knead for 10 minutes and return to the clean bowl. Let rise a second time, repeating the process.

4. Preheat oven to 350° F. Divide the dough into three equal portions. Roll and stretch each portion to about 15 inches. Grease a large cookie sheet and lay each portion side by side on the sheet. Stack 3 ends on top of each other and press them together. Braid the three portions together and end by stacking the 3 remaining ends. Press each end so the braid is secure and does not come undone during rising and cooking. (The braid will stretch the entire length of the cookie sheet.) Lightly oil the top of the bread with a pastry feather or small brush. Let rise for 30 minutes.

5. Bake for 30 to 40 minutes in the center of the oven or until the top of the bread is a medium golden brown.

Gagi's Gumbo

D. Trinidad Hunt

My treasure chest of memories is full of little Gagi stories that warm my heart and bring a smile to my face. A collage of impressions surface when I think of her. Gagi, my grandmother, was a woman ahead of her time, courageous, outspoken and gifted in many ways. Born in Canada, she was raised on the Canadian prairies where she got her can-do attitude and innovative spirit. She spoke fluent French and was trained in the art of French cuisine by the Roman Catholic priests in a French monastic order in Saskatchewan.

Gagi was known for her pioneering spirit and brilliant mind. It was this spirit that propelled Gagi and her family across the Pacific on the savings from the sales of her French candy to settle in the Hawaiian Islands. Once in the islands, Gagi began earning money for the family by caring for children. She started one of Hawaii's first day-care centers—and it still flourishes to this day.

But it was Gagi's stories and her cooking that I remember so vividly. My brothers and I often went to Gagi's for dinner when my parents were working late. Her home was a safe haven from the world during my early years of growing and self-discovery.

"Tell us a story, Gagi!" became our family's favorite words, and then we'd wait patiently as Gagi searched her mental files for *just the right one.*

One night, after much begging from my brothers, Gagi's eyes twinkled as she dipped a piece of bread into her famous Gumbo. It was the look of a story brewing in her eyes. "Do you have a request?" she asked.

"The *wolf* one," my brother answered quickly. It was one of our favorites and we all waited with bated breath.

" . . . The nights were long and lonely on the Saskatchewan prairie." Gagi's voice was full of mystery and adventure as she began. "And during the icy winters we rarely ventured far from our house, for the prairie animals were lean and hungry. The later it was in winter, the leaner and hungrier they were." She glowed as the story came to life.

"But one afternoon," she continued, "my mother and I were forced to go to the home of a friend. Mother had heard that our neighbor Henry had been running a fever and she thought he might need help. So she and I hitched the horse to our wagon and ventured out with food and supplies. When we arrived we found Henry up and about. He'd been sick but he was better now.

"Before we knew it, late afternoon was upon us. The sky was growing dark and ominous. Night settled in at about 4:30 on the winter prairie; we knew we had to go. Henry didn't feel right about letting his two neighbor ladies out alone at such a late hour, so he hitched up our horse and we all set out together.

"It was three or four miles between houses on the prairie, and soon the clouds rolled in. First the flatland turned into a glowing violet blue, and then night fell, covering the land in pitch black. Then it started, the sound of wolves in the distance. Our horse shivered and shifted in her stride as the sound grew closer."

My brothers and I fidgeted nervously in our seats. "We were still a couple of miles from home and I knew from the look on Henry's face that we were in trouble.

"'It sounds like a large pack, hungry from the winter famine,' he murmured as he whipped the horse into a full run. Soon we could see their dark angry forms racing to catch up with us from behind." Gagi's eyes were wide with fear as she spoke.

"They were about 60 feet behind us and my mother and I clung to each other as Henry screamed and cracked the whip, urging the horse to push beyond his limits." My brothers and I leaned forward in our seats, the breath of the wild wolves on our backs.

"We raced as the wolves pulled closer and closer, their starvation driving them as they snapped at the back wheels of our wagon. Just

then the horse spotted our farm house ahead, and with a final burst
of energy, lunged forward with all his strength and raced for the
barn. As we pulled through the farmyard fence, the wolves suddenly veered off to the right and ran off into the night, howling."

My brothers and I heaved a group sigh and threw ourselves back
in our chairs, exhausted by the hairy escape.

"And the moral of the story is . . ." my grandmother continued,
"Don't ever go out on the prairie alone on a wild winter night."

It never occurred to us that we were in Hawaii where there
wasn't a real winter, let alone wolves, so we all solemnly
promised and breathed a sigh of relief at having escaped the
wolves one more time.

The storytelling tradition is found in every culture, and I came to
know it personally through the spirit of my Gagi's soup. The spirit
of the soup is always in the story.

Gagi's Gumbo

Makes 4 servings

❧

Serve with a large loaf of warm bread and one wonderful story, shared from the heart.

5 large potatoes, peeled and
  cut into large chunks
1½ sticks (12 tablespoons) butter
1 medium onion, sliced
⅓ head cabbage, shredded
1 stalk broccoli, chopped
¼ head cauliflower, cut
  in cubes
4 carrots, peeled and cut
  in cubes
2 cups bean sprouts
1 (12- to 14-ounce) can
  chunky tuna packed in water
4 to 8 ounces fresh fish, cut
  in cubes

4 cloves fresh crushed garlic
2 tablespoons chopped fresh
  basil (or 2 teaspoons dried,
  crumbled)
1 tablespoon fresh oregano
  (or ½ teaspoon dried,
  crumbled)
¾ teaspoon salt
½ teaspoon sweet paprika
½ teaspoon ground black pepper
⅛ teaspoon cayenne pepper
1 pound shelled, deveined shrimp
Thinly sliced scallions to
  sprinkle over each serving

1. Place potatoes in a soup pot with water to cover; boil until soft. Pour off and measure the water, returning 4 cups of it to the pot. Mash the potatoes, leaving some of them in large chunks. Stir in butter.

2. Add the onions, cabbage, broccoli, cauliflower, carrots and bean sprouts to the pot. Bring to a simmer and cook for 45 minutes.

3. Drain and discard the water from the can of chunky tuna; add tuna to the pot. Add the fresh fish, cut in cubes, along with 1 to 2 cups water as needed for consistency. Add the remaining ingredients except shrimp and scallions; simmer 30 minutes longer.

4. Add shrimp; simmer 10 to 15 minutes. Serve in soup bowls; sprinkle the top of each serving with thinly sliced scallions.

Grandma Yehle's Summer Kitchen

Pam Finger

Some of my fondest childhood memories are of spending week-ends with my four sisters at my grandparents' house in the city. My own family lived in a small village, so going to the city for a week-end was a thrill.

My grandparents lived in a big, old home with lots of room for playing hide-and-seek, and a bright, sunny attic full of books and dis-carded toys from my mom, aunts and uncles. Even the basement had several rooms, one of which contained a mangle that my grandma used to press shirts and sheets for all the beds in the house.

My sisters and I spent hours learning to play the grand piano that stood in the entrance hall. Grandma patiently taught us the practice scales and all the tunes from "The Sound of Music." She would even listen to the melodies that we "created."

One of the highlights of the weekend was having "Coffee with Curtis"—a radio talk show—on Sunday mornings. So that we could all share in the fun, we were each given a demitasse cup filled mostly with milk and a small amount of coffee. How grown up we felt drink-ing coffee with Curtis in the breakfast room!

The walls were covered with maps of the world, and my grand-father would tell us about different countries and world history. Grandpa was a children's court judge and very much the taskmaster of the household. I'm sure having his home invaded by five lively girls on weekends tried his patience. "The Judge," as he was affec-tionately called, spent Saturday afternoons in the big overstuffed chair outside his office listening intently to Syracuse University football and basketball games. He was famous for falling asleep after a large holiday meal and I distinctly remember encouraging a cousin of mine to try and throw a ping-pong ball into his open mouth while he napped. Luckily it never went in and he never woke up.

My grandmother loved to play practical jokes. One of her favorites was to put a piece of flannel in the batter of one of my Grandfather's pancakes. How we twittered waiting for him to bite into the right piece. Grandma loved to bake and always had several batches of homemade cookies on hand to offer us. She was famous for her Christmas cookies and filled many tins each year.

Each year we went to the Sample Fair held in the carriage house behind one of the big city mansions. As children we talked for days about all the treasures we could collect there. Each of us got a shopping bag when entering and we proceeded to fill it with hundreds of samples—everything from mini loaves of bread from a local bakery to yardsticks from the paint store. We spent hours choosing and deciding which treasures to take.

Another favorite activity was to spend time with my grandparents at their summer cottage in the Thousand Islands. Grandma let us accompany her, regardless of the weather, on her daily 6 A.M. dip in the St. Lawrence River. What an invigorating way to start a summer day!

She loved to let us help her bake too. A highlight of Sunday mornings was helping her make doughnuts—a real family treat. We'd take the warm doughnuts and roll them in powdered sugar or cinnamon, then sit down to a cup of coffee with a radio program and we were on our way to another wonderful summer Sunday.

Although I didn't turn out to be much of a baker, I really appreciate the work and love that goes into making treats for others. Every year when the Christmas cookies come out or we get a bag of doughnuts from the local bakery, I am reminded of Grandma's wonderful recipes and all the good times we had together.

Grandma Yehle's
Summer Doughnuts

Makes 18 doughnuts

∽

This recipe is from Florence Markham Smith, my grandmother's mother (and my great-grandmother, of course).

3 cups pre-sifted flour	*½ teaspoon cinnamon*
1 cup sugar	*½ teaspoon nutmeg*
1 cup milk	*Extra flour, for rolling out*
2 tablespoons melted butter	*dough*
2 eggs	*Vegetable shortening, for*
2 teaspoons cream of tartar	*frying*
1 teaspoon baking soda	*Sugar to roll the doughnuts in*
½ teaspoon salt	*while still warm (optional)*

1. In a large mixing bowl combine all ingredients except shortening for cooking. Stir it all together as much as you can with a spoon. Sprinkle the dough lightly with flour and turn out onto a board, kneading it into one cohesive mass. Do not allow to stand.

2. Roll out the dough about ½-inch thick and cut with a doughnut cutter. Reroll and cut the scraps. Heat 2 cups vegetable shortening in an electric skillet set at 375° F (or in another deep frying pan into which you've inserted a deep fat thermometer). Use a slotted pancake turner dipped in hot fat to transfer 4 doughnuts to the hot fat. Fry on one side until brown, then turn over to cook other side. Drain on several layers of paper towels. Continue cooking doughnuts, replacing fat in the pan as needed. If desired, roll the doughnuts in sugar while still warm.

Grandma Yehle's German Animal Christmas Cookies

Makes more than 200 cookies

❧

4 cups sugar	*1½ teaspoons baking soda*
4 eggs	*1½ teaspoons cream of tartar*
½ pound butter	*2 teaspoons vanilla, or to taste*
½ pound vegetable shortening	*½ teaspoon salt*
2 cups milk	*About 10 cups pre-sifted flour*

1. In a very large mixing bowl, beat together sugar and eggs. In a small saucepan melt together the butter and vegetable shortening and let cool; when cool, add to the butter and eggs and mix well. Heat milk to lukewarm; stir in baking soda and cream of tartar until dissolved. Add to egg, butter and shortening mixture and blend well. Add vanilla and salt.

2. Gradually add flour until the dough is the right consistency for rolling. Roll out ¼-inch thick onto a floured surface. Cut with animal (or other) cookie cutters. Place on greased cookie sheets and bake for 8 to 10 minutes. (Frost with a butter frosting if desired.)

Almost Grandma's Apple Pie

Kirby Howard

Sometimes in the dead heat of summer, I feel a faint, warm breeze in which I smell the precious scent of lemon, cinnamon, butter and chicken feed. What a marvelous blend of aromas, sending me back through time to my grandmother's kitchen.

From dawn to dusk, the iron wood-burning stove turned out delicious foods—sugar cookies, chocolate cake, cherry pies, turnip greens, and, oh Lord, the best apple pie in the universe! There was never a time that I went into that kitchen that I did not see proudly displayed at least one gorgeous pie, next to the melt-in-your-mouth cookies, and if you were truly blessed, the apple pie—which none of us in the family have ever been truly able to duplicate.

We comfort ourselves by telling each other that it's the stove, and that's why we can't reproduce her apple pie on our modern, emotionless stoves with their cold buttons and knobs. Maybe it was the stove. But I think that there was another force at work, namely good old-fashioned love, hard work, sacrifice and many selfless hours of giving so that others might enjoy life more easily and more often. And most importantly, she represented that life could be sustained, because in my grandmother's day, life was to be sustained at all costs.

I have often marveled at how much she accomplished each day—caring for 10 children and Lord knows how many others she took in. All under her care wore clean, ironed shirts and trousers or dresses. All of them ate three substantial meals a day, for hers was a farming family and they had to eat heartily—there were chickens to be fed, eggs to be gathered, butter to be churned and wash to be done in well water—no air conditioner, no ice maker and no mixer or food processor.

My grandmother never dwelled on what she did not have; she simply made the most of what she did have—a strong body and an incredible spirit of giving, selflessness and humility. I will always remember how wonderful it felt to talk with her. I would pump her for stories of her childhood and she would oblige with endless tales that I wish to this day I had written down.

Now that she is gone I long for those conversations with her in her kitchen and on her porch with the wicker furniture and devil's backbone plants. She was not a woman who tested you or judged you—no way—she just loved you! It was an unconditional Godlike love that she didn't even think about. She didn't agonize over her daily chores, she just did them. And as unbelievable as it is to remember, given today's world, she did her work comfortably in a flour-sack dress with an apron tied around her ample middle.

In reflective moments, when I take a look at my own life, I wonder, could I really be kin to her? How very different our lives are! That I don't have 10 children and a wood-burning stove is only the tip of the iceberg. What I wouldn't give to have her stamina and generous nature! How many more things besides the apple pie can I not quite master in my life that she mastered in hers?

I greatly admire her life of service to others and I honor her memory as one of the dearest influences of my childhood. I am thrilled whenever my own mother tells me that I am just like my grandmother. I wish it were closer to the truth, but at least Grandma gave me a mark to shoot for. I believe that she is with me often and I still hold long-winded conversations with her. They are just somewhat one-sided now. I long for the day when we can hug again and she finally tells me what *exactly* I am doing wrong with this apple pie recipe.

Almost Grandma's Apple Pie

Makes one 9-inch pie

❧

PIE CRUST:
2 cups flour
¾ cup solid vegetable shortening
1 teaspoon salt

5 tablespoons ice water
Sugar, to sprinkle over the top

FILLING:
6 cups sliced, peeled apples
1 cup sugar
¼ cup flour
3 tablespoons cinnamon

2 tablespoons butter, melted
½ teaspoon nutmeg
½ teaspoon salt

1. For crust, use a pastry cutter or two knives to cut flour, short-ening, and salt together until the shortening is the size of small peas. Sprinkle in water one tablespoon at a time while tossing with a fork until the mixture holds together.

2. Roll out about two-thirds of dough to line a pie pan, saving the other portion to cut in strips and weave into a lattice over the top of the pie.

3. For the filling, mix all ingredients together until the apples are coated with a syrup-like glaze. Pour into the pie pan. Top with a lattice crust. Sprinkle with sugar to make it glisten. Bake at 375°F for 1 hour.

4
Family

A home is a place where a pot of fresh soup simmers gently on the hob, filling the kitchen with soft aromas . . . and filling your heart, and later your tummy, with joy.

—Keith Floyd

The bond that links your true family is not one of blood, but of respect and joy in each other's life.

—Richard Bach

For as long as I can remember, my grandfather, John A. Mark, said the following blessing at every meal. To this day I can hear his voice, complete with every pause and emphasis, speaking the words. A relative recently told me that my Great-Grandpa Mark developed the blessing through the course of his life, and that he said it before every meal. It continues to be used today at our family gatherings.

We thank you Father for the privilege of meeting around this board. Bless this food to our use; may it strengthen us for our several duties in life. And at last when the race is run, take us to thy home on high. We ask it in your name, Amen.

—Matthew S. Diener

*F*amily Prayer

Lord, behold our family here assembled.
We thank you for this place in which we dwell, for
the love that unites us,
for the peace accorded us this day,
for the hope with which we expect the morrow;
for the health, the work, the food and the bright skies
that make our lives delightful;
for our friends in all parts of the earth, Amen.

—Robert Louis Stevenson (1850–1894)

From Dancer to Cook

Patti Rypinski

I loved my mother-in-law. Beautiful, exciting, adventurous, fun. She was a true treasure. We certainly had our differences, but through 35 years, our cautious friendship ripened into mutual respect and genuine love.

Did I mention that Florence Forman was a star? Well, she was . . . from the tip of her toes to the top of her head. She never forgot her stage etiquette—on leaving a room, she would turn and make her exit with a little bow and a wave.

Encouraged by her Russian ballet instructor, she tried out for an acting part at age 14. At that time she met another aspiring actress, Harriet Hilliard Nelson, who would later become the mom of the famous Nelson family. Florence and Harriet remained close, true friends from age 14 until and beyond Florence's death at 84 in 1993. At the time Harriet said, "How Florence loved top billing!"

On her honeymoon in the South of France in 1920-something, Florence met another lifelong friend—Marjorie Husted, the original Betty Crocker, who first introduced Bisquick, and whom Florence credited as her cooking inspiration.

Because she adored entertaining, cooking and interesting people, Florence's parties were famous. Not only did everyone want to attend, they wanted to share her recipes. Most of us would copy a few and hand them out. In 1981, Florence wrote and published her own cookbook, *Dancer to Cook*. Demand grew over the years, with the book going into six printings, each one larger than the last. She was down to her last copy which she gave to her favorite nurse, Elizabeth, five days before her death.

For six months after Florence died, I could not make it through a day without tears and a wrenching heart. All of us in the family had been with her almost constantly in the three months before she succumbed to cancer. Even though I thought I had said all I wanted to her and done all I could, the regret and sadness that engulfed me grew more and more intolerable. I seemed to be taking her death harder than anyone else.

We all loved and missed her, but they had all done something I was unable to do. Yes, I had told her, as had the others, how I loved her, how she influenced me, how I would carry on remembering and cherishing her. What I had forgotten and could not bring myself to tell her was . . . goodbye.

With the help of a very wise friend, I was able to realize that in not letting her go, in not saying goodbye, I was hanging onto the grief (something Florence would abhor). So, I sat quietly for a long time, visualizing Florence and telling her goodbye.

That night, I slept deeply and had the most wonderful dream. Florence appeared refreshed, rested, glowing and vital, with the old twinkle in her eyes. She turned, in full Technicolor, and before leaving a perfect movie set—a garden laden with trees, vines, flowers and birds, complete with a rainbow—blew me a kiss and ascended a flight of stairs, giving me that little exit wave. Smiling, she continued walking upward and away. The stairs became narrow, disappearing into heavenly clouds. What a finale!

I released her, and in doing so released my grief. She was content, smiling and at total peace; her love for me reached out to fill up my anguish. My sorrow dissolved into fond memories that enrich my daily life as well as my soul, teaching me beyond life about love.

Aloha, dear Florence, our *kaanei* (meaning "special one" in

Hawaiian), a name chosen and given to her by her wonderful friend, Mahi Beamer.

My husband Alan's favorite chocolate cake is the following one from Florence's book. He compares every chocolate cake he tastes to it, and he's never found one that satisfies him quite so deeply.

Harold Lloyd's Chocolate Cake
Makes about 12 servings

Harold Lloyd was, besides Florence's friend, a star of silent screen—the comic in round black glasses who hung from the clock face atop the skyscraper.

CAKE:

1 (1-pound) box brown sugar
1 stick (½ cup) butter
2 eggs
2 squares unsweetened chocolate

1¾ cups cake flour
1 teaspoon baking soda
¼ teaspoon salt
1 cup sour milk or buttermilk

CHOCOLATE FILLING:

1 tablespoon (1 package)
  unflavored gelatin
¾ cup sugar
½ cup flour
½ cup water

1½ squares unsweetened
  chocolate, coarsely chopped
1 tablespoon butter
½ cup heavy cream
  (whipping cream)

CHOCOLATE FROSTING:

3 ounces (3 squares)
  unsweetened chocolate
2 tablespoons butter

½ cup milk (or more if needed)
3 cups powdered sugar
2 teaspoons vanilla

1. Preheat oven to 350°F. Butter and flour (or line with buttered parchment) two 8-inch round cake pans. In a large bowl, cream together brown sugar and butter with an electric mixer. Add eggs and melted chocolate. Sift together flour, baking soda and salt. Add

the flour mixture alternately with sour milk or buttermilk, beating all the while. Pour the batter into the prepared pans and smooth the tops. Bake for 25 to 30 minutes until a toothpick inserted near the center comes out clean.

2. While the cake is baking, make the filling. Sprinkle gelatin over ¼ cup cold water and set aside to soften. Stir sugar and flour together in a saucepan. Add ½ cup water, chocolate and butter, and heat, stirring until chocolate is melted and the mixture is smooth. Remove from heat. Stir in the softened gelatin and let *cool completely* to room temperature. (It needs to attain a pudding-like consistency.) When both the filling and the cakes are cool, beat the heavy cream (whipping cream) until it holds a shape, and mix the cream into the filling. Spread between the two chocolate layers.

3. To make chocolate frosting, melt the chocolate, butter and milk together in a saucepan over very low heat, stirring often. Cool to lukewarm, then blend in the powdered sugar and vanilla, beating until thick and smooth enough to spread. Use a spatula to spread the frosting over the top and sides of the cake.

Homemade Children

Naomi Rhode

As I write this recipe there is bread "raising" on my hearth and children "raising" in my home. Neither progeny is finished, but the ingredients have been carefully selected, measured and blended. The good recipe book promises: "Train up a child in the way he should go, and when he is grown he will not depart from it" (Proverbs, 22:6). Having experience in following that recipe book, I trust the author!

1. Measure into a home, parents who love, followed by a few children (use own discretion on number—we prefer 3).

2. Add, stirring constantly, yeast (we recommend faith in God). Stir in wisdom (as much as possible from God's Word, previous training and lots of common sense), truth (very important for consistent results), patience (ample portions needed throughout), kindness (large volumes), gentleness (soften before adding), discipline (with fairness, measured in a clean container), love (full measure, pressed down, shaken together and overflowing the cup), and laughter (knead in as much as possible and let permeate throughout the whole batch).

3. All ingredients should be measured using a container of prayer (no substitutions, please). For excellent eating and preserving quality keep dough as soft and pliable as possible, but not sticky—just so you, with God's help, can handle it.

4. Mix until smooth and elastic (about 18 years). Place in a greased bowl (symbolic of life's struggles) and cover with a damp cloth (we learn through failures as well as victories). Let rise in *warm* place (the temperature for "raising" is very important) until double in size (about four to eight years after high school).

5. Dough will be ready to be divided and made into all shapes of beautiful young men and women for use as the Staff of Life in other people's lives. Guaranteed—wonderful results!

The Sound of Snowflakes and Warm Cranberry Pie

Avril Johannes

Have you ever heard a snowflake fall? I have.

My husband, Joe, our three children and I drove one day until the logging road ended among the spruce trees. Walking into an area that few people travel during the winter months, we could enjoy the peace and quiet of the countryside.

It began to snow. Being all bundled up in snowsuits, hats, gloves and snug-fitting, fur-lined boots, neither the cold nor the snow bothered us. Sounds were muffled by the falling snow. The air was very still. Evergreens stood majestically in their winter splendor, their boughs drooping under the weight. Aspen and birches were naked except for an occasional frozen leaf.

Animal tracks were disappearing in the light snowfall, but we could still see where a fox had run between some trees, and a moose had left its telltale prints. Further on, under a willow bush, we saw the shiny, coal-black eyes and black-trimmed ears of a snowshoe hare. A red squirrel scampered down a tree trunk and dashed off to its midden, where it sat on its furry bottom, folding its hands and admonishing us for the intrusion. We heard the swishing sound of raven wings above.

Ahead, the children played tag, running, rolling and pushing each other. Laughter filled the air as they opened their mouths to catch a

snowflake and feel it melt on their tongues. Leaving them to their games, Joe and I walked on until we were out of hearing range. Finding an old tree stump, we sat to rest.

It was so still there, we could hear the snowflakes touching the ground as they fell. Maybe it was because we were straining to hear the children, or maybe it was one of those rare occasions when one blends with nature and the senses are as acute as God meant them to be.

It was not long before the silence was shattered by three boisterous, giggling, shouting youngsters running and stumbling into view. They were ready to return home to the comfort of a warm fire, dry clothes, hot chocolate and their favorite goody, warm Cranberry Pie.

As we strolled hand-in-hand back to the car, each deep in our own thoughts, we saw a moose and her yearling calf walk out from the trees into full view and then disappear again like shadows.

Later that evening, after the children had gone to bed, we sat in front of the fire and talked about the serenity of the moose and her baby, how a snowshoe hare changes colors to blend in with the seasons, and the magic of hearing a snowflake.

Cranberry Pie
Makes two 9-inch pies

2 cups flour
1 cup sugar
2 teaspoons baking powder
1 cup cold whole milk

1 tablespoon melted butter
2½ cups raw whole cranberries
½ cup chopped walnuts
  (optional)

SAUCE:
1 cup sugar
1 stick (½ cup) butter

¾ cup evaporated milk
1 teaspoon vanilla

1. Preheat oven to 350°F. To make the pie, in a large mixing bowl combine the flour, sugar and baking powder. Stir in the milk, melted

butter, cranberries and walnuts. Mix well and transfer to 2 ungreased 9-inch pie pans. Bake for 30 minutes.

2. To make the sauce, in a small saucepan combine the sugar, butter and evaporated milk. Bring to a boil and simmer for about 3 minutes, until sugar dissolves. Remove from the heat and stir in vanilla. Pour the sauce over the two pies. Cut in wedges and serve hot.

> . . . *when I was a tiny child I turned from the window out of which I was watching a snowstorm and hopefully asked, "Momma, do we believe in Winter?"*
>
> —Philip Roth

Happy Hooligan—
Dog Gourmet

Floren Harper

Happy Hooligan was a fox terrier—black on the back, brown-sugar face, white underside and paws. He was probably the most brilliant, sleek, athletic canine ever born. Everyone in the town of Laurelton, Long Island, knew him. He'd sail over hedges showing off his terrier powers, defying gravity. Graceful . . . he was graceful and kind and thoughtful. He was my best friend. I could tell him anything. And he was probably the most enthusiastic eater in the family—no one else talked or cared much about what we ate.

We always had simple meals—chicken, vegetable, potato, a side salad and Jell-O or applesauce for dessert, sometimes ice cream. There was milk for my brother and me, tea for the folks. The menus varied a little but not much. Food was no big thing. Mom didn't care much about cooking; Dad never lifted a pan. We had a Canadian housekeeper, Ada, who cooked simple meals.

Once in a while, Happy Hooligan would get mildly excited about smells in the kitchen; but I don't remember my brother or me sniffing anything with anticipation upstairs in our rooms during the homework hours before dinner.

And because he was generally a well-behaved, mature creature, Happy only sniffed around the table when the appetizer was deposited on the service plates. He might even go so far as to jump up on one of the gargoyle-carved chairs and bring his nose dangerously close to what was already on the table. But, as far as I know, he never attacked the food. Of course, we couldn't know if he was just terribly well-behaved or as unmoved by the food as we were.

Each evening, when Dad came home, like clockwork we'd run downstairs to see if he brought home chewing gum or ice cream. We loved chewing gum, peanut butter and jelly and, of course, ice cream.

One spring evening at around 6 P.M. we were pestering Dad for treats when suddenly a pained wail tore through the house. Ada was in tears, howling and chasing Happy with a meat mallet.

It seemed that Happy had downed the appetizers on all four serving plates—ate every last morsel—and left only the lettuce leaves. And because we knew Happy to be a creature of elevated temperament and refined taste, my brother Karl and I were sure that we'd probably missed the only gourmet meal ever to grace our dining room table.

Happy Hooligan died a week later. That was one of the hardest days of my life, but I'll always remember him. And I trust that he left us with a memory of a meal suited to the perfection he was.

Here is the meal Happy Hooligan loved.

Chicken Liver Pâté Hooligan

Makes 1½ cups

8 ounces chicken livers
1 large shallot or the white
   part of 3 scallions
2 teaspoons dry mustard
1 teaspoon salt
⅛ teaspoon ground allspice
⅛ teaspoon freshly grated
   nutmeg

⅛ teaspoon cayenne pepper
3 tablespoons port or brandy
2 sticks (½ pound) sweet
   (unsalted) butter, at room
   temperature
1 tablespoon minced fresh
   parsley
Crusty French bread, for serving

1. Rinse chicken livers and place in a small saucepan in cold water to cover. Bring to a boil, then lower heat and simmer slowly for 10 minutes.

2. Meanwhile, mince shallot or scallions in a blender or food processor fitted with a steel blade. Add dry mustard, salt, allspice, nutmeg and cayenne pepper. Drain the chicken livers well and add them to the blender or food processor. Process to a smooth paste, then add port or brandy and continue processing, stopping the motor from time to time to scrape down the sides of the container with a rubber spatula. Let cool to room temperature.

3. Add butter, ½ stick at a time, processing until very smooth and scraping the sides of the container often. Stir in minced fresh parsley.

4. If you wish to serve this simply as a spread with crusty French bread, transfer to small crocks for serving; press plastic wrap into the surface to keep fresh and prevent discoloration. Serve chilled. Another, fancier way to serve this as first course or picnic fare is to make bread tubes by hollowing out two 6-inch lengths of crisp French bread baguettes to fill with the mixture. Cover one end of each tube with plastic wrap held in place with a rubber band. Spoon the pâté into the tubes, tapping lightly to remove any air bubbles that form, and fill them to the top. Cover the filled bread crusts with plastic wrap and place upright in the refrigerator to chill until the pâté is firm. When cold, remove rubber bands and use a serrated slicing knife to cut crosswise into ¼- to ½-inch slices.

Our Italian-American Table

Carol Miller

My Italian-New Jersey upbringing left me with fond memories of delectable and sumptuous food consumed around my family's large kitchen table. When one dish, such as Parmesan-stuffed artichokes, was finished, a plate of glistening marinated red and yellow roasted peppers with mozzarella was next on the table as a prelude to several main entrees: eggplant parmigiana, stuffed ricotta pasta shells and bell peppers filled with rice and sausage.

Friends and relatives were always welcome, and mealtime conversations were always lively, sometimes argumentative and often humorous. Cousin Mario, a saxophonist *par excellence*, would fascinate us with tales of his nightclub performances; he dazzled audiences by simultaneously playing two saxophones. When Cousin Steve was late (which was every time), he was quickly forgiven because of funny jokes.

My mother (also known as Aunt Rosie) was happiest preparing food for large gatherings of relatives. Little did I know that these early experiences were steering me toward catering as a profession. I am grateful that my Italian heritage has provided me with the exposure to the joys and adventures found in fine food and good company.

Here is one of my company's most popular appetizers.

Sun-Dried Tomato and Basil Torta with Toasted Crostini

Makes 15 or more servings

∽

8 ounces cream cheese, at
  room temperature
1 small clove garlic, peeled
¼ cup loosely packed fresh basil
1 cup freshly grated
Parmesan cheese
Crostini, for serving
  (recipe follows)

4 ounces blue cheese, at
  room temperature
¾ cup loosely packed fresh
  Italian parsley
¼ cup drained and slivered
  sun-dried tomatoes
¼ cup finely chopped walnuts
¼ cup olive oil

1. In a mixing bowl combine cream cheese and blue cheese and allow to come to room temperature. Mix until thoroughly blended and set aside.

2. Drop one small clove garlic into the *dry* bowl of an electric food processor with the motor running. Instant minced garlic! You may, of course, mince the garlic and chop the remaining ingredients by hand. Combine parsley, basil and sun-dried tomatoes in the bowl of the processor with the garlic; process until smooth, then with the motor running pour in the olive oil. Transfer the mixture to a small bowl. Stir in Parmesan and walnuts.

3. Line a 5½- x 2½-inch loaf pan with plastic wrap, leaving extra wrap hanging over the sides. Divide the cheese mixture into three equal portions. Spread one-third of cheese mixture on bottom of pan; spread half of tomato-basil mixture over cheese. Repeat the cheese layer and the tomato-basil layer. Top with the remaining third of cheese. Cover with plastic wrap and refrigerate for 24 hours (or freeze).

4. To serve, allow the torta to come to room temperature for 30 minutes (2 hours if frozen). Invert onto a platter, provide a spreader and serve with crostini.

Crostini

1 French bread baguette
2 tablespoons Herbes de Provence
  (or other herb blend you like)

¼ cup olive oil
1 tablespoon minced garlic

1. Preheat oven to 350°F. Cut French bread into thin slices and place on a cookie sheet.

2. In a small bowl, combine olive oil, herbs and garlic. Spread or brush each slice lightly with the herb-garlic mixture and bake for 5 to 7 minutes until golden.

> *Tomatoes and oregano make it Italian; wine and tarragon make it French. Sour cream makes it Russian; lemon and cinnamon make it Greek. Soy sauce makes it Chinese; garlic makes it good.*

—Alice May Brock

My Grandpa Bentura and the Carrot Cake

Frank Trujillo

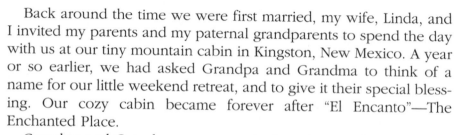

Back around the time we were first married, my wife, Linda, and I invited my parents and my paternal grandparents to spend the day with us at our tiny mountain cabin in Kingston, New Mexico. A year or so earlier, we had asked Grandpa and Grandma to think of a name for our little weekend retreat, and to give it their special blessing. Our cozy cabin became forever after "El Encanto"—The Enchanted Place.

Grandpa and Grandma were amazingly unique and special individuals. They were always eager to help a neighbor or family member in a time of need—they were full of life and energy, and witty and wise. Alone, each was a delightful individual, but together they were just magnificent. They were especially significant in my eyes, for I was their *ahijado*, their godchild, and they were my godparents, my *padrinos.* Along with my parents, they were my first—and my best—teachers. And they loved Linda. From the moment I first introduced her, they adopted her and treated her as their very own. They were that way—loving, giving, welcoming each new member of their extending family.

I have some favorite stories about them too . . . like the time my 80-year-old grandma took a hoe to a rattlesnake that had cousin Stevie and me cornered and screaming for our lives out behind Grandpa's old tool shed. And the time Grandpa and I sold three truckloads of *chiles verdes* (green chili peppers) and *pepinos* (cucumbers) in just two days, by peddling our fresh-picked produce door-to-door. Bentura and Adamacia (Tafoya) Trujillo were special, all right.

One splendid afternoon in Kingston is a time with them I shall never forget. The night before making the trip to our cabin, Linda busied herself concocting our favorite dessert: carrot cake. I packed our little pickup full of provisions in anticipation of the 75-mile trip into the Black Range mountains to our little weekend retreat, located almost exactly halfway between Silver City, where I was born, and Monticello and Hot Springs, towns where I had lived most of my life.

The next day, we all met at *El Encanto*. Three generations converged—four, if you count Mr. Bumpus, our white, curly-tailed dog. I have a couple of photographs of my father, then in his late 50s, jumping rope, and a photo of Grandma spinning a hula-hoop while my mother, Linda, Grandpa—and it appeared even Bumpus— clapped and shouted their encouragement . . . typical of how we always had fun together.

One day I remember all of us sitting down to dinner. Grandpa had found an old wooden table and three chairs at a yard sale. He had rough-painted them the brightest red imaginable. During one of our visits Grandpa had told me to back up my little '54 Ford pickup to his toolshed because he had something for us—fire-red kitchen furniture. The enamel paint was brushed on so thick that years later it was somehow still pliable, especially on a hot day. Grandpa must have spent weeks painting it.

We were sitting at that very table that night. There was nothing particularly eventful about our meal, but I remember Grandpa finishing way before the rest of us were done. He got up and walked through the kitchen and outside onto the deck. After a few moments we began wondering whether he was feeling well; after all, Grandpa was in his mid-80s.

Linda went outside to check on him and the rest of us remained at the table, finishing our dinner and looking forward to dessert. Within seconds Linda was back. "Shhhh!" she said. "Come over to the window and take a look at Grandpa." There he was, his back to us, sitting in the warm fading sunlight, his chair drawn up close to a small TV tray. He was eating—he was polishing off the very

last morsel of Linda's loaf-sized carrot cake. Linda had intended to slice the small loaf into six equal portions.

Of course, we never said a word. Smiling, we quietly retreated to the kitchen and got to work on the dishes. A while later we looked out and saw Grandpa napping—his head resting on the side of old, fluffy Mr. Bumpus. Contentment personified.

Every time I eat carrot cake I think of Grandpa that day. And I wonder what Grandpa would have said or done had he ever known . . . and I wonder what deep, sweet, enchanted dreams he dreamed that day.

Here is Linda's recipe for carrot cake—except now she always makes two.

Twin Carrot Loaves

Makes two 9 x 5-inch loaves

2½ cups flour
1½ teaspoons baking powder
½ teaspoon baking soda
½ teaspoon salt
1 teaspoon ground cinnamon
4 large eggs, separated
1½ cups vegetable oil

2½ cups sugar
⅓ cup hot water
1½ cups grated carrots
1 cup chopped walnuts or
 pecans
1 teaspoon fresh lemon juice

GLAZE:
¾ cup powdered sugar
1 tablespoon fresh lemon juice

¼ cup grated carrot

1. Preheat oven to 350°F. Grease two 9 x 5-inch loaf pans with butter or shortening and dust with flour.

2. Sift together the flour, baking powder, baking soda, salt and cinnamon. Set aside.

3. Separate eggs. In the large bowl, beat oil, sugar, hot water and egg yolks with an electric mixer until creamy. While beating, add

carrots alternately with the dry ingredients. Then stir in the nuts.

4. Beat the egg whites with fresh lemon juice until they hold stiff peaks when the beater is lifted. Fold half the whites into the batter, mixing thoroughly. Fold in the remaining whites gently until no lumps of white can be seen. Divide the mixture between the prepared pans. Bake for 60 to 70 minutes or until firm when pressed in the center. Remove from the oven and let rest in the pans for 15 minutes; then turn them out on a rack to cool slightly before glazing.

5. For the glaze, mix together powdered sugar, lemon juice and grated carrot and beat until smooth. Drizzle over the loaves while they are still warm.

6. For best flavor, wrap in foil and store at least 24 hours at room temperature before serving.

Tea Party Fare

Jamie Drew

A truly great man never puts away the simplicity of a child.

—Chinese proverb

Bob Drew and I met thanks to the hilarious efforts of Bob's former wife and a mutual friend. As they both predicted, we met, fell in love, got married and have merged two collections of children. Combined, we now have a total of 10 children and 12 grandchildren.

When Bob retired, we moved to Prescott, Arizona, and tried to have long-distance chats with our grandchildren. But they couldn't remember who we were from one call to the next. Conversations were stilted and it was difficult to get a little kid of three or four to say anything but "yes" or "no" or "ummm."

Early in the game we got them interested in us by talking about tea parties. In our travels we searched for small, inexpensive and preferably unbreakable tea sets and sent them from Spain, Australia, Mexico, even the local dime store. Once we found a beautiful, tiny sterling tea pot, creamer, sugar and tray.

But it wasn't the tea set that was important—the fun was in asking, "Have you had a tea party lately?" "Who did you invite?" "Let's pretend to invite Bess, the dog, and Abu, the cat, and who else?" "What will you serve for tea? A cake? Some cookies? And lots of tea!" "Who else would you like to invite?" "Oh, the new boy in your class? The little girl down the street?"

This past Christmas when one of our 11-year-old grandchildren was visiting, we asked what she remembered best about us. She said, "A special tea party we had long ago when we sang 'Happy Unbirthday' to me."

When we went to Minnesota and saw some of the grandchildren who barely knew us, what fun it was to begin talking about having a tea party with those two lovely girls. We quickly went into the playroom, set up a tea set, and had pretend tea with pretend cakes and all the dolls in the room.

This same scenario has taken place all across the country, many times just over the telephone. "Who would you like to invite to our tea party?" "Grandpa?" "Oh, you'd better ask Grandpa yourself!"

Next week another young grandchild is coming to Prescott for a visit and everyone can hardly wait, because we are going to have—guess what? A tea party! Only, for this party, we shall have real herb tea and Popovers, which any little boy or girl loves to make. Such fun!

How to Have a Tea Party

1. If you are visiting, please take a new tea set to share. Pieces get lost and mothers take it personally when they can't be found.

2. Go outside together and pick a few small branches of greenery or a flower and place in a small vase of any kind.

3. Find a corner on a towel, a table with a cloth or just a location that is special and private.

4. Any cups will do to begin with. Great gifts to older grandchildren can be small decorative cups that ultimately can grow into nice collections.

5. Serve cookies or small slices of cake or petit fours from the bakery. Better yet, Popovers are easy, economical and always turn out well.

Mamasan's Foolproof Tea Party Popovers

Makes 6 popovers

*Vegetable shortening for the
   muffin tins or cups*
2 eggs
1 cup milk
1 cup flour

1½ teaspoons salt
*Butter or margarine, jam,
   honey or warm syrup to pour
   over or inside popover*

1. Tie a tea towel or apron on the little cook. Grease 6 popover cups, muffin pans or custard cups generously with vegetable shortening.

2. Break eggs into a large bowl. Beat with a whisk or a fork until they are frothy. Add milk.

3. Sift flour into the egg mixture. Add salt. Mix well. Fill prepared cups one-third full. Place in a cold oven; do not preheat. Cook at 450°F for 25 minutes; reduce heat to 350°F and cook an additional 15 minutes. The popovers should be crisp and brown.

4. Remove from oven and make a small slit in the side of each popover. Turn out onto a wire rack to cool slightly. Set out your accompaniments and pour some tea.

5. Enjoy your family tea party. Remember to kiss the cook and clean up the kitchen together.

For Our Children
*We give thanks for our children.
May we continue to be blessed
by their simple wonder
so that we might not take
for granted one single moment
of this miracle to which
we've been born.*

—Steve Myrvang

Abraham Lincoln and the Mashed Potatoes

Bobbie Probstein

Uncle Bill is my "bragging relative." I brag about him all the time because he has done things no one else I know has ever accomplished.

I feel like I'm related to a celebrity because he competed in the 1908 Olympics in four different sports, won medals and set a world record that has never been broken in the 26-foot rope climb (they discontinued the event many years later, so his record is safe). I brag because even though he didn't finish high school because he had to work to support his family, he nevertheless received honorary degrees from several universities for his scholarship.

His specialties were Abraham Lincoln and the Civil War, and he was often asked to lecture about his favorite subjects. We heard he was very well-received. He sent us his clippings; we got pictures of him at a Civil War round-table panel with Adlai Stevenson, the governor, and another newspaper clipping with two young men whom he had saved one winter from drowning in Lake Michigan.

Uncle Bill was just *different*, and the differences seemed greater to me because of the huge disparity in our ages. He was actually my great-uncle and when he came from Chicago to visit us once a year, I knew I would be prodded to exercise and to talk about my studies. He loved nothing better than teaching and inspiring others, but he had never had children and didn't really know how to talk

to kids about what *really* mattered, like games and dances. I think he came West for mother's delicious home cooking, especially pot roast and mashed potatoes.

When I was in high school in San Francisco, he wanted to speak before the student body on Lincoln's birthday. I was mortified, because with his long silver hair and rumpled dark suit Uncle Bill didn't look like any teacher I knew. I was afraid I would be embarrassed, and I embarrassed easily in those days. But the principal wanted him to speak, and so he came.

When the dreaded morning came, I cringed in the auditorium seat.

Uncle Bill was wonderful. There was just no other word for him. His flow of language, total knowledge of his subjects, love of history and passion for the greatness of Lincoln encouraged us to study and learn more about our country. He received a standing ovation.

I basked in being his relative.

Mother, who had to work, couldn't attend the lecture at school, but that night she made Uncle Bill's favorite pot roast and mashed potatoes with gravy and apple pie for dessert. He was a simple man, with simple tastes.

He worked and lectured in Chicago until his late 70s, but the icy winters took their toll, so he moved to Santa Barbara, California, where he could swim outdoors all year. He became chaplain of the local veteran's group. Although he had served his country in the medical corps during both World Wars, he was a man of peace.

A few years later, during the Vietnam War, a young man walked up to him and spat in his face because he was wearing his old lieutenant colonel's uniform. Shocked, my uncle said, "Young man, in my 84 years no one has ever questioned my integrity or physically attacked me." He decked the man with a right to the jaw and marched on to the chapel. A few bystanders saw the episode and reported it to the Santa Barbara newspaper. Uncle Bill was praised and famous again.

At 85 he swam 100 laps at the local pool. It took him a long time, he said, but then, what was time for? I wondered if he thought about the Civil War as he swam, to keep from getting bored.

In his late 80s, he and another elderly man were unwisely carrying a refrigerator down a flight of stairs when the other man fell, and the load tumbled Uncle Bill to the ground and broke his hip. He was hospitalized for a long time, and his mind faded as the hip only partially healed.

After the fall he was never really the same. He began to live entirely in his past, and was observed catching baseball games and giving signals to his invisible pitcher from the wheelchair to which he was confined.

I visited him often, although he no longer recognized me. When I identified myself as a relative he was gallant, and would tell me he had just taken his mother (my great-grandmother) for a drive around the lake. She had been dead for more than 40 years.

I dreaded his 90th birthday at the convalescence hospital. He seemed utterly senile; his once muscular body sagged, and several teeth were missing.

All the nurses, and the patients who could remember the words, sang "Happy Birthday." Uncle Bill smiled and tried to struggle to his feet. Two orderlies held him up as he straightened his old body as best he could and, staying nearly vertical, began reciting the Gettysburg address.

The room fell silent. All eyes were on him, even those that were half-blind with cataracts.

Each word was a ringing declaration of faith, of hope, of pain for those fallen in the Civil War. His voice had power; his memory was precise. I had never felt the words so emotionally and I began to cry. I noticed others crying, too.

When Uncle Bill finished, he received a long, stirring ovation. When the applause ended, he collapsed back into his wheelchair.

Someone asked him what he wanted for his birthday present after such an inspiring speech. "Pot roast and mashed potatoes with gravy!" he said. "I'm hungry right now!"

Pot Roast with Gravy

Makes 6 to 8 servings

ᐰ

A 4-pound boned and rolled
beef roast (chuck, rump or
eye of round)
2 tablespoons oil or beef
drippings

1 onion, chopped
1 bay leaf
1 teaspoon salt
Freshly ground black pepper
Mashed potatoes, for serving

GRAVY:
1 tablespoon drippings
3 cups beef broth, divided

6 tablespoons flour

1. Pat the roast dry, and brown it in oil or beef drippings in a heavy pot over medium-high heat. Remove the roast and lightly brown the onion in the drippings. Return the beef to the pot along with ¼ cup water, bay leaf, salt and pepper. Cover the pot tightly, reduce the heat to low and simmer slowly for 3 hours, turning meat every half hour or so and adding a tablespoon or two of water if needed.

2. When the beef is tender, lift it out of the pan and onto a heated platter, cover loosely with foil and keep warm in a low oven. Skim all but 1 tablespoon fat from the drippings. Add 2 cups beef broth to the pan and heat, stirring to scrape up any browned bits. In a jar, shake together 1 cup beef broth with the flour, and stir slowly into the simmering broth, whisking until thickened. Simmer 2 to 3 minutes while you add more seasoning to taste.

3. Slice the pot roast and serve with mashed potatoes and gravy.

Blessings in Disguise

June Shoffeitt

In 1971, while convalescing from a nearly fatal coronary, my husband was put on a salt-free diet. Bill suddenly realized why he'd had so many requests to make seasoners without salt. It didn't take him long to start an entire line of salt-free seasoners for people on low- or no-sodium diets. His heart attack ended up being a blessing in disguise. The gratitude of patients when they taste food with flavor again makes all the years of hard work, disappointments and failures worthwhile.

Bill and I started Shoffeitt Gourmet Seasonings 28 years ago, and even though Bill has since passed away, the company is still family owned and operated. Now it is an all-woman company: our daughter, Bobbie; her daughter, Tonja; and Tonja's daughter, Danielle, will all be working. This will be a four-generation summer.

Our motto has always been "train them young." Boy, do we mean it! When my first great-granddaughter, Danielle, was born, we moved her crib into the ladies' lounge. After her nap, Danielle would be placed in a baby backpack and we would all take turns wearing her while running the production line.

As a family, we do trade shows two or three times a year to demonstrate our seasonings. At one in San Francisco, my three daughters and two co-workers all piled into an elevator loaded with all their luggage, show supplies, dishes and cameras. Up, up, they went, all tired and subdued. When they got to the sixth floor and the doors opened, Sandy was the first one out. No one was watching her because they were all getting a handle on their bags and other equipment. Sandy spotted a new shiny penny on the floor

❧

and reached down to pick it up. At that moment, Sondra and Pam, with their arms loaded, started to walk out of the elevator, tripped on Sandy and fell right over the top of her, at which point Bobbie and Janet went sprawling over the rest of them. Suddenly there were bodies, luggage, dishes and cameras everywhere! The gentleman who was waiting to get on the elevator was so alarmed when he saw this spectacle, he literally ran to the stairs—he just couldn't get away from them fast enough.

That event was a blessing in disguise, too, because even after all these years, we still have things to laugh about. And we often do.

Chicken with Stir-Fry Vegetables

Makes 4 servings

4 chicken breast halves, boned
  and thinly sliced
¼ cup oil
1 large onion, sliced
1 bell pepper, sliced into rings
1 (6-ounce) can water chest-
  nuts, drained and sliced
4 medium zucchini, thickly sliced
2 cups celery, diagonally sliced
1 cup mushrooms, sliced
2 cups carrots, diagonally
  sliced
Salt-free Shoffeitt Lemon
  Teriyaki seasoner

Heat oil in a wok or heavy skillet. Stir-fry chicken in hot oil until tender. Add the remaining ingredients; sprinkle generously with Shoffeitt Lemon Teriyaki seasoner. Stir-fry until done to your liking. Do not cover the pan or overcook.

"I Love You"

Bonnie Cox

A few days before Christmas, my husband Michael and I flew to Minneapolis to spend the holidays with his brother and family. We looked forward to the visit, and on the plane Michael told me that what he would like more than anything else for Christmas would be to have an opportunity to really connect with his brother. Though they love and respect each other, they have always been opposites when it comes to feelings; Michael wears his feelings on his sleeve, David is more private and reserved.

We were welcomed not only by David, his wife Vickie and their children, but by Bogie, a flamboyantly colored macaw parrot.

"I love you, Michael!" Bogie called as we came through the door. Unfortunately, Bogie's enthusiasm was mostly limited to men; no matter what I did, he always ignored me.

At the dinner table Vickie confided that she had some sad news about someone in her family. She was obviously distressed and something about the conversation angered David. Michael could sense that some bottled-up feelings were coming to the surface. Their voices escalated and they began to yell at each another.

My eyes welled up with tears. On one hand, I could tell that the anger was good and would probably be cathartic, but yelling at the dinner table was too much a reminder to me of some childhood memories and triggered some old discomforts. Needing to flee, I cleared some dishes from the table and headed for the kitchen.

Standing by the sink, I took a deep breath and tried to calm down. *Oh, dear*, I thought . . . *why is it that holidays always bring up old memories?* Then behind me, I heard a most kind, loving and

gentle voice say, "I love you." How sweet! I turned to see who had followed me into the kitchen. No one was there.

A few moments passed, then Bogie said it again. "I love you." What could I do but laugh? Eager to tell the others, I returned to the dining room where another miracle had occurred. Mike and David had their arms around each other and were joking again. That Christmas Michael got his heart's desire!

Here is a colorful fruit salad the whole family loves, especially Bogie!

Bogie's Tropical Fruit Salad
Makes 8 servings

3 cups thinly sliced red cabbage
1 cup thinly sliced celery
½ cup roasted peanuts
¼ cup dried currants or raisins
2 oranges, peeled and sectioned
  without membrane or the
  drained contents of an
  11-ounce can of mandarin
  orange sections

1 (8½-ounce) can pineapple
  chunks, drained; reserve
  2 tablespoons syrup
1 tablespoon lemon juice
1 banana, sliced
1 (8-ounce) carton orange,
  lemon or pineapple yogurt

1. In a large salad bowl, combine red cabbage, celery, peanuts, currants or raisins, orange sections and drained pineapple.

2. Mix the reserved pineapple syrup with the lemon juice and pour over the sliced banana in a small bowl. Lift the bananas out with a slotted spoon and add them to the salad.

3. Stir yogurt into the remaining syrup, and toss this dressing with the cabbage mixture until coated. Chill before serving.

5
Holiday Traditions

My kitchen is a mystical place. It is a place where the sounds and odors carry meaning that transfers from the past and bridges into the future.

—Pearl Bailey

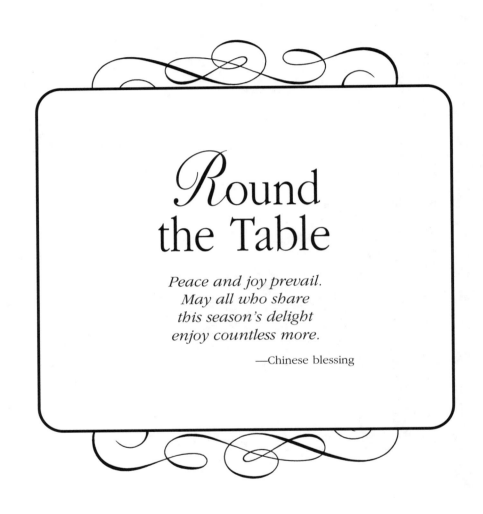

Round
the Table

Peace and joy prevail.
May all who share
this season's delight
enjoy countless more.

—Chinese blessing

Christmas Eve

Ann Hyatt

The miracle of Christmas is the gift of love.

—Anonymous

One of our family's Christmas traditions is a festive gathering and program on Christmas Eve. We each perform in order, from youngest to oldest, with the final number being the Christmas story read from the Bible by Grandma. Over the years we've had dancers, singers and players of almost every instrument; poetry readings; and our own unique comic rendition of "The Twelve Days of Christmas." We always include a few sing-along numbers as a group that range from traditional Christmas and winter songs, to Santa and the gang favorites, to more sacred interpretations of the birth of Jesus.

Through the innocent delight of the children present we are able to enter the new and intriguing world they see and hear. For instance, "round yon Virgin" becomes "round John Virgin." "Cattle are lowing, the poor baby wakes" becomes "cattle are glowing, the poor baby breaks." "Far, far away on Judea's plains" becomes "far, far away on Judy's plates." And, Rudolph the red-nosed reindeer has a pain-in-the-neck friend named Olive. She was discovered in a Christmas drawing when a child presented his picture of Rudolph and his friends, and there was a straggler reindeer behind the rest with an olive green nose. When I asked who that was, the response was "Olive, the other reindeer." Seeing the blank look on our faces, he added, "You know, the one who used to laugh and call him names!"

When the program ends, we all kneel in prayer, and then all the socks are hung by the chimney, chairs, piano and anything else we can find to hang stockings from with care. Then moms and dads head for the kitchen to cook, and all the children make plans when to stand in front of their parents' room on Christmas morning to sing at the top of their lungs "Little Tom Tinker sat on a clinker and he began to cry Ma, Pa, poor little innocent guy." The children know they can't empty their stockings until everyone is lined up to open their presents together. They are truly motivated singers.

After all the plans are made, and one Christmas Eve present is opened by each child, we all stuff ourselves on the homemade goodies, then retire to bed. The older kids and adults play cards, waiting for all the children to go to sleep so the wrapping can begin.

Here are some of our family's favorite recipes: a punch used at many family get-togethers, two desserts popular with younger and older kids and a family favorite holiday cake.

Almond Orange Punch
Makes 4 quarts, or 16 servings

ᑐᗨ

2 cups sugar	*¾ cup fresh lemon juice*
2 cups water	*1 tablespoon vanilla*
2 cups frozen orange juice	*1 tablespoon almond extract*
concentrate	*2 quarts chilled 7-Up*

1. In a medium saucepan, boil together sugar and water until sugar is dissolved; cool.

2. In a 4-quart container, combine orange juice concentrate, lemon juice, vanilla, almond extract and the cooled sugar syrup; chill. Before serving, stir in 7-Up. (If you want the punch to have the texture of a slush, freeze the mixture, then add 7-Up.)

Chocolate-Dipped Peanut Butter Balls

Makes 40 to 50 candies

∽

2 cups peanut butter
1 stick (¼ pound) butter
  or *margarine*

3 cups powdered sugar
1 (12-ounce) package semi-
  sweet chocolate chips

1. Melt together peanut butter and butter or margarine in a large bowl in a microwave oven or in a double boiler; stir until smooth. Add powdered sugar, stirring until very well combined. Roll into balls about the size of a small walnut; place on wax paper and chill thoroughly.

2. Melt chocolate chips as above. Dip the chilled balls in melted chocolate and transfer to wax paper to harden. Yummmmm.

Chocolate Bars

Makes 3 dozen bar cookies

∽

2 cups dark brown sugar
2 sticks (1 cup) soft butter or
  margarine
2 eggs
1 teaspoon vanilla
1 teaspoon baking soda
½ teaspoon salt

2½ cups flour
3 cups oatmeal
16 ounces chocolate chips
1 (14-ounce) can sweetened
  condensed milk
2 tablespoons butter or
  margarine

1. Preheat oven to 350°F. Grease a 9 x 13-inch baking pan. In a large mixing bowl, beat together brown sugar, butter or margarine, eggs and vanilla until the mixture is creamy. Add baking soda, salt, flour and oatmeal, mixing until well combined.

2. Press two-thirds of the batter into the prepared pan. Combine chocolate chips, condensed milk and 2 tablespoons butter or margarine; spread this filling mixture over the batter in the pan. Spread or pour remaining batter on top of filling. Bake for 25 minutes. Cool before cutting.

Wacky Cake

Makes one 8-inch square cake
Double recipe for a double layer or 9 x 13-inch oblong cake

1½ cups flour
1 cup sugar
¼ cup cocoa
1 teaspoon baking soda
½ teaspoon salt

1 tablespoon vanilla
1 tablespoon vinegar
1 cup water
⅓ cup vegetable oil

1. Preheat oven to 350°F. Grease an 8-inch square baking pan.
2. Combine all ingredients in a bowl and mix well.
3. Pour into greased pan and bake for 30 minutes.

The Christmas Cookie Workshop

Natalie Hartanov Haughton

In my house, cookies are synonymous with Christmas. Some of my earliest and fondest childhood memories include baking special cookies during the holiday season. As my mother turned the kitchen into a Christmas workshop (the aromas wafting through the kitchen were wonderful) my sister, two brothers and I were welcomed as assistant bakers. Like most children, one of the things we liked best was eating the raw dough—and the slightly cooled cookies right out of the oven.

Each of us had our favorite cookie that had to be included in the Christmas baking marathon. I loved Chocolate Pecan Chews while my sister was fond of Bullets (similar to cookies known as Mexican wedding cakes). My brother preferred Toffee Squares and Mrs. Arnold's Spritz Cookies. I always made four or five recipes of the Pecan Chews so there were a few extras for me. They were so good I could eat an entire recipe. To this day I still love them.

Once cookie baking was finished, Mother filled a collection of cookie tins. One two-foot high, round, red tin stood out. I have never seen another like it. No matter how well she tried to hide the tins, my brother and I would find them, sneak a cookie or two from time to time over the next few weeks prior to Christmas, and think Mother would never notice. Well, Mother did notice when she was making up her cookie platters for holiday parties and gifts and found the tins only half full. No matter how much we were reprimanded, the scenario continued yearly.

Years of cookie baking, cookie gift-giving and cookie-recipe collecting since childhood led to my writing a cookbook, *Cookies*, and my being known among my circle of friends as the Cookie Lady. My two children also started making cookies at an early age, and now they are chocolate chip cookie and brownies-from-scratch experts. Here are my childhood favorites.

Chocolate Pecan Chews

Makes 48 (1¼-inch) cookies

From Cookies, *by Natalie Hartanov Haughton (HP Books).*

1 (14-ounce) can sweetened condensed (not evaporated) milk	Pinch of salt
	2 teaspoons vanilla
	2 cups coarsely chopped pecans
2 ounces unsweetened chocolate	

1. Preheat oven to 325°F. Line baking sheets with foil; grease foil generously. In top of a double boiler, combine condensed milk and chocolate. Place over boiling water on medium-high to high heat. Cook until mixture thickens, about 6 minutes, stirring frequently. Stir in salt, vanilla and pecans. Drop by teaspoonfuls, about 2 inches apart, onto foil-lined baking sheets.

2. Bake for 12 to 14 minutes or until edges begin to brown, watching carefully to avoid burning. Cookies will be very soft, but will become firm as they cool. Cool 5 minutes on baking sheets; then carefully remove to racks to cool completely.

Chocolate Raspberry Streusel Bars

Makes 48 bar cookies

∾

From 365 Great Chocolate Desserts, *by Natalie Haughton (HarperCollins).*

1½ cups flour
½ cup sugar
1 stick (½ cup) soft butter
 (cut in pieces)
3 tablespoons whipping cream

1 teaspoon vanilla
½ cup seedless raspberry jam
1¼ cups (7½ ounces)
 semi-sweet chocolate chips

TOPPING:
¾ cup flour
5⅓ tablespoons (⅔ stick)
 soft butter, in pieces

⅓ cup sugar
1 teaspoon vanilla
½ cup chopped walnuts

1. Preheat oven to 350°F. Line a 9 x 13-inch baking pan with foil. To make the shortbread base, combine the flour and sugar in a mixing bowl or a food processor fitted with the steel blade; mix well. Add butter, whipping cream and vanilla, and mix or process until the mixture holds together.

2. Press the dough evenly over the bottom of the prepared baking pan. Bake for 12 to 15 minutes or until very light golden.

3. Place raspberry jam by spoonfuls on top of the warm crust; spread evenly with a table knife. Sprinkle chocolate chips evenly over the jam.

4. To make the crumb topping, combine the ingredients in a mixing bowl or food processor. Mix or process in quick on/off motions until mixture resembles coarse crumbs. Sprinkle the topping evenly over all.

5. Return pan to oven and bake 18 to 20 minutes longer until crumb topping is golden. Cool completely, then cut into bars.

Rebecca's Christmas Cut-Out Cookies

Elaine Cannon

For 20 years my daughter-in-law, Rebecca Russell Cannon, birth mother of seven, stepmother of three, grandmother to several, has been affectionately crowned Mother Christmas because of her annual Christmas Cookie Party. As early as October people begin asking for the date—they would never want to miss their favorite party of the season. To an assortment of nieces, nephews, cousins and friends, she sets the tone for a joyous holiday.

Rebecca has a large, well-appointed kitchen with a huge round table that seats 12, plus a breakfast bar with extra stools and plenty of standing room too.

At her Christmas gathering, Becky happily mixes, cuts, bakes, cools, stacks and dispenses sugar cookies in the shapes of Christmas. Delighted guests of all ages are encouraged to dig into the frosting pots, the candy sprinkles and the shredded coconut to design their own creations.

Cookie frostings are not limited to primary colors like holly green and berry red—paper plate palettes cover the spectrum: mauve, sage green and blue for bulging socks; silvery pearl for shining stars; chimney grey for Santa's boots; brick red for his suit; yellow for an angel's hair. And there is pure white and skin pink for the Baby Jesus cookies.

Her party is wonderful fun. The level of conversation between preschoolers, teenagers and grandparents is charming and civil. Everyone is a child in such a setting. Everyone is an artist. Everyone is a success as inevitable exclamations of approval erupt over every finished cookie.

Everyone is a bit of a philosopher about The Season, too. People eat as they go, sip cider or milk and take home their own prized plateful. Oh, yes, the annual cookie party is an enormous nuisance. Yes, it's an incredible mess! Certainly Becky is exhausted . . . but she's exhilarated by love, too.

How can one measure the worth of this kind of mothering? It bonds not only one family, but in-laws, neighbors, first cousins once removed and near-strangers seeking heart-shelter in such a home. As a pebble falling in a pool, the ripples from her devotion travel farther than Becky will ever know. As the grandmother (and her proud mother-in-law), I do so testify.

Rebecca's Christmas Cut-Out Cookies

Makes approximately 4 dozen cookies

1½ cup powdered sugar
2 sticks (1 cup) butter or
  margarine
1 egg
1 teaspoon vanilla

½ teaspoon almond flavoring
2½ cups flour
1 teaspoon baking soda
1 teaspoon cream of tartar

1. In the large bowl of an electric mixer, cream together thoroughly the powdered sugar, butter, egg, vanilla and almond flavoring.

2. Add the flour, soda and cream of tartar and mix thoroughly. Form into 2 large patties, wrap, and refrigerate for 3 hours.

3. Preheat oven to 325°F. Roll out the dough on a floured cloth to ½-inch thickness. Bake 7 to 10 minutes. When cool, frost with Butter Frosting.

Butter Frosting

4 cups powdered sugar
1 stick (½ cup) butter
1 teaspoon vanilla

Milk, as needed to make a
spreading consistency
Food coloring, as desired

1. In a mixing bowl combine the sugar, butter and vanilla. Beat together, adding enough milk to make a spreadable consistency.

2. Place frosting in different bowls and add food coloring as desired.

Tamales, El Loco and the Dreaded Scarves

Frank Trujillo

At Christmas all people smile in the same language.

—Anonymous

When I was five years old, my family lived in a proud little village by the name of Monticello, New Mexico, where it was a short walk from our comfortable little tin-roofed *adobe* home to the tiny church at the corner of the village square.

That Christmas season my parents had worked for weeks on end making extensive preparations for a big community celebration that was to follow Christmas Mass. There were only about 50 families in the little town of Monticello, and Mass was celebrated in our town only one Sunday a month, as we shared a priest with the other villages nearby. Christmas Mass this year was to be celebrated in Monticello, and for us kids—for all of Monticello—it was a big deal!

My parents had volunteered to prepare most of the food for the festivities. For what seemed like weeks, my brother, David, and I had helped Mother and Father with the preparations. Cleaning the hominy to be used in making the *posole*; selecting only the largest

Tamales, El Loco and the Dreaded Scarves excerpted from *Half the Love*, a story scheduled to appear in the book *Messages for a Troubled World* by Frank Trujillo, to be published in 1996.

corn husks for *tamales* in which the *masa* and other ingredients would eventually be wrapped. There were dozens of important chores assigned to the two of us. Making Mother's tamales just perfect required the attention of the entire family—and there was no time for funny business.

I remember Father telling David in no uncertain terms, "Your job is to look after Frankie and make sure *El Loco* doesn't catch him! And make sure," he said, "make real sure you do your best to keep him from constantly tasting all the food, or there won't be anything left for all the others!"

El Loco was this crazy rooster we had in our backyard who, with tremendous passion and vigor, at least twice a day, would demonstrate his intense dislike of me. Looking back, I am quite sure old El Loco just couldn't find it in his heart to forgive me for one act or another of childish indiscretion—a choke-hold perhaps, or a kick—inflicted upon him when he was but a chick.

I was very small for my age and I remember being deathly afraid of all chickens, especially El Loco. I was, therefore, only too happy to stay inside and help. David, however, had his hands full. He would much rather have been assigned any outdoor chore, however tedious . . . especially one not involving the immediate supervision of his mischievous brother.

I can smell those tamales now. We helped make dozens and dozens of them—tamales of every possible variety. There were savory pork tamales and delicious tamales made of beef. There were, as well, sweet tamales, David's delight, and there were plenty of my favorite type: tamales just chock-full of *chile colorado*, tamales ripe with spicy red chile! Mmmmmm. I remember it all as if it were only yesterday. Making all those tamales was truly a special time of family togetherness.

Winters were always cold in south-central New Mexico, and this particular winter was no exception. Christmas Day arrived with a cold, brisk wind screaming down *La Cañada Alamosa*, where Geronimo and Cochise once rode, ripping over the snow-covered San Mateo mountains, and swirling down into the Monticello valley.

It was freezing cold, and I remember that neither David nor I had a hat to wear. So when it came time for the family to take the huge pots of food to the church, Mother announced she was going to outfit us boys each in a scarf to help protect our heads from the bitter cold. Yes, we were going to the village square in scarves!

A bolt of greenish-yellow plaid, a store-bought fabric out of which Mama had been contemplating a dress, soon made its unwelcome appearance. The material looked almost exactly like the plaid fabric that Volkswagen used in upholstering their early 1970s vintage vans and buses. It was truly ugly.

Well, never were two boys more upset than we. We threatened to boycott even going to the church; we pleaded; we whined; we cried. We begged Father to intervene; after all, our manhood was at stake—we would be ridiculed at school. But we saw that familiar knowing look pass between my mother and father that we had seen a hundred times before. We knew we were sunk—they had made up their minds. We were going to church . . . we were going to wear those scarves . . . end of discussion.

Now in those days there were no grocery carts like those you see today—or at least there were none in rural New Mexico. So to carry the big pots of tamales the half mile down to the church, my mother came upon the ingenious idea of pressing my bicycle into service. It was an old, rickety hand-me-down version with solid rubber tires and skinny, splayed training wheels. I had been lobbying my father for quite a long while to take those ugly old training wheels off my bike, but to no avail. I now realize that my mother was pregnant at the time with my soon-to-be sister, Judy Mae, and my father could see no logic in removing the training wheels if in a short three or four years he would have to reattach them for her. To my father it made perfect sense. Myself, I would sooner have died than to have anyone see me riding on a bicycle with training wheels.

So off we go on Christmas day. Just imagine this scenario: Mary, my mother, pulling the bicycle, using one of Father's old World War II Army belts strapped to the handlebars . . . David and I steering the bicycle, and doing our best to balance these two huge pots of tamales on the complaining bike . . . my father at the tail end of this curious squeaky procession, Christ-like, with two heavy cast-iron pots of *posole* balanced somewhat precariously on a metal bar digging painfully into his stooped shoulders . . . all of us inching our way slowly down the icy dirt road to the church hall and to the hungry, festive throng in the village square.

And David and I—for all the world to see—in *scarves.*

I remember there were lots of people. I remember pulling the scarf deep down over my nose, and I remember praying real hard that no one I knew in Monticello would see me there.

Although I did not realize it at the time, my childhood days were some of the happiest, most secure times of my life. My parents always, without fail, took personal responsibility for the health and welfare of all their children—even if it meant making us wear the dreaded scarves to keep us from catching a cold. They knew what it meant to discipline and love and protect their children.

Aside, of course, from having to put up with El Loco and all those other chickens, could anyone in one's childhood have asked for more? Well, perhaps more of those remarkable tamales . . .

Here is Mary's and my recipe.

Tamales con Chile Colorado

Makes about 24 tamales

24 dried corn husks, the largest you can find

Masa preparada *specially for tamales from a Latino market (for a homemade equivalent, follow directions on a bag of Quaker Masa Harina for making tamale dough)*

2 pounds chopped pork shoulder

3 to 5 tablespoons New Mexico chili powder (see Note)

2 tablespoons cominos (whole cumin seed)

1 tablespoon salt

Broth, as needed

Reserved broth from the filling, as needed

Note: *Yes, it* has *to be New Mexico chili powder to guarantee best results! Add as much chili powder as you like to make your tamales as hot or* picante *as desired. New Mexico chili powder is available in mild, hot and* con mucho cuidado *(Frankie's favorite), which translates to "You better watch out!" (Just kidding!).*

1. Rinse and clean corn husks. Soak in very warm water until they are soft and very pliable.

2. To make the filling, place pork, cumin seeds, salt and 3 to 4 cups water (to cover) in a large saucepan over medium heat. Bring to a boil, then cover, reduce heat and cook, stirring from time to time for an hour or so, until the meat is very tender. Drain, reserving the broth. Stir in chili powder and enough broth to make a smooth mixture. Season to taste with salt and pepper. Let cool.

3. Drain the corn husks, rinse and place on paper towels. Use a rubber spatula to spread a small amount of filling (about 2 tablespoons) of masa on a large husk, leaving a 1-inch border at the narrow end. Spread and flatten the masa on the husk to create a thin, even layer. Now add a small spoonful of the pork and chili mixture to the center of the masa, varying the amount according to the size of tamale you wish to create. Finally, roll the corn husk lengthwise and fold over the pointed end to cover the seam. If you wish (this is optional), you can now tie the ends with ¼-inch strips of corn husk.

4. Continue making tamales until all the filling and masa are used. (If not using immediately, tamales may be frozen individually, then placed together in freezer bags.)

5. Gently place tamales, seam-side down, in a large steamer, or on a rack in a covered pan over boiling water. Cover and steam over boiling water for 45 minutes to an hour, or until the masa of a test tamale does not stick to the corn husk. (Steaming time will vary depending on the amount of masa used in each tamale.) Enjoy your tamales right away, or refrigerate or freeze them. Always steam (or microwave) until hot before serving.

Credo at Christmas

Daniel Roselle

At Christmas time I believe the things that children do. *I believe with English children* that holly placed in windows will protect our homes from evil.

I believe with Swiss children that the touch of edelweiss will charm a person with love.

I believe with Italian children that La Befana is not an ugly doll but a good fairy who will gladden the hearts of all.

I believe with Greek children that coins concealed in freshly baked loaves of bread will bring good luck to anyone who finds them.

I believe with German children that the sight of a Christmas tree will lessen hostility among adults.

I believe with French children that lentils soaked and planted in a bowl will rekindle life in people who have lost hope.

I believe with Dutch children that the horse Sleipner will fly through the sky and fill the earth with joy.

I believe with Swedish children that Jultomte will come and deliver gifts to the poor as well as to the rich.

I believe with Finnish children that parties held on St. Stephen's Day will erase sorrow.

I believe with Danish children that the music of a band playing from a church tower will strengthen humankind.

I believe with Bulgarian children that sparks from a Christmas log will create warmth in human souls.

I believe with American children that the sending of Christmas cards will build friendships.

I believe with all children that there will be peace on earth.

"Juanito's" Tamales Verdes

Ernie Nagamatsu

My growing-up years at Checker Board Truck Farms in Garden Grove, California, were filled with warm memories. My father, who was Japanese-American, took exceptional pride in his truck farm, the vegetables he grew, and the workers who labored there. Long before affirmative action and the notion of job discrimination, Dad took personal interest in and special care of each worker. I remember well the lecture I would receive if ever he found the workers' drinking water level getting low.

At the end of harvest season, the eyes of all the workers seemed sad as they bid us goodbye. They always promised to return the next year and work for Jorge, my father, the very best *patrón*.

Because of the *bracero* program, many of our workers were from Mexico, but my father also hired several local Latinos from nearby La Colonia. One, who I knew all my life, was Juanito, a tiny, stooped man who continued to work well into his 70s.

Juanito taught me ("Little patrón," as I was known) and the braceros an important lesson. As we would hoe to thin out the corn fields, Juanito could not quite keep up. The workers nearby would take turns hoeing five yards for him so he could keep up with the crew. And the workers, picking vegetables in the adjacent row would pick some for Juanito, put them into his lug box, then take his box to the end of the row when it was filled. Juanito graciously accepted their assistance and never lost their respect. Every now and then he would throw a dirt clod or threaten with his hoe in jest, letting us all know he was still due full courtesy.

Every Christmas, as regularly as the swallows return to Capistrano, Juanito and his wife would walk four miles from La Colonia to bring a gift of his wife's homemade tamales. It was his way of showing that the high regard he felt from my father was mutual.

It was a crisp, cold December morning when I last watched Juanito and his wife walk down our long dirt driveway. I marveled at his dignity and made a wish that Juanito would return for work again next year. I never saw him again.

Juanito lives on in our Christmas traditions, however. In our home, Christmas means tamales, and I have learned to make some that taste just like the ones Juanito and his wife used to bring.

"Juanito's" Tamales Verdes

Makes 15 servings

4 chicken breasts
1 pound fresh tomatillos or
  1 small can of tomatillo sauce
1 medium can or bottle of
  salsa verde
¾ cup chopped cilantro
1 cup chicken broth
1½ tablespoons oil
4 minced cloves garlic
7 mild green chiles (Anaheim,
  poblano or other mild long
  green chiles—see Note*) or*
  2 (4-ounce) cans mild green
  chile strips

2 pounds masa preparada *(You*
  can find it prepared especially
  for tamales in a Latino market.
  For a homemade equivalent,
  follow directions on a bag of
  Quaker Masa Harina for
  making tamale dough.)
About 20 packaged, dried
  corn husks
15 to 20 pitted black olives

Note: *If using fresh chiles, they must be roasted and peeled.* All chiles should be handled with care—*they contain a chemical irritant that can cause a painful rash on those who are highly sensitive.*

Wear rubber gloves when handling them until you determine your degree of sensitivity. To peel the skin from chiles, char over a direct flame, on a rack over an electric burner, or under the broiler, turning often to blacken the skin evenly. Place the chiles in a plastic bag and let them steam for a few minutes, separating the flesh from the skin. Peel by scraping off the skin with the back of a knife on a flat surface, or by rubbing under cold running water. Most of the hotness is in the membranes and seeds, so slit the chiles down one side and open to remove the seeds if you want a milder flavor.

1. Prepare the filling for the tamales one day ahead. Steam chicken breasts until cooked, about 20 minutes. Cool, remove skin and shred into strips.

2. Trim (remove thin parchment-like outer covering) tomatillos. Wash and place in a pot with 2 cups water; boil for 3 minutes and drain. In a blender, coarsely blend the tomatillos (in several batches if necessary) with *salsa verde*, cilantro and chicken broth.

3. In a large skillet, heat oil and sauté onion until lightly browned. Add garlic and sauté briefly. Stir in the blended tomatillo sauce and simmer for 8 minutes. Add the shredded chicken and season with salt to taste. Allow the filling to cool, then refrigerate until needed.

4. If using fresh, roasted chiles, cut the flesh in long strips.

5. Set out or make masa for tamales. Rinse and clean packaged dried corn husks. Place husks in warm water until easy to fold. Spread a small amount of masa with a rubber spatula on a large husk, leaving a 1-inch border at the narrow end. Spread and flatten the masa on the husk to create a thin, even layer. Add a small spoonful of the chicken mixture to the center of the masa, varying the amount to the size of the tamale—you will soon develop an eye for this. Top the filling with a strip of green chile and a pitted olive. Roll the corn husk lengthwise and fold over the pointed end to cover the seam.

6. Gently place tamales in a large steamer with the seam-side down. Steam, covered, over boiling water, for approximately 1 hour, or until the masa of a test tamale does not stick to the corn husk. Steaming time will vary according to the amount of masa used in each tamale. Enjoy them right away, or refrigerate or freeze the tamales; steam until hot before serving.

Aunt Catherine's Sugar Cookies

Caroline A. Goering

I grew up in a small town in Pennsylvania. We lived in a neighborhood where we were able to walk to town or to the train station to go to Philadelphia. The milk man, the fruit and vegetable peddler and the meat man all delivered food to our door. We did not have a car and my relatives lived miles away. As a result, my neighbors became my extended family. They were the ones to whom my mother sent me to borrow a cup of sugar or flour, or an egg, until the next grocery delivery came to our house.

Two women in particular, who I called Aunt Catherine and Aunt Myrl, became my special "Aunties" and I became their special "Cookie." I loved going to their homes with my family for dinner or simply to borrow ingredients for my mother. They made me feel loved no matter what I had or had not done.

After filling up my measuring cup or giving me the egg my mother needed, Aunt Catherine would always let me take a cookie from her cookie jar. She'd often say, "Take another!" and I'd go home with two. There was something special about those cookies. It wasn't just the taste—deep down inside I felt unconditionally loved.

This past Christmas season, I invited several families with children from my parenting classes to come and bake cookies with me. On three different occasions we mixed, cut, decorated, baked and ate Aunt Catherine's Sugar Cookies.

The delicious smell of baking cookies filled the house. We put the last red sugar candy on Rudolph's nose and sat in the living room around Aunt Catherine's coffee table, I in Aunt Myrl's red wing chair and the children in chairs my father made. As we sat, sipping hot chocolate from Danish china cups, eating our handiwork, watching the electric train run around under the tree, enjoying the lights and decorations, I suddenly realized that I had become "Aunt" Caroline, and these children were now my special "Cookies."

Parents have told me since that they have overheard their children say, "Let's play going to Caroline's house. I'll be Caroline and you come to the door and knock, and we'll make cookies." Another mother wrote me, "The tea party was a highlight—a magical memory to be cherished. We all left feeling that we were somebody special."

Are you the "cookie person" in some child's life? If not, consider inviting one or more children to mix, decorate, bake and enjoy some of Aunt Catherine's sugar cookies with you. As you let them know they are somebody special, you'll discover the magic in Aunt Catherine's cookies too.

Aunt Catherine's Sugar Cookies

Makes approximately 4 dozen medium cookies

3¼ cups sifted all-purpose flour
2½ teaspoons double-acting baking powder
¼ teaspoon salt

1½ sticks (12 tablespoons) butter
1½ teaspoons vanilla
1½ cups sugar
2 large eggs
Colored sugar, to decorate

1. Preheat oven to 400°F. Sift together onto wax paper the flour, baking powder and salt; set aside.

2. In a large bowl, cream the butter with an electric mixer until fluffy. Add vanilla and sugar and beat well. Add the eggs, one at a time, beating well after each addition. Gradually add the sifted flour mixture, stirring only until thoroughly mixed.

3. Divide dough in half, form into patties and wrap each separately

in wax paper. Chill (in the refrigerator, not in the freezer) for 3 hours. (Make one batch before children come.)

4. Roll out the dough to your desired cookie thickness on lightly floured pastry cloth with a floured rolling pin. (Younger children may watch the rolling and focus their energies on cutting and decorating.) Cut with a variety of cookie cutters, depending on the season. Decorate with colored sugar lightly pressed into the surface. Place on greased baking sheet.

5. Bake 8 to 12 minutes or until lightly browned. Using a wide spatula, transfer to rack to cool. Enjoy with hot chocolate and the smiles and laughter of children.

Memories of Holiday Mincemeat

Hazel Court Taylor

I began my life in a beautiful place called Sutton Coldfield in the county of Warwickshire, England. The area was semi-rural and everybody knew their neighbors. Autumn was always a special time in our family, as it came as a prelude to Christmas and all the traditions that went with that time of the year—and there were many in those days. Shopping malls didn't exist, and so life during autumn was centered around making presents and decorations, gathering holly, mistletoe, yule logs and, of course, cooking festive dishes.

Our kitchen was large with an old-fashioned table in the center of the room. As a toddler, life seemed to totally revolve around this piece of furniture where I played my games and painted my pictures. I would eat breakfast, lunch, have tea and dinner there, and stash food I didn't care for on the ledge underneath.

The big range always had a coal fire burning, and the wonderful smell of bread baking invariably came from the oven that joined the fire. It was a wonderful, cozy room full of friendly aromas like furniture polish made from beeswax and turpentine, and black lead, a substance my mother used to polished the range until we could see our faces reflected on it like gray ghosts. It was in this room that we cooked our festive foods.

First came the Christmas cake in the second week of October—cooked, wrapped in a cotton cloth, lightly soaked in sherry and placed in a colorful tin. The third week was Christmas pudding time, and the last week was the mincemeat party.

My mother prepared the mincemeat from my Welsh grandma's 1842 recipe. Traditionally, after all the ingredients were put in a very large china bowl, silver threepenny coins were scrubbed clean and placed beside the bowl. All our neighbors were invited to come in the evening and give the mincemeat a stir. At the same time, they would make their wish for the coming year, and the threepenny coins would be dropped into the mincemeat. Whoever found one of these small coins later in their mincemeat pie would have an incredibly lucky year.

Each neighbor, upon entering our house, was given a glass of sherry and a piece of Madeira cake. Laughter was loud and musical and a special loving atmosphere surrounded my family's lace-covered table.

I loved this night. It was the beginning of late autumn as it drifted into winter—crunchy golden leaves outside—great, hot fires inside. Two wonderful parents created these special memories for me in a time gone by when there was not a lot of money, but there was a lot of love and understanding; a time when a Christmas stocking was filled with sweets, chocolate, nuts and apples. I'm so very glad I was part of those simpler times.

Mincemeat

Makes five 1-pint jars to make 5 pies

1 pound very finely chopped
  beef suet
1 pound dried currants
1 pound finely chopped raisins
1 pound peeled and minced apples
½ pound golden brown sugar
4 ounces each diced candied
  citron, lemon and orange peel

1 teaspoon each grated nutmeg, ground cloves, ground ginger and ground allspice
Juice and finely chopped peel of 1 lemon
1 cup brandy
½ cup orange Curaçao
3 ounces sherry

1. In a very large mixing bowl combine the ingredients in the order listed.

2. Pack the mincemeat into 1-pint jars, seal and store in a cool place for two months.

Filling for Mincemeat Pie
Makes one 9-inch pie

2 cups mincemeat
1½ cups fresh peeled, grated
  apple

½ cup chopped walnuts

1. Combine ingredients. Pour into pastry-lined 9-inch pie pan.
2. Top with a lattice crust. Bake the pie at 425°F for 45 minutes. Let stand at least 1 hour before cutting.

Mincemeat Bars with Vanilla Glaze
Makes 36 bars

Recipe submitted by Alice Simmons.

2¼ cups flour
1 cup sugar
1 tablespoon baking powder
½ teaspoon salt

GLAZE:
1 cup powdered sugar
1 tablespoon milk

1¼ cup milk or buttermilk
3 tablespoons room-temperature
  butter or margarine
1 large egg

½ teaspoon vanilla

1. Preheat oven to 375°F. Grease a 13×9-inch pan. In a mixing bowl, combine flour, sugar, baking powder and salt; stir. Add milk or buttermilk, butter or margarine, and egg; mix until the dry ingredients are moistened. The dough will be soft and sticky.

2. Spread half the dough in the bottom of the pan to within ½ inch of the sides of the pan (it will spread during baking). Spread the mincemeat to the edge of the dough. Spread out the other half of the dough on wax paper the same size; turn over onto mincemeat and pull off the wax paper carefully. Bake for 30 minutes.

3. While the cookies bake, prepare the glaze. Combine in a small mixing bowl powdered sugar, milk and vanilla. Stir until smooth, adding a little extra milk if needed to make a smooth spreading consistency.

4. When the cookies come from the oven, let them cool slightly, then spread the glaze over the surface of the warm pastry. Cut, while still warm, into 36 bars.

Poor Man's Spice Cake

Warren Farrell

I grew up on simple and healthy food. My mom would listen to a nutritionist named Carlton Fredericks almost every day on the radio. Those were the days when the milkman delivered full-fat whole milk to the back door, the bread man delivered full-of-air white bread to our front door, and sex came after marriage. Well, both Mom and Dad agreed on the first and the third, but as for that full-of-air white bread . . . Mom told the bread man that that white bread just had to go.

Our family was the only one I knew of that had heard of whole-wheat bread, no less actually swallowed it. I knew I was doomed to sissyhood. I knew it for sure one day when Bobby Mack, the best football player in town, said yes when I asked, "Wanna drop by for lunch after tomorrow's game?"

I thought I was home free when Mom gave in to my pleading to get white bread just once. But Bobby spotted the old whole-wheat bread hidden in a cupboard. When he begged for it, said it was great for building muscle, and made me plot to tell his mom to get it for him, well, I developed a sudden fondness for whole-wheat bread and gained an intuitive understanding of the value of celebrity endorsements, even from guys who hurt themselves to get attention.

As great as Mom was about nutrition, when it came to cooking for crowds (defined as anything more than a family of four), it overwhelmed her. So Dad cooked on the holidays—the greatest homemade white and whole-wheat bread, turkey, stuffing and what he called "Poor Man's Spice Cake." Fortunately, I didn't know what a calorie was, much less a fat gram, so after a 50,000-calorie meal and a week's worth of fat grams, nothing deterred me from my favorite Poor Man's Spice Cake.

When I got married, I enjoyed my wife's family's fabulous Christmases. By Thanksgiving I could smell Christmas coming . . . well, almost. One smell was missing. When my wife asked me what it was, the only thing I could remember was something about powder and a musket. Wrong smell, she said. Dad's was the last stop on Christmas rounds, and when I went to the oven, there it was, the smell of Christmas, the moistness of Christmas, the taste of a cake that knew to never let the orchestra of baking powder drown out the song of the Muscat raisin.

Poor Man's Spice Cake

Makes 8 to 10 servings

1 box (15 to 16 ounces) seedless
  Muscat raisins
1 stick (½ cup) butter
1 cup sugar
1 teaspoon ground allspice
1 teaspoon ground cinnamon

½ teaspoon ground cloves
2 cups water
2 cups flour
½ teaspoon baking soda
½ teaspoon baking powder
½ teaspoon salt

1. Preheat oven to 350°F. Grease a 9 x 5-inch bread pan.
2. In a medium saucepan, combine raisins, butter, sugar, spices and water. Bring mixture to a boil. Let cool.
3. Mix together the flour, baking soda, baking powder and salt and mix into the spice mixture. Bake for 1 hour, or until just firm—spice cake is best when moist.

Vinetarta, the Icelandic Christmas Torte

Naomi Rhode

When love adorns a home, other ornaments are a secondary matter.

—Anonymous

In the early 1900s, many Icelandic Viking people left their homeland, immigrating mostly to the North Dakota plains. Two of the adventurers who took passage on ships to America were Anna and George Goodman. They came to homestead in North Dakota and try their fortune in this wonderful new land.

They built sod houses, farmed the land in spring, summer and fall, and had 14 children. My mother, Ellenborg (Elskaborg in Icelandic), was their oldest girl.

Winter was always a valiant struggle through the sub-zero cold in their tiny dark home. Through the deep heavy snow they built tunnels connecting them with the barn so the cows could be milked and cared for. Because of the harsh living conditions, celebrations, laughter, storytelling and dancing were cherished pastimes. Food became much more than nourishment; it became *food for the soul*!

The whole month of December, Christmas was celebrated with trees, candles, homemade decorations and endless baking. The center of all the culinary festivities was the Christmas torte—Vinetarta. The festive ceremony of making the Vinetarta was joined in by the children, cousins, aunts and grandmas. It was a celebration in and of itself.

The completed Vinetarta was cut in thin, decorative slices approximately seven to nine layers thick and served with Icelandic coffee (the ultimate drink of friendship and hospitality) at every possible occasion and time of the day.

Because Vinetarta is moist and lasts so well, the traditional cake would be served with finesse, flair and sentiment well past Christmas and into the New Year. And always, it was served as dessert on Christmas Day and New Year's Day with roast goose from the family farm.

Ellenborg passed along this ceremonial recipe to me, and I have continued it with my family with a twinge of nostalgia for the special Icelandic tradition. Enjoy this bit of Iceland along with my blessings for a happy Christmas and a prosperous New Year.

Vinetarta

Makes approximately 12 servings

DOUGH:

1 cup butter	*¼ cup milk*
1½ cups sugar	*3 eggs, beaten*
½ teaspoon vanilla	*5 cups flour*

FILLING:

2 pounds prunes	*Rum flavoring, to taste*
1½ cups sugar	*Cardamon spice, to taste*

1. Mix the dough ingredients and chill. (Chilled dough absorbs less flour, giving more tender layers to the torte.)

2. Divide the dough into 7 to 9 pieces. On a floured board, roll each piece to approximately ⅛- to ¼-inch thick.

3. Using the bottom of a round cake pan as a pattern, cut the torte layers.

4. Bake each layer as you would a large sugar cookie on a greased cookie sheet. Bake at 375°F for approximately 5 to 7 minutes or until edges are lightly browned. Cool.

5. To make the filling: Boil the prunes until soft. Mash and beat the prunes well. Add sugar and simmer until glossy. Cool and then add the rum flavoring and cardamon spice to taste.

6. Assemble the Vinetarta Christmas Torte by stacking the cake layers, with the prune filling spread in between.

7. A thin layer of powdered sugar sprinkled on top of the torte makes a beautiful finish to this traditional ceremonial Christmas pastry.

8. Wrap the torte in aluminum foil, store in refrigerator and slice in thin pieces. Serve with delicious strong coffee.

Passover in the Playroom

Bobbie Jensen Lippman

*Bo-ruch a-toh A-do-noy, E-lo-hay-noo me-lech ho-o-lom,
Bo-ray p'ree ha-go-fen.*

How strange those words sounded the first time I heard them 25 years ago. Early in 1970, when we lived in Los Angeles, she came into my life. It was instant friendship although we had little in common. I'm tall, she's short. I'm thin, she's not. I have one kid, she has six. I'm Protestant, she's Jewish. What we had in common was auburn hair, a love of life and a zany sense of humor.

That spring, this new friend, Roz, invited me, my 10-year-old daughter, Rocki, and my new husband, Burt, to our first Seder—the celebration of Passover. On the way to Roz's house I reminisced about Presbyterian Sunday School in Nebraska, trying to recall what Passover was all about.

I expected a solemn evening at Roz's house—it was anything *but!* Children were everywhere, including the six who belonged to Roz. There were uncles, aunts, grandparents, cousins, babies, and peeking out from under a coffee table, watching all the activity, was a comical-looking dog.

We were immediately caught up in introductions and greetings. The shout of "Hello buh-bee!" made me spin around, thinking someone had mispronounced my name, but there stood two bearded men heartily embracing each other. It was the first time I'd heard the phrase *"shalom aleichem."*

We took our seats in a large playroom, at several round tables on which were blue cloths, bottles of Manischewitz wine, grape juice and unfamiliar foods. Rocki looked at the food, tugged at my sleeve and asked, "What's all that weird stuff?" I automatically shushed her, not that anyone would have heard her question, what with all the noise. The adults settled down, but not the kids, who were laughing and shrieking, poking each other, or lingering reluctantly in a grand-parent's arms for one more kiss.

My attention was on Roz's husband, Bob, sitting patiently at the head table, waiting for the din to die down. Which it didn't. Suddenly, he stood up, looked very stern, raised his arms, and yelled, ". . . and it came to pass!" Rocki jumped a foot out of her chair.

How were we to know this was Bob's way of calling order, and not an official part of the Seder? When everyone finally was quiet, we all opened a book called "The Haggadah for the American Family." By the end of the evening we knew about Israel's redemption from bondage in Egypt. As everyone took a turn reading the story of Passover, it became clear to me that the foods on the table had a symbolic meaning, such as the *moror*, bitter herbs, that recall the bitterness of life in Egypt, and *matzo*, the unleavened bread, signifying the hasty departure of the people persecuted by the Pharaoh.

As soon as the ceremony ended, out came all the traditional Passover foods. An older woman at our table looked at the matzo ball in her chicken soup and announced loudly, "Hmmmph, Rozzie makes floaters. *Mine* are always sinkers!" You didn't have to be Jewish to catch the humor. Soup was followed by gefilte fish, brisket, potato kugel, matzo farfel, carrot tsimmes, stewed fruit, macaroons and honey cakes. *Oy vey!*

Until our move to Oregon, we attended every Seder at Roz's house, and somewhere along the line she affectionately dubbed me the "Swedish *shiksa*."

The Seder in the playroom has seen many changes during these years. Grandpa Sammy is no longer present to hug his grandchildren, toddlers have become teenagers, and three couples have divorced. Bob died of cancer not long ago. I'm thinking of Roz now as Passover nears once again, and am trying to picture what the

Seder will be like with all the changes in her family. The faces around her table may be different, but the ancient story will be retold, just as it has been for thousands of years.

Bo-ruch a-toh A-do-noy, E-lo-hay-noo me-lech ho-o-lom, Bo-ray p'ree ha-go-fen . . . "Blessed art Thou, O Lord our God, King of the universe, Who createth the fruit of the vine."

To people of all faiths now when our world is in such need of healing, the words *shalom aleichem,* "Peace unto you," seem fitting.

Chicken Soup the Way Roz Makes It

Makes 12 servings

∽

1 large chicken and some
  additional wings and legs,
  if desired
2 to 3 large onions, quartered
8 large carrots cut in 2-inch
  pieces
1 parsnip, peeled and cut in
  1-inch pieces

1 bunch parsley
Salt and pepper
4 chicken bouillon cubes
2 tablespoons reserved fat
  for Matzo Balls
  (recipe follows)

1. In a large pot, place chicken and enough cold water to cover by an inch. Bring to a boil and use a large spoon to skim off any fat that rises to the top. Add onions, carrots, parsnip and parsley. Cover, leaving lid ajar, and lower heat to a simmer; cook 1 hour. Season lightly with salt and pepper (bouillon cubes will be added later) and cook 1 hour longer.

2. Using a slotted spoon, remove the chicken from the soup to cool. Strain the soup and discard the vegetables, except for 3 or 4 pieces of carrot. Add bouillon cubes to the soup and taste for seasoning, adding more cubes if needed for a richer flavor.

3. When chicken is cool enough to handle, remove skin and bones and tear into shreds; place chicken back in the soup. Refrigerate, skim off the fat that hardens on the surface and save 2 tablespoons of the fat for Matzo Balls.

4. To serve, bring to a simmer. Remove carrots and slice thinly, placing only a few slices in each heated soup bowl with one Matzo Ball. Ladle in the soup and serve.

Matzo Balls . . . Hopefully Floaters

Makes 12

4 eggs	*2 tablespoons chopped parsley*
2 tablespoons chicken fat	*1 teaspoon salt*
1 cup matzo meal	*6 tablespoons chicken soup*

1. In a mixing bowl, lightly beat eggs, then beat in chicken fat. Stir in matzo meal, chopped parsley and salt. Add chicken soup to make a soft dough. Refrigerate an hour or more.

2. With wet hands, shape matzo mixture into 1½-inch balls. Bring 4 quarts of water to a slow boil. Gently drop in matzo balls, cover, reduce heat and simmer for about 10 minutes without lifting lid. Add one to each serving of chicken soup.

Alice Wentworth's Yummy Yams

Diana von Welanetz Wentworth

Our first Thanksgiving together, a few weeks before our wedding, we invited both our families to Ted's ranch in the hills above Temecula. I was excited about getting everyone together for the first time and cooking a huge traditional turkey feast.

The ranch house had been used only for weekends, and I didn't know whether the kitchen was stocked with the equipment I would need. I was concerned I might forget something, so I made scrupulous lists of every ingredient and piece of kitchen equipment that I'd need.

As we were packing the car the day before Thanksgiving, I said, "I'm worried I'm going to forget something really big."

Traffic was bumper-to-bumper at sundown as we progressed slowly along the freeway on the way out of town. We'd gone only 10 miles or so in an hour and a half and were concerned about our late start.

Suddenly, Ted's face went pale. "Diana, we forgot something."

"What?"

"It's really big, Diana! Really, really BIG!" I was alarmed by the look on his face.

"What did we forget?"

"My mother."

"Your *mother*? I had no idea she was coming with us! Can't someone else bring her?"

"Nope. . . . It would hurt her feelings."

Now we were going to be really late and would miss dinner with our three daughters who were waiting there all ready to go out.

But Ted had a Keystone Cops solution. Traffic was light going the other direction. We picked up his mother, Alice, her luggage and the pan full of Candied Yams she'd made. Then we headed for John Wayne Airport where Ted kept his plane. We loaded everything, all my cooking equipment, an extra oven, food processor and groceries into the luggage compartment and the back seat. There wasn't a square inch to spare after we cozied Alice into the back seat and convinced her she'd have to hold the yams on her lap.

We took off, soaring high above the long, long lines of headlights on the freeways below, and approached the airport in Temecula only 20 minutes later. On his approach, the plane hit some turbulence and we heard a squeal from the back seat. The sticky sauce on the yams had spilled onto Alice's lap.

The girls were waiting at the little private airport with two cars for all the luggage and were eager to get to dinner. Alice was a good sport about her predicament. She headed for the rest room to clean her pants and remove her underwear, then said she wasn't uncomfortable and didn't mind going to the restaurant the way she looked.

Well, wouldn't you know, the waitress reached across someone to pour ice water while looking the other way and poured it right on Alice's lap. That was when I discovered where Ted gets his sense of humor. Tears of laughter rolled down her cheeks.

Alice's Yams have long been a tradition in the Wentworth family. I've been reading recipes all my life, and this is probably the most decadent recipe I've ever encountered. Surely there is not a drop of nutrition in them, but they are so full of love and pure yumminess, who cares!

Alice Wentworth's Yummy Yams

Makes at least 16 servings

❧

These are beyond wonderful reheated the next day. There are never enough!

4 pounds yams	*1 box dark brown sugar*
1 stick (¼ pound) butter	*1 cup real maple syrup*

1. Boil the yams in their skins until just tender when pierced with a knife. Drain, and if not using them right away, cool in their skins and refrigerate in a plastic bag.

2. Peel the yams and cut them crosswise into 1-inch slices. Arrange them in a large skillet (Alice uses an electric frying pan), cut-side up and edges touching. Add the butter to the skillet along with the brown sugar and maple syrup.

3. Cook, uncovered, over medium heat (350°F in the electric frying pan) for about an hour, nudging the yam slices this way and that when you think of it and taking care not to let the sauce burn. The dish is done when the sauce is dark and no longer watery. Turn off heat—the sauce will thicken more as it cools. Keep warm until serving.

Thanksgiving Day Prayer

*We take so much for granted
of life and liberty,
and think that we deserve it;
that all was done "for me."
Think how they must have struggled,
new pilgrims in this land.
So many died from hardships
yet still they made a stand.
When all the work was finished,
new crops sowed in the ground,
they gathered with their neighbors,
asked blessings all around.
Oh, God, help us be grateful
for gifts you've sent our way.
For these we want to thank you
on this Thanksgiving day.*

—Kris Ediger

6
Men in the Kitchen

If a man be sensible and one fine morning, while he is lying in bed, count at the tips of his fingers how many things in this life truly will give him enjoyment, invariably he will find food is the first one.

—Lin Yutang

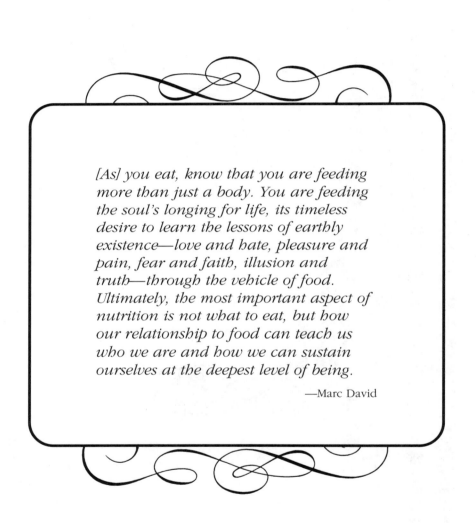

*[As] you eat, know that you are feeding
more than just a body. You are feeding
the soul's longing for life, its timeless
desire to learn the lessons of earthly
existence—love and hate, pleasure and
pain, fear and faith, illusion and
truth—through the vehicle of food.
Ultimately, the most important aspect of
nutrition is not what to eat, but how
our relationship to food can teach us
who we are and how we can sustain
ourselves at the deepest level of being.*

—Marc David

Dad's Chicken Cacciatore

Sam Keen

During my adolescent years I spent succulent summers at Bethany Beach, Delaware, body surfing, riding waves of hormones, pretending to be the man I wanted to become. My dad ruled the small kingdom of Beachcombers Flat, the nest and crash pad for the family. One unbroken rule of beach life was that Dad did the cooking, the kids did the cleaning up and the dishes, and Mother rested.

My father's style of cooking can be best described as intuitive, inventive, passionate and chaotic. When he gathered beach plums for the yearly batch of jam, day after day large pots of the warlock's brew simmered on the stove, and the kitchen looked like the playpen of a child who had spilled purple paint.

Whenever guests were expected, Dad would begin early in the morning to make Chicken Cacciatore. The largest skillets and pots came out. Mountains of chicken were cut up and browned in olive oil with as much garlic as was available in southern Delaware. Whole fields of tomatoes, onions, celery, peppers and mushrooms disappeared into the caldron, in no particular order or proportion. Salt, pepper, basil and varieties of spices unknown to the Frugal Gourmet were added—to taste. Always to taste. Every hour or so, the concoction was tasted and discerning comment was gathered from any family member or visiting friend who happened by.

As the sun lost its intensity, the sea grew calm and emerald—the dinner hour arrived. What I remember most was the appetite we brought to the table, the rich simmered symphony of the Cacciatore, the profusion of talk, the plenty-for-all, sweet chaos of the feast around the kitchen table—the wine and wafer of food prepared with wild love.

Chicken Cacciatore

Makes 10 to 12 servings

2 (3½-pound) chickens
Olive oil, as needed
4 pounds ripe tomatoes, chopped,
   along with their juices
4 ounces tomato paste
6 carrots
1 pound mushrooms
3 medium red onions
4 stalks celery

1 green bell pepper
1 orange bell pepper
4 cloves (or more, to taste)
   garlic, minced
Salt and pepper to taste
Chicken broth, as needed
½ cup minced fresh basil
Warm homemade corn bread,
   for serving

1. Cut up chickens into serving pieces; discard skin and wing tips. Pour olive oil into a large frying pan. Brown the chicken in batches, adding more olive oil as necessary. Transfer the pieces as you brown them into a large pot. To the pot add tomatoes and tomato paste.

2. Prepare vegetables as follows: slice carrots and mushrooms, chop onions, celery, green and orange bell peppers. Add the vegetables to the pot with the chicken and tomatoes along with minced garlic, salt and pepper. Stir, and if the liquid does not cover the ingredients, add some chicken broth as needed. Cover, and simmer over very low heat while you spend a lazy afternoon doing nothing in particular, or until the chicken is tender and begins to fall off the bones.

3. To serve, remove the chicken bones from the pot. Stir in the minced fresh basil. Serve in bowls, accompanied by warm homemade corn bread. Give thanks before eating.

A Spiced Chocolate Applesauce Cake for Dad

Claudia Stromberg

Among the many people who knew and loved him, my father was famous for three things: his generous heart, his conservative politics and his passion for chocolate.

When we were children, my sister, my many cousins and I all shared in the stash of Tootsie Rolls, Chocolate Necco Wafers and other "penny candies" he kept in a cigar box under the front seat of his car.

He traveled a great deal when I was young, and a critical part of the ritual in the excited preparations for his return was my mother baking a chocolate cake. Invariably the cake would crack and have to be "glued" together with still more of the fudge frosting which was being slathered on top and around the sides.

He kept rocky road fudge or Hershey bars in the drawer of his bedside nightstand, and no matter how quietly he would try to sneak some candy, our dog Suzi, snoring in the corner of my parents' bedroom, would wake up to get her share, which Dad would hand over with a rueful grin.

He attended conventions, industry meetings and political dinners. To guard against the disappointment of some fruit tart or other pale imitation of a dessert, he always made sure there was something chocolate to eat by bringing cases of Hershey bars to pass out to everyone there.

And when he died, among the masses of beautiful flowers at his memorial service, one arrangement stood out: a beautiful bouquet, sent anonymously, with a Hershey bar nestled among the blooms—a sweet farewell to a very special man.

For my father, dessert had to be chocolate—the darker, the richer the better. I created this recipe in his honor.

Spiced Chocolate Applesauce Cake

Makes 10 to 12 servings

CAKE:

3 ounces unsweetened chocolate
2 cups flour
1½ cups sugar
2 teaspoons cinnamon
1 teaspoon salt
1 teaspoon soda
3 large eggs

1 cup vegetable oil
1 cup buttermilk
1 cup applesauce
1 teaspoon vanilla
1 cup chopped walnuts
6-ounce package of chocolate chips

SAUCE:

1 cup sugar
½ cup buttermilk
½ stick (¼ cup) butter

1 ounce unsweetened chocolate
½ teaspoon baking soda
1 teaspoon vanilla

1. Preheat oven to 350°F and butter a 12-cup Bundt pan. In a small saucepan, melt 3 ounces unsweetened chocolate over low heat; set aside to cool.

2. In large mixing bowl, combine flour, sugar, cinnamon, salt and soda. In another bowl, beat the eggs and add vegetable oil, buttermilk, applesauce and vanilla. Stir into dry ingredients. Stir in cooled

chocolate. Add chopped walnuts and chocolate chips. Pour batter into the prepared pan and bake for 50 to 60 minutes or until a toothpick inserted near the center of the cake comes out clean. Leave the cake in the pan.

3. To make the sauce, combine the ingredients in a saucepan. Bring the mixture to a boil and simmer for 8 minutes. Poke cake (still in the pan) all over with a toothpick or skewer. Pour half of hot sauce over the warm cake. Allow to cool in pan for 30 minutes. Turn out onto serving platter. Drizzle remaining sauce over the cake.

My First Cooking Class

Dick Martin

My adventure into the art of gourmet food preparation began in 1974 when my wife Dolly and I took cooking lessons from cookbook authors Diana and Paul von Welanetz. While I certainly consider myself open to new experiences, taking a cooking class was a bit out of bounds for me—after all, I was a comedian—what did I know about cooking? But the class was to change my life in more ways than one.

Despite my trepidation, my passion for cooking, especially for Chinese-style cooking, was born that first class. Paul demonstrated how to make Hot and Sour Soup. He told us it was the one thing his Diana wanted him to fix for her when she was sick in bed, it was her soul food. Of the thousands of versions of Chicken Soup in the world, this remains my favorite.

Paul showed about a dozen of us how to sharpen knives and Chinese cleavers. In Chinese cooking, you prepare everything you will be using ahead of time, placing the ingredients in small bowls next to your cooking area.

Every utensil, every bottle of seasoning, must be within arm's reach because Chinese cooking is done in mere seconds. The reason for this is that in China there was seldom much cooking fuel, and what was used needed to be used economically. Whatever the reason, I always find it calming to prepare and line up all the ingredients neatly in small bowls I bought in Chinatown. And, I enjoy the *macho*, methodical act of sharpening my knives.

Oh, and the other way the cooking class changed my life? Along with learning the joys of cooking, I soon inherited part of the von Welanetz lifestyle—the joys of dog ownership, and standard poodle ownership in particular. Paul and Diana owned a beautiful black standard poodle named Misty. The dog was very intelligent and trained in a way I found astonishing. Paul would open the door and say, "Misty, go to the bathroom!" and with that she would run to an authorized area and do whatever she had to do, whether she had to or not.

Although we'd owned dogs before, we were so impressed by Misty's style that we went right out and bought a standard poodle ourselves. We named him Paddy, after an island halfway between Ireland and Scotland near a place we like to golf. When Paddy passed away we got Bristol, named for Bristol, England, which is famous for three things: an active seaport during World War II, the birthplace of Cary Grant and, best of all for me, the birthplace of my beautiful wife, Dolly. Both dogs were quick to learn Misty's trick and impressed all our neighbors as Misty had impressed us.

Without further ado, here is the Hot and Sour Soup recipe with my own additions. As Julia would say, *"bon appétit!"*

Hot and Sour Soup

Makes about 8 servings

◆

A dozen dried mushrooms, approximately 1½ inches in diameter

4 chicken breast halves, boned and skinned

1 (10½-ounce) package tofu, drained

BOWL 1:

3 tablespoons white vinegar

3 tablespoons dry sake

1 tablespoon soy sauce

½ teaspoon to 1 tablespoon ground white pepper (depending on how hot you like your soup)

BOWL 2:
3 tablespoons cornstarch   *¼ cup dry sake*

BOWL 3:
1 egg, lightly beaten

BOWL 4:
5 cups of a combination of
  good chicken broth and the
  mushroom soaking liquid

BOWL 5:
Thinly sliced scallions, for serving

1. Pop the dried mushrooms into 2 cups of hot water and allow them to soak for 20 minutes or so. Drain the liquid, reserving it to use as part of the broth. Cut away and discard the tough mushroom stems. Place the caps on a chopping board and cut into thin slices.

2. Slice chicken breasts into ½-inch cubes. Slice the tofu into ¼-inch slices, then turn it on its side and slice again. Turn the tofu around and make about 1-inch cuts. You will end up with several 1-inch strips of tofu.

3. Assemble the ingredients in bowls as listed above. (I told Diana I use 1 tablespoon ground white pepper, but Diana doesn't believe me!)

4. About 15 minutes before serving, bring chicken broth and mushroom soaking liquid to a boil in a wok or saucepan. Add the mushrooms and chicken, lower the heat to a simmer and cover for 10 minutes. Add the tofu and let it simmer for 3 more minutes. Add the vinegar/pepper mixture. Stir the cornstarch mixture and add, stirring all the while.

5. Now, get the whole soup moving clockwise with a spoon, and as it is moving, drizzle in the egg—instant egg drop soup. Scatter a handful of thinly sliced scallions over the top and it is ready to serve. Remember, what makes this Hot and Sour is the pepper and white vinegar, so adjust those two flavorings to your taste.

Foule and the Art of Living

John Catenacci

I learned to make *Foule* (pronounced, roughly, FOOL) from Ghalib Al-Awan, a Saudi Arabian friend who prepared it for me as I watched—and, of course, then, so as not embarrass him, ate most of it. It is an ancient dish that is eaten throughout the Middle East made from fava beans, fresh garlic, olive oil and ground cumin. A great food for any time of the day—we ate it that day warm for breakfast.

We sat together next to his kitchen window, looking at the low mountains that skirt Calgary, easily seen across the treeless landscape sweeping out of the city across the brown winter plateau. In the frozen north of Alberta, Canada, we were both a long way from our homes and we found ourselves brought together by a stroke of fate.

The morning light broke through night and danced off the far mountains to the west. Speaking in subdued voices, not wanting to wake the house, we sat and dipped warmed pieces of Lebanese bread in the still-warm Foule, accompanied by fresh pieces of feta cheese and slices of raw tomato.

As we ate and sipped hot tea, it occurred to me that he was not unlike the dish we shared together—gentle, subtle, healthy in mind and spirit, and vibrantly alive. While I err often in the food I eat, I was reminded how simple food made in this way, with fresh ingredients, feeds not only the body but the soul. Perhaps it makes a difference too to share good food with friends in the presence of nature, so we may be more in touch with our own natures.

What Foule really helped me to notice is that life can be art—it can be lived with skill as an expression of beauty and truth. And I noticed I live it that way often enough.

I have read that the Lakota Sioux have a saying, "You are what you eat." I suspect native people in touch with ancient traditions know the deepest meaning of this. "Six Billion Big Macs Sold" may explain the increasing homogenation of our processed minds and lives. Maybe not. Maybe we just make too much of food.

In any case, Foule is an excellent way to enjoy a Calgary sunrise . . . and to experience a friendship. I'll wager it can punctuate many life-giving experiences—and move you a little closer to the Art of Life.

Like many traditional foods, Foule may vary considerably from country to country and region to region. Most often it is accompanied by *hummus bi tahini*, a thick, creamy sauce of ground chickpeas seasoned with lemon juice, garlic and olive oil, which is used as a dip or spread. It is good with some fresh green onions on the side, and, of course, hot tea.

Foule

Makes 4 to 5 servings

༄

1 (28- to 32-ounce) can small fava beans (or start with dry beans and cook according to package directions for 3 to 4 hours until soft)	½ to 1 teaspoon black pepper
	½ large bunch of parsley
	2 cloves garlic (or more, to taste)
	6 tablespoons fresh lemon juice
	10 to 12 tablespoons fine olive oil
2 teaspoons salt	1 tablespoon white vinegar
1 teaspoon ground cumin	1 large, ripe tomato, diced

1. In a frying pan, place the beans with a cup of their own liquid; heat until the liquid is gently simmering. Add salt, ground cumin and black pepper. Mash some of the beans with the back of a large spoon as they are being heated—they should look like lumpy refried beans.

2. Rinse parsley well and shake dry. Strip the leaves from the

stems by laying the parsley flat on a wooden cutting board and sliding a knife pressed tightly against the board across the parsley
leaves, cutting them off. Discard the stems and chop the leaves finely.
Grind the parsley and at least 2 cloves garlic (or more, to taste),
using a mortar and pestle. Add lemon juice, olive oil and white
vinegar (to "sweeten" the flavor, my friend told me) to the garlic and
parsley, grinding the mixture thoroughly. (You may use less oil if
avoiding fat, but maintain a ratio of 2 parts olive oil to 1 part lemon
juice.)

3. Add the chopped tomato to the parsley mixture. (One must
pay dearly for a decent tomato in January in Calgary, but only one
is required, and the result is well worth the cost.)

4. When most of the moisture has simmered from the beans,
remove the pan from the heat. Stir the parsley mixture into the hot
crushed beans. Eat while still warm or after cooling—it tastes
wonderful no matter what!

Family Secret Sesame Chicken

Ronald W. Jue

My father was a French chef for several major restaurants in the San Francisco Bay area. He was second-generation Chinese, born and raised in Los Angeles by parents who had migrated from Canton in the early 1900s. He developed his French cooking skills through the back door by apprenticing with some of the major French chefs in the Bay area.

He was a quiet, hard-working man who worked many hours, but he was also an innovative cook in our home. I remember the compliments from our guests and how my mother would joke about my father's patience teaching her to cook. Whenever he was asked for a recipe, he would say it was a family secret. Once, when our neighbors wanted to learn, he asked them to observe his cooking methods: a pinch of this, a shake of that, a twist of something else. His students then translated his intuitive style into tablespoons and cups.

He had a unique way of integrating his family's own style of Chinese cooking, constantly experimenting by mixing French approaches with oriental ingredients. Salad dressings were flavored with Japanese rice vinegar and scallions; chicken was fried with sesame seeds, soy sauce and French wine; Denver omelettes were made with Chinese pork sausages—the list went on. When serving, each prepared dish would complement the preceding or succeeding one: Subtle textures would follow strong flavors, sweet would follow sour and hot would follow cold.

My father infused his work with affection, and through his

cooking he taught me how to integrate his principles:

- Recipes for life are only guidelines, life is an intuitive dance, and each step, or ingredient taken, makes a statement of who you are.
- In each moment there are complementary ways to solve a problem, be it between different foods or different people. You may call it approaching life with yin (reception) or yang (direction) energy. The combination of these energies becomes the wellspring of something new and creative.
- Through working or cooking from the place of the heart, you will touch the people you serve, and by bringing joy to your work, you will give the bounty of good fortune and fullness to all.

Here is one of my favorite recipes created by my father.

Sesame Chicken

Makes 5 to 6 servings

3 pounds (15 to 18 pieces)
  small drum sticks or chicken
  wings, wing tips removed
1 egg, beaten

Salt and pepper
Flour, for dredging
¼ cup olive oil

SAUCE:
½ cup soy sauce
¼ cup sugar

¼ cup sherry
1 tablespoon white sesame seeds

1. Preheat oven to 325°F. Dip chicken in beaten egg that has been seasoned with salt and pepper to your liking; dredge in flour and shake off excess. Heat olive oil in a large skillet; brown chicken pieces in hot oil. Drain on paper towels.

2. Combine sauce ingredients. Dip browned chicken in sauce and place in a 10 x 13-inch baking pan. Bake 30 to 40 minutes. Serve hot, or refrigerate and serve cold.

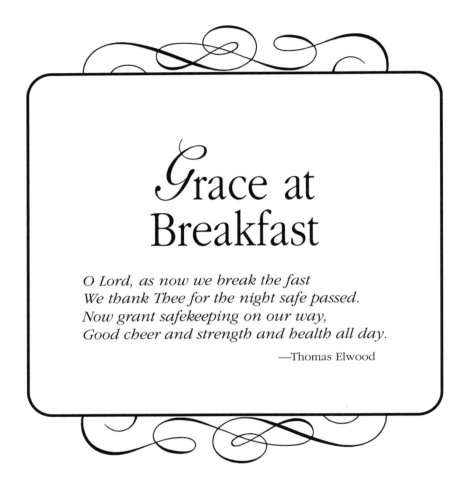

Grace at Breakfast

O Lord, as now we break the fast
We thank Thee for the night safe passed.
Now grant safekeeping on our way,
Good cheer and strength and health all day.

—Thomas Elwood

Health Nut Pancakes

Rama J. Vernon

As the daughter of holistic health practitioners, I grew up with more than an average emphasis on the value of food and conscious eating. Our cupboards and refrigerators were filled with homemade yogurt, wheat germ, molasses, brown rice, goat's milk, powders and potions known to be the natural cure-all for whatever ailed one. My father's authority dominated the table at mealtimes as he told us every vitamin and mineral lurking in each colorful item on our plate. As he sprinkled the latest elixir for health and eternal life into his morning drink and over our whole grain cereal, my mother would comment, half-joking and the other half not, "One day Daddy's going to blow up."

My father was one of the earliest pioneers of chiropractic to successfully campaign for the licensing of chiropractors in California. My mother, a physical therapist, was a protégé of the originators of Reflexology. Their combined practice blossomed into a highly respected school for naturopathy and holistic healing in our large Southern California home. Our living rooms became a haven for those trying to break free from tradition and who were to later pioneer new paths, not only in healing, health and diet, but in holographic thinking or what we now call "New Thought." Adele Davis and Gaylord Houser, Norman Vincent Peale, and Ernest Holmes, founder of the Church of Religious Science, were just some of the luminaries of the 1940s and 50s who graced the portals of our home.

My parents' work attracted a multifaceted array of psychics, mystics and healers, as well as serious "food faddists," as they were called at the time. I remember sitting at mealtimes with chin in hand, pouting over steaming platters of brown rice, tofu and organic vegetables while dreaming of white bread, canned Spaghetti-Os and Hostess Twinkies. My father was always experimenting with new food cures purported to reverse the aging process and treat disease. He believed that aging was a conditioned state of mind and that if enough people overcame the concept of old age and death, the world would reach a critical mass, lifting humanity into new vitality and longevity.

During the summer, my father would awaken the household at sunrise insisting that our family of six join him on his quest for the fountain of health and youth. He would usher us onto the front lawn, instructing us to stomp barefooted on the grass to absorb the *prana* of the earth's radiation from the early morning dew. He would then take off his shirt—signalling it was time for us children to take off ours in order to absorb the first rays of dawn. We were then led through a series of yoga breathing exercises while jogging around our Wilshire Boulevard neighborhood. Neighbors in pajamas and bathrobes waved their encouragement as we huffed and puffed in single file past their windows. For children in their first decade of life, this was more than a little embarrassing.

My mother was sympathetic to our groaning and complaining and would have our favorite breakfast of pancakes waiting upon our return. These were not ordinary pancakes. They nourished our bodies and fed our soul because they contained the most important ingredient of all—her love.

Even though they were the healthiest pancakes in the world, made from freshly stone-ground grains, nuts and seeds, we still thought they were delicious. Since they had no leavening, such as baking powder or baking soda, we could eat more because they did not create a sensation of fullness. The secret of their light, fluffy texture was the beaten egg whites and the turning of the cakes at just the right moment with a flip of the wrist—which puffed them like a soufflé.

My brothers and sister and I watched with enthusiasm as my mother sprinkled pecans or walnuts on the cakes before turning. Our joy diminished, however, whenever she chose to sprinkle sunflower or flax seeds, or oat or wheat bran on the top. The pancakes were always different in taste and texture depending upon the combination of grains used. My mother would throw a variety of grains into the stone grinder just before mixing them into the milk and beaten egg white to maintain the maximum nutrients. They were so simple and so good.

Health Nut Pancakes

Makes 10 to 12 pancakes

Serve with butter or margarine, pure maple syrup and love!

3 eggs, separated
1½ cups milk
1¼ cups whole grain flour
  of any combination: wheat,
  brown rice, millet, etc.
¼ cup bran or cornmeal
  (for texture)

Chopped pecans or walnuts,
  sesame seeds, sunflower or
  flax seeds
Canola, sesame or corn oil

1. Place the yolks in a large bowl and whip them with a fork. Beat the whites separately in a grease-free bowl until they hold stiff peaks. Stir milk into the yolks, followed by the whole grain flour and bran or cornmeal. Fold in the beaten egg whites gently with a fork using a light whipping motion until well mixed.

2. Heat and oil a griddle with oil. Spoon the batter onto the griddle to form pancakes not more than 3 inches in diameter so they will cook evenly. Sprinkle on top your choice of nuts or seeds. As the pancakes puff up and begin to bubble on the top, turn them with a flick of the wrist. Watch them closely until the bottoms become dark and seem to cry out, "I'm done!"

Beer Bread

Charles Champlin

My father, who died when I was 12, was a wine chemist by profession and quite a good amateur chef, I'm told. He could dirty 10 pans in the preparation of one small sauce.

During Prohibition, when the family winery was all but extinct, selling only the occasional bottle of altar wine, my father had the sensible idea of using some of the winery's vast reserves of wine vinegar to produce salad dressing. He and my grandmother filled her kitchen with wonderful aromas as they concocted the perfect blend, so a cousin of mine remembers. Alas, my father, unlike Paul Newman, never figured out how to market the stuff, and for lack of sales outlets, the project never got off the ground. I know all this only second-hand, of course; my sole link to the project are memories of cruet-shaped bottles gathering dust in the dirt-floored basement where my brother and I played on rainy days.

None of my father's kitchen talents have passed on to me or to my brother, whose idea of a great meal is two peanut butter sandwiches instead of one. I can handle pancakes and scrambled eggs, and I once roasted a rack of lamb without damaging it too much. But in truth, my only star turn in the kitchen is that I can make bread. Friends laugh when I say this, until I explain that it is Beer Bread, which I can pop into the oven within ten minutes of deciding to whip up a loaf. No tiresome messing about with yeast and wet towels over the dough while it rises; no endless kneading and re-kneading rituals that I used to watch with fascination at my maternal grandmother's house, keenly aware of how swell the bread would taste still warm from the oven.

My grandmother would almost certainly be aghast at the idea of my quick bread, just as she was of store-bought pickles as a substitute for her own nine-day wonders, as she called them. But my bread is very tasty, as I think she would have been honest enough to admit.

I was introduced to Beer Bread by a friend when I praised the bread she was serving and asked what brand it was. She replied quite smugly that it was her own. I was properly impressed, and would have said she was a careerist and not the bread-making type, until she revealed her secret, and the recipe.

For many reasons, I'm sorry I never had a chance to know my father better. I could have told him about Beer Bread and he could have introduced me to his sauces and salad dressing.

Beer Bread

Makes one 9 x 5-inch loaf

~

3 cups self-rising flour
  (see Note 1)
3 heaping tablespoons sugar
  (I use raw sugar, but any
  kind will do)

1 (12-ounce) bottle or can of any
  beer: regular, lite, dark (which
  makes a darker loaf), foreign
  or domestic (see Note 2)
2 tablespoons milk

Note 1: *There's a formula for converting regular flour into self-rising flour by adding 1½ teaspoons of baking powder and ½ teaspoon of salt per cup of regular flour. This is good to know, especially if you are on a no-salt or low-salt diet. You can simply reduce the amount of salt you add, or eliminate it altogether. My wife thinks self-rising flour tends to make a fairly salty loaf.*

Note 2: *I use whatever I find in the house, preferably a bottle or can that hasn't been in the refrigerator. Warm beer seems to add a little more* oomph *when the baking begins.*

1. Preheat oven to 375°F. Grease loaf pan. In a bowl, combine flour, sugar and beer. I stir the bejeezus out of the mix for 5 minutes,

until it's smooth and bubble free. If the mix seems dry and hard to stir, I splash in a little water; the recipe is indestructible—an amateur's delight.

2. Pour the batter into the greased pan and slap it into the oven. My friend recommended baking for an hour at 375°F or 70 minutes at 350°F. I usually opt for the faster bake. The key to getting a nice crusty loaf, I find, is to cover the pan lightly with aluminum foil (allowing space for the bread to rise without hitting the foil, to which it tends to stick) for the first 45 minutes. Remove the foil and brush the loaf with milk (I use low-fat) before you finish the baking. The old toothpick test is infallible; if it comes out clean, you're home free. It makes particularly wonderful toast, just like my grandmother's.

The One That Got Away

Ralph Waterhouse

I grew up in Yorkshire, England, in an area bordering country fields that extended for miles and miles. Throughout my youth I roamed the meadows, observing birds, rabbits, hedgehogs, field mice and all kinds of wildlife.

Bird watching eventually led to bird sketching and then evolved to include other creatures. Those early years led to my lifelong passion for small creatures and to my long career as a wildlife artist. Through my painting I endeavor to create an awareness that our environment is sacred, and if we damage it we are damaging our very selves.

Not long ago, a client of mine in England who had purchased several of my wildlife paintings commissioned me to do a special painting of a salmon he had caught in Scotland. It was an especially beautiful specimen, large and pink and delicate. I took it home wondering what to do with it until I was ready to paint it.

Well, that fish was just meant to be eaten. I decided that all I would really need for identifying marks would be the head and tail. I cut them off, wrapped them carefully in aluminum foil and stored them in the freezer. With the succulent center, I set about making one of my favorite dishes, Salmon Steaks in Cider. It was exquisite.

A few weeks later, I set up to begin the painting and went to the freezer for my subject. It wasn't there! I searched frantically, looking through everything three or four times, thinking my mind must be playing tricks on me. When my wife came home, the mystery was solved, You see, I hadn't told her what I'd done and she had no idea she was throwing away my model when she cleaned out the freezer.

I bought another salmon at the fishmongers (which was not nearly as nice) to pose for me. At the viewing, my client said, "Hmmm. How did you miss seeing that little round mark the salmon had on his head?"

Foiled! I had to confess that I'd eaten his prize. He graciously caught me another, which I ate as well, but this time I painted it first.

Salmon Steaks in Cider

Makes 4 servings

Diced yellow Finnish potatoes and tiny peas with fresh mint are lovely with this.

4 salmon steaks, 1 inch thick	1 lemon, thinly sliced
2 tablespoons soft butter	½ cup apple cider
3 or 4 sprigs fresh tarragon, dill or thyme	Mayonnaise or Hollandaise sauce

1. Preheat oven to 325°F. Butter a shallow casserole dish with a tight-fitting lid (or use foil to make a tight seal).

2. Place salmon steaks in casserole dish and spread with butter. Season to taste with salt and pepper. Place a sprig of herb on top of each steak and cover with 2 slices of lemon.

3. Heat the cider and pour into the bottom of the casserole dish; cover tightly. Bake about 25 to 30 minutes until the salmon flakes easily. Serve with pan juices and either mayonnaise or Hollandaise sauce.

A priest who had spent a fruitless day fishing picked out three fat fish in the market. "Before you wrap them," he said to the store manager, "toss them to me, one by one. That way I'll be able to tell the Monsignor I caught them and I'll be speaking the truth."

Long Beach, British Columbia, Salmon Supreme

Val van de Wall

A number of years ago I ventured with a few dear friends to a part of Canada that most Canadians do not know exists. Long Beach is, as one would expect, a long stretch of beach, rivaling those of our sister country to the south, only with a different interpretation of nature's hand in the sand. Nature speaks in this part of our land through rough seas of ice blue strands, caressed with blue-white touches of foam, and through evergreens obscuring totems carved long ago.

One crisp dark night, we ventured up the beach by the light of the moon. As we came upon a row of totems, we marveled at the spirit of our aboriginal forebears. Walking north along the beach, we came upon an aboriginal brother preparing a meal in the sand by barbecuing large chunks of salmon impaled on sticks downwind of a bonfire, allowing them to be caressed by cold white smoke and warm gentle flame.

Being a consummate collector of food flavors, I wondered why I hadn't thought of that. We conversed with our host and received a taste of this bountiful bonfire salmon. The flavor flowed through my body, and I resolved, then and there, to duplicate this recipe for my family.

For weeks after I returned home I tried to re-create the ancient method in order to share from the past of our native land. After many struggles I at last cultivated the exact taste. From the soul of the past, I share from my heart to your table this ancient art of cookery.

To re-create the setting of the beach you will need a charcoal-burning smoker, plus kindling and hardwood—mesquite, cherry wood or alder wood. You will also need lungs that can handle lots of smoke.

Long Beach, British Columbia, Salmon Supreme

Makes 6 to 10 servings, depending on size of the salmon

I suggest that you serve this with plain vegetables with no special sauces, just butter and salt and pepper to taste, because there is a world of flavor in the fish. Serve with a crisp, cold Chardonnay.

1 whole red or pink fresh salmon,
   3 to 5 pounds (see Note*)*
Sea salt and freshly ground pepper
The freshest possible dried dill,
   to taste

Garlic powder, to taste
   (Do not *use garlic salt or a*
   squeezed garlic clove—
   fresh garlic is too severe)

Note: *Have your vendor scale the salmon completely and remove all fins, including the tail fin. Filleting the fish is optional because all bones will lift out after cooking.*

1. As in all preparation of foods, energy is involved—the song of your soul as you prepare the food. For instance, if a mother is vexed and upset when breast-feeding her child, she passes her upset feelings to the child. It benefits all of us if we prepare our food with an attitude of love and joy so that we energize the bodies of those we love with constructive, health-giving energy.

2. Lay the fish, spine down, on a paper towel placed over a

cutting board. With your favorite sharp kitchen knife, open the salmon up the belly. Thoroughly wash the cavity of the fish under cold running water and pat dry. Take the tip of your knife and run it down the spine so that the fish lays completely flat.

3. Take a large piece of aluminum foil and double it widthwise. This will be your roasting pan to place on the grill of your smoker. Use your fingers to coat the foil with oil. Place the salmon, skin side down, on the foil. Sprinkle the fish generously with garlic powder and dill.

4. This recipe will need constant care before you can share the beauty of this treat. You will need a very bright light over your barbecue smoker in order to administer the loving care this recipe requires. It is the smoke that must do most of the cooking here. The golden key is the fire—it must never be too hot. Once the charcoal is safely under way, assemble your kindling wood around the charcoal to ignite your hardwood—you need enough wood to create an abundance of cool smoke. When the smoke from the hardwood begins to burn, place the salmon on its foil pan on the grill. Close the hood and all vents to contain the smoke around the fish. The reason we close the air vents is so we do not have an excess of heat, which could overcook or burn the fish.

5. It is time to turn on the bright light on top of your barbecue. Check to make sure there are no hot spots on the foil from the charcoal—they could burn the meat. With a cold, crisp glass of Chardonnay, a table fork and your bright light you are ready to monitor your progress. A milky white substance will develop and cover the whole surface of the meat.

6. You must not overcook or undercook the salmon. The color of the meat, when done, must be bright pink, not red or gray pink.

7. When the fish is done to your taste, take the salmon to the kitchen and remove the entire bone structure. You will be surprised that the meat does not taste like garlic, but has a delicious pungency, heretofore unknown to salmon, and the quality of your hardwood has given it a subtle smoky flavor.

Tomato Mix-Up

Art Linkletter

In June, 1929, I graduated from San Diego High School at the age of 16. I was 5′ 9″, weighed about 140 pounds and looked from certain angles like an immature raccoon. The girls in my class who were 17 or 18 wouldn't give me a second look, much less a dance at the senior party. In school productions I played the child parts, and on the courts I was pushed back away from the crowds who watched the varsity team play. So, I decided to take a year off and see the world. In other words, I would grow into college instead of going to college. But I had another serious problem—I was broke. My adoptive parents were poor and I could never remember having more than a half dollar in my pocket at any one time. How was I to see the world?

Simple! I became a hobo, and for the next year and a half I rode freight trains, stopping off to work in small towns across America as a busboy, a typist and a handyman. When the going got lean and rough between hopping freights and being thrown off them by railroad cops, I would occasionally bed down under a railroad trestle at the edge of town with other transients and, over an open fire, cook up whatever was available.

It was during one of these gastronomic adventures when I wondered what in the world was in that pot, that I ran into what we called Tomato Mix-Up. It was like a big, bubbling stew made of tomatoes and torn-up bits of bread and a few condiments, and it was one of the most delicious dishes I had ever tasted.

It's still one of my favorite dishes, except that now as I sit in my home in Bel Air overlooking all of Los Angeles, surrounded by the mansions of the very rich and the very famous, I can recall those early days and I can almost hear the whistle of a freight train leaving the division point of the rail yards. The camaraderie of a mixed group of travelers with no destinations, of tall stories, of exciting days jumping on fast trains, soften the rough times that we were really going through during those lean days in the deepest depression America had ever seen. And yet, with all its vicissitudes, life was full of unexpected adventures and warm friendships.

I don't expect anyone who tries this recipe to have the same memories stirred by the food, but I think you will be amazed at what a homey, comfortable and unassuming dish it turns out to be. Inelegant? Too simple and easy? So is a peanut butter sandwich and a glass of milk on a hot day. So is a cookie and a glass of lemonade. Sometimes the simplest things in life are the best, especially (for me) when they bring back wonderful memories.

Tomato Mix-Up

Several cans of stewed tomatoes
A lot of torn-up bread pieces or rolls

Butter, to taste
Sugar, to taste

1. Open stewed tomatoes and transfer to a large pot or saucepan (not iron). Add a lot of torn-up bread pieces or rolls, plus sugar and butter to taste.

2. Heat, stirring, until the bread has absorbed the juices into big marshmallow-sized chunks, all a beautiful tomato red.

Things My Father Taught Me, Including "Cabin Stew"

Bobbie Jensen Lippman

You hear so many stories about fathers beating their kids. My father only hit me once. Corporal punishment was left up to Mom, who, when pushed far enough, resorted to putting us over her knee and using a long-handled wooden canning spoon on our you-know-whats.

The day my father slugged me was a hot Nebraska afternoon when my parents were getting ready to attend a wedding. "Would you hose off the car, please?" called Dad, from an upstairs window of our old house.

On the day of "The Slugging" I was 10 years old, and loved any excuse to play with the hose in 90-degree heat. It's important to mention here that I was raised with older brothers who frequently felt they had good reason to beat on me—which our parents tolerated but only if the boys followed this rule: "You can hit your sister on the muscle in her right arm, but that's all!"

There I was, washing our dusty old Ford in the driveway, when Dad came out the side door. "That's good enough," he said. "Shut off the hose."

I obediently turned to the faucet, oblivious of the hose that was now pointing directly (and full blast) at my father. The sight of him dripping wet in his best suit was so shocking that I was speechless

—and so was he. Without saying one word, he punched the puny muscle in my right arm, then marched back into the house to change clothes. And that was that.

Although I was the only girl in the family, I was not excluded from my brother's activities. My father taught me the same things he taught my brothers, which meant being included on overnight camping trips. Sometimes we camped out in the open under the stars, but most of the time we headed for what I now realize was one of my father's few investments, but definitely one of his greatest passions—a ramshackle shanty on the banks of the Elkhorn River. The camping-out menu rarely varied and was referred to as "Cabin Stew" (accompanied by fresh bakery rolls and some sort of a salad). But it was the smell of Dad's Cabin Stew simmering on an open fire that set every hungry mouth watering.

In addition to letting me come along on camping and fishing trips, Dad made sure my skinny little self got in on all softball games, touch football and even "boy chores" such as mowing the grass, shoveling snow and helping pitch coal into the old belching basement furnace. It was from Dad I learned about hard work, sports and competition.

He taught us kids to respect and take care of guns. Dad patiently worked with me and a .22 rifle until I became almost as good a marksman as he and the boys. But *never* were we allowed to shoot at a bird or any living thing. From my father, I learned young to love and respect animals.

In 1926, Dad organized a Boy Scout troop, which was also a rag-tag drum and bugle corps. The troop was so poor that the bass drum was played with a ball of twine on the end of a stick. Since Dad loved kids and band music, he managed to convince Union Pacific Railroad (where he worked) to sponsor a children's marching band. My brothers and I became instant members.

How many fathers teach their small daughters to play a drum, a bugle and a glockenspiel? Eventually, I talked Dad into springing for a few baton twirling lessons (at a whopping 50 cents a lesson) so I could march in the glamour spot at the front of the band. From my father I learned enormous lessons in self-confidence. To this day I can't watch a parade without choking up, especially when a children's drum and bugle corps marches by. And, I can still twirl a mean baton.

I treasure many personal memories of my father. The outdoor smell of his overcoat when he came home from the office on a cold winter day. How he was always working around the house, holding out his left arm as a balance while carrying anything heavy in his right hand, like a tool box or a bucket of paint.

One day, in my early teens, Dad came home from work and handed me a small manicure set that he had bought on his lunch hour. No words, no big announcement and no special occasion, just his silent way of saying "I love you." From that experience, I learned the fun—and the specialness—of giving happy "Unbirthday" love gifts.

When I was 13, there were some dramatic changes in our family. My frail, elderly grandmother lived with us, and I was home the day she died in my father's arms. I sat at the end of her bed, holding her feet, but my grief was for my father who was sobbing, "Mama, Mama." It was the first time I'd seen a grown man cry or anyone die. From Dad, I learned my first lesson in dealing with older people and how to accept the human experience of death. For the past 25 years I have been active in hospice work. Whenever I sit by the bedside of a dying person, I know in my heart that somehow my father influenced me to do what I call "this work of the heart."

On hot summer nights (in the days before television), our family would sit out on the front porch, with my father burning punk to keep the mosquitoes at bay. On those nights—if we kids got lucky—he told ghost stories, some of them about great-grandfather in the old country who was the town coffin maker. We would breathlessly await the part about robbers who crept into the church basement to steal rings and jewelry from the newly deceased. From my father, I learned the art of storytelling.

In my teenage years, Dad grew especially strict. I'm personally convinced men remember all too well their adolescent feelings, and are paranoid about protecting their own daughters from predatory males. My first real date was with a neighbor boy. At 11:00 P.M. (my curfew!) the streetcar let us off two miles from home. I ran all the way, easily half a block ahead of my poor date. There was Dad, waiting on the porch steps, looking very stern and announcing I was grounded for three weeks. So much for my first date, but from my father I learned a big lesson in responsibility.

That same year, when I was a freshman in high school, my kid brother, Paul, was born. I watched my father with this tiny baby, and learned about male tenderness.

My father died not long ago, at 90, and I miss him terribly. But to this day whenever somebody, anybody is browning hamburger meat and onions, suddenly I'm a little girl again sitting by a campfire and waiting for my tall, handsome father to stop stirring the contents of that old black cast-iron kettle and announce, "Come and get it! Cabin stew's ready!"

Chris Jensen's Cabin Stew

Makes 8 to 12 servings

All ingredient amounts are approximate, depending on size of crowd.

2 pounds lean ground beef	*Salt and pepper*
2 to 3 onions, finely chopped	*Worcestershire sauce*
2 to 3 (15-ounce) cans red beans,	*Ketchup*
or pork and beans, or both	*Mustard*
2 to 3 (16-ounce) cans	
stewed tomatoes	

1. In a large skillet, sauté meat and onions, breaking up the meat with the back of your spoon. Dump in the beans and tomatoes and bring to a simmer.

2. Season to taste with salt and pepper, Worcestershire sauce, ketchup and mustard, and be sure to holler out, "Come and get it! Cabin Stew's ready!"

Shake and shake
the catsup bottle.
None will come,
and then a lot'll.

—Richard Armour

7
Friends

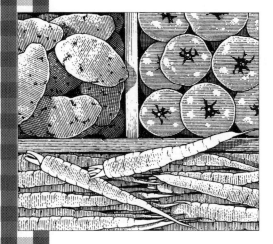

A smiling face is half the meal.
—Latvian proverb

An Irish Blessing

May there always be work for your hands to do
May your purse always hold a coin or two
May the sun always shine upon your window
  pane
May a rainbow be certain to follow each rain
May the hand of a friend always be near to you
  and
May God fill your heart with gladness to cheer
  you.

—Author unknown

Elvis Pie

Diana von Welanetz Wentworth

One spring day in 1959 while lounging on the top bunk in my room at the sorority house, I asked whoever was playing the radio to turn it down. Someone said, "Diana just doesn't like Elvis Presley." A sudden thought entered my mind that I was going to know him and I said, "On the contrary, I'm going to *date* him someday." All my pledge sisters laughed. *Where did* that *come from?* I wondered.

A few months later, my mother took me to Europe for the first time on what was called a Cook's tour. We flew to Paris and checked into the Hotel Prince de Galles near the Champs Elysées. There we met the other tour members including Bobby, a boy of 14, whom I adopted as a pal.

As Mother and I entered the hotel lobby one afternoon, Bobby came running up all excited because Elvis Presley was in the dining room. "I'd give anything for his autograph, but I can't get up the nerve to ask!"

Elvis was in Paris on his first Army leave and looked handsome in his uniform with hair cut short on the sides. I approached him smiling and said, "Hi! My friend Bobby would like your autograph!" He was very friendly and seemed happy to chat with Americans. He signed the paper Bobby gave him and said he'd see me later.

That evening our group went to the early show at the famous

Folies-Bergére, and, as it happened, so did Elvis. His bodyguard recognized me in the lobby, so when our tour bus returned to the hotel, Elvis was waiting in the lobby. He asked Mom if he might take me to the late show at the Lido, the most famous Parisian nightclub.

It felt wonderful to be on his arm. He was impeccably polite and kind to me even as he was being mobbed for autographs. We were shown to a table that was practically on stage where bare-breasted showgirls writhing within inches of the table flirted wildly with Elvis throughout the performance.

On our return to the hotel, Elvis invited me to his room where we talked for a while and he actually sang "Imagination" to me while accompanying himself on the guitar. (This is true—cross my heart!) I had stars in my eyes as he walked me to my room.

The next day I was boarding a bus to leave for the next city on our tour, when Elvis' bodyguard came running up with a note from Elvis giving me his phone number in Bad Nauheim, Germany, and asking me to call when our group reached Wiesbaden. I called just after our train arrived and we made a date for dinner the next evening.

Elvis arrived at the hotel to pick me up in a Mercedes with a driver and his bodyguard, Lamar Fike. Word spread quickly that he was in town, and by the time Lamar escorted me to the car a throng of onlookers had gathered outside our hotel.

Elvis had been smoking a cigar—probably an experiment because he was definitely green and clearly feeling queasy. Instead of his Army uniform, he was wearing a very strange turquoise sweater with black lacings over bare skin down the sleeves. This was not the clean-cut soldier of a few weeks past, and as I walked toward him I remember feeling a flash of fear at leaving the safety of my mother and our hotel.

He took my hand and said, "Good to see you, darlin'!" with that funny little curl he had to his lip. *Oh my,* I thought, *what am I doing here?* We rode for an hour or so before we reached the small town of Bad Nauheim and the little house he'd rented where he lived off-base. Locals who wanted a look at him were gathered outside.

Lamar put out some dinner for us, then Elvis sang to me for hours in the living room, accompanying himself on both piano and guitar.

It was the strangest experience. I couldn't think of a thing to do but smile at him, and after awhile my cheeks ached. From time to time he would yank back the curtains and laughingly surprise the folks who had their noses pressed against the windows. We were late getting back to my hotel and had to knock. The guard who answered our ring was curt until he recognized Elvis; then he politely turned away. Yes, Elvis kissed me. And yes, it was very nice.

I didn't see Elvis again for two years. We stayed in touch with Christmas cards, and I wrote to him the next year when I got engaged. When his time in the Army was complete, he returned to Hollywood to make a movie and rented a house on Perugia Way in Bel Air. I had just broken my engagement when he called to renew our friendship.

I enjoyed how excited my father and brother got about meeting him, and was actually quite surprised. After all, what did my father really know of him except that he was called Elvis the Pelvis? The two of them didn't want to just hang around and stare, so there was a good deal of discussion about how they could seem just naturally present. It was decided that my brother would answer the door and escort Elvis to the den to meet Papa. Gene would offer him some lemonade. Mother would then come in to say hello, and finally I could make my entrance.

All went as orchestrated. I waved goodbye and rode in a limousine to Elvis' house, where there must have been 10 relatives and bodyguards living with him, as well as his father, Vernon, who was visiting. We watched television and ate pizza, sitting on the couch in his den. One of his buddies, Joe Esposito, kindly took me aside and gave me a gold record that had arrived that day to give me the thrill of presenting it to Elvis myself. Another of his buddies dressed up in a gorilla suit and lunged at me through the window next to where I was sitting, and, as expected, I was so startled I jumped a mile!

The next time I saw Elvis, he had moved to an even larger house in Bel Air. He had even more people living with him, as well as a pet chimpanzee who misunderstood and bit me when I took his bowl of potato chips to refill it. Elvis and several of the guys had to pull him off me—his teeth marks lasted for days.

My sorority sisters had never been completely convinced that I was telling the truth about dating Elvis, so one evening after a movie I drove a few of them past his house. As it happened, it was January 8 and there was a huge party going on for his birthday. My friends insisted I ring the doorbell. Joe and Lamar recognized me and welcomed us all.

That was the last time I ever saw Elvis, though the Christmas cards continued for a few years until I married. What I remember most is how gentlemanly he always acted toward me.

Like many of the significant events in my life, meeting Elvis was foretold by one of those moments of knowing, when sudden clarity appears like a burst of sunlight and then vanishes just as quickly, leaving me with a remnant of sureness. Yet our friendship was not earth-shattering nor formative to my life in any real way. I certainly had no idea then how much of a legend he would become.

Even then, I imagined knowing him would provide a fun story for me to share with grandchildren one day. It is even more fun to share the story in this book because by the time I have grandchildren (hint, hint), they will probably just say, "Who?"

One of Elvis's favorite food combinations was peanut butter and bananas. He liked them in sandwiches, but I'll bet he would have *loved* this pie. I created this peanut butter-flavored banana cream pie with gratitude for the kindness shown to me by a sweet man we all knew so long ago.

Elvis Pie

Makes a 9-inch pie to serve 8

∾

¾ cup Reese's peanut butter chips	1 tablespoon butter
	1 teaspoon vanilla
½ cup sugar	2 ripe bananas, sliced
⅓ cup flour	1½ cups heavy (whipping) cream
2 cups milk	3 tablespoons sugar
2 egg yolks	1½ teaspoons vanilla

CRUST:

1½ cups Zwieback crumbs made from a 6-ounce box of Zwieback baby biscuits or graham cracker crumbs (grind in blender or food processor)

3 tablespoons sugar
½ cup ground peanuts
¼ teaspoon ground cinnamon
¾ stick (6 tablespoons) butter or margarine, melted

1. To make the crumb crust, mix the ingredients in a small mixing bowl. Spoon into a 9-inch pie pan and, using the back of a spoon, press firmly into the bottom and sides, but not above the rim. Bake 8 to 10 minutes. Cool before filling.

2. Sprinkle all but 1 tablespoon of the peanut butter chips over the bottom prepared crust.

3. In a medium-sized heavy saucepan, combine ½ cup sugar and the flour; stir in the milk. Heat over medium heat, stirring often with a whisk, until it just starts to bubble and has thickened. Whisk a small amount of the hot mixture into the egg yolks in a small bowl, then whisk the yolks into the hot mixture in the saucepan and cook, stirring constantly, for 2 to 3 minutes. Remove from the heat, whisk in 1 tablespoon butter and 1 tablespoon vanilla and let cool 10 minutes. Pour half the warm custard into the pie shell over the peanut butter chips. Arrange sliced bananas evenly over the custard; top with remaining custard; chill thoroughly.

4. Before serving, whip the cream with 3 tablespoons sugar and 1½ teaspoons vanilla until it holds its shape. Mound the whipped cream over the pie, making decorative swirls. Sprinkle more peanut butter chips evenly over the surface. Serve, or chill up to 8 hours before serving. Brace yourself for cheers and applause!

In Hella's Kitchen

Sharon Huffman

No matter where I take my guests,
It seems they like my kitchen best.

—Pennsylvania Dutch saying

For years, whenever I felt the weight of the world on my shoulders I would find my way to Hella's kitchen. I knew that, there, whatever ailed me would be healed.

Hella Hammid was a special lady—gracious, wise, humble, full of life and love. Books have been written about her and her abilities as a world-renowned photographer and psychic hired by governments. Even the Ali Khan hired her to find his stolen race horse, inspiring the film "The Black Stallion." But to me, she was a wonderful friend.

I would arrive at her home, where she would immediately sit me down in her little kitchen and welcome me with tea. Then, as she concocted one of her remarkable soups, I would tell her my troubles. She listened patiently as she chopped and stirred. Always, as we would sit together sipping hearty, nurturing soup with warm, crusty bread fresh from the oven, she would offer simple words of wisdom that lifted my spirits. By the time I left Hella's kitchen, I felt renewed, refreshed and ready to face the world again.

It was in her kitchen over a steaming bowl of soup that I learned about the healing power of women. I learned there that it is the woman who sets the tone of a relationship and the home, that a woman has the ability to uplift and inspire and bring out the best in everyone around her. She showed me that it is a woman's role to inspire her man to be his best, and if she sees him being less, she may lovingly guide him to be more. Hella taught me that it is the responsibility of a woman to create a loving world, starting in her own kitchen.

Hella understood the healing power of food when love becomes the main ingredient. Food prepared with love fills us with love as we eat it, nourishing body, mind and spirit, and making healthy, loving individuals.

She always brought her best disposition to her kitchen. She put the respect and caring she felt for her guests into every dish she served. As she stirred her soup pot, she mixed in her highest hopes and aspirations. I don't remember a harsh word ever spoken there. Every movement in her kitchen was done in loving reverence for life and for all who would enter there. To step into her kitchen was to step into the essence of love.

To this day, whenever I feel weary from the world and in need of healing, I head for the kitchen to prepare some soup, re-creating Hella's magic in my own way. And though she is gone, when I now play the same role for others that she once played for me, I feel her quiet presence.

Here is a recipe for Basic Cream of Vegetable Soup; make it with whatever seasonal vegetable you like. And may you be healed as I was in Hella's kitchen.

When her friends would ask her for her flan recipe, Hella would always say, "I'll leave it on my epitaph." And she did. Her epitaph, engraved in brass and fastened to a tree outside her bedroom window, is the recipe for Hella's Flan.

Basic Cream of Vegetable Soup
Makes 8 servings

2 tablespoons butter or margarine
4 cups any vegetable, cleaned,
  peeled if necessary, and chopped.
  Suggested vegetables are any
  combination of broccoli, cauliflower, mushrooms, summer
  squash, sorrel, spinach and
  watercress.
1 large leek, halved, thoroughly
  rinsed, and thinly sliced
2 stalks celery, chopped
2 quarts chicken broth

1 pound baking potatoes,
  peeled and cut in ½-inch cubes
¼ cup minced parsley
1 tablespoon chopped fresh
  herbs of your choice or ¾ to
  1 teaspoon dried herbs,
  crumbled
1 cup light cream (half and
  half) or whole milk
Salt and white pepper to taste
Freshly grated nutmeg, to
  taste (optional)

1. Melt the butter in a large, heavy Dutch oven or soup pot and sauté the vegetable of your choice with the leek and celery over medium heat for a minute or so. Cover and cook over low heat for 5 minutes. Add the broth and potato, bring to a boil, cover and simmer very slowly for 20 minutes. Add parsley and herbs; simmer, uncovered, 10 minutes longer.

2. Ladle about 3 cups of soup at a time into an electric blender; cover tightly and blend until smooth. Pour into a clean saucepan, add half and half or milk and season to taste with salt, white pepper and freshly grated nutmeg. (Season more assertively if the soup is to be served cold.) Bring just to a simmer, then remove from the heat. Serve hot or chilled.

HELLA'S FLAN

PREHEAT OVEN TO 350 DEGREES.

1 QT. HALF AND HALF~SCALD

7 WHOLE LARGE EGGS ⎫ BEAT WELL AND ADD
½ CUP SUGAR ⎬ SCALDED CREAM
PINCH OF SALT ⎭

POUR INTO CARAMEL LINED BAKING DISH. SET DISH
INTO HOT WATER IN SLIGHTLY LARGER PAN AS HIGH AS
POSSIBLE. BAKE FOR 20-35 MINUTES DEPENDING ON
DEPTH OF DISH. WHEN INSERTED KNIFE COMES OUT
GOOKY, REMOVE FROM OVEN AND FROM HOT WATER
BATH. IF KNIFE COMES OUT CLEAN, FLAN IS OVERCOOKED!

CARAMEL: IN ENAMEL OR STAINLESS STEEL (NOT ALUMINUM)
PAN (SMALL), PUT 1 CUP SUGAR AND 4 TABLESPOONS
WATER. BOIL TILL CARAMELIZED. WATCH CAREFULLY
SO IT DOESN'T BURN. POUR INTO DISH. LET SET.

BE CAREFUL~ VERY HOT!

Friendship Forever Fondue

Sharon Civalleri

A good friend—what a treasure! I've had a good friend since the fourth grade (and that's a considerable piece of time since we are now in our 50s). Joyce and I see each other only occasionally, but when we're together it's as if we just saw each other yesterday. Being with her is as beautiful as a colorful rainbow, a fresh box of crayons or a cool shower on a hot day—refreshing.

One of our favorite things to do is play in the kitchen together. Lots of problems can be solved while you're chopping and slicing. Sharing a recipe is sharing your life. Are those tears from the onion or from that memory? Does it matter because soon there is only laughter. There is always a sense of understanding, of peace and comfort, of feeling completely at home. Most of all, there is acceptance, no matter what we've done. There is unconditional love. Always.

Friends sharing joy, sorrow, laughter and tears. Through the good—weddings, births and successes; the off-beat—TM, vegetarianism, yoga; the sad—loss of a mother, loss of a child, loss of our youth: we rage on together. We share beauty secrets—after all, we can't let gravity and the years show too much. That's how it is when you share time in the kitchen with a friend who will be a friend forever.

Friendship Forever Fondue

Makes 12 servings

❧

Serve this with 1½-inch pieces of toasted French bread, a variety of fresh vegetables cut in bite-size pieces or tortilla chips

2 (10¾-ounce) cans of
 Cheddar cheese soup
1 pound shredded Swiss cheese
1 (8-ounce) can tomatoes,
 crushed (or mild Mexican
 salsa)

1 pound shredded Cheddar
 cheese
1 (7-ounce) can diced green
 chiles
⅓ cup white wine (optional)
1 small onion, minced

1. Combine all fondue ingredients in a heavy saucepan. Stir over low heat until cheeses are melted and all is smooth.

2. Pour into a bowl and place in the center of a platter surrounded by bread, vegetables or chips for dipping.

Cyndi's Quickie Quiche

Cyndi James Gossett

Three years ago my whole life changed. I was getting a divorce and coming to grips with the fact that my life was altering drastically. I was experiencing a spiritual transformation, and all of my beliefs were being tested on every level. Suddenly I was a single parent who was busier than ever.

My children were also in crisis, and there were times when it seemed like I was incapable of being there for them because of my own confusion. I was so grateful to have a tremendous support group of women friends. They held me, listened to me and on many occasions prayed with me.

I bought a new home and wanted to make it as comfortable as possible for me and my children. For me, it was important to be able to provide a peaceful, comfortable environment for us. I knew I was going to have to work hard to balance my career and family life.

My friends helped me move and set up my kitchen. I no longer had a housekeeper or cook, and my teenage sons were still eating like there was no tomorrow. I had to find ways to make healthy meals for friends and family that were quick and easy. We decided together to become vegetarians and eliminated all meat in our diet except fish. I invented my Quickie Quiche recipe which has become one of our favorites.

Time has moved quickly and now I feel so blessed. I can look back and say this is the best time of my life. My children are happy and healthy. We weathered one of life's storms together and have emerged stronger and closer than ever.

Cyndi's Quickie Quiche

Makes 4 to 6 servings

❧

*1 frozen, prepared pie crust
(or make one from a mix)
1 cup grated low-fat Cheddar
cheese
1 cup grated low-fat
mozzarella cheese (soy
cheese may also be used)
½ onion, minced
1 clove garlic
1 tablespoon canola oil
or butter*

*¼ cup water
A handful (about 2 cups)
spinach leaves, well washed
Bragg Liquid Aminos (salt
substitute) and Spike
seasoning to taste (see Note)
Cayenne pepper to taste
2 eggs
1 cup soy milk*

Note: *Available in health food stores. If you don't have these seasonings, use whatever tastes good to you.*

1. Preheat oven to 350°F. Set out pie crust. Mix together the grated cheeses and spread half the mixture over the bottom of the pie shell.

2. In a skillet, sauté the onion and garlic in canola oil or butter. Add water and spinach leaves, well washed, tossing until the leaves have wilted. Add Bragg Liquid Aminos, some Spike seasoning and cayenne pepper to taste. Spread the spinach mixture over the cheese in the shell, topping with half the remaining cheese.

3. Beat together the eggs and soy milk; pour into the crust. Bake for 15 to 20 minutes. Top with remaining cheese and close the oven door for a few more minutes, until cheese is melted and the filling has set. You can serve right away or reheat in microwave. It's just as good the second day.

The Finnish Connection

Dennis Mannering

If you have much, give of your wealth; if you have little, give of your heart.

—Arabic proverb

Several years ago as I was going through a particularly rough time in my life, I met a young elementary school teacher who later consented to marry me. She took me home to meet her parents, and that was the beginning of a lifelong lesson in what it really means to be a "citizen of the world."

Mom and Dad (Carl and Agnes) Pokela grew up in Finnish homes where Finnish was spoken often and, in Dad's case, spoken exclusively. He went to school and didn't know English, so he had to learn it without the benefit of hearing it spoken when he returned home.

Going to school in a small farm town minimized the selection of people to date and possible spouses but, as Dad says, "Once I saw Mom on the swing with her pigtails flying in the wind, there wasn't another girl that I ever considered."

All three of their children grew up in the same little village in northwest Wisconsin in the same house they still occupy today. In our itinerant society they are part of that dwindling group who have roots.

When I married into the family, I was fascinated by the traditions they kept: singing Finnish songs at family reunions, eating *Kropsu* for breakfast, taking saunas and sharing their unflagging hospitality.

Stories abound about the number of people Carl and Aggie have taken in for lunch or lodging. Dad Pokela says it was a part of their marital agreement that no one would ever enter their house without getting at least a cup of coffee and something to eat.

One such story involves a German boy who was visiting America, bicycling from the East Coast to the West Coast. His journey took him down Highway 8 in northern Wisconsin, where Dad Pokela was working at the end of his driveway. It was near noon and hunger was setting in, so the young man approached Dad and asked if he knew of a restaurant nearby. Knowing there was no restaurant for the next 16 to 20 miles, and knowing that his wife was the best cook around, Dad replied, "You can get a great lunch right here at the house." Once again, Dad had invited someone to lunch without warning Mom. Not that she minded—her policy was, "Always make more than you'll eat; you never know who might drop in!" (It must have been common knowledge there was ample food at the Pokela's, the way people "dropped in," so often close to meal time.)

The young man not only had lunch, but stayed overnight. After being entertained by Dad and his accordion and fed Kropsu for breakfast, he rode off with several packed sandwiches for his continued travels. Several months later, Mom and Dad received a letter from Germany thanking them for their warm hospitality. The young man said in the note, "Of all the wonderful sights and experiences I had, you were the highlight of my trip."

Following is the recipe for Kropsu, which you may be served if you stop by Carl and Aggie's on a Saturday or Sunday morning. It takes a while to bake in the oven, so there is plenty of time for visiting.

Kropsu
(Finnish Baked Pancake)

Pronounced krup'soo *with a rolled "r."*
Makes 2 to 3 servings

❧

3 tablespoons butter or
  margarine
2 to 3 eggs (more egg gives a
  more custard-like consistency)
1½ tablespoons sugar

½ teaspoon salt
1 cup milk (whole, low-fat
  or skim)
½ cup flour

FOR SERVING:
*Syrup, crushed strawberries, crushed raspberries, blueberry pie fill-
ing or create your own topping of your favorite fresh fruit*

Note: *To make 4 to 6 servings, double the recipe and use a 9 × 13-
inch cast-iron or glass pan.*

1. Preheat oven to 400°F. Place the butter or margarine in a heavy
9- to 10-inch cast-iron skillet or heavy glass pan (lightweight pans
will burn the bottom of pancake) in the oven until butter is melted.

2. In a mixing bowl, beat the eggs. Stir in the sugar and salt. Add
the milk alternately with the flour, mixing well after each addition.

3. Pour the batter into the hot butter in the pan. Bake for 20
minutes.

4. Cut into wedges and serve with your choice of toppings.

A Gaelic Blessing

May the road rise to meet you,
May the wind be always at your back,
May the sun shine warm upon your face
And the rain fall soft upon your fields;
And until we meet again,
May God hold you in the palm of his hand.

—Author unknown

Cooking for a Friend Is More than Just Feeding a Friend

Barbara Swain

Do not wait for extraordinary circumstances to do good; try to use ordinary situations.

—Jean Paul Richter

I've given a lot of thought lately to how fortunate I am that cooking is one of the skills I've developed and enjoy. I grew up in a home where all special occasions were celebrated at the dinner table with family and friends. Sharing food has always seemed a natural thing to do.

During the Christmas holidays about 15 years ago, I was struck in a different way by the power of cooking. I received a call from a man I'd never met. He was from Chicago, and a mutual friend there had suggested he call me when he was in Los Angeles. I responded by doing what seemed normal—I invited him to dinner. When he arrived I had a fire going in the fireplace. I'd put a small dining table in front of the fire and had decorated it with a few Christmas things.

As is usual with me, I was still deeply involved with the food preparation. He settled down on a stool in the kitchen and we talked over a little wine and some snacks while I stirred the Mornay sauce for the fish and tossed the Caesar salad. He said he was divorced and we talked about the changes that had meant in his life. It wasn't until somewhere in the middle of dinner, as we sat in front of the fire, that it dawned on me that this was his very first Christmas alone—away from the home he had known for years and the children he had raised.

At that moment I realized that I had provided more than just simple nourishment and hospitality. Although he hardly knew me, I sensed that I had probably given this man the nicest gift I could— not just the food, but the comfort of a kitchen with someone who was cooking for him, the special table with the warmth of the fire, and an evening at home where he was the focus.

Since that Christmas, I have grown more and more aware of the pain in others' lives, whether from a loss of health, financial security, usefulness or, most important, the loss of a loved one. I am so grateful that by doing something as simple as having someone to dinner, I can make a life a little less hopeless, a little less lonely and a little more loving.

The wonderful surprise in this process is that the bonus to me for such giving is precisely the same as it is for the receiver. And that's one of the reasons I feel blessed to be able to enjoy cooking.

Here's a great recipe to share with someone who is hurting. It's comfort food at its best!

Chicken and Dumplings

Makes 2 servings

∿

If you like, speed up the recipe by not browning the chicken.

2 tablespoons butter or oil
2 chicken legs or chicken-
  breast halves, or 1 of each
Salt and freshly ground black
  pepper to taste
½ cup coarsely chopped onion
3 tablespoons all-purpose flour
1¼ cups chicken stock, homemade, canned or reconstituted

1 or 2 celery stalks, cut in
  chunks
2 to 4 carrots (½ pound),
  peeled and cut into 2-inch
  chunks
Dumplings (recipe follows)
½ cup frozen peas
Minced parsley or chives for
  garnish (optional)

1. In a 2- to 3-quart saucepan or Dutch oven, heat butter or oil on medium heat. Season chicken pieces with salt and pepper and brown on all sides; set chicken aside.

2. Add onion to Dutch oven and sauté until translucent. Add flour to pan and cook 1 minute, stirring constantly.

3. Add stock, bring to boil and cook, stirring to dissolve any crust on bottom of pan. Continue to cook, stirring constantly, until thickened.

4. Return chicken to pan and add celery and carrots; season with salt and pepper. Cover pan, reduce heat to maintain a simmer and cook 1 hour.

5. Meanwhile, prepare dumpling dough. After chicken has cooked 1 hour, divide dough into 4 equal portions and spoon onto chicken and vegetables, leaving space around each dumpling for expansion. Simmer, uncovered, 10 minutes. Then cover and simmer 10 minutes longer.

6. Spoon dumplings, chicken and vegetables onto 2 serving plates; cover and keep warm. Stir frozen peas into gravy and heat through. Blend additional water into gravy if it is too thick; pour over chicken, vegetables and dumplings. Garnish with minced

parsley or chives, if desired. Serve immediately.

Variation: CHICKEN AND DUMPLINGS WITH CANNED SOUP
Omit flour and chicken stock. Substitute 1 (10-ounce) can cream of
chicken, celery or mushroom soup diluted with ¼ cup water.
Complete recipe as above.

Dumplings

Makes 2 servings

(*This recipe is excerpted from* Intimate Dining—Memorable Meals
for Two, *by Barbara Swain [Fisher Books].*)

½ cup all-purpose flour	¼ teaspoon poultry seasoning
½ teaspoon baking powder	(optional)
G teaspoon salt	1 tablespoon melted butter or oil
⅛ teaspoon pepper	3 tablespoons milk

1. Measure flour, baking powder and salt into a medium mixing
bowl; mix together until no lumps remain.

2. Stir in pepper and poultry seasoning, if desired. Add butter, or
oil, and milk to dry ingredients, and stir just until dry ingredients are
moistened.

Variations: Add any of the following to dumplings recipe before
adding fat and liquid: ¼ teaspoon ground pepper, ½ teaspoon
ground poultry seasoning, ½ teaspoon dried leaf thyme, 1 tablespoon minced fresh parsley, 1 tablespoon minced chives, 1 tablespoon minced canned pimentos, 2 tablespoons shredded sharp
Cheddar cheese.

BISCUIT-MIX DUMPLINGS: Stir together ⅔ cup biscuit mix and
any of the optional ingredients above in a small bowl. Add ¼ cup
milk and stir just until dry ingredients are moistened. Proceed as in
master recipe.

8
Inspirations and Insights

The invariable mark of wisdom is to see the miraculous in the common.

—Ralph Waldo Emerson

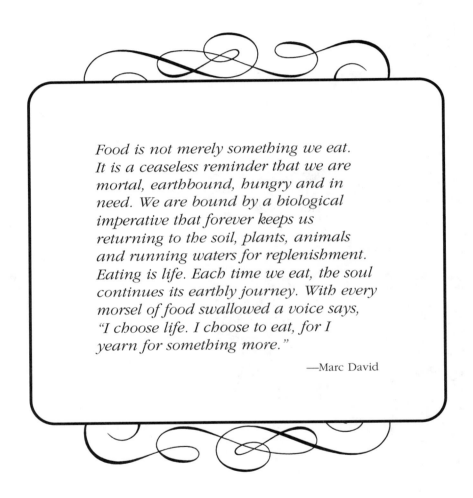

Food is not merely something we eat.
It is a ceaseless reminder that we are
mortal, earthbound, hungry and in
need. We are bound by a biological
imperative that forever keeps us
returning to the soil, plants, animals
and running waters for replenishment.
Eating is life. Each time we eat, the soul
continues its earthly journey. With every
morsel of food swallowed a voice says,
"I choose life. I choose to eat, for I
yearn for something more."

—Marc David

Mothers' Day

Diana von Welanetz Wentworth

Susie Gross and I met more than 30 years ago when I was 19 and she was 29. I was immediately drawn to her, sensing she would become my lifelong friend.

Tall, boyishly slim and graceful, with a pixie face and naturally curly hair, Susie breezed along fashion-show runways as one of Los Angeles' most popular society models. She had a handsome and devoted husband, a four-year-old daughter and a newly adopted baby boy. Her home reflected her flair for cooking, decorating, crafts and gardening. Best of all, Susie always was and continues to be even more beautiful on the inside than on the outside. She moves between her many interests like a bee from flower to flower, leaving a bit of her essence wherever she goes, a piece that touches and lives on without clinging. By example, she has shown me how to let go of what is old and done and used, and move on to the next phase of life.

Susie and I met for tea recently to share news. I was eager to hear the latest stories about her grandchildren whom she so obviously enjoys. Susie was especially excited as she told me how she had been playing with Violet, age three, and Lily, age one, a few weeks before, when she was suddenly overwhelmingly grateful and so filled with love for them. She couldn't help feeling sad at the thought of her son Bill's birthmother missing all the joy of these adorable babies—his birthmother did not even know they existed. In that moment, Susie made a vow to herself to find Bill's natural mother, Victoria (her name has been changed to protect her privacy).

At the time of the adoption, the doctor had told Susie the woman's name. A few years later, her friend Louise had brought Susie a picture of Bill's mother from a newspaper, saying, "Do you know who this is?"

Susie, seeing the strong resemblance, declared, "That's Billy's mother!" If Louise had saved that clipping—and it was likely because "Louise is the kind who saves everything, even her Little Orphan Annie Ovaltine shaker cup"—it could give Susie the lead she needed.

Louise still had the fragile yellowed clipping, and with only a few phone calls, during which she identified herself simply as an old friend, Susie had the right number to call.

Calling the number, Susie reached an answering machine. Overcome with emotion at hearing the soft voice, Susie took a deep breath and left a poignant but discreet message, "Victoria, you don't know me . . . but you did me an enormous favor 33 years ago. Now, the time has come for me to return that favor. . . ."

Later that day, Susie's phone rang. Victoria was overwhelmed to hear that her son was well and happy and that she (miracle of miracles!) also had a daughter-in-law and two beautiful granddaughters who looked just like her. In the two hours they talked, Susie was able to hear Victoria's story for the first time. "I always assured Bill that his mother didn't want to give him up," Susie told me, "that she really had no choice. And it was true.

"In 1959, Victoria was 18 and the daughter of a prominent family on the East Coast. When she became pregnant, her father, whose word was law in the household, wouldn't hear of her marrying. The idea of having an abortion never entered Victoria's mind. Though she pleaded to keep the child, it was decided that she must give the child up for private adoption. Victoria had no choice. She saw her baby boy only once.

"Halfway through the pregnancy she phoned her mother and said, 'I want to keep this child and raise it myself.'

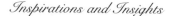
" 'If you do that, Victoria,' her mother replied, 'we won't support you, and you can't bring the child home.' So Victoria had no choice. She saw her baby boy only once."

Susie told Billy often as he was growing up that she believed his real mother had loved him and hadn't wanted to give him up. Bill thrived, and eventually married DeAnne, a young woman who was musically inclined. Together they discovered a favorite song, "From God's Arms to My Arms to Yours," about a woman who gave up her child. DeAnne loved to hum the chorus:

> *And maybe, you can tell your baby,*
> *When you love him so, that he's been loved before*
> *By someone who delivered your son*
> *From God's arms to my arms to yours.*

> —"From God's Arms to My Arms to Yours" by Michael McLean © 1990

Victoria had no more children and held no hope of seeing her son again. Yet one bright spring day, the whole Gross family, arms brimming with flowers, embraced her at the airport in Los Angeles. After the tearful first moments, Victoria pressed a note into Susie's hand:

> *What can I possibly say or give you to express my eternal gratitude for your quite extraordinary generosity and kindness. Ultimately, I can only look you in the eye, hold your hand and say thank you. My respect and affection for you is unlimited and I personally feel that you have set a standard for women throughout the world.*

The bishop at Susie's church had been asking her for years to be the lay member who addresses the congregation. Susie had always protested, "Whatever would I say?" Now she knew.

Her speech was set for Mother's Day. Susie told her story beautifully, giving tribute to Victoria as a very special kind of mother.

"Thirty-three years ago, on September third, a woman delivered a baby boy into this world and looked into his face—looking into the face of your first newborn is like looking into the face of God. And then, due to a set of circumstances, she relinquished him into the arms of another woman to love and raise as her own. It must have taken tremendous faith . . . and it must have broken her heart. Few people have to make that kind of sacrifice in life. My heart aches for her pain.

"I'm the mother who took her baby home to love and raise. I had been miserable because I couldn't have another child, but, thank God, my prayers were heard.

"In the weeks since I found Billy's mother, I have experienced a collage of emotions, and now I know there is one supreme fact in the universe. It eclipses all other truths, all thought, all being, all emotion—God lives. He loves us and directs our lives. Victoria was prompted to come to California to give birth and therefore found me and gave me her baby. And I know God directed me to find Victoria and give her this joy."

Then Bill spoke spontaneously and lovingly of his jubilation in finding a second mother, and of his admiration for "my mom, Susie, the kindest person I know." The service ended with a song from DeAnne:

This may not be the answer for another girl like me
I'm not on a soapbox saying how we all should be
I'm just trusting in my feelings and I'm trusting God above
and I'm trusting you can give this baby both his mothers' love.
And maybe, you can tell your baby,
When you love him so, that he's been loved before
By someone who delivered your son
From God's arms to my arms to yours.

—"From God's Arms to My Arms to Yours" by Michael McLean ©1990

Susie's Rosemary Chicken

Makes 4 servings

❧

Over the many years of our friendship, Susie has shared numerous recipes that have appeared in my cookbooks, including her Sherried Walnuts, Curried Turkey Salad, Apricot Marmalade, and now her Rosemary Chicken. "The recipe has been adapted from Marion Cunningham's Supper Cookbook," *she tells me. "Rosemary is the easiest herb to grow, so we have masses of it in the garden year-round. Its tiny violet flowers are edible and beautiful to sprinkle over chicken as a garnish. Tarragon and other fresh herbs in season would be delicious, too."*

1 (3-pound) chicken
4 medium red potatoes cut in
   quarters (or 8 small ones, halved)
3 to 4 medium leeks, white
   part only, cut in half lengthwise and thoroughly rinsed
   (save the green part of the
   leeks for making soup)
3 cloves garlic, minced

1 tablespoon chopped fresh
   rosemary (or 2 teaspoons
   dried, crumbled)
Salt and pepper
1 to 2 tablespoons olive oil
Fresh sprigs of rosemary and
   a sprinkling of rosemary
   flowers, if the herb is in
   bloom, to garnish

1. Preheat oven to 425°F. Use poultry shears to cut along both sides of the backbone of the chicken. Discard the backbone and remove any extra fat. Rinse the chicken and flatten it out.

2. In the center of a 9 x 13-inch roasting pan or baking dish, place red potatoes. Surround the potatoes with the leeks. Sprinkle the potatoes with minced garlic, rosemary and salt and pepper to taste. Drizzle with a tablespoon or so of olive oil.

3. Place the flattened chicken on top of the vegetables. Sprinkle with salt and pepper. Bake for 45 minutes (or for 1 hour at 350°F).

4. Drain juices into a measuring cup, let stand a few minutes while you cut the chicken into quarters, and serve with potatoes

and leeks. Skim the fat from the pan juices and discard; pass the juices at the table. Garnish with fresh sprigs of rosemary and a sprinkling of rosemary flowers.

Grandma Victoria's Coffee Cake
Makes a 9-inch coffee cake

∾

The second recipe is from Billy's birth mother—it is shared with us by DeAnne Gross.

Shortening or nonstick coating for the pan	½ cup (1 stick) butter
2 cups flour	1 cup sugar
1 teaspoon baking soda	2 eggs
1 teaspoon baking powder	1 cup sour cream
½ teaspoon salt	1 teaspoon vanilla

TOPPING:

⅓ cup brown sugar	¼ cup finely chopped pecans
¼ cup white sugar	1 teaspoon cinnamon

1. Preheat oven to 350°F. Grease a 9-inch round cake pan with a heavy coating of shortening or a generous spray of nonstick coating.

2. Sift together flour, baking soda, baking powder and salt. In a large bowl, cream the butter and sugar with an electric mixer until very smooth and fluffy. Add the eggs, beating until very smooth. Alternately beat in the sifted ingredients with the sour cream. When all is smooth and well-combined, stir in vanilla.

3. Combine topping ingredients.

4. Pour half the batter in the prepared pan; sprinkle with half of topping mixture; pour remaining batter on top and sprinkle evenly with remaining topping mixture. Bake for 35 to 40 minutes, until firm.

Miracle Cookies

Helice Bridges

There are people who put their dreams in a little box and say, "Yes, I've got dreams, of course. I've got dreams." Then they put the box away and bring it out once in a while to look in it, and yep, they're still there. These are great *dreams, but they never even get out of the box. It takes an uncommon amount of guts to put your dreams on the line, to hold them up and say, "How good or bad am I?" That's where the courage comes in.*

—Erma Bombeck

On a park bench—200 feet above the roaring Pacific Ocean—I sat quietly, relaxing and breathing in the rays of the sun. The day was clear, calm, sweet. Sunset was only an hour away.

I noticed that on a bench only 50 feet further along the path was an older woman. She was frail and bent over from the weight of her shoulders. She had a large, witch-like beak nose. Despite her appearance, something about this woman drew me to her.

I walked to where she was seated. As I sat beside her, I kept my focus on the ocean. For a very long time I didn't say anything. Without thinking, I spontaneously turned to this old woman and quietly asked, "If we never saw each other again, what would you really like me to know about who you really are?"

There was no answer—silence lingered in the air for what seemed like an hour. Suddenly, tears rolled down her cheeks. "No one has ever cared that much about me," she sobbed. I placed my hand lightly on her shoulder to comfort her and said, "I care."

After introducing herself as Isabel, she whimpered, "Ever since I was a little girl I have always wanted to be a ballerina. But my mother told me I was too clumsy. I was never given the chance to learn how to dance. But I have a secret. I've never told anyone this before. You see, ever since I've been four years old I've been practicing my dance. I used to hide in my closet and practice so my mother wouldn't see me."

"Isabel, show me your dance," I urged.

Isabel looked at me in surprise. "You want to see me dance?"

"Absolutely," I insisted.

That was when I saw the miracle. Isabel's face seemed to shed years of pain. Her face softened. She sat up proud, head erect, shoulders back. Then she stood up, turned and faced me. It was as if the world stood still for her. This was the stage that she had been waiting for all her life. I could see it in her face. She wanted to dance. She wanted to dance for me.

Isabel stood before me, took a long deep breath and relaxed. Only moments before, her brown eyes were sunk deep into her skull; now they were bright and alive. Elegantly she pointed her toe forward while gracefully stretching out her hand. The move was masterful. She took my breath away. I was witnessing a miracle before my eyes. One minute, she was an ugly, old, miserable woman; the next, she was Cinderella wearing glass slippers.

Her dance took a lifetime to learn and only a moment to do. But she had fulfilled her life's dream. She had danced.

Isabel began to laugh and cry almost at the same time. In my presence, she had become human again. We continued to speak about math and science and all the things that Isabel loved. I listened and hung on her every word. "You are a very great dancer, Isabel. I am proud to have met you." And I really meant it.

I never saw Isabel after that. I still remember smiling and waving goodbye to her. Since that day, I have taken the time to stop and acknowledge people everywhere. I have asked them what their dreams are. I have rooted them on. Each time I do this, I witness a miracle. Like Isabel, people stand taller, smile and somehow begin to believe in themselves again.

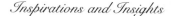

To each of these people I have awarded a *Who I Am Makes a Difference* blue ribbon. I have taught over three million people how to show their appreciation for others. You can be a miracle maker, too. There are great people everywhere. There is an Isabel in everyone. Perhaps you will change the life of someone today. Perhaps you will make them some Miracle Cookies, which are miraculously easy, to remind them that who they are makes a difference and that dreams really do come true.

> *We awaken in others the same attitude of mind we hold toward them.*
>
> —Elbert Hubbard

Miracle Cookies
Makes about 3 dozen cookies

Made as directed, these make 3-inch cookies. You can make them larger and mold them, while still warm, over the back of small bowls. When they harden, use for serving ice cream with fresh berries.

¼ cup firmly packed dark
  brown sugar
¼ cup light corn syrup
½ stick (4 tablespoons)
  butter, melted

½ cup flour
½ cup finely chopped pecans
2 teaspoons vanilla

1. Preheat oven to 350°F. Line two cookie sheets with foil. In a small saucepan, combine the brown sugar, corn syrup and butter. Stir constantly over high heat until the mixture boils; remove from the heat. Stir in the flour and nuts until blended, then stir in the vanilla.

2. Drop by level teaspoonfuls onto the foil, placing about 3 inches apart (they spread!). Bake for about 8 minutes until the cookies are a rich golden brown.

3. Remove from the oven. Let cool about 2 minutes until firm, then lift with a spatula to paper towels to drain off excess butter. When cool, pack in airtight tins to preserve crispness.

Starving Student Chicken

John and Kyoko Enright

Many years ago, in Japan, a starving student lived in a tiny garret room that happened to be just above a very fancy restaurant where rich folk came to dine. (That students starve seems to be truly a cultural universal.) The student had only one meal a day—a meager bowl of rice, which he ate in the evening before studying.

One day the student was on his way home for his frugal meal, when he chanced to meet a friend just outside the restaurant. They stopped to chat. Not surprisingly, being just before the student's mealtime, they talked of food.

"It is so wonderful that I live over this restaurant," said the student to his friend. "Each night as I eat my little bowl of plain rice, I can smell the delicious odor of the wonderful food this restaurant serves, and I can imagine myself eating those tasty dishes down here with the rich folk instead of eating my rice alone up in my room. There is one chicken dish that I especially love. The garlic and pepper smell seems to creep right into my rice bowl and nourish me!"

Unfortunately, the greedy restaurant owner happened to be standing right near the door of the restaurant greeting his customers, and he heard the student's words. He marched out, grabbed the student by the ear and demanded payment.

The student, horrified, protested that he had no money, but the owner simply marched him to the nearest police box and filed a complaint, insisting on payment.

By chance, court was in session at that very time, presided over by Judge Ohta. The case could be heard immediately. Judge Ohta had a wide reputation for both justice and wisdom, but the student was too caught up in his misery to realize this as the hearing started.

The owner was surprisingly eloquent in his accusation. He cited the terrible load of expenses borne by the restaurant and the need for all who used the restaurant in any way to help meet these costs. The student's defense was pitiable: it was simply a plea that he had no money and could not pay. Judge Ohta looked thoughtful for a moment, and then began his judgment.

"Clearly," he addressed the student, "you must pay for the value you have received from the owner." If possible, the student looked even more frightened and dejected than before, while the owner, if possible, looked even more smug and righteous. "Do you have any money with you?"

The student found a couple *sen* (far less than a penny) at the bottom of his very limp purse and took them out. "Rattle them together," said the judge. Bewildered, the student did so, producing a pathetically thin sound. "Good!" said Judge Ohta. "The sound of money is sufficient payment for the smell of food. Case closed."

The chicken dish so favored by the student could not have been exactly this one, but it might have been close to it.

Starving Student Chicken

Makes 4 servings

1 to 1½ pounds boned, skinned, defatted chicken breasts
½ cup sake or white wine
1 pound spaghetti, linguine or other pasta of your choice
1 tablespoon butter or margarine
½ cup olive oil

8 to 10 minced garlic cloves
½ to 1 teaspoon crushed dried red chili flakes
1 teaspoon soy sauce
½ to ¾ cup minced parsley
Grated Parmesan or Romano cheese (optional)

1. Cut the chicken breasts into small pieces, about the size of the first joint of your ring finger. Sprinkle with the sake or white wine and marinate for 2 to 4 hours.

2. Cook the spaghetti, linguine or other pasta of your choice according to package directions. Rinse and drain in colander; toss with butter or margarine to keep pasta separate.

3. While the pasta is cooking, in a large frying pan heat the olive oil, minced garlic and chili flakes to taste depending on how hot you like it (it becomes stronger in flavor as it stands). Turn heat as high as possible and add the chicken, reserving the marinade. Cook until chicken is no longer pink in the center.

4. Add the cooked pasta to the frying pan and season to taste with the salt and pepper. Stir in any remaining marinade, the soy sauce and minced parsley. Serve immediately (with grated Parmesan or Romano cheese, if desired) and prepare for compliments in the local language!

See How They Run

Bobbie Jensen Lippman

Who can ignore the fitness craze going on? Everywhere you look, people are jogging, power-walking, bicycling, Rollerblading, playing tennis. For us semi-couch potatoes, it can be semi-depressing.

One day my friend Roz and I were sitting in a deli commiserating about our need to lose some weight while also scarfing Danish, drinking coffee and waiting for our friend Sherrie to show up. We consider Sherrie a semi-jock because she jogs three times a week, while Roz and I do little more than walk a mile or two.

Sherrie sat down, dug around in her purse and plunked a flyer on the table. It said: "THE GREAT PUMPKIN CHASE. A 10K FUN RUN WITH NO HILLS. T-SHIRTS FOR ALL PARTICIPANTS." Until that moment the term "10K" was not in my vocabulary. It simply was not relevant in *my* life that 10K added up to 6.2 miles . . . of running.

"Listen," Sherrie said, "It's two months away. Why don't we get in shape and try for it?"

We looked at each other. Maybe it would be a way to lose some weight, I thought. By the time we finished the Danish, we agreed to launch a campaign. We would meet three times a week and start slow. And we would stop eating Danish. I even forced myself to come up with some sort of a power drink to satisfy my sweet tooth and keep me from reaching for sugar-loaded sweets.

As the weeks went by we gradually built up to four miles of jogging. We weren't fast, but at least we were doing it. On the day we managed to go four miles, we had to quit because my glasses fogged up, Sherrie got a sideache and Roz had to go to the bathroom. During our "conditioning" we never managed to jog more than four miles. But the pounds were beginning to fall off!

Race day arrived. We each had our own concerns. I worried about my glasses fogging up and my socks falling down. I also worried about bra straps breaking and everything falling down. Sherrie worried about sideaches, and Roz worried about the availability of bathrooms. We all worried about going the distance.

The registration table marked "WOMEN 40-49" was not exactly teeming with activity. Most of the crowd was clustered around the other tables, signing in and pinning on race numbers. Everywhere we looked, runners were bending, stretching and hopping up and down.

The loudspeaker sputtered and a voice blared out that beginners should start at the back of the pack to avoid getting knocked over. *Swell,* I thought. However, the moment we got to the back of the pack, the starting gun went off and two thousand people surged forward. We three had planned to stick together for moral support, but we soon were separated in the crush of bodies.

An official-looking person was stationed at each mile point, calling out the distance and time. The first three miles were almost fun—until perspiration leaked into my eyes and fogged up my glasses. The bra straps held, but my left sock slithered down around my ankle.

Runners were strung out along the street, and I hadn't seen Roz or Sherrie since the first mile. I anxiously scanned the faces of policemen at blocked-off intersections, hoping for an encouraging smile. A cute young girl at the curb, in a red velour warmup suit, called out "MILE FOUR!" Why wasn't I doing that instead of this?

Up ahead I could barely make out the mile-five person, who was waving and shouting at people as they ran past. I glanced down, fully expecting to see lead weights strapped to each leg because that's exactly what my legs felt like. It was time for a decision. If I could just make it to the mile-five person, that would be it! Enough already. No way could I haul my body farther than that.

Suddenly I heard the sound of soft footsteps padding behind me. An elderly man—who had to be at least 75—passed on my left. He was stripped to the waist, his brown back accordion-pleated with age. He was nearly bald except for a little white tuft of hair on top of his head. And he was smiling.

I said to myself, "Self . . . if that old man can do it, you can do it!"

Focusing my fogged-up gaze on his leathery back, I pictured myself as Joanne Woodward in the movie, "See How She Runs." The lead weights fell away and, somehow, I managed to follow the old man right across the finish line.

There was Sherrie, excitedly jumping up and down, cheering me on. A few moments later, Roz came stumbling into our outstretched arms. "We did it! We did it!" we yelled at each other.

It doesn't matter that we started and finished at the back of the pack. What matters is that we set a goal and went for it. And in the process, we got slimmer and healthier.

I looked around for the old man, wanting to tell him what an inspiration he had been, but he had disappeared into the crowd. For some reason, I have this vision of him collecting his 10K T-shirt and heading for home on a skateboard.

Bobbie's Power Drink

Makes 1 drink

❧

I keep over-ripe bananas in the freezer for Power Drink purposes. One minute on "high" in the microwave and the formerly frozen banana will slide right out of its peel and into the blender.

1 to 2 cups low-fat milk or non-fat plain yogurt	*½ to 1 scoop of chocolate Slim Fast (or protein powder of your choice)*
1 banana	*A bit of sweetener (optional)*
1 or 2 tablespoons peanut butter	*A few ice cubes*

1. Place milk or yogurt in a blender. Toss in remaining ingredients and let 'er rip.

2. For a change of pace (and fewer calories), I also make my power drink with blueberries, strawberries, grapes, peaches or strawberry-flavored Slim Fast. And, of course, leave out the peanut butter.

Bon appétit, and keep moving!

A Silver Belt

Cheewa James

I had wandered into a small Indian shop in the foothills of the Sierras in Northern California and struck up a conversation with the Native American woman who owned the shop. My own Modoc Indian heritage and love of Indian jewelry prompted me to tell her of the pain I suffered when my mother's silver Navajo concho belt was stolen. My mother had worn it almost every day of her life. It had passed on to me when she had passed through the arch of life to the other side.

I remember as a small girl putting my arms around my mother's waist and feeling the warmth of her body through the silver platelets. Having her belt gave me great comfort after her death.

As I talked with the Indian woman, I could sense her empathy. But when I finished expressing my grief at having lost the belt, her message was not the one of sympathy I expected. What she gave me was a new beginning and an insight into my mother.

"Remember," she said, "the true gift you were given was things of the spirit. Don't ever cry over things that can't cry over you."

My mother is not a belt. My mother is reflected in the woman who now stands in her place—me. My true heritage is the talents and strengths that she left to me. I no longer cry over things that can't cry over me. I cherish the fortitude and the love a woman left to me.

Harvest Bake

Makes 6 servings

ᕲ

1 large onion, chopped
2 tablespoons oil
1 teaspoon oregano, crumbled
1 teaspoon chili powder
½ teaspoon cumin seed
2 large zucchini or yellow
   summer squash, chopped

1 green bell pepper, seeded
   and cut in thin strips
1 cup fresh corn, cut from cob
2 large tomatoes, sliced
¼ cup grated Longhorn cheese

1. Preheat oven to 325°F. In a skillet, sauté the onion in oil until golden. Stir in the oregano, chili powder and cumin.

2. Combine the vegetables, except the tomatoes, in a shallow baking dish and top with the onion mixture. Bake for 1 hour. Top with sliced tomatoes, followed by cheese, and bake uncovered 20 to 30 minutes longer until the cheese is melted and bubbling.

American Indian Fry Bread

ᕲ

This is the most traditional of all Indian dishes.

3 cups flour, either all-white
   or half whole wheat
1¼ teaspoons baking powder

½ teaspoon salt
1⅓ cups warm water

1. Mix flour, baking powder and salt. Add warm water and knead until dough is soft but not sticky.

2. Stretch and pat dough until thin. Tear off one piece at a time, poke a hole through the middle and drop into a kettle of sizzling hot lard or cooking oil. Brown on both sides. Serve hot.

The Pheasant

Bettie B. Youngs

Growing up on a farm gave me a daily opportunity to see how mankind and nature are interrelated. Both of my parents had a supreme sense of respect for Mother Nature and everything in her realm. This was demonstrated time and time again in childhood, and was personified by the events of one particularly memorable early spring day.

The bright sun filtered through the clouds, warming the fields of alfalfa that my father was mowing. Within a day or two it would be put into bales of hay, gathered from the field, stored in the hay loft and used to feed our livestock. I stood at the fence-line with the lunch my mother had prepared for my father, watching as he cautiously guided the tractor up and down the field, head down, eyes closely observing the movements of the mower. As he neared the end of the field, Dad saw me holding out the lunch for him. He stopped and motioned that it was safe for me to bring it to him.

"Please, Daddy, take me for a ride," I begged as he ate his lunch. I loved riding on the tractor with my father. It was quite a treat because children were forbidden from riding it alone; it was for grown-ups only. Extremely safety conscious, Dad rarely allowed us children to even come near it, let alone climb up on this big "dangerous" machine. He was so protective of his family that he seldom asked my mother to drive the tractor even short distances—such as to fuel it—around the farmstead.

I also liked riding on the tractor because I loved the feel of the wind blowing through my hair and the warm sun on my face, arms and legs. Most of all, I loved being close to my father; sitting near him on the tractor seat inside his protective arms. I adored my daddy and everything about him. I found his energy and passion for the outdoors contagious, his charisma exciting, and his running commentary about everything around him interesting—nothing escaped his attention—birds, bees, flowers, clouds, passing cars and trucks. All became fodder for a comment, story or lesson.

"Please Daddy, can't I ride with you?" I asked again.

"No, no. It's not safe for you to be on the open tractor; I never know when the mower sickle will come dangerously close to a nesting pheasant or a rabbit or a fox. When that happens I have to stop suddenly and that could cause you to fall. No, I'll give you a ride another time."

"Oh please Daddy. I'll be so careful. I'll stay out of your way. Take me with you for a little ways, and then I'll get off and I won't complain even if it's a long way home."

It never took too much begging with my father. When his children wanted to be with him, he was a softy.

I sat on the edge of the tractor seat between my father's legs, holding on to his knees, trying as hard as I could not to get in his way as he shifted from side to side. With the skill of a surgeon, Dad began by first looking ahead as he aligned the tractor with the meticulously straight line of still-standing alfalfa—a sharp contrast to the stems, cut off from their life source by the mower, now laying flat against the ground. After he did this he shifted to look behind, always watching the long row of razor-sharp sickle blades as they deftly sliced thousands of hearty alfalfa stalks the instant they came into contact. One powerful arm steered the tractor while the other arm wrapped around his 10-year-old daughter, protecting her in its grip.

Suddenly a pheasant squawked and jerked skyward, and in the same instant my father instinctively stepped on the clutch. As the tractor lurched to a halt, my father flung both his arms around me, stopping me from being thrown into the steering wheel or off the tractor.

Protecting me had made it impossible to save the female pheasant minding her nest. As quickly and sharply as she rose into the sky, she fell from it, hitting the ground with a deadening thump, then violently and aimlessly thrashing around. Both her legs had been severed near her body.

"Oh, no," my father said softly, getting down from the tractor and lifting me off with him. He hurried over to the wounded bird, picked her up and, with tears in his eyes, stroked her beautiful sleek feathers, apologizing to her for pain he had caused.

He shook his head and said in a voice that housed as much disgust as it did passion, "She can never live this way." He was talking as much to the universe as he was to me. "She'll be easy prey to any predator." And in his next breath, he took hers. With one quick flick of my father's wrist, she no longer had to contemplate her fate in the wild.

He flung the head of the now-decapitated bird far away from us. Then gently pulling the bird's wings together, he held her upside down so that her blood would drain from her body and not be absorbed into the meat, which would have made it inedible.

Over the years I had often experienced the killing of foul: chickens, turkeys, geese and ducks all made their way to our table in a similar fashion. So I was saddened as much by my father's sense of devastation as from having witnessed the bird's death.

Dad gathered up the three orphaned eggs from the pheasant's nest, which now lay in disarray, and placed them in the empty lunch box which sat alongside the pheasant, and home we went.

My mother prepared the pheasant for dinner that evening. At the supper table, my father talked about Mother Nature, and our role in protecting and comforting all of her creatures. His sadness had been replaced by his appreciation for such an excellent dinner, and the safety of family at his side.

We children were taken by surprise. We had come to the table fully prepared to mourn alongside our father. I had shared with all my brothers and sisters the sequence of events and Dad's reaction; we felt sad for him as well as the pheasant. But our father wasn't sad at all; in fact, he seemed jubilant. We children didn't understand his changed mood, after all we were all still a bit sad—and not at all sure if we were going to take a helping of the roasted pheasant now nestling in the glass baking dish.

"Daddy, why didn't we let the pheasant live?" my sister Judy inquired. "She could still sit on her eggs and hatch them, even without legs."

"Without legs," Dad answered, "the mother pheasant would no longer be able to teach her chicks to hunt after they hatched. And worse, without legs, she couldn't protect herself against predators, like the fox. No, I'm afraid she wouldn't make it out there without legs."

Always the humanitarian, my brother Mark chided, "Daddy, no one, not even a hungry old fox, would hurt a poor pheasant who didn't have legs."

"Legs or no legs," responded my father, "a fox will eat a pheasant any day, any time of day."

"That's not very nice," cried my littlest brother.

"Why?" I questioned. "Why would a fox want a wounded bird?"

"Because," replied my father, "It's in his nature."

We all looked confounded. Sensing that he hadn't been completely understood, our father leaned forward, rested both elbows on the table and, with his best storytelling voice began, "Once upon a time, there was a pheasant who, while out foraging for food, broke both her wings. And since her wings were broken, she couldn't fly. Now this was a real big problem because her home was on the other side of the lake, and she wanted to get there. She stood by the edge of the lake thinking what to do. She flapped and flapped her wings, but it was no use; she was too injured to fly.

"Along came a fox who, seeing the pheasant's problem, said, 'Looks like you have a problem. What's the matter?'

"'Oh,' said the pheasant, 'I live on the other side of the lake and I've broken my wings and now I can't fly home.'

"'What a coincidence!' said the fox. 'I live on the other side of the lake, too, and I'm on my way home. Why don't you hop on my back and I'll give you a ride.'

"'But you're a fox and you will eat me,' said the pheasant.

"'No, no,' said the fox. 'Don't be afraid. Hop on. I'll take you home.'

"'So the pheasant, anxious to get home, hopped on the fox's

back and he began the swim home. But, just before they reached the shore on the other side of the lake, the fox shook the pheasant from his back, causing her to fall into the water. Frightened, the pheasant cried out, 'Oh please don't eat me.'

"'I'm afraid I have to,' said the fox.

"'But why?' pleaded the pheasant.

"'Because,' grinned the fox, 'it's in my nature.'"

With different degrees of understanding—and deep in thought—we children quietly began eating, absorbing the visions of the story we had just heard. And so it was that the taste of the pheasant was made delicious to me—and became symbolic of the nature of Mother Nature and of my father's understanding and respect for it.

The pheasant's three eggs were given to a plump old goose who dutifully sat on the eggs around the clock, getting up from the nest only briefly to turn the eggs and to eat. Within weeks, three pheasant chicks emerged. After several weeks of caretaking, we released them into the wild, making the cycle complete; my father had taken from Mother Nature and given back to her as well. In making the exchange, he taught us a bit more about the nature of Mother Nature and our role in protecting and comforting those in it. And to hold her in the highest regard—as much as we did our father.

Roasted Pheasant

Makes 3 servings

෴

1 (2- to 3-pound) pheasant,
 cleaned and dressed, cut up
1 cup flour seasoned with
 ½ teaspoon salt and
 ¼ teaspoon pepper
3 tablespoons butter or
 ½ cup vegetable oil

1½ cups chicken stock
1 small onion, finely chopped
¼ cup finely diced celery
2 cups (1 pint) cream

1. Preheat oven to 375°F. Lightly roll pheasant in seasoned flour. Heat butter or oil in a fry pan and sauté for 6 to 8 minutes.

2. Transfer the pieces to roasting pan, add chicken stock, onion and celery. Roast in oven for 45 minutes. Add cream, lower the heat to 350°F and continue cooking 15 minutes longer.

3. Serve on a bed of long-grain wild rice or mashed potatoes, accompanied by a platter of steamed carrots and/or asparagus tips. For dessert try Rhubarb Pie (see page 43)!

My father had faith in me and loved me. Maybe you don't exactly learn from that, but it allows you to take on the world. I grew up knowing I was accepted and loved, and that made an incredible difference.

—Bernie Siegel

We Miss You, Dina!

Susan Zolla and Kathy Jensen

*Everything has its wonders, even darkness and silence.
I learn that whatever state I may be in, therein to be
content.*

—Helen Keller

The Channel Road Inn, a bed-and-breakfast in an historic home by the sea, has been privileged to be the site of many a romantic weekend and countless happy celebrations: wedding nights, birthdays, anniversaries, graduations, even the arrival of first grandchildren. But not all our guests stay at the Inn to celebrate happy occasions—some stay here while they're in town for medical treatments.

Such was the case of Dina Wigmore, who came to stay once a month for cancer therapy. Sometimes she came with her husband, sometimes her daughter Mary stayed, and sometimes she came alone. We could tell by her appearance that the therapy was not working. Dina was noticeably thinner and weaker on each visit.

The Northridge earthquake struck the Channel Road Inn on Monday morning, January 17, 1994, with a vengeance. Parts of Santa Monica were as badly affected as Northridge, and the Inn was no exception. Guests were thrown from their beds, furniture slid, pictures and mirrors flew, windows broke, and the chimney smashed against two rooms and then pulled away from the house. The 100-gallon hot water heater located on the second floor turned over, sending gallons of hot water down the stairs and through the living room ceiling.

The structure remained sound, but the interior destruction and lack of utilities forced us to close that night and begin cleanup immediately. The entire staff reported to work Tuesday morning, regardless of their work schedules. Workmen also were summoned to install a new hot water heater, remove the damaged walls, tear down the chimney and replace all the broken glass.

It wasn't until late Tuesday evening that someone noticed that Dina Wigmore was scheduled to arrive the next day. On Wednesday morning we all frantically worked on getting her room ready. Her favorite was Room 5 because of its light and especially because of its patio where she enjoyed the warmth of the sun and the view of the trees, the garden and the ocean.

Room 5's plaster was hardly dry when Dina came through the back door as usual at one in the afternoon, stepping over the mounds of debris, plaster dust and drop cloths as she walked to her room. We apologized profusely for the mess. She looked at us with soft brown eyes made more prominent by her thinness, and answered that no earthquake could affect her; she was fighting bigger battles. As I later looked up to her porch and saw her with her kerchief on, facing the sun and the ocean, I knew then that an earthquake could not affect us, either.

Dina died a month later lying in her own bed, which also faced the ocean. She always loved the Inn's Apple French Toast, saying that warm homemade food gave her strength. She never knew that she really fed some of her inner strength to us. She ultimately gave us the perspective we sorely needed during that devastating earthquake week, and from her example of courage and dignity, we were able to go forward stronger than before. We miss you, Dina.

Baked Apple French Toast
Makes 8 servings

∾

Cling peaches may be substituted for the apples, or fruit can even be eliminated altogether. This breakfast casserole may be baked immediately or covered with plastic wrap and refrigerated overnight.

3 large green apples
1 stick (½ cup) butter
½ cup (or more) brown sugar
12 ounces cream cheese
12 slices firm bread (your
    choice—plain white, wheat,
    French, sourdough, cinnamon
    or your favorite)

8 eggs
1 quart milk
2 tablespoons vanilla
Cinnamon

1. Set rack in lower third of oven and preheat oven to 350°F. Butter a 13×9-inch baking pan. Core and cut the apples into thin wedges, leaving the skin on.

2. In a skillet, melt butter with brown sugar and 1 tablespoon water. Add the apples and cook, stirring for 2 to 3 minutes. Transfer to the baking dish and let cool.

3. Cut cream cheese into cubes and arrange evenly over the apples. Cut the slices of bread in half diagonally and layer over the apples to cover the whole dish.

4. In a large mixing bowl, beat together eggs, milk and vanilla. Pour the egg mixture over the bread, taking care to dampen all the bread. Sprinkle with cinnamon. Bake for 40 to 50 minutes, until golden and puffed. Let cool 10 minutes before serving. (This reheats beautifully.)

A Legacy of Tomato Aspic and Meatloaf

Elaine Cannon

During my senior year at the University of Utah, I was president of Chi Omega sorority and developed a close relationship with the house mother, Mamie C. Robinson. She lived on the premises, supervising the food preparation and ambiance that helped college coeds survive tough schedules, scholarship crises and the fear of war. It was a tender time of lost loves, broken hearts and hasty marriages.

Because of World War II there were food rationings and shortages. Mrs. Robinson had to be innovative with food, yet she was able to mother us with appetizing meals.

I married my soldier between winter and spring quarters and for 50 years have guarded Mrs. Robinson's gift to me. It was a treasure in my time, a small, black leather six-ring binder containing more than 100 recipes written in her own neat hand. Her inscription in the front read:

> *I hope that your house will always be full of good food. The way to a man's heart, so they say, is through his stomach. My interest and love are with you. May you have loads of happy meals.*

That little book helped me through the beginnings of family life, and now, near the ending, it steadies me. Fifty years of use in my various kitchens, with my assorted family configurations and occasions, leaves it stained and stuck with frostings, fillings, sauces, juices, pastries, candies and soufflés.

The recipes in my precious book reflect the times—World War II.

The recipes are largely low in fat because fat was used for ammunition and was heavily rationed. Now, with a fitness-focused generation, some of these fat-free recipes are making a comeback. Tomato Aspic, for example, is a favorite at our house all over again.

Other recipes in the book offer heartier fare, such as Meatloaf to serve with old-fashioned scalloped potatoes, or to savor in slabs between thick sourdough slices. Meatloaf offers the comfort of a good burger without the risk of raw beef in the center of the patty.

At the top of the Meatloaf recipe in Mamie's book, I've scribbled a quote from Paul Newman. I found it in Utah's red rock country in the guest book at the Homespun Restaurant, a café much admired by movie stars on location for its hearty home-cooking. Said Newman, "The best way to deal with the original Homespun Restaurant was to starve for a week and then go straight facedown in the Meatloaf!"

Mamie Robinson's Tomato Aspic
Makes 8 servings

In our early years, our aspic was made from our home-grown and home-preserved tomato juice—rich in flavor, but inexpensive. An advantage to aspic was that it could be made ahead—way ahead. It is colorful, nutritious, satisfying and slimming.

2 tablespoons (2 packages) unflavored gelatin
1 quart (4 cups) tomato juice, divided
Zest (finely grated yellow peel) and juice of ½ a lemon

½ teaspoon Worcestershire sauce
Salt and pepper to taste
A dash of onion salt to taste

1. Soften gelatin in ½ cup cold tomato juice for 5 minutes. In a small saucepan, heat 3½ cups tomato juice; stir in gelatin mixture until dissolved. Cool. Add the zest and lemon juice, Worcestershire sauce, salt and pepper and onion salt to taste. Pour into a ring mold that holds 6 to 8 cups; chill until set.

2. When ready to serve, unmold on a round platter and fill the center of the ring with a mixed salad of your choice. (We like bay shrimp mixed with Thousand Island dressing, or cabbage and green pea slaw.)

Mamie's Best-Ever Meatloaf

Makes 2 loaves
Freeze one for baking later

❧

1½ cups dried mixed bread pieces (packaged croutons work well)
1 cup canned evaporated milk
2 large eggs, lightly beaten
2½ pounds lean ground beef
½ pound ground sausage (breakfast bulk sausage)
½ cup grated or chopped raw carrot (optional)

½ cup chopped fresh parsley
1 tablespoon each garlic salt and dried marjoram
½ teaspoon each dried thyme, dried basil and Italian seasoning
¼ teaspoon ground black pepper

TOPPING:
2 strips bacon

4 tablespoons ketchup

SAUCE:
2 tablespoons flour

1 (10¾-ounce) can beef consommé or beef broth

1. Preheat oven to 400°F. In a large mixing bowl, soak bread pieces in evaporated milk until soft and fluffy. Add eggs, ground beef, ground sausage, raw carrot and chopped fresh parsley. Mix in

seasonings. Divide mixture between two foil 8 x 3⅞ x 2⅜-inch loaf pans. Top each loaf with 1 strip of bacon and 2 tablespoons ketchup.

2. Place pans in oven and immediately lower temperature to 325°F; bake for 1 hour. Remove loaves from pans to warm platter and allow to stand for 10 minutes before slicing.

3. Pour the pan juices into a small saucepan and (off the heat) stir in 2 tablespoons of flour. Add beef consommé and bring to a simmer while whisking. When the sauce boils and thickens, thin with water as needed.

Debbie's Creamed Corn

Kimberly Kirberger

The quality of presence determines the quality of life.

—Jack Kornfield

I have never been a patient person. I am always in a hurry, think-ing about the next thing I have to do, rather than doing what I am doing. This was not the case with Debbie. Everything she did was so purposeful, so filled with concentration. I used to love to watch her play the piano, arrange flowers, put on her make-up; but most of all, I used to love to watch her cook.

I don't really like to cook; well I do, but it just takes so long, requires such concentration and I have learned over the years that you really need to follow directions. With Debbie, it was as if she loved each tiny little step as much as, if not more than, the delicious result. It was as if she savored each moment. I watched her with utter fascination. Every year on Thanksgiving she made creamed corn for about 20 people, and I would watch her patiently extract-ing every drop of liquid from the freshest corn she could buy.

Debbie was killed in a car accident nine years ago. I still miss her so much. Now every year on Thanksgiving, I make creamed corn just like Debbie did. I become very calm and patient. I am not in a hurry to finish, no matter how many people I am cooking for. I savor every moment and actually enjoy cooking. I often think of Debbie at these times and wonder if my guests will notice how much love is in this simple dish . . . it seems they always do.

Debbie's Creamed Corn

Makes 12 servings (figure on 3 ears of corn per person)

❧

3 dozen ears of the very
*   sweetest corn you*
*   can find*

Butter
Sugar (if corn is not sweet)
Salt and pepper to taste

1. Remove the leaves and all the silk from the corn. Hold an ear of corn on its end, and with a serrated knife, slice downward, removing only the very top part of each kernel, placing the kernels in a large saucepan. (Don't think about how many ears you still have to do; just do one at a time, savoring each moment.)

2. After removing every kernel from every ear, use the back of the knife to scrape each ear and extract any creamy liquid that is left, saving the liquid. (Once again, scrape as if this is the only thing in the world you want to be doing right now, feel peaceful and happy to be scraping.)

3. Add the corn liquid to the saucepan with the corn and place over medium-low heat. You may add a little butter if you wish, and some sugar if the corn you found is not very sweet. Salt and pepper to taste, and cook for 15 minutes or so until it tastes right to you.

A Fish, a Fish, Lord, I Need a Fish!

Martha A. Burich

In an elementary school art class, the students were told to draw a dog. A visitor came in and complimented a girl on her excellent drawing. The girl looked at the visitor and said quite earnestly, "I really can't draw a dog. So when I have to draw a dog, I just draw a horse and it always looks like a dog."

—Author Unknown

As a substitute teacher I see many children of all ages. One beautiful spring morning, I was called to fill-in for an elementary school art teacher. I taught art to almost every grade that day, but the one I remember most was the kindergarten class that arrived right after lunch.

The assignment was to draw a fish. I demonstrated and explained the finer points of drawing a fish on paper. I then let the class work on their own as I walked about the room supervising and giving assistance. All the children were excitedly creating fish with pencil, chalk and crayon. All the children except Jerrod. Jerrod had laid his little five-year-old head down on the table and was softly crying. When I asked him what was wrong, he raised his tear-stained face to me and cried, "I can't draw a fish. It's too hard!"

Only five years old, I thought, yet "can't" and failure are already too familiar to him. I knew I couldn't let him fail. At the same time,

I didn't want to deny what he believed was reality by disagreeing with him. So I quietly replied, "I know it's hard to draw a fish, Jerrod. But I bet you can do it." I pointed out a few fish the other children were drawing and mentioned to Jerrod that maybe, if he watched the others, he could see many different ways to draw a fish. I busied myself with other students and chores. Jerrod cried a while, then seemed to take an interest in what the other children were drawing.

I forgot about Jerrod until about 15 minutes later when I heard an excited yell. "I did it! I did it! I drew a fish! Mrs. Burich, I drew a fish!" I looked over and there was Jerrod proudly displaying his crudely drawn picture of a fish . . . in a garden.

"Yes," I responded, "no doubt about it, Jerrod. You drew a fish." I then silently said a prayer of thanks to God.

Ever since then, whenever I eat fish, I think of Jerrod and smile.

Mrs. Burich's Fish in a Garden

Makes 3 to 4 servings

❧

FOR STIR FRY:

1 small yellow squash, sliced into ¼-inch rounds
1 medium onion, finely chopped
8 to 10 ounces fresh broccoli florets, cut into bite-size pieces
½ pound crab meat or surami

½ pound peeled raw shrimp
½ pound scallops (cut up if large)
1 tablespoon light sesame or canola oil
1 tablespoon soy sauce

FOR SERVING:

2 single-serving packages shrimp-flavored ramen noodles, cooked according to package directions

1. In a large wok or skillet, stir-fry the vegetables in sesame or canola oil over medium heat for 5 minutes. Add fish and soy sauce and continue cooking until fish is cooked (when shrimp is pink), about 5 to 10 minutes longer.

2. Meanwhile, in another pan cook ramen noodles according to package directions. Drain and transfer noodles to a serving plate. Mound the fish and vegetables on top.

To Russia with Love

Diana von Welanetz Wentworth

I expect to pass through life but once. If, therefore, there can be any kindness I can show, or any good thing I can do to any fellow being, let me do it now, as I shall not pass this way again.

—William Penn

Leningrad, *May 1985. This broad-streeted European city is swept daily by old women with faces as gray as December. Clearly, these* babushkas *hold no illusions of immortality. They know the treasures of this earth are love, courage and waking up alive in the morning without planes overhead.*

Three days in this war-torn city, and we are no longer secure in the beliefs we have held. Brought here by the Center for Soviet-American Dialogue, our mission is to be a presence of love and goodwill within a country, which, like our own, has the power to destroy the earth. If we leave without touching the hearts of these strangers we shall have failed.

Our tour leaders, both American and Russian, encourage us to explore the city on our own, so Paul and I head for the subway system in hopes of meeting people. We walk apprehensively down a windy spring street beneath a sky full of darting crows. Old eyes follow our movements; young eyes stare at our shoes as if we are film stars. Paul takes a firmer grip on my hand.

"I forgot the camera," I say. "Let's go back to the room."

I've bought a few moments' reprieve. Why would a stranger be drawn to talk with us? We look so foreign that we are hardly approachable!

Re-entering our room, we are greeted by hundreds of smiling glass eyes. We are the keepers of armloads of handmade dolls made by church groups in Seattle and carried across the border individually, to be given away at the first opportunity at various peace committee meetings as gifts for schoolchildren.

"That's it! We'll take along a doll and look for a child to give it to!" I pick up an adorable Cabbage Patch girl in a hand-sewn blue gingham dress.

"I'll bet whoever made this one would love to see it go directly into the arms of a child."

Back on the street, we venture down the steps to the Metro, the Soviet subway system. We are obviously Americans: I in my white waterproof trench coat with Paul's lilac muffler around my neck, Paul in brown turtleneck and tweeds. We follow the crowd and ride down a long, long escalator to a chandeliered lobby. We drop 5-ruble coins in the turnstiles and pass through to the platform.

The train arrives. We find seats on the bench along one side, the door whispers shut and we're off. I look around—one, two children here are possibilities. Which shall it be? The girl to the left pretends not to see me. The one across the car stares glassily through me when I smile—she's somewhere else. No luck so far.

The car slows to a stop. A family—child, mother, father, friend— their faces aglow to be out on a Sunday excursion, enter to take seats diagonally from us, to the right of the doors. The dark-eyed girl looks with open interest at the doll in my lap. Delighted to have found a like-ly recipient, I wave the dolls tiny arm at her and smile too enthusias-tically. Shyness overcomes her and she presses her face into the side of her mother's coat, but Mama gently encourages friendliness.

With a glance at each other, Paul and I decide to make our move, then exit at the next stop. As the car slows, we stand and step toward the child. I offer the doll wordlessly by holding it out to her. Her face dis-appears again behind her mother. Chagrined, my gift still extended, I extend the doll to the mother.

"Pashowsta," I say. It is one of the few Russian words I know, a combination of "please" and "you are welcome."

A sudden light in her eyes, and our gift is accepted. Without a word, she and the father simultaneously stand and touch their open hands to their hearts. Beaming smiles at them, eyes gleaming, Paul and I touch our hearts and step through the sliding door with damp lashes.

Too moved to speak, Paul and I make our way in silence to another subway track. I find myself wondering how the family will describe the experience to their friends. Sensing my thought, Paul says aloud, "You will be known as the Madonna of the Metro."

We enjoyed many bowls of hearty cabbage soup in Leningrad and Moscow that spring. Here is our version.

Cabbage Patch Soup

Makes 4 quarts, or 8 to 12 servings

*2 tablespoons butter or
   margarine*
*3 large baking potatoes, peeled
   and cut in ½-inch cubes*
*4 medium carrots, peeled and
   cut in ½-inch slices*
*2 medium leeks, washed and
   cut in ½-inch slices*

2 quarts water
*1 medium cabbage, finely
   chopped*
*2 (or more) minced cloves
   garlic*
Salt and pepper

1. Melt butter or margarine over medium heat in a heavy 6-quart pot. Add the potatoes, carrots and leeks. Cook gently for 5 minutes, stirring the pot often.

2. Add the water and bring to a boil. Lower the heat and simmer slowly, uncovered, for 1 hour. Add the cabbage to the pot along with the garlic. Simmer 30 minutes longer. Season to taste with salt and pepper. Serve hot with crisp slices of Cheesy Pumpernickel.

Cheesy Pumpernickel
Makes about 30 slices

∿

A 1-pound loaf of unsliced
pumpernickel, black bread
or any good rye bread
2 sticks room-temperature butter or
margarine (not the "light" type)

1½ cups finely grated
Parmesan cheese

1. Preheat oven to 300°F. Cut loaf in half. Spread one cut end generously with soft butter or margarine. Hold a long thin knife under hot running water and use it immediately to cut the buttered end into a slice of bread no more than ⅛ inch thick.

2. Spread the Parmesan evenly on a plate. Press the buttered side of the bread slice into the Parmesan cheese, coating it densely, and place, cheese side up, on a baking sheet. Continue buttering, slicing and coating in the same manner until the baking sheet is filled with slices.

3. Bake for 15 to 20 minutes until the bread is crisp and curled on the edges. Remove from the oven and cool. Continue making slices in the same manner until all ingredients are used.

4. When cool, the slices may be stored in an airtight container at room temperature for a day or two.

Neighborhood Soup

Linda McNamar

In January 1994, the Northridge quake struck Southern California. The day after this horrendous earthquake, my family and I rode through the devastated area on our way to help our niece and nephew clean up. Their home was all but leveled; everything in it was shaken, scattered or shattered. They told us that as their world jolted and shuddered during the quake, they heard their three-year-old son calling from his bedroom, "It's okay, Mommy. I'm alright, Daddy. I'll stay right here." That calm little voice in the midst of fear kept their panic from spilling over.

In the aftermath of the quake, there was tremendous work, grief and fear. But through it all a depth of human caring and resilience had been tapped. In the voice of their child, in the hands of their neighbors, in the strain of their losses, they found an inner strength and a deeper love than they had known before. Neighbors, living in tents on the front lawns, began to behave as if they were on a great American camp-out. Water was shared from backyard pools. Stories, shovels and safety tips were passed from person to person in a sense of camaraderie and benevolent spirit. Since they didn't have much available to them for the first few days, they also shared food, and in one case made Neighborhood Soup, a sort of mulligan stew that nourished the body, heart and spirit. In sharing their meals, they found a deep sense of security and a bonding among families that will last for years.

Time has passed and the evidence of the destruction has disappeared. New chimneys sit atop the houses; driveways and foundations are once again straight and smooth. But some evidence of the aftermath still exists: the neighbors still meet in the street. Now they share child care, neighborhood barbecues, street parties and household tips. We read of the terrible devastation of these events, and it's true. But what also happens, though it is not always reported, is how lives are changed for the better when the barriers that divide us come crashing down.

Neighborhood Soup

Makes 6 to 8 servings

～

This soup may be made with all fresh vegetables, or more quickly with all canned vegetables. Serve with sourdough bread and a salad.

1 chopped onion
2 cloves garlic
1 tablespoon olive oil
3 (14-ounce) cans vegetable broth
2 cups water
6 tablespoons barley
1 bay leaf
1 (28-ounce) can diced or crushed tomatoes with their juice
1 cup carrots, halved lengthwise and cut into ¼-inch slices
1 cup chopped broccoli
1 (10-ounce) package frozen cut green beans

½ teaspoon crumbled dried rosemary leaves, or 1 teaspoon fresh
½ teaspoon crumbled dried oregano leaves
½ teaspoon salt
¼ teaspoon ground black pepper
3 white or red rose potatoes, cut into bite-size pieces
1 medium zucchini, halved lengthwise and cut into ¼-inch slices
1 (14-ounce) can black beans, drained and rinsed

1. In a large stock pot, sauté the onion and garlic in the olive oil over medium-high heat until the onions are translucent, about 5 minutes. Add vegetable broth, water, barley and bay leaf. Bring to a boil, cover and lower heat to medium-low; simmer for 1 hour.

2. Add diced or crushed tomatoes with their juice, carrots, broccoli, green beans, rosemary, oregano, salt and pepper. Continue to simmer for 30 minutes.

3. Add potatoes, zucchini and black beans; simmer 30 minutes longer.

Heart-Shaped Scones for Helen

Diana von Welanetz Wentworth

The best and most beautiful things in the world cannot be seen, nor touched . . . but are felt in the heart.

—Helen Keller

One rainy afternoon, after four or five days of continual downpours, I had been too long at my writing. I yearned for a change of scenery, some hot tea and a bit of exercise. I headed for Crystal Court, a local mall I had never visited before, because I knew it was completely enclosed and would provide a safe haven.

As I wandered through three floors of shops that were new to me, I had no inkling how fate had led me there. I had recently become enthusiastic about letters—both writing them and reading them—and found myself in an excellent bookstore where I found several books on historic letters. Leaving there with a bag full of books and the idea of a cozy corner in a restaurant in which to peruse them, I noticed an unusual shop next door, The Gallery of History. It specialized in framed original documents of famous people.

Most were business letters, receipts and such, but one ranked far, far above all the others in both appearance and content. It was a frame containing a photograph and a typewritten, hand-signed letter from Helen Keller to her publisher and friend, Frank Nelson Doubleday, written while she was on vacation in Scotland. It was addressed to "Effendi," the Turkish word meaning "master" or "chief," which was a nickname given to Doubleday by his friend

Rudyard Kipling because it sounded similar to his initials: F.N.D.

Over a plate of scones with Devonshire cream I was haunted by the letter and touched by how much of her generous nature she had revealed in her words:

> *South Arcan, Muir of Ord, Rose-shire, Scotland*
> *January 21, 1934*
>
> *Dear Effendi,*
>
> *I'm glad you've done it again. Your "Indiscreet Recollections" are delightful, and I enjoy walking with you along the road of Memory. It is pleasant to find that some of the friends you write about were mine also. What wonderful book adventures you have had!*
>
> *One of the reviewers of "Midstream" said that I knew many distinguished people uneventfully. I wonder what that means. Like Conrad, neither you or I have had intrigues or scandals or thrilling romances with the people we knew, it is true, but is not friendship itself the highest of adventures? And is not meeting and exchanging ideas with a great personality an event?*
>
> *I am pleased to hear that the Lindberghs are agreeable young people. It was dear of them to want to fly to the hospital when you were ill. Others have given me quite a different impression of them.*
>
> *Colonel Lindbergh seems not to have made many friends among newspaper men. I have thought—but I may be mistaken—that his attitude towards publicity is indefensible. If any one does something extraordinary, be it reprehensible or admirable, it is natural that the public should be interested, and want to know as much as possible about him. This would be an insufferably dull world, would it not, if there was no curiosity.*
>
> *I am only too familiar with the annoyances of being hounded by reporters, but I find that an attitude of courtesy and kindness works wonders with them, and I believe I have a host of good friends among them.*
>
> *I have in mind an incident which points my meaning. A friend of my sister's was chosen by a reception committee to present Colonel Lindbergh with a bouquet of roses. He asked coldly, "Is it official?" Of course he was bored to death by pretty girls offering him all manner of things from kisses to roses, but surely it would not have taken any more*

of his time or vitality to be friendly. The acceptance of a hundred bouquets would not have cost him more than refusing them, and the fragrance of good-will would have followed him into his quiet hours.

If you have read any accounts of my winter retreat in the American newspapers, you will smile at the bleak picture the reporters have of the Highlands of Scotland. This is one of the many warm days of a mild winter. I can almost smell spring on the wing. In imagination I see the avalanche of golden broom that will soon tumble down the hill-sides into the straths and the streams, the harebells that will ring in every field, the primroses that will carpet the roadsides. Already the sap is running up the trees, the grass is green in many places, and there is a new bird here every day. We are feeding blackbirds, finches and thrushes, and expect a glorious chorus in March.

Please give Mrs. Doubleday my love. I hope she keeps well, and that the New Year will be rich in blessings for you both. My teacher and Polly send kindest greetings with mine. I wish one of the thousand pigeons around here was fitted with a pair of sea wings and the intelligence to carry my love to you.

Affectionately yours,

Helen Heller

Several days later, I decided I would love to own the letter and justified the purchase by its investment value. It hangs above the antique roll-top desk in my office, reminding me to write as my most authentic and expansive self.

I created these heart-shaped scones in memory of that fated rainy afternoon.

Heart-Shaped Scones for Helen

Makes 9 or 10 scones

❧

Serve warm or at room temperature with Devonshire cream (now available in many supermarkets) or unsweetened whipped cream.

2 cups flour
½ cup sugar
1 tablespoon baking powder
Zest (finely grated rind)
  of 1 orange
¼ teaspoon salt
½ stick (4 tablespoons) cold
  butter, cut in pieces

2 eggs
⅔ cup sour cream (or orange-
  or lemon-flavored low-fat
  yogurt)
½ cup dried cranberries or
  currants
1 tablespoon coarse or regular
  sugar, for topping

1. Preheat oven to 400°F. Line a baking sheet with parchment paper, or grease it lightly. In a mixing bowl, or food processor fitted with the steel blade, combine flour, sugar, baking powder, zest, salt and butter pieces. Use a pastry cutter, or process in short bursts, until the butter looks like crumbs.

2. Separate the eggs, setting aside one egg white; beat the whole egg and extra yolk together in a small bowl. Add sour cream (or yogurt) and dried fruit. Stir these wet ingredients into the dry ingredients to make a sticky dough.

3. Turn out onto a lightly floured surface and pat dough into a circle about 1 inch thick. Cut out with a heart-shaped (or round) 2½-inch cutter. Place 1 inch apart on the baking sheet. Beat the reserved egg white with a fork until frothy; brush over the top of the scones. Sprinkle with 1 tablespoon sugar.

4. Bake for 15 to 20 minutes, until puffed and lightly browned.

Udana's Yummy Waffles

Udana Power

For-Those-Who-Are-Allergic-to-Everything

Okay, so I don't have a heartwarming, jovial story about my grandmother cooking me these waffles when I was a little girl, although my mother did have an old, round waffle iron that we would fill with Bisquick batter, which oozed out the sides where we would scoop it up with our fingers. Yum.

As I got older I forgot about waffles, mainly because I went through periods when I wouldn't eat sugar, couldn't eat wheat, wouldn't eat oil—and knew I shouldn't eat eggs or white flour. Put them all together and they spell: W-A-F-F-L-E.

Ultimately, I found that the hundred books I read on how to eat all contradicted each other. Though I followed most of them at different times, I finally realized that I just wanted to have fun with food again.

One of these books talked about whole grain flours and how waffles were one of the most nourishing, inexpensive, easy-to-make fun foods you could eat. Hmmm . . . I started looking at recipes. I didn't want whole wheat flour. No, no, no, no. (Chocolate chips? Yes. But not whole wheat flour. Don't ask.) I liked the idea of not eating eggs (admonitions from a vegan friend). I could use canola oil. I was feeling much healthier already. And vanilla soy milk. Or even Rice Dream. Yes! No dairy for this girl—except for the milk in my coffee. (Perfection is boring.)

Out of this eclectic mix came one of my favorite foods of all time.

As a matter of fact, all my friends love them. Jim actually bought himself a $50 waffle iron and all the ingredients, and he travels with them. He calls our little twosome The Waffle Club.

I like to think of waffles as a cross between a piece of toast and a muffin. When I have a long day ahead of me on a soundstage where the craftperson piles a table with doughnuts and other things too decadent to mention, I prepare my waffles, let them cool on a rack and pack them in a plastic baggie. While everyone else is going into sugar shock, I'm sailing away on an even surge of energy that lasts all day. They're delicious. I don't even feel deprived.

Now for what you all have been waiting for: The Waffle Recipe. I buy all the ingredients and have them on hand at all times. I never know when the urge is going to hit. I like them just the way they are. Nothing on them at all. So does my friend Joel. My mom loves them with molasses. My roommate loves them any way he can get them. Hah. No, he really likes them with pure maple syrup. My boyfriend and his kids like them with everything, including jam. I even bought them a waffle iron and the ingredients, and lo and behold Charles, the 15-year-old, enjoys making them for his dad and brother. Whadda stud.

Udana's Yummy Waffles
Makes 4 waffles

༖

1 cup vanilla Rice Dream or vanilla soy milk (from a health food store)
¼ cup canola oil
2 teaspoons powdered egg substitute
1 tablespoon Bragg's liquid aminos (from a health food store)
1 teaspoon vanilla
½ cup brown rice flour

½ cup millet flour
2 teaspoons baking powder
4 or 5 shakes (approximately ½ teaspoon) Dr. Bronner's powdered barley malt sweetener (again, from a health food store)
Optional additions: 2 tablespoons peanut butter, sesame tahini or chocolate chips

1. Plug in a waffle iron and set timer for 6 minutes.

2. In a mixing bowl combine Rice Dream or soy milk, oil, egg substitute, liquid amino seasoning and vanilla; blend all this with an egg beater. Add brown rice flour, millet flour (Remember: keep all your flours in the freezer. It keeps them from getting stale and they maintain their hint of sweetness.) baking powder and malt sweetener.

3. Add (for sheer pleasure) one of the following: peanut butter, chocolate chips or sesame tahini, or replace vanilla extract with almond extract.

4. After 6 minutes of heating, wipe the inside of the waffle iron with a pastry brush dipped in oil (or butter), then dole out the waffle goop onto the grid, close the lid and let cook for 3 minutes. When done, take out the waffle and lay it on a cake rack to cool. (If you lay it directly on a dish it will "sweat" and get a teensy bit soggy.)

Variations: I have concocted several variations: Gingerbread Waffles, Carrot Cake Waffles, and Tamale Waffles, which are really good, but the *KILLER CORN WAFFLES* are everyone's favorites.

KILLER CORN WAFFLES: Substitute corn meal for the rice flour. Sometimes I even substitute barley flour for millet flour. (Oh, I'm getting so snazzy.) I also add a small can of sweet corn, drained.

I cook these a little bit longer because of all that corn in the batter—but oo la la, you and your family will be glad you took the time to read this.

Best wishes. Have fun! And enjoy all that energy they will give you. The Waffle Club salutes you.

P.S. I'm driving up to Carmel tomorrow morning. Guess what I'm going to make for the journey? Easy to eat while I'm driving and far superior to anything I can get on the run.

Blue-Ribbon Apple-Kiwi Pie

Linda Bruce

As a newlywed I wasn't a very experienced cook, and I was surprised someone asked me to bring a lemon meringue pie for Thanksgiving. Not being satisfied with the amount of lemon recommended in the cookbook, I added more—so much more that no one could unpucker their cheeks. Then at Christmas I was asked to bring a pecan pie. Well, it looked and tasted delicious, but I forgot to remove the paper from the top of the frozen pie shell before baking the pie which made it a little tricky to eat.

I thought my pie-baking days were over and that I'd never redeem myself, until I came across this recipe for Apple-Kiwi Pie. It was so delicious that I decided to enter it in the contest at the county fair. Now I know a good pie when I taste one, but when I won a blue ribbon you would have thought I'd won a million dollars! I called my whole family with the exciting news and, of course, was asked to bake the pie for our next get-together. Over the years it's become a real family favorite, along with the stories of my first attempts at pie-making.

Recently the pie came to mean much more. My mother was dying of cancer, and as we kept vigil by her side those last nights it was a very stressful time. I went into her kitchen and baked that pie two nights in a row. The wonderful smell that filled the house from those pies was comforting to all of us. And I know that from the smell my mother knew we were there and that we were going to be alright.

Get your taste buds ready. This is a winner!

Blue-Ribbon Apple-Kiwi Pie

Makes one 8- or 9-inch pie

❧

1 cup sugar	1 tablespoon fresh lemon
3 tablespoons quick-cooking	juice
tapioca	Pastry for a 2-crust pie (see Note)
1 teaspoon ground cinnamon	2 tablespoons butter, cut in
¼ teaspoon ground nutmeg	small pieces
7 peeled and sliced kiwis	1 egg white
2 peeled and sliced tart apples	2 tablespoons sugar

Note: *Purchased, ready-made refrigerated pie crusts make this pie quick and easy to put together. But don't forget to remove the paper lining.*

1. Preheat oven to 375°F. In a bowl, mix together sugar, tapioca, cinnamon and nutmeg. Add kiwis, apples and lemon juice. Toss gently and let stand 15 minutes.

2. Roll out and line a pie pan with pastry. Mound the kiwi-apple mixture in the pan; dot with butter. Roll out a second round of pastry and place over the mixture; seal edge decoratively. Make a slit in the crust for venting. For a crunchy sugar crust, brush the top pastry with beaten egg white and sprinkle with 2 tablespoons sugar.

3. To prevent over-browning, cover edge of pie with a strip of foil. Bake the pie in the center of the oven for 20 minutes; remove foil strip and continue baking 25 to 30 minutes longer until the crust is golden.

Artful Antipasto

Vaughn Greditzer

I have fallen in love many times in my long and peripatetic life—but only one passion has lasted for over half a century. I was born with an extraordinary sensual sensitivity and began to cook when I was ten years old. Oh, the exquisite smells, sights and tastes!

I am an artist, and in my kitchen I create as excitedly as I do in my studio, and with equally undiminished pleasure. Although I haven't literally used food or other raw materials on my canvases, as certain modern painters do, I surely bring my color and artistry into my kitchen, planning and arranging each detail as though it were indeed a canvas—flowers, candles, linens, dishes and an awareness of the food I am to serve.

Once I spent 17 hours turning rock cornish game hens into swans and arranging them (20 or so!) directly on the surface of our black lacquered dining table, as though it were a lake. Spectacular!

My memory is crammed with recipes I have tried and many I have not as yet, and my cookbooks are old friends whom I have consulted over and over through the years. In cooking, as in life, things don't always turn out the way you had hoped; but if we persist in experimentation, elimination, enthusiasm, curiosity and tenacity, chances are we will become talented culinary creators. Here is a palette I love to arrange. It is always a show-stopper!

Artful Antipasto

Amounts will depend upon the number of guests

❧

Various kinds of lettuce leaves
Thick slices of juicy (preferably
  beefsteak) tomatoes
Thick slices of orange
Anchovy fillets (reserve oil from
  canned anchovies for the
  dressing)
Slices of sweet onion
Slices of hot-house cucumber

Mozzarella cheese
Canned whole Italian red
  peppers (pimentos)
Thinly sliced Italian salami
Assorted Italian peppers—
  hot, mild, cherry
Extra-virgin olive oil
Juice of one lemon
Warm chunks of Italian bread

1. Cover a large round platter with various kinds of lettuce leaves. On top, alternate thick slices of tomatoes with thick slices of orange. Top each orange with two crisscrossed anchovy fillets. Top each tomato with a thin slice of sweet onion and a scored and sliced hot-house cucumber.

2. Cut thin strips of red peppers and strips of mozzarella cheese 4 inches long and ½ inch thick, using both to separate the tomato and orange stacks attractively.

3. Inside the tomato and orange stacks create a smaller circle of thinly sliced Italian salami. Make a mound of more sliced cucumbers in the center of the platter and encircle them with assorted Italian peppers. Look at your creation and add extra cheese, pepper strips or small peppers where needed to add beauty to the arrangement.

4. Pour the oil from the canned anchovies over the top of all, plus a drizzle of extra-virgin olive oil, followed by the lemon juice. Refrigerate until serving time.

5. Place in the center of the table and enjoy! Encourage your guests to wipe up remaining juices with warm chunks of Italian bread. This is called *scarpete*, and my Italian father-in-law told me this is not only *not* bad manners, but is *de rigueur!*

A Post-Earthquake Chilean Quinoa Tabouleh Shared from the Heart

Carlos Warter

When I was in medical school in the mid-1960s, an earthquake that measured 8.9 on the Richter scale hit Chile. As is common in my native country, I enlisted with other students in solidarity teams to help the villagers whose homes had been damaged. Because it was winter and the earthquake had destroyed houses and washed away agricultural fields, many people were in need of aid.

I was assigned to a town in the mountains with other volunteers. Our responsibilities included helping take care of the sick and rebuilding some barracks so they could be used for temporary shelters.

The village was very poor and was populated by a mixed ethnic population. Some were descendants from a native culture that traced back to the Mapuches, a tribe who had been influenced by the Incas. Others were second- and third-generation Chilean-born immigrants who were called—much to their displeasure—*turks*. They were given this name because they were descendants of Palestinians, Lebanese, Syrians or other Middle-Eastern people who had entered South America before World War I but continued to hold Ottoman passports.

The beauty of the village was that the people had been living in harmony and intermarrying for a few generations. The only sadness evident was due to the fact that their homes had been affected by this quake and now they were sharing a refugee shelter.

After a long day of volunteer work, we were tired and hungry. There was a real scarcity of food, so we were surprised when the villagers told us to stop our labor, clean up and come to share a meal with the poor.

Though we appreciated their offer, we at first declined, explaining that it was not necessary for them to share with us what little food they had since each of the students in our group had brought some canned food with them. One of the villagers then said, "Share a meal with the poor. Our food has heart; it will taste better than your canned food."

One woman told us that we would be eating a meal from the Middle East. Another said we were going to share an ancient Incan dish. As the meal unfolded, we realized that we were really in for a feast.

While in the midst of disaster, these village people were appreciating what there was. Even though it was a dish of the poor and of those who had lost their homes, a synthesis was created between the cultures which gave rise to one of the most heartfelt dinners in all our lives.

Quinoa (keenoah) can be found in the natural or health-food section in any store in America. It is a delicate pearly grain that is delicious served hot or cold in salads. Originally grown high in the Andes as a major element in the Incan diet, it became on this occasion a Chilean Middle-Eastern inspired dish served with avocados, tomatoes, corn, cucumbers and cilantro. When making this recipe, don't mix it vigorously. This will allow the quinoa to stay fluffy. And as one of the peasants said, if you don't eat it all at once, it can be used the next morning.

Quinoa Tabouleh

Makes about 10 servings

❦

These ingredients were all we had. It was fascinating to see the sharing and heartwarming to see how cultures mingled to come up with this combination plate which fed our whole group with care. Though you may find some of the following directions unusual, I feel they were essential to the joy and unity we felt. I encourage you to follow these steps as I have written them so that you can experience the same sense of sharing.

2 cups quinoa	2 teaspoons minced garlic
4 cups water	1 ripe avocado, peeled and cut
½ teaspoon salt	into ½-inch dice
¼ teaspoon fresh black pepper	1 cup fresh corn kernels, cooked
5 tablespoons fresh lemon juice	1 cup diced cucumbers
⅓ cup olive oil	½ cup fresh red onion, chopped
½ cup coarsely chopped fresh	4 plum tomatoes, cut into
cilantro leaves	½-inch dice

1. Rinse the quinoa under cold water and drain. Place it in a medium-sized pan. Add the water and bring to a boil. Reduce heat to low and simmer, covered, for about 10 minutes until the liquid is absorbed.

2. When the quinoa is cooked, sprinkle the grains with the salt and pepper and stir. Add 4 tablespoons of the lemon juice and the olive oil. Fold in cilantro and garlic.

3. Mix the diced avocado with the remaining 1 tablespoon lemon juice.

4. Add corn, cucumbers, avocado, onion and tomatoes to the quinoa mix. Add seasoning to taste. Allow to stand at room temperature for 2 to 3 hours before serving.

If you want to share in the spirit of the food and the group as we experienced it, follow these two steps as well.

5. Appreciate each person who will partake of the meal.

6. Tell stories. (In our particular case, the stories came from the Andes and the Middle East and were told with open hearts. They demonstrated our solidarity and the true essence of the people present. You may want to share stories from the *Chicken Soup for the Soul* books.)

The Rainbow

Joan Fountain

As a child I was told and believed that there was a trea-
sure buried beneath every rainbow. I believed it so
much that I have been unsuccessfully chasing rainbows
most of my life. I wonder why no one ever told me that
the rainbow and the treasure were both within me.

—Gerald G. Jampolsky

I was speaking in San Diego on a moored riverboat. It was a
rainy day and I was feeling blue from traveling and working continually for 10 straight days. The conference was well-attended, but
I felt tired and out of touch. As my speech ended the rain finally
stopped. While visiting with members of the audience who came up
to speak with me, I could only think about how good it would feel
to get home. The last person finally left: Free at last.

As I walked down the gangplank I took a deep breath, enjoying
the beginning of my leisure time. Since the rain had stopped and
there was some sunshine, I looked for a rainbow.

Though I looked and looked, I could not see a rainbow.
Suddenly, very quietly from behind me on the gangplank I heard a
woman's voice, "If you want to see the rainbow, you must look into
the dark clouds."

It was one of those moments when you realize that what was said
meant so much more than what was said. And how did she get
behind me on the gangplank? I was the last one to leave.

I was, before that moment, doing what most of us do—rushing to
look away from the difficult times for the joy that must be coming in

the future, desiring to remember only the successes of the past and to bury the uncomfortable times.

I looked back into the dark clouds. There it was—the rainbow. Beautiful! I turned to thank the woman for giving me the secret of how to find a rainbow in nature and in life. There was no sign of her anywhere. Had she really been there? Was it a voice from my imagination? Or had I heard the voice of an angel? I like to think it was the latter—it is more comforting.

Chicken Posole is also very comforting—a great soup to have on a rainy day. It is low in fat and very nourishing for both body and soul.

Chicken Posole

Makes 10 to 12 servings

8 cups chicken broth, divided
1 tablespoon chili powder
1 tablespoon dried leaf oregano, crumbled
2 teaspoons ground cumin
3 bay leaves
4 minced cloves garlic
Cayenne (ground red pepper to taste)
12 stalks celery, cut in ½-inch slices
8 medium carrots, cut in ½-inch slices
1 medium onion, cut in ¾-inch pieces

1 pound bell peppers, cut in ¾-inch pieces
6 cups (four 15-ounce cans) drained yellow and/or white hominy
3 pounds skinless, boneless chicken breasts, cut into 1-inch cubes
1 bunch cilantro (also known as fresh coriander or Chinese parsley), leaves only
Juice of 1 lime (optional)
Warm corn or flour tortillas and lime wedges, for serving

1. Place 1 cup chicken broth in a large stock pot and bring to a rapid boil. Add chili powder, oregano, cumin, bay leaves, garlic and cayenne to the boiling broth and boil for 1 minute to bring out

the flavor of the spices. Add the remaining 7 cups broth and bring to a boil.

2. Add carrots, celery and onion; simmer for 20 minutes. Add bell peppers and drained hominy. Bring to a boil and simmer until the vegetables are tender. Add chicken and the cilantro. Simmer, skimming any foam that rises to the surface, for about 10 minutes or just until the chicken is tender. Take care not to overcook.

3. Taste and adjust seasonings to your liking. *Optional:* Add the juice of 1 lime to the pot. (For very best flavor, refrigerate and reheat for serving the next day.)

4. To serve, ladle hot posole into soup bowls. Garnish with a sprinkling of fresh, chopped cilantro. Serve with warm corn or flour tortillas and lime wedges for guests to season the soup.

Sarson Ka Saag

Rita and Mallika Chopra

"Bhabhiji, why do you always set aside a portion of food at dinner?" It was a tradition she had always kept.

She stared beyond the slowly spinning fan above, her voice barely audible at first as she reeled in images from another world. A frail figure: lost in a sheer white sari, she sat on a hard bed, several pillows supporting her worn body. A stagnant room, white plastered walls, incense teasing a tattered picture of her husband, *rudraksha* beads wrapped around her fingers. Shooting fleeting glances in our direction just long enough to make sure we understood the words she wanted us to hear, Bhabhiji (our grandmother and great-grandmother) told us a story that has been passed down through our family for generations.

"He must have been six, seven years old at the time. They said he had the clearest of faces—innocent and joyful. The kind of clearness that a sage remembers when he attains enlightenment. Deep, dark eyes—eyes of shimmering black that twinkled like lone stars brightening up an infinite universe.

"Seven generations ago, there was a war in northwest India. Massive killings, bloody tortures, innocent victims. Turbulent and violent times that are common throughout history—one group of people being persecuted by another because of their religion. Our family had seen loved ones dragged from their homes and beaten alive—savage realities that are too horrible to imagine.

"They, too, were in danger. And so, in an effort to save their children, they decided to leave their home and flee deeper into India where such persecution did not exist. A perilous journey—if they were caught they would undoubtedly be killed. They left with neither money nor possessions—only their seven sons and a desire to survive.

"It was a rainy night, full of thunder, crying winds and wandering spirits. They left their home, perhaps on foot, perhaps in a cart. They walked for hours. They heard from other refugees that it was a risky night—others had been discovered and killed for trying to escape.

"Eventually they came to a river. To continue, they had to find some way to cross it. They found a boatman, an older man, pale and somber, with an empty and desolate expression. He had a good-sized boat that could take them across the river.

"The boatman eyed this family that approached him to save their lives. He saw a family with seven sons—a family committed to one another. He saw the fear in their eyes, but more clearly he felt the love that emanated from their souls. He envied the emotion they had for each other. He had had a wife and a child, but both were dead now. He was all alone in this world—a soul wilting away, hungry for companionship. An unbearable loneliness was slowly killing him.

"This desperate family could not understand the boatman's desperation. They begged him to take them across the river. They had no money and could think of no way to repay him. The old man eyed the children. In an attempt to save himself, he asked for one of the sons as payment.

"At first they were horrified. To give away a son was to lose a part of themselves. War, however, brings new insights to people. Our family could see the pain and suffering in the old eyes of the man. They feared for their own lives because they had so much to live for, but a more insidious and calculating death preyed upon this man—he had nothing to hope for, nothing to live for. In a moment of desperation, compassion and salvation, they agreed to give their youngest son to this man. To save the lives of their children and to save his life as well."

And so the story has been told for seven generations, and our family began a tradition that Bhabhiji continued to follow throughout her lifetime. During every meal, one plate of food was set aside for the little boy who was left behind. During every meal, he was remembered and honored. At six years old, the little boy's favorite dish was Sarson Ka Saag, a traditional north Indian dish of spinach usually prepared in winter. In memory of a little boy who saved the life of his family and a lonely old man, Sarson Ka Saag has become a special dish in our family tradition.

Sarson Ka Saag

Makes 4 to 6 servings

ᘛᐧᘚ

1 pound mustard greens, washed and chopped	*3 tablespoons* ghee *(see* Note 1*)*
¼ pound spinach, washed and chopped	*2 tablespoons flour or corn starch*
	Salt to taste
1 teaspoon fresh ginger, chopped	Garam masala *(optional) (see* Note 2*)*

Note 1: Ghee *may be purchased in East Indian markets, or make your own by removing the milk solids from melted butter and using only the clear, golden oil. To make* ghee, *cook unsalted (sweet) butter over very low heat until all water is dissipated and milk solids have turned almond-brown and cling to the sides or have fallen to the bottom of the pan. Strain off the remaining clear liquid for use in cooking.*

Note 2: Garam masala *is a mixture of ground aromatic spices used as a seasoning in Indian foods. It is often a combination of lightly roasted cumin seeds, coriander seeds, cardamom, cinnamon, black pepper and cloves that have been ground together.*

1. Place mustard greens and spinach in a pressure cooker or large covered pot with the fresh ginger. Cook for 30 minutes in pressure cooker, or 60 minutes in large pot. The greens will be very soft.

2. Heat *ghee* in a wok over medium heat. Add flour and cook for 1 minute. Add the greens and cook, mashing gently, until all the excess liquid has been cooked away, approximately 15 minutes. Season with salt to taste. Serve in an earthenware bowl. If you wish, sprinkle some *garam masala* over the top.

The Wooden Spoon

Tony Luna

I can remember my parents spanking me only twice. Once was when I was acting up during a church service—I wore a suit that didn't fit me, and I was having a fit that didn't suit my parents. My father took me outside, placed me across his lap and proceeded to give me some uncomfortable whacks across the rear end. I knelt during the rest of the service. I don't remember how I was disobedient the second time, but I clearly recall my mother giving me a sharp rap on the backside with an old wooden spoon she kept on top of the stove.

The wooden spoon incident was a clear example of Mom's version of behavior modification. Whenever I began to act up she would warn me, "If you don't straighten up young man, I'll get the wooden spoon." As far as I can recall, the mere mention of that device would elicit the correct conditioned response. Pavlov and Skinner would have been proud of Mom.

Years passed, and I generally led a pretty straight life. I walked between the white lines in the crosswalk, changed out of my good clothes after school and into my grubbies to play, and used the proper hand signals while maneuvering my bike through traffic. I always received good conduct and citizenship grades, and I was usually not a prime suspect when someone made a foul noise in class while the teacher's back was turned. If anything, I led an uneventful, almost pious, childhood; other parents embarrassingly compared me with their own children, saying, "Now son, why can't you behave like Mrs. Luna's son?"

From childhood through adolescence I still pretty much walked the straight and narrow. I was no saint, but I also had a knack for avoiding trouble in cases when my peers would walk in and embrace it. It never occurred to me to be anything other than a good kid, and I never thought of anything close to rebellion until my mid-20s.

Sometime after college and assorted jobs, and during my active duty in the army, I got this itch to question convention that coincided with the hippie movement, free love and the weekly anti-government, anti-establishment demonstrations. Let's just say that the money I saved in haircuts purchased a lot of jasmine and patchouli. It was a time of great idealism and experimentation.

I made a pilgrimage to the Revolutionary People's Constitutional Convention in Berkeley, in November 1970, where I met a number of conventionality breakers. I was moved as much by their commitment as I was by their diversity. There were self-interest groups seizing the podium to gain a voice; there were flyers, petitions and speeches on behalf of the Black Panthers, the Gray Panthers, the Brown Berets and the Gay Male Vegetarians, just to name a few.

Because I hadn't been taking very good care of myself when I returned from Berkeley, I came down with mononucleosis. My spleen had become infected, and without medication I would certainly need surgery.

While in the hospital, the fever and my over-indulgent way of life would yank me in and out of manifest reality. At one moment I was calm and surrounded by angels, the next I was being judged by devils. Sometimes I was visited by doctors and nurses, sometimes by archetypal shamans clad in Day-Glo vestments.

On one occasion, I saw my mom and a priest standing by my bedside—the priest was praying over me. The prospect of hearing the Last Rites at such a young age enraged me—I bolted upright and yelled profanities. I wasn't going to let anyone surrender my chance to continue my life as I saw fit. Later I was ashamed at my behavior, but I was too proud to admit it.

After I was released from the hospital, I tried to resume my life where I had left off, but I didn't feel the same—I had crossed over a line. I had no words to define it, but the world would never be the same again.

The following Christmas the family got together as usual. I showed up in a tie-dyed army undershirt, bib overalls and moccasins. I took every opportunity to explain why I didn't believe in Christmas (a capitalist plot driven by guilt) or any of its trappings. My family was patient. After dinner we all sat around the tree (I had an opinion about that, too).

The presents were handed out and I smugly watched while the ritual was played out. When I was handed what appeared to be a tie box wrapped in corny Christmas paper with a recycled tag from Mom and Dad tied to the ribbon, I smirked. "Oh great. A tie. Just what I need!" I pulled off the ribbon, tore through the paper, opened the box and was startled by the gift inside. It was the wooden spoon. The wooden spoon that had ruled and guided my young life. The old wooden spoon with burns on the handle that had sat atop the stove for so many years was now lying in my hands. I sheepishly turned to my parents. "It's yours now," my mother said. "You are in charge of the wooden spoon."

With those words, they gave me the scepter of responsibility, empowered me and, at the same time, showed me the awesome strength that comes with being in charge of one's own destiny. In one swift act they had simultaneously elevated me and exposed my weaknesses. The two unassuming people who had given me life gave me the authority to either waste or build my own life. I started to cry. We hugged for a long time.

Years later, my wife had a special Plexiglas box made for the wooden spoon. It now hangs prominently in my office as a reminder of values, responsibility and unconditional love.

I am grateful that I requested Mom's recipes for this cookbook. Before she wrote them down for me, there was no written record of the meals I so fondly remembered from my childhood—they had been passed down through generations—but now I can pass them along to my daughter. Reading it over, I can almost smell the roasting chiles, the meat and the bay leaf as they sauté.

Mama Dee and Papa Julio's Caldillo
(Chile Verde con Carne)

Makes 4 servings

6 medium tomatillos
4 fresh jalapeno chiles
1 fresh chile pasilla
3 tablespoons olive oil
2 small cloves garlic, peeled
1½ teaspoons salt

½ teaspoon ground cumin
1 pound top sirloin, cut in
  ½-inch cubes
2 bunches (about ½ pound)
  fresh spinach
3 bay leaves

1. Peel and wash the tomatillos. In a saucepan, boil the tomatillos and chiles in about ½ cup water to cover, until tender (test by piercing with a fork). Transfer to a blender with 2 tablespoons of the olive oil, the garlic, salt and cumin. Turn on the motor briefly to make a mixture that has the consistency of a salsa. Set aside.

2. Sauté the sirloin in 1 tablespoon olive oil for approximately 10 minutes, or until browned. Meanwhile, wash the spinach leaves well, shaking off the excess water; discard stems. Add the spinach to the pan with the meat, sauté briefly, then add the chile mixture and the bay leaves, and cook for about 20 minutes or until the meat is tender when pierced with a fork. Add water as needed and stir with a wooden spoon to prevent sticking. Remove the bay leaves before serving.

What on Earth Is Shoo-Fly Pie Anyway?

Mary Helen Livingston

The doctor closed his bag and turned to me, "Call me if he gets any worse this afternoon or tonight. I'll stop by in the morning to see him. If he's no better, I'll have to put him in the hospital. He needs fluids, and he must eat."

"I've given him everything I can think of, but he just can't keep anything down."

"You must keep on trying. He is getting weak and dehydrated. Do your best, I'll see you tomorrow morning."

I sat down in the rocking chair by the sofa where my little son lay. Bobby had always been thin and undersized. Now, after days of battling an especially severe form of influenza, he looked wan and wasted. What would I do if he had to be hospitalized? I was a nursing student at Florida State University in Tallahassee and had no hospitalization insurance and very little money. What if the hospital refused to admit him?

I prayed silently, "Lord, show me what to do."

"Bobby, suppose I go to the store and buy a different kind of soup for you. And maybe some Jell-O. Don't you think you might be able to eat some?"

"No, Mama."

"Can't you think of anything you'd like?"

"Make me some shoo-fly pie, Mama. I could eat that. I know I could."

Bobby had never eaten shoo-fly pie in his life. He could not desire something he had never seen nor tasted. Yet I knew why he had asked. To pass the long, weary hours of illness, I had been reading stories to him from library books—*Yonie Wondernose* by Marguerite De Angeli was his favorite. It was the story of Johnny, a little Amish boy from the Pennsylvania Dutch area, and it described vividly the customs, dress, food and daily activities of the Amish.

My life had been spent in Georgia and Florida. I knew nothing of the Amish, had never seen an Amish person, had never tasted a Pennsylvania Dutch dish. What on earth is shoo-fly pie? The little story had mentioned shoo-fly pie, but had failed to list the ingredients. I doubted the wisdom of experimenting with strange, exotic foods in the middle of a serious illness. However, it was the only food Bobby had requested and maybe it was worth trying. Whatever was in it, it was probably not going to stay in him long enough to do any harm.

Having made the decision to act on Bobby's request, I set about locating a recipe. The Leon County Library did not have a book on Pennsylvania Dutch cookery and neither did the State Library. The library at Florida State University had such a cookbook, but it was in use and not due back for two weeks. I called nearby bookstores. They had no Pennsylvania Dutch cookbooks. I called my neighbors, friends, relatives. Some of them had heard of shoo-fly pie, but none of them knew what it was.

"Bobby, there isn't a recipe for shoo-fly pie in this town. I'm just as sorry as I can be. After you are well, we will try again, but right now we are going to have to do with what we can get. I'm going to the grocery store now and I'll try to find something easy for you to eat. Your grandfather will sit with you while I'm gone."

"What store are you going to, Mama? I'll ask God to send you a recipe there. He'll send you one."

"Oh, no, Bobby," I said in alarm, "please don't do that." I couldn't bear the thought of his faith being shattered. And there was obviously no way for God to provide a recipe in the grocery store. I had already tried all the likely places. It would be best for Bobby not to ask for the impossible.

"God will know how to send you a recipe, Mama. Are you going to Winn-Dixie?"

"Yes, I'm going to Winn-Dixie. Don't ask God, honey. I'll be back soon with something good."

In Winn-Dixie I pushed my shopping cart, filling it with red and green Jell-O, butterscotch pudding, chicken noodle soup. And then, nearing the checkout counter, I stood still, not believing what I saw. Walking in the door were two women, one wearing a black prayer cap, the other a white one, just like the pictures in *Yonie Wondernose.* Hurrying toward them, I asked, "Are you Amish?"

"Yes, we are Amish."

"And do you know how to make shoo-fly pie?"

"Of course. All Amish women know how to make shoo-fly pie."

"Could you write me a recipe?"

"Why, yes, certainly. If you have paper, I'll write it down, and then we will help you find the things you need to make a nice pie."

As we walked around gathering brown sugar, molasses and spices, I asked them if they lived in Tallahassee.

"Oh, goodness no. We are just passing through. We have been down in Florida and are on our way back home to Pennsylvania. I don't know why we stopped in here, but all of a sudden, my companion said, 'Let's stop at that Winn-Dixie.' So here we are. I really don't know why we came in."

Awestruck, humbled and ashamed, I knew why. Bobby had disobeyed me. He had asked—and asked—and received.

When I walked into the living room with the groceries, Bobby said, "You got the recipe God sent, didn't you, Mama?"

The recipe made not one, but two large shoo-fly pies. Bobby ate almost the whole pie during the late afternoon and early evening and drank several cups of weak tea. Moreover, he retained all he ate and drank. The pie, high in carbohydrates, provided energy, and the tea replaced lost body fluids. By morning, Bobby was able to drink fruit juices and eat poached eggs and toast. His improvement thereafter was dramatic. And so, after all these years there's a letter I want to write:

Dear Amish Ladies:

This story is really a long-overdue letter to you. It should have been written immediately after this incident, which happened so many years ago. I thought it was in 1954; Bobby says it was 1955. His grandfather would remember exactly, but he died in 1976 and I cannot ask him. Please forgive me for not getting your names and addresses. How could I have been so preoccupied with my problems that I failed to provide myself with the means of thanking you two for the parts you played in this drama?

Perhaps, not knowing the beginning or end of the story, you regarded it as a trivial incident and pushed it away into the vast storehouse of forgetfulness. I want to jog your memory. You had been on a pleasure trip to Florida with friends and were driving back home. You passed through the business district of Tallahassee, Florida. You were driving north on Monroe Street, the highway to Thomasville, Georgia, when you came to a Winn-Dixie on your right. Do you remember?

I want you to remember, because for me this was not a happenstance, a coincidence.

Through the years, when my faith has faltered, when cynicism has threatened me, I find myself thinking of a very sick child making a simple request that he knew would be granted. Unlike me, Bobby wasn't concerned with how God was going to go about it; he trusted in His infinite power. It reminds me that I have no right to wish my own human limitations on God, for with God all things are possible. Thank you, dear Amish ladies, for being his messengers.

Amish Shoo-Fly Pie
Makes two 8-inch pies

CRUMB MIXTURE:
2 cups flour
¾ cup brown sugar
⅓ cup lard, shortening
  or butter

½ teaspoon nutmeg (optional)
1 teaspoon cinnamon (optional)

SYRUP MIXTURE:
1 cup molasses
½ cup brown sugar
2 eggs

1 cup hot water
1 teaspoon baking soda
  dissolved in hot water

1. Thoroughly mix crumb mixture ingredients together in a bowl until crumbs are formed. Line two 8-inch pie plates with half the crumb mixture, reserving the remaining half for topping.

2. In a separate bowl, mix syrup ingredients thoroughly. Pour half of the syrup mixture into each unbaked crumb-lined pie plate, then sprinkle remaining crumb mixture on top. Bake at 400°F for 10 minutes, then reduce heat to 350°F and continue baking for 50 minutes more. Cool before eating.

9
Love, Romance and Marriage

*We are each of us angels with only one wing. And
we can fly only by embracing each other.*

—Luciano deCrescenzo

We Thank Thee

For health and food,
For love and friends,
For everything
Thy goodness sends.
Father in Heaven,
We thank Thee.

—Ralph Waldo Emerson

"We're out of flowers."

Magical Vegetarian Moussaka

Sirah Vettese

One day as I sat working at a health center in Del Mar, California, a wonderful man walked up and put a rich, dark chocolate birthday cake with candles on top in front of me. Though we hadn't met, I knew the man was Harold Bloomfield and that he had opened up his practice there that very week. I was astounded and delighted by the cake because it was my birthday that day, but no one in the office knew about it. How could he have known?

When I noticed that the cake was missing one very small slice, I asked him what had happened to it. He just smiled and left me wondering. At that moment, I was struck in the heart by an arrow!

After our meetings, I could not stop thinking about him. I felt like I was under a trance of some sort. Later on when we finally spoke, he told me it had been his birthday the day before and it was just a coincidence that he had offered me cake on my own birthday. Well in my book there are no accidents, just events that lead us to our destiny.

What followed could have been a scene from the film *Like Water for Chocolate*. I spent the entire weekend preparing a special dish for him. I chose to make a vegetarian version of the popular Greek dish *moussaka*. As I chopped and stirred and tasted, I poured my thoughts, desires and whatever else was simmering inside of me into the delicious sauce. I felt as if I was under a spell.

When I delivered the dish to Harold and watched him take his first bite, I knew that through my cooking I had imbued the same intoxication in him that I felt: his eyes rolled back and he moaned with delight as he savored the moussaka.

Here is my formula for adding culinary magic:

1. Envision the person you are cooking for.

2. Be aware of exactly what you wish to convey through your food: sensual pleasure, passion, laughter, unbounded love, deep unexpressed emotions, joy.

3. As you mix, stir, peel, chop, blend and cook, focus on that person and see your energy received through the food with all your intentions behind it.

The magic of my Vegetarian Moussaka has lasted a long time. Harold is *still* under its spell. Our love blossoms anew each day, and he always looks forward to re-experiencing its enchanting taste. I have not been able to reproduce it exactly, but the following recipe is the basic dish. It's up to you to add your own desires and magic.

Magical Vegetarian Moussaka
Makes 6 servings

∾

1 cup dried black beans (you
  may substitute 3 cups
  cooked beans)
2½ cups vegetable broth
  (I save liquid from cooked
  vegetables in my freezer)
A teaspoon or so of olive oil,
  to prevent boiling over
1 pound eggplant, sliced thinly
Salt
3 medium onions, chopped
2 tablespoons extra-virgin
  olive oil
2 cloves garlic, minced

1 (6-ounce) can tomato paste
¼ to ½ teaspoon ground
  cinnamon or allspice, to taste
Salt and pepper
A pinch of sugar
2 more tablespoons olive oil
3 cups mashed potatoes
1½ cups plain yogurt
A generous sprinkling of
  freshly grated nutmeg
⅓ cup freshly grated
  Parmesan cheese
A light sprinkling of paprika,
  for color

1. Rinse and pick over the black beans and place in a soup pot with the vegetable broth. Bring to a boil, skimming any foam that rises to the surface. Add a teaspoon or so of olive oil to prevent boiling over and lower the heat to simmer. Cover and simmer slowly for 1½ to 2 hours, until tender. (Or, you may substitute 3 cups of cooked or canned beans.) Drain, reserving extra liquid.

2. Sprinkle eggplant slices generously with salt and place on plastic wrap or other non-metal surface for 30 minutes; rinse with cold water and pat dry with paper towels. This will draw out excess juices.

3. Meanwhile, sauté onions in olive oil for 10 minutes or so until they begin to brown. Add garlic, tomato paste and cinnamon or allspice to taste. Stir in the drained beans and mash them into the mixture with the back of a large cooking spoon. Season to your liking with salt and pepper, and perhaps a pinch of sugar. Add a bit of the reserved liquid if the mixture seems dry.

4. Preheat oven to 350°F. Oil a 9×13-inch oven-proof casserole dish. Sauté the slices of eggplant in olive oil for a few minutes on each side until they are tender; remove and drain on paper towels. Arrange a single layer of eggplant slices on the bottom of the casserole dish. Spread an even layer of half the bean mixture. Repeat the layers and top with the final pieces of eggplant.

5. Spread mashed potatoes over the eggplant. In a small bowl beat together the plain yogurt, a generous sprinkling of freshly grated nutmeg, and salt and pepper to taste; spread the yogurt mixture over the mashed potatoes. Sprinkle Parmesan cheese over the top, followed by a light sprinkling of paprika for color. Bake for 40 to 45 minutes.

Reunion

Burt Dubin

Be willing to do what your soul directs you to do if you want
to create what you are asking for.

—Sanyana Roman

I did not call her until after I completed my speaking engagement.

Knowing I'd be in Boston to give a speech, I'd negotiated an extra two nights in the hotel as part of my fee. I so wanted to see her. I wanted to touch her, to look into her eyes at least one more time. I hoped against hope that maybe, just maybe . . .

We hadn't seen one another since our Atlantic City High School reunion five years earlier. I'd stayed away from every previous reunion. An intuitive pull, a sense that I was to be at this reunion, compelled me to send in the reservation to attend my first reunion ever. Along with my confirmation came a list of those who had signed up to be there.

Her name was there, *her maiden name!* What thoughts flowed through my mind . . . what memories flooded back to me! I had never really been able to forget her. She was the unattainable dream, the vision of my high school senior year.

We knew each other only slightly and had a few mutual friends, but we were never together socially. I don't remember ever speaking to her—just admiring her from afar. A year or two later, I became very aware of her life. We'd both moved to Philadelphia. I had a job selling furniture for my uncle while starting to put myself through Temple University. She had married a successful young man with whom my uncle did business. As the office gofer, I got to be at her husband's office every week. Her picture hung on the wall. *(Wringing of hands! Blue notes in minor key on the strings, please.)*

She, of course, knew nothing of me. After a few years, I married and moved to California.

Every five years another invitation arrived to attend my high school reunion. I ignored them all. Her graduation was a year after mine. But this fateful year they sent her an invitation to attend the wrong reunion. *Mine.*

Now alone, as was I, she'd been living in Boston for several years. She didn't realize it was not *her* reunion so she sent in her reservation. When she *did* realize it, she decided to attend anyway. She just *felt* like attending. Meanwhile, I asked the reunion chair to seat her *at my table.*

All through that dinner, I looked at her on the far side of the table, not daring to speak. Finally, I screwed up my courage and asked her to dance. *It was the last dance.* It became the most significant dance of my life. Of *hers,* too.

We did infinitely more talking than dancing and kept on talking after the music stopped. Phone numbers and addresses were exchanged, 3,000 miles apart. Maryam—yes, that's her name—later said that when she returned to Boston she told her married daughter of the deep, meaningful conversation she'd shared with a classmate she hardly knew—one of the deepest conversations she'd ever had. She sensed that most people never get to that level even with those they've known for years.

We wrote back and forth for a while. After a few months, the letters stopped. Five years of *nothing* ensued. Until my phone call that January night.

When she answered her phone, I told her I was in town for just that one night and asked if I could see her. She told me she was busy cooking for a dinner party at her home and invited me to attend—and to arrive an hour early so we'd have a chance to talk while she prepared the food.

Our conversation began where the last one had left off. I'd been enchanted five years ago, and I was more so now. The aroma of the Tamale Pie she was making added a mouth-watering sensuality, rendering me incapable of rational thought.

The party was a success. Though I hardly shared a moment with her once the other guests arrived, I enjoyed meeting her friends.

The evening wound down. The last guest left and finally we were alone. I got right to the point—there was no time for small talk. Looking straight at her, I asked, "Would you be receptive to a courtship?"

She replied, "I have no gentleman callers at the moment . . ." (Be still, my beating heart!)

It had grown late. She drove me to the cab stand in Harvard Square. I kissed her warmly on her mouth. We both anticipated a long courtship. After all, there was so much we had to learn about each other. Even whether we were right for each other. She lived on one coast, I on the other.

Fate had other plans.

Sunday morning I flew back to L.A. I had no idea what to do next. First thing next morning, my office phone rang. It was a CEO who had heard my keynote. He asked me to come East and do some consulting for his company. We made the arrangements.

I called *her*, said I'd be only an hour away from her in a few days, and asked if she'd be receptive to a visit. She *would*.

Yes, she'd make me a reservation at a convenient hotel. Yes, she'd make us a reservation at the nicest restaurant in Cambridge (the Charles). That evening, we enjoyed a fine dinner. Lingering over wine and dessert, I heard my voice saying unplanned words: "Will you be my wife?"

She looked at me for a long moment. My heart was in my mouth. I was dazzled by the possibilities of this unplanned proposal. She suddenly said, "*Yes!*" Not once, not twice, but *three* times "*Yes*, yes, YES!" We looked at each other in wonderment. Both of us are intellectual types, neither of us is that brash. What had we done? These "yes's" were spoken not by her rational mind, but by some deeper part of her being over which she had no control.

We followed through. We felt—and still feel—that we were led to each other. We've been happily married for three years now, and it just keeps getting better. I love telling this story, *our* story; I never tire of it. Both Maryam and I are happy to share this recipe with you, the recipe that has such special memories for us both.

Each time she prepares this Tamale Pie, it tastes as wonderful as the first time I savored it that night at her dinner party. One reason is that she always cooks with *love*. And, though love is not listed as one of the ingredients, it is the most essential component.

Tamale Pie

Makes 6 servings

1 medium onion, chopped
1 small green pepper, chopped
2 to 3 tablespoons canola or
  olive oil
15 ounces kidney or pinto
  beans, cooked (drained,
  if canned)
2 cups seasoned tomato sauce
  or 2 (8-ounce) cans
1½ cups whole cooked corn or
  a 15½-ounce can, drained

½ cup pitted black olives,
  coarsely chopped
1 tablespoon sugar, honey or
  barley malt
2 to 3 teaspoons chili powder
1 teaspoon salt
1½ cups shredded Cheddar
  cheese (or substitute soy
  Cheddar)

CORN MEAL TOPPING:
¾ cup yellow corn meal
2 cups cold water

1 tablespoon butter
½ teaspoon salt

1. Preheat the oven to 375°F. In a large skillet, sauté the onion and green pepper in oil until tender. Stir in beans, tomato sauce, corn, olives, sweetener, chili powder and salt; simmer 20 to 25 minutes, until thickened. Add cheese, stirring until melted, and pour into an ungreased 8½ x 11-inch baking dish.

2. In a medium saucepan, stir corn meal into cold water. Cook, stirring until thickened. Stir in butter and salt. Spoon over the bean mixture in narrow lengthwise and crosswise strips. Bake for 40 minutes or until browned. Serve with salad and warm bread.

Salmon Wellington, Chez Jo

Ozzie Jurock

Arriving in Canada from Germany, I came, I saw a gorgeous Filipina and I conquered (or rather I lucked out, as she somehow agreed to be my wife). And I was happy. But we humans are more than creatures of heart: we also have stomachs. Hoping to satisfy both, and thus make my happiness complete—and thinking of my pre-bachelor days and my mother's fine home cooking—I asked Jo, my new bride, to make me fish accompanied by spinach (my favorite vegetable) for our first dinner together. Despite her unfamiliarity with Western-style cooking, she proceeded to do so— exactly. Fish and spinach . . . both from a tin (separate tins, granted, but the overall effect was still, well, rather unusual).

It was hard concealing my bewilderment and surprise when faced with that plate. Being a good sport (and having no desire to disrupt our domestic tranquility), I picked up my fork and started into the green and glutinous pile. Yum.

Now Jo is both perceptive and tenacious. She caught my look of shock and immediately decided she was going to conquer Western-style cooking and become a chef. Right then and there she proved what an undaunted personality she had and still has: she announced that her first dish would be Salmon Wellington.

Even for skilled chefs, Salmon Wellington is not an easy dish to prepare. The ingredients in themselves are simple, but as with anything else in this life of ours it's how you put them together that makes or breaks the dish. Be it a relationship or a *roux*, all it takes is one irrevocable misstep—a touch too much or too little season-ing—and what could have been memorable simply becomes forgettable. Or worse.

I didn't want her to risk it. Start out slowly, I suggested. Fish and chips are fine. Cut up a fish, slice a spud or two, toss them in hot oil and there you go (actually, that's not quite true). But I could not dissuade her: She had decided on Salmon Wellington, and Salmon Wellington it was going to be. Catching the look in her eye I promptly shut up.

She spent every night of the next week at the library researching the various combinations and regional variations on this "simple," yet subtly complex dish. I meanwhile made do with toast and eggs.

The fateful Sunday finally rolled around. Jo withdrew to the kitchen while I fidgeted in our tiny dining room, preparing for the worst and mentally rehearsing various feeble platitudes and well-meaning "atta-girl's."

Then the door opened and Jo marched in bearing a plate. On it, steaming and fragrant, . . . Salmon Wellington. And not just a good Salmon Wellington, but a great one.

The change from that unhappy canned salmon and spinach to this veritable feast was so dramatic, so tremendous, it made me appreciate what a determined personality Jo has. As our years together have gone by (27 and counting, with two children, one grandchild and more on the way), this appreciation has only grown. During this time we have experienced much growth together in our private and business lives. And thanks to her increasing culinary skills, my waistline has also grown somewhat as well.

But needless to say, my favorite meal remains to this day Salmon Wellington. Over time, the recipe has changed a bit. Jo says it's sim-pler now, faster and easier to prepare. But to me, it will always rep-resent the power of determination and love.

Salmon Wellington, Chez Jo

Makes 8 to 10 servings

Head north, catch a wild salmon and fillet it. If that's not possible, angle down to your nearest fish shop and find a (relatively) lively fish. A fresh salmon should have clear eyes, firm flesh and a pleasant smell—just like any good dining companion.

2 pounds fresh salmon fillets
½ cup low-fat milk
Salt and pepper
2 (8-ounce or 215-gram) packages frozen puff pastry, thawed

3 hard-cooked eggs, halved
   lengthwise
1 egg, beaten, for glaze

BÉCHAMEL SAUCE:
1 tablespoon butter
1 teaspoon flour

½ cup low-fat milk

MUSHROOM FILLING:
1 tablespoon butter
½ cup chopped onions
½ cup thinly sliced
   mushrooms

2 teaspoons fresh lemon juice
Salt and pepper to taste

MUSHROOM CREAM SAUCE:
2 tablespoons butter
1½ cups sliced mushrooms

2 tablespoons flour
1 cup light cream (or
   low-fat milk)

1. Preheat oven to 400°F. Thaw frozen puffed pastry. Hard cook the eggs and let cool.

2. Divide the salmon into two portions of 1½ pounds and ½ pounds (750 and 250 grams). Finely chop or grind the small portion and blend in milk. Season with salt and pepper. Thinly slice the large piece of the salmon.

3. Prepare béchamel sauce by melting the butter in a small skillet, adding flour and blending in the milk. Set aside.

4. To make the mushroom filling, melt the butter in a skillet and sauté the onions until soft but not brown. Add the mushrooms and lemon juice. Stir in the béchamel sauce and simmer for 5 minutes. Season with salt and pepper. Remove from heat and set aside.

5. Divide the puff pastry into two portions, one slightly larger than the other. Roll out the smaller piece (12×6 inches, or 30×15 cm for the stoutly metric) and place on a greased baking sheet. Place half the salmon slices along the center of the pastry. Top with half the mushroom mixture. Cover with the minced salmon/milk mixture. Top with two rows of egg, halved lengthwise. Spread remaining mushroom mixture over the egg halves and cover with the remaining salmon slices.

6. Roll out remaining pastry 14×8 inches (35.5 × 20 cm) and drape it over the salmon layers. Brush the edges with beaten egg; press the edges and seal. With a fork, poke steam holes in the pastry. Be artistic—decorate the top with scraps of dough cut into shapes. Brush the pastry with remaining beaten egg. Bake for 25 minutes.

7. To make the cream sauce that will accompany the Wellington, melt the butter and sauté the mushrooms for 2 to 3 minutes. Stir in flour, then gradually pour in light cream or milk. Stir continuously until thickened. Season with salt and pepper.

8. Remove the Salmon Wellington from the oven and serve with sauce.

The Case of the Missing Chocolate

Diana von Welanetz Wentworth

I came home the other night after my writing class to find my husband Ted in bed, playing Gameboy with a very satisfied look on his face. I thought, *Uh-oh,* walked to the kitchen and discovered his trail of foil and chocolate crumbs. He had discovered the brownies I'd made for the Saturday picnic. *I should have known,* I thought, as I looked at the remains.

Ted peeked around the kitchen door. "My doctor says I'll never outgrow my need for chocolate . . . it's medicinal!"

"He really said that?"

"Yep. He says there's nothing that can be done."

This is not the first time it has occurred to me that having a husband is a bit like having a big dog.

Ted's case history of chocolate addiction is lengthy. Mid-afternoon, when he dives into the bowl of M&Ms and Hershey's Chocolate Kisses at his office, Paula, his secretary of 26 years, rolls her eyes . . . she knows he will soon be bouncing off the walls.

Usually a generous soul, Ted gets territorial only over chocolate. One night I served him a particularly beautiful chocolate éclair I'd found that day. I was dieting and the sight became too much for me. I said, "I wish I had a bite of that."

He emitted a little growl and said, "Sure you do . . ." as he placed his arm protectively around his plate, "like a frog wishes he had wings so he wouldn't bump his butt along the ground."

He gives up chocolate every New Year's Day. That usually lasts until Valentine's Day, when he begins eating it slowly, like normal people do, and tells me he has it under control. Gradually, I begin to notice that every night after dinner he asks, "Do we have any chocolate?" Non-fat frozen yogurt with non-fat hot fudge topping is not for him; he points the car toward the local Italian ice cream parlor where he asks for a taste of every chocolate *gelato* they have.

Eventually he notices chocolate has become an obsession and he talks about giving it up again. Which he does, until Easter, and then we are off again. We make it fairly well through the summer months, but with the approach of autumn and Thanksgiving, then Christmas, he falls off the wagon with a thud.

Here is Ted's very favorite chocolate dessert. It is a tiny warm chocolate cake with a gooey center and a warm chocolate sauce that our friend Margo Rogoff introduced him to at mad.61, the trendiest new restaurant in New York City at this writing, located in Barney's department store at 61st and Madison. I have photos of Ted using his fingers to scrape up the very last lick.

Warm Valhrona Chocolate Cakes
Makes 6 servings

Recipe courtesy of mad.61 pastry chef, Patti Jackson.

Butter and sugar for 6 brioche *molds*

8 ounces Valhrona bittersweet chocolate (Caraibe—see Note)

6 ounces (¾ stick) sweet (unsalted) butter

5 eggs plus 3 egg yolks

¼ cup sugar

2 tablespoons strong brewed coffee

¾ cup sifted pastry flour

CHOCOLATE SAUCE:

¾ cup heavy (whipping) cream

6 ounces Valhrona chocolate, coarsely chopped

2 tablespoons sweet butter

1 teaspoon vanilla or Myers dark rum

Note: *Valhrona chocolate is dark, rich and not too sweet. If not available, use any excellent bittersweet chocolate.*

1. Preheat oven to 375°F. Butter 6 (4-ounce) *brioche* molds (or other molds about 1 inch high) heavily and sprinkle with sugar; set aside. In the top of a double boiler, melt together the chocolate, cut in small pieces, and butter.

2. In a mixer, beat together whole eggs, egg yolks, and sugar until light and lemon-colored. Add and mix in the coffee, followed by the chocolate/butter mixture and sifted pastry flour. Pour the batter into the prepared molds, filling them within ⅛ inch of the top. (These may now be left at room temperature for up to 3 hours or refrigerated for up to 48 hours.)

3. To make the Chocolate Sauce, heat the cream just to a boil and pour over the chocolate pieces. Add butter and vanilla or rum; stir until smooth. Use while warm; if sauce should cool, reheat over simmering water or in a microwave oven on low heat, taking care not to overheat or it will separate.

4. Just before serving, place the cakes in preheated oven and bake for 8 minutes until set around the edges—center of cakes should be runny. Turn out of molds immediately onto serving plates. Top with chocolate sauce and serve warm with ice cream.

Love from Afar

Diana von Welanetz Wentworth

When I married Ted, he had never been to Paris. I had lived there many years before and was eager to show him the City of Lights. We arrived at Orly Airport one busy Saturday, six days before Christmas. So much seemed just as it was years before, and through Ted's eyes I found myself experiencing the romance of Paris all over again. Breakfast of fresh oranges, *pain au chocolat* and *café au lait*; dinner before a performance at the Paris Opéra at *Le Soufflé*, where they still serve the most delicious soufflés of all, a different one for each course.

Early our first morning in Paris, we hopped on a Cityrama bus so Ted could have an overview of the entire city. From then on we walked everywhere, and that afternoon I led him up the winding streets of Montmartre, the historic and picturesque village atop a butte overlooking all of metropolitan Paris. Since the late 19th century it has been the haunt of artists and home of the exquisite Sacre Coeur Basilica.

Rounding a curve on a steep cobblestone street, Ted encountered his first of many Parisian crêpe vendors, a fetching blond woman with an inviting smile. Explaining the concept of crêpes to Ted, I ordered one for him with sugar and Grand Marnier, the aromatic orange-flavored cognac. He watched, wide-eyed, as she ladled smooth cream-colored batter onto a huge round griddle then spread it to the edges with a T-shaped wooden stick.

"Look! She's using a bird perch!" Ted said.

She deftly flipped the huge pancake, wiped it with butter, and sprinkled it liberally with sugar and Grand Marnier. After cooking it briefly on the second side, she folded it neatly into sixths, enveloped it in paper and handed it to him. One bite and Ted got that far away look in his eyes that he gets when he eats chocolate.

I waited while he savored each mouthful until he eventually remembered I was there and offered me a bite.

"Uh . . . I don't know how to tell you this, Diana . . . but I think I'm in love with another woman."

I have developed a recipe to make for him at home that he says he likes just as well. But once in a while, I catch him with that look and know he is thinking about her. Ah . . . love from afar.

Crêpes au Grand Marnier

Makes about 20 crêpes

BASIC CRÊPES:

1½ cups Wondra instant-blending flour or sifted all-purpose flour
Pinch of salt

2 cups milk, or more if needed
2 eggs, lightly beaten
2 tablespoons vegetable oil

FOR SERVING:

Melted butter
Sugar

Grand Marnier

1. Place flour and salt in a mixing bowl. Combine remaining ingredients and add slowly, beating with a whisk until smooth. Let stand at room temperature for 15 minutes.

2. Brush the inside of a heavy 5- or 6-inch skillet or crêpe pan with vegetable oil and set over medium heat, until a drop of water dances on the surface. Stir the batter, then add about 2 tablespoons batter to the skillet, just enough to cover the bottom of the pan, while twisting the skillet. The crêpe should be very thin. Ignore any small holes. It may feel awkward at first while you get the feel of it, but you'll catch on!

3. Brown lightly on one side, then turn with a spatula to brown the

other side. Turn out onto paper towels, with the pretty side down so that when the crêpe is folded it will be on the outside. Cook remaining batter the same way. (They may be refrigerated or frozen at this point, and may be used in many recipes, either sweet or savory.)

4. Just before serving, reheat the crêpes on a griddle, two or three at a time, with the pretty side down. Brush with melted butter, sprinkle with super-fine sugar and drizzle with Grand Marnier. Fold into quarters and transfer to serving plates, allowing three per person.

Cooking is like love. It should be entered into with abandon or not at all.

—Harriet Van Horne

Twice in a Lifetime

Rhonda Nielsen Bisnar

When I met my husband John in 1992 both of us noticed an other-worldly feeling . . . a déjà-vu sense that we had met before.

We both had been previously married and had lived in various places. As our relationship progressed we discussed the paths our lives had taken, and the places we had lived. We were surprised to learn how often our paths had almost, but not quite, crossed.

He told me of a night in 1969, when as a young soldier stationed in Honolulu, he decided to walk alone from his apartment near Waikiki to Kalakaua Boulevard in the direction of the International Market Place. On a street corner along the way he saw a young woman about 16 or 17 whose image stayed with him through the years. He could still see her clearly in his mind—long blond hair, dressed in a very unusual sort of fishnet dress worn over a body suit, laughing up at an unusually tall, young oriental man. He told me how he was instantly drawn to her and could not take his eyes away. "I found her compelling and felt as if there was something I was supposed to do," he said, "as if she held the key to a once-in-a-lifetime opportunity . . . if only I could have known what to do or say."

I told him I had lived in Hawaii in 1969, and was a senior at Punahou High School. I lived on Kalakaua Avenue at the foot of Diamond Head, not far from where John remembered his blond vision. And I even had a vague memory of a dress like the one he described, and having a friend, Eddie Ebisui, who could have been the young man John remembered.

What could he have said or done that night? Clearly nothing—we were worlds apart and would have had nothing in common. Now,

25 years later, John and I are married, we are both lawyers and our families of two boys and three girls have merged magically. We are convinced there was destiny in our meeting, but it could not be rushed. It is only now that our time has come.

We returned to Honolulu together not long ago for my high school reunion. I introduced him to Eddie, now also a lawyer, who remembered that special dress, as well as my passion for tropical fruits. Here is a healthy, low-calorie salad I love. John and I call it Twice-in-a-Lifetime Fruit Salad.

Twice-in-a-Lifetime Fruit Salad

Makes 2 large servings

*1 mango, peeled and sliced
  (reserve ½ cup for dressing)*
*1 papaya, peeled, seeded
  and sliced*
*¼ pineapple, cored, peeled
  and sliced*

1 banana, peeled and sliced
1 orange, peeled and sectioned
*1 cup fresh berries (raspberries,
  strawberries, blackberries
  or a combination)*

MANGO YOGURT DRESSING:
½ cup mango
1 cup non-fat yogurt

2 tablespoons honey

Arrange fruit decoratively on two serving plates. Spoon on dressing.

Working Miracles for the Judge

Andrea Bell

There is only one happiness in life, to love and be loved.

—George Sand

Celebrating the most important passages in people's lives is what I love about my work as a chef and event coordinator. Love was the operative word to describe the Judge's last party. And the saying "Love can work miracles" described the only possibility that it would, in fact, ever take place.

The Judge was a large, brusque, loud and autocratic man. One instantly knew he would have no trouble controlling *his* courtroom! Through the planning and execution of the many weddings I catered for his large family, he called the shots. His kind, intelligent and caring wife seemed to possess a special inner wisdom, but she always let the Judge preside. His presence was always required for even the smallest decisions.

Though fiercely opinionated, bellicose and gruff, the Judge had another side. He believed in celebrations—of life, of love, of friends, of transitions and, most of all, of family. He found many an occasion to gather them all together—to savor the food, friends, family and festivities that he carefully orchestrated.

For his upcoming retirement from the bench, the planning to celebrate another passage of life began months in advance. The Judge, his wife and I sat at their kitchen table and discussed his culinary favorites.

"We must have your Carrot Orange Bisque," he insisted. I mulled over the simplicity of this exquisite soup, bursting with flavor—a longtime favorite of the Judge. We went on to plan a menu of Oyster Shooters, Rare Leg of Lamb on Garlic Sourdough Croustades with Pear Chutney and Minted Mayonnaise, as well as other eclectic delicacies for his party. The Judge became engrossed, as usual, with all the details. The party was still months away, but as I left, I knew I would be busy carrying out the Judge's orders. As I went out the door, he yelled, "Don't forget the Carrot Orange Bisque!"

I ironed out each detail for months. As the party grew near, I called the Judge to discuss one of the myriad items with him. I was terribly distressed to find out he was in the hospital, that he had been diagnosed with terminal cancer and that he might not even be able to attend his party. The Judge, of course, insisted that he would indeed be attending his party, so the planning continued.

During the party, he pulled me to the side to share a secret dream. His 40th anniversary would be the next occasion to celebrate. He wanted to throw a surprise tribute to "my angel of a wife who I dearly love." I quickly agreed to conspire with him, but when he told me the date—nearly half a year away—I was too stunned to say a word. I knew his prognosis, and it was apparent how thin, frail and weak he was. It would take a miracle for this party to ever take place! As I left I was deeply saddened, but the Judge was chipper as he insisted that the Carrot Orange Bisque be the first course for the anniversary celebration.

I received clandestine telephone calls from his hospital bed. He planned a loving tribute to his wife between courses of Carrot Orange Bisque and Mesquite Grilled Salmon with Porcini Mushroom Ravioli. As the planning continued, the Judge grew weaker. He insisted, however, that we meet at his son's home where the party was to take place so he could help decide where the tables would be, where the band would play and what color of tableclothes would be used. On that day, the Judge was so frail that a driver had to bring him and help him walk into the room. How was he ever going to make it for three more months until the party? I left this final meeting in tears. He had planned such a loving evening to celebrate the wife who had cherished him through sickness and health—yet chances were slim that he would live to see the party.

As the phone calls continued, I could hear increasing tiredness in the Judge's voice, but his mind remained clear and focused. He was fiercely determined that the love of his life would have her surprise party—a lasting tribute and testimony to all she had meant to this once-giant of a man.

The party day arrived, and so did the Judge. Although in a wheelchair, his spirit was unhampered. He spoke eloquently of his sweet wife in the loving tribute he shared with family and friends. There were few dry eyes. The party was an outrageous success. Everyone there knew that this would be their last opportunity to celebrate with the Judge. The Judge thanked me as he left and declared that the Carrot Orange Bisque was the best it had ever been. A few days later, the Judge died peacefully.

Carrot Orange Bisque
Makes 3 quarts, or about 10 to 12 servings

2 large onions, chopped
½ stick butter or ¼ cup olive oil
1 tablespoon ground cumin
1 tablespoon fresh tarragon
  (or 1 teaspoon dried)
1 teaspoon fresh thyme, stems
  removed (or ⅓ teaspoon
  dried)
1 tablespoon sugar or honey
2 teaspoons salt
1 teaspoon freshly ground
  black pepper or to taste
¼ teaspoon freshly grated
  nutmeg

1 tablespoon fresh orange zest
  (the finely grated outermost
  skin of an orange)
1½ pounds carrots, peeled
  and shredded
7 cups chicken broth (turkey or
  vegetable broth may be
  substituted)
½ cup raw white rice
½ cup whipping cream
½ cup sour cream
2 cups freshly squeezed orange
  juice

GARNISH:
A swirl of créme fraîche *or*
  sour cream

Sprigs of fresh tarragon,
  if desired

1. In a 4- or 5-quart saucepan, sauté onions in butter or olive oil until translucent. Add cumin, tarragon, fresh thyme, sugar or honey, salt, freshly ground black pepper, nutmeg and orange zest. Add carrots and cook over medium heat for 3 or 4 minutes, stirring often. Add chicken broth and bring to a boil. Add rice, stir, then lower the heat to a simmer, cover and cook about 30 minutes, at which time the rice will be overcooked and the carrots will be falling apart.

2. Purée the soup in small batches in a blender, taking care not to process too much hot soup at a time or it may overflow. Return the puréed soup to the cooking pot and bring to a simmer; whisk in whipping cream and sour cream.

3. Just before serving, whisk in freshly squeezed orange juice. Garnish with a swirl of *creme fraîche* or sour cream and sprigs of fresh herbs. (This soup freezes beautifully, but do so before adding the cream and orange juice.)

10

A Love Story with Recipes

To love abundantly is to live abundantly, and to love forever is to live forever.

—Henry Drummond

A Love Story with Recipes

Diana von Welanetz Wentworth

I met my current husband (he claims to be my *late* husband, insisting that my first husband was my *early* husband) over breakfast, appropriately enough. His opening line was, "Will you live with me?"

Ted had just turned 50. He'd been a widower two years, since losing his wife, Sharon, to a prolonged illness. His long marriage had agreed with him, so he was deep into the process of "interviewing" as many likely women as he could find for the position of new wife/best friend.

At the start of his search, friends assured him it would be easy, that the women of the world were waiting eagerly for such a superb catch as he, a nice-looking, medium-tall strawberry blond, with a successful 30-year law career, father of two grown daughters and the owner of a home with a view. He was told to expect candidates to line up around the block with casseroles in hand.

Though a few did appear, not all of them liked him and no one seemed quite right, so he made his quest known to everyone he met, inviting suggestions for likely prospects. He was single-minded in his pursuit. He checked out church groups and every lead he got. He knew she was out there somewhere and he was determined to find her.

❧

At this point, it will help you to know some of my history to fully understand the circumstances of Ted and me coming together. In November, the year before I met Ted, my husband Paul von Welanetz and I celebrated our 25th anniversary. Our marriage was the result of a storybook romance. I knew the moment I saw Paul in a hotel lobby in Hong Kong in 1962 that he was *the one*. I watched him step off an elevator and felt suddenly dizzy from the impact; he took my breath away. He asked me where I was from, invited me to dinner, and three days later we were engaged.

The days that followed are a blur now. He had been in Hong Kong on business; I was on a tour of the Orient with my parents. Now our reasons for being there were forgotten. We wandered the city holding hands and grinning at each other, crossing Hong Kong Bay on the Star Ferry and riding the cable car on the island to the top of Victoria Peak, where we carved our initials on a rock.

DW
PW
62

Paul was an artist, and in the months that followed he penned exquisite letters on thin blue, fold-up airmail envelopes that he covered with sweet cartoons. I called him Tiger, he called me Kitten, and we were sure no two people had ever been so deeply in love. We were married one year from the day we met in a small church that no longer exists in my hometown of Beverly Hills. The minister told us, "Your marriage will be your ministry."

Paul and I knew with certainty that we were soul mates, that there was a destiny to our meeting. And it was a truly happy marriage. We felt joined at the hip from our wedding day on—as if we shared a single soul—and eventually built a career out of our togetherness. For, soon after we were married, I began attending what became five years of classes with Chef Grégoire LeBalch, head chef at the famed Escoffier Room at the Beverly Hilton Hotel. Paul followed me into the kitchen, chopping, kneading and adding his artistic touches to the dishes I learned to prepare. During that same time, Julia Child began appearing on public television with her first series *The French Chef*, spawning interest all over America in classic French culinary techniques.

My cooking classes began almost by accident, on the day I quit smoking. Our daughter Lexi had just been born and I was suddenly housebound and coping with all the realities and responsibilities of being a new mother. Lexi was napping and I wanted a diversion to keep my hands busy, so I put three crêpe pans on the stove and started making crêpes to store in the freezer—pouring the batter in the first, flipping the second, turning the third out onto a towel to be brushed with melted butter. The busy rhythm of my movements allowed no time to think about lighting a cigarette. Two friends dropped in and were intrigued with the process. Hundreds of crêpes later, we decided, with great enthusiasm, to meet the next day for a class in omelette-making and the following week for soufflés. We had so much fun that word spread quickly, and soon strangers began calling to inquire about lessons.

Because teaching classes answered a new need on my part for personal expression and creativity, Paul encouraged me to pursue this opportunity for meeting new people without having to leave the house. Paul located some folding desk chairs to set up in our kitchen, and I was off on a new vocation. I was teaching four and five classes a week while a babysitter played with Lexi.

Paul became a welcome addition to my evening classes with his advice about wines and knife sharpening and his flair for creating decorations and garnishes on the platters of food. Paul would artistically flute the mushroom caps to sauté and serve atop our favorite chicken dish.

Chicken Breasts in Champagne

Makes 4 servings

ↄ彡

*4 whole chicken breasts, boned
  (see* Note*) and skinned
¼ cup flour
1 teaspoon salt
½ teaspoon pepper
1 stick (½ cup) butter or
  margarine
2 tablespoons oil
½ pound mushrooms*

*1 cup whipping cream
½ cup champagne
8 large mushrooms
1 tablespoon butter
Lemon juice
Salt and pepper to taste
Chopped parsley or other herb,
  to garnish*

Note: *Boning is easy to do with your fingers instead of a boning knife—just keep running and pushing your index finger along the ribs and the meat will separate from the bones easily.*

1. Place the 8 chicken breast halves between two pieces of wax paper and flatten them slightly with the side of a mallet or the bottom of a skillet. Place the flour, salt and pepper in a bowl and dredge the breasts in the mixture, shaking off excess flour.

2. In a large skillet with a lid, melt the butter or margarine with the oil over medium-high heat. Lightly brown the floured breasts on both sides. Wash the mushrooms quickly under cold running water, rubbing off any grit with your fingers. Dry them immediately so they do not absorb water, trim away the stem ends, and cut them into quarters through the stem. (If you use shiitake mushrooms, cut out and discard the stems.) When the breasts are lightly browned, add the mushrooms, cover the pan, lower the heat, and cook slowly for 10 minutes. Uncover and remove most of the excess butter with a spoon. Add the cream and champagne (which may be saved from another occasion in the refrigerator for this purpose—bubbles are unnecessary) and simmer slowly, uncovered, for 5 more minutes. Remove from the heat.

3. While the breasts are cooking, remove the stems from large mushrooms to use as decoration. Sauté the mushroom caps in a small pan with 1 tablespoon of butter and a squeeze of lemon juice for 2 to 3 minutes.

4. Remove the chicken breasts to warm plates for serving. Season the sauce with salt and pepper to taste. If it has become too thick, thin it with a little milk or cream. Pour the sauce over each breast and top with a mushroom cap. Sprinkle with a little chopped parsley or other herb. This is lovely served with fresh asparagus at the beginning of spring.

❧

Word traveled quickly about the couple who enjoyed cooking together and the fun we had with our students. It wasn't long before there was a waiting list for our classes. Those early classes in our kitchen led to our 25-year career, in which we wrote six cookbooks, ran successful cooking schools both in a cookware shop on Sunset Boulevard and at Robinson's, a large department store chain, and co-hosted a daily, national television series for three years, *The New Way Gourmet*.

We loved our work and traveled all over the United States, hauling our pots, pans and ingredients with us to appear nationally on *Good Morning America* and local morning talk shows everywhere. It was challenging to travel with sharp knives, a food processor, and all the fruits and vegetables we needed to assemble centerpieces on camera. Often our clothes had the distinct aroma of molding parsley. Paul used to joke, "Why don't we take up something less complicated like ant farming for our next career so we can travel lighter."

We were the headliners of newspaper-promoted food fairs in cities such as Toledo, Ohio, and Milwaukee, Wisconsin, where we put on shows for audiences of 3,500 to 4,500 people, twice a day, two or three days in a row. I treasure a photo of one marquee in front of the huge auditorium in Toledo, promoting our appearance followed by some very famous pianists:

The Toledo Blade Food Fair
Starring Diana and Paul von Welanetz
Next week: Ferrante and Teicher

Often the best demonstrations we gave were when something went wrong, and I developed a reputation for being unflappable. I would calmly repair whatever didn't turn out right, or demonstrate how to turn it into something else. "Never apologize," I would say. "Nothing is more boring than a cook who tells you the food isn't right."

On only one occasion was I so flustered that I couldn't regain my composure. A lovely deaf woman who had attended classes for years always sat in the front row so she could read my lips; she watched me one day as I prepared omelette after omelette, flaming them with brandy, and then flipped them onto a waiting plate with a showy wide-armed swing.

"Haven't you ever dropped one?" she asked.

"Never!" I boasted, as the one in the pan landed across the top of her foot, leaking butter all over her perfect pink silk shoe.

Unflappable, Unflippable Flaming Apple Omelette
Makes 4 omelettes

FILLING:
1 (24-ounce) jar chunky-style applesauce
1 tablespoon sugar
1 teaspoon ground cinnamon
2 tablespoons fresh lemon juice

Finely grated peel (yellow part only) of 1 lemon
Cognac or brandy to flambé the omelette
¼ cup of sour cream

OMELETTE:

3 eggs, per omelette *1 tablespoon butter or margarine, per omelette*

1. Make the filling first: Combine the applesauce, sugar, cinnamon, lemon juice and grated peel in a small saucepan. Bring to a simmer and cook slowly for 2 minutes to dissolve the sugar. Set out a bottle of cognac or brandy to flambé the omelette and ¼ cup of sour cream for each serving.

2. To make each omelette, place an omelette pan over medium-high heat. Break 3 eggs into a mixing bowl and beat with a whisk for 30 to 40 strokes. When the pan is quite hot, drop in 1 tablespoon butter or margarine and swirl the pan to coat the bottom and sides. When the butter has melted, pour in the eggs. Stir the eggs slowly with the end of a spatula until the egg starts cooking. Now, while rotating the pan gently in a circular fashion, lift the edges of the omelette with the spatula to allow the uncooked egg to run underneath—akin to sweeping dust under a rug. (Avoid the tendency to pull the cooked part toward the center of the pan or it will be too thick in the center.) When the egg is just firm, reduce the heat and add about ½ cup of filling in a strip down the center. Use the spatula to fold the sides in over the filling.

3. To remove the omelette from the pan, shake it gently to loosen. The most dramatic way to turn it out is to hold a warm serving plate in your left hand (left-handed cooks, use your right hand), swing the pan up in an arc and invert the omelette onto the plate. This takes practice and a little courage. A more cautious method is to shake the omelette to the edges of the pan and simply turn it over carefully on the plate. To become comfortable with your technique, sacrifice 1 or 2 dozen eggs to practice.

4. To flame the omelette, heat a tablespoon or two of cognac or brandy in a ladle over a candle or your gas flame and ignite it with a match. Hold the pan away from you and quickly pour the flaming liquid over the omelette. Move your hand away immediately to avoid the high flames that result when the liquid is ladled into the pan. Shake the pan gently until the flames die down. Turn the omelette out on a serving plate and top with a dollop of sour cream.

Once, on stage in front of a huge audience in Milwaukee, Paul and I were wearing cordless microphones so our cables wouldn't tangle as we weaved this way and that around each other in the small display kitchen. Suddenly, Paul disappeared behind the curtain. We were at a place in the program when it was his turn to demonstrate. I looked around for him, then looked at the audience and asked, "Where'd he go?" People shrugged their shoulders.

A moment later, we all heard, magnified greatly, "AHHHHH-CHOOOO!" He had tactfully withdrawn to sneeze but forgot he was wearing his mike. The following week, the food editor wrote in her column, Milwaukee owes Paul von Welanetz a giant *Gesündheit*, and printed our home address. We received hundreds of cards.

My most unflappable moment happened on the kitchen set of our television series. The show's director had given us firm orders to never "stop tape." It was not up to us to decide that one of our actions needed to be shot again. Well, one of the shows just went haywire from the very beginning, one disaster after another: Paul dropped some eggs and was cleaning them up as I was making crêpes, thin French pancakes, in a pan that had not been properly seasoned. The crêpe stuck to the pan and I had to scrape it out in shreds—what a mess! Paul and I started laughing and I said, "We really are in deep Bandini."

Still, we heard no directions to stop the show, so Paul and I proceeded through a series of dropped dishes and nervous giggles. Finally, my last move was to walk by the stovetop which had caught on fire. On the way past, I said, "Hmmm, that's quite a little blaze we have going there."

Paul did his final garnish, we raised our glasses in a toast, and we heard, "It's a wrap!" The producer aired that show just as it was, and everyone—the producers, the network, the audience—loved it!

We spent three years as the "Gourmet Gurus" for Robinson's, a large department store chain, appearing in all their advertising and in-store videos, doing numerous demonstrations for hundreds of people at a time, and serving each person in the audience a taste of all the dishes we prepared. We had a full-time assistant to help us cook the samples and check the detailed packing lists that included, besides ovens, gas burners, overhead mirrors, an elaborate sound system with microphones that Paul would set up in auditoriums while I prepped trays of supplies we would need. All our equipment fit compactly into a portable folding kitchen on wheels that we rolled up a ramp into our Volkswagen bus with the license plate PWDW62. There must have been easier ways to make a living, but it was fun and never boring.

We even got to travel internationally by hosting a series of "Gourmet Cruises" for Princess Cruise Lines, on which we invited cooking friends, James Beard, Craig Claiborne and Wolfgang Puck to join us at different destinations at sea. With all the delicious pastas served daily on the cruise ships, travel became a broadening experience in more ways than one!

We named this dish after the Italian flag because of its distinct white, green and red colors. It is wonderful to use as a pasta salad anytime, and the recipe may be multiplied to infinity. Leftovers are not to be sniffed at.

Shipboard Pasta Tricolore

Makes 8 servings

ℭ✍

⅔ cup extra-virgin olive oil
2 cloves garlic
Leaves of 2 large bunches of
 fresh basil
½ bunch fresh parsley
½ medium red onion

5 large, ripe tomatoes
1 to 2 teaspoons salt
¾ teaspoon freshly ground pepper
1½ pounds dried pasta of
 your choice (penne is a
 good choice)

1. Pour the olive oil in a large serving bowl. Mince the garlic, and chop the fresh basil, parsley, onion and tomatoes very finely. Add to the serving bowl with salt and freshly ground pepper. Cover and

leave at room temperature for at least an hour to blend the flavors.

2. Just before serving, cook the pasta in plenty of boiling water until barely tender and still chewy (*al dente*). Drain and rinse; toss immediately with the sauce. Serve warm. Any leftovers can be refrigerated to serve as a pasta salad the next day.

Our cooking career was a great adventure while it lasted, but by the early 1980s, the interest in home cooking throughout America began to change. Women were entering the workforce in record numbers, and they were now not wanting to cook so much as to be wonderfully fed. Restaurants serving all types of ethnic food and variations of The New French Cuisine began to thrive. Chefs were suddenly superstars.

By 1985, our career did not feel meaningful to us anymore; the art of fine dining was becoming less of an art and more of an exercise in trendiness. Food had become the new art form, and we felt driven in our career to compete in that arena. It just wasn't fun anymore, and it was time for a change.

Serendipitously, we were invited to attend The First International Peace Conference in the Soviet Union as part of a proposed television documentary. Our group came from many walks of life, and most were people we had heard of and admired. They included actors Dennis Weaver, Mike Farrell and Shelly Fabares, authors Alan Cohen (*The Dragon Doesn't Live Here Anymore*), futurist Barbara Marx Hubbard, international lecturer Patricia Sun, professionals in many fields, housewives, humanitarians and activists in the human potential movement. The invitation was irresistible.

It was May 1985—Cold War ideology still dominated international relations. Our role as part of this grassroots project was to be citizen diplomats and to mingle with people we met there to create some sort of citizen-to-citizen communication that might lead to more dialogue for peace between the governments of the two most powerful nations on earth.

Going to Russia seemed a highly adventurous and positive thing to do. Our friends and families were not thrilled, and the television news stations thought the idea strange and provocative enough to interview many of us before we left.

We departed with a group of 80 for Helsinki, where we received three days of indoctrination about protocol, language and logistics in the USSR. We then embarked on a railroad journey across the border first to Leningrad then Moscow. Being *Amerikanski* in the Evil Empire became one of the most demanding—and eventually enriching—experiences of our lives. We presented banners to numerous peace committees, visited churches, and had tea at home with Vladimir Posner, who was then the official liaison between the Soviet government and touring American citizens.

What we discovered on our life-altering journey was that the Soviet people were just like us. We learned that during World War II they had endured 900 straight days of bombing in Leningrad, when more than a million people had died of injuries or starvation. There wasn't a person we met who hadn't lost loved ones to the devastation. Their eyes mirrored a lifetime of grief.

Having a history of being invaded over and over again, Russians were not prone to trust foreigners, especially those from a country engaged in an arms race with theirs. They were taught English in their schools and had studied our history. They knew that there had never been a major war on American soil. "Why is your country building so many weapons?" they would ask.

One day, viewing a mass grave in Leningrad that contained 475,000 bodies, we were so saddened that our feelings about what really matters in life were forever changed. When we returned home we were more confused than ever about the direction we wanted to take in our careers. More than anything, we wanted to do something meaningful.

Soon we were attending a motivational seminar in Hollywood for people in the entertainment industry, which met three days a week from 6 to 8 A.M. It was exhilarating to be up before dawn and greeted by hundreds of high-energy people who were also actively making changes in their lives.

One day, after months of soul-searching, we had a brainstorm. Power Breakfasts were becoming the rage in New York, Los Angeles and other big cities. With our talent as hosts and our experience at producing entertainment, hauling sound systems, etc., we could create a weekly, early-morning breakfast club for people who were consciously working to improve the quality of their lives and the world around them. We would, we assumed, still have the rest of the day free to write or do whatever else we decided.

We found a distinguished restaurant, which agreed to open for a weekly breakfast, and sent out invitations to everyone we knew who shared our interests. Many of our early members weren't well-known yet, but were at the beginning of very successful careers: media psychologist Dr. Barbara DeAngelis, best-selling authors Louise L. Hay and Dr. Susan Jeffers, motivational speakers Jack Canfield and Dr. Mark Victor Hansen, and Drs. Harold Bloomfield and Sirah Vettese.

We called it "The Inside Edge." We had no idea how successful and all-consuming it would become. Within three months, we opened a second chapter 50 miles south of Los Angeles in Orange County, and then a third, 120 miles south of L.A. in San Diego. Three days a week we rose at 3:30 A.M. and drove through the dark to arrive early enough to set up microphones, name tags and everything needed for the meetings. We put in 14 hour days, at least six days a week.

By February 1986, we had more than 500 members and business was booming. *Los Angeles Magazine* did a special Valentine's Day article, featuring Paul and me as "One of the Most Romantic Couples in L.A."

We had plenty of energy and enthusiasm for our new business, but had little solid business experience, so the next four years were fraught with challenges. We joked that we were getting our doctorate degree from MTU (Making Things Up). Those were the best times and the most difficult times of our lives.

In May 1988, we completed a pilot for a television show to be called "The Breakfast Club" with producer Vin DiBona, the creator of the hit show, *America's Funniest Home Videos*. We had high hopes for the future.

That November, Paul and I celebrated our 25th anniversary. Congratulations poured in from everywhere—from friends, relatives, people who knew us through our writing and television career, people who loved us and felt they owned a part of us. We were living proof, as two devoted people who adored each other, that fairy-tale romances could come true *and* endure.

I used to laughingly say to Paul, "If you die before I do, I'll never speak to you again!" We enjoyed our little joke, because we were so sure that we'd die together at some distant time, in a plane crash or earthquake, painlessly, and never be parted. A double coffin we half-expected.

We spent our anniversary at a beachfront apartment with a sweeping ocean view loaned to us by friends in Laguna Beach. As we sipped champagne and watched the sunset, we performed an anniversary ritual of lighting a candle and spending the next few hours reminiscing about our golden moments, the triumphs we'd celebrated, and the struggles we'd endured. Overwhelmed with gratitude for our lives together, the twists and turns of our career paths, our pride in our 20-year-old daughter, we laughed and cried and congratulated each other.

"What would we have changed about those years?" we asked ourselves. The answer was simple, "Only our resistance to whatever was happening at the time."

We dressed for dinner, Paul in his tuxedo and I in a new dress, and went out for a candlelight dinner at a restaurant we both loved that served a combination of Chinese and European cuisine. It reminded us of our courtship in Hong Kong, and offered new evidence that international boundaries were not only beginning to come down, but creating a blend. The menu featured such exotic fare as the following, which is an adventure to make if Chinese ingredients are available.

Peking Pizza

Makes a 12-inch pizza

༄

A 12-inch commercial pizza crust
(such as Boboli, available fresh
in most supermarkets)

TOPPINGS:

1 tablespoon dark sesame oil
3 tablespoons hoisin *sauce*
1 tablespoon minced fresh ginger
1 bunch thinly sliced scallions
  (including some of the
  green tops)
1 tablespoon toasted sesame seeds
½ a Chinese roast duck
  (meat shredded and skin
  reserved)

6 fresh shiitake mushrooms,
  sliced (or dried shiitake,
  soaked, squeezed and sliced,
  with stems discarded)
8 ounces shredded part-skim
  mozzarella cheese
Reserved pieces of duck skin
1 tablespoon finely chopped
  cilantro (fresh coriander),
  to garnish

1. Preheat oven to 450°F and place rack in bottom third of oven. On a pizza crust arrange toppings in the following order, leaving a 1-inch margin all around: sesame oil, *hoisin* sauce, fresh ginger, sliced scallions, sesame seeds, shredded roast duck meat, sliced mushrooms, mozzarella cheese, reserved pieces of duck skin.

2. Bake approximately 20 minutes, or until the crust is browned and the duck skin very crisp. Sprinkle the top of the pizza with cilantro (fresh coriander). Let rest 10 minutes before cutting into wedges to serve.

༄

After dinner, we returned to the same spot on the couch to light a second candle with which we intended to set some goals for the *next* 25 years, but neither one of us had much to say. A foreboding thought came into my mind, "Is that all? Are we complete?" As we got into bed, I was haunted by those questions, wondering where they came from.

Two days later, Paul fell ill. What was first thought to be pneumonia turned out to be lung cancer. He lived only four months more.

Ten days before he died, Paul and I had a heart-to-heart discussion about how he wanted his affairs handled if he were to die. Though he was sedated and in pain, he forced himself to stay present with me, and seemed his old self for an hour or so while we phoned an attorney and made arrangements. That difficult job completed, I thanked him for the heroic effort he'd made. He closed his eyes, and, thinking he had drifted into a fog of sedation once more, I rose and walked toward the kitchen.

"I don't want you to be alone!" His words were firm and clear.

"Then, *send* somebody!" I replied instantly, surprising myself.

"I *will!*" he answered.

He did.

At the moment Paul died, I felt suddenly expanded, as though he merged right into me. I walked out of the hospital alone after midnight, the bright moonlit night was clear and windy; it had a surreal feeling, the air sparkling and electric with change. A deep peace descended on me and I sensed there would be yet a new part to our love relationship.

As much as I missed his physical presence, I didn't feel lonely for him because I could feel him with me. Perhaps in losing each other physically, we could be together in a new way, a way that transcends physical death.

Paul seemed to be with me every minute of the days that followed. When alone, I found myself speaking out loud to him and feeling his responses. The night before his memorial service, as I got ready for bed, I suddenly felt a void where I had sensed his presence. "*Where's Paul?*" I wondered

"Where are you?" I asked. No response.

But, when I awoke the next morning I could feel him back again. I perceived him encouraging and comforting Lexi and me as we made last-minute preparations for the service.

I had written to everyone we knew:

Paul and I believed that each life is a work of art. Our marriage was our masterpiece, a rich tapestry of love, aliveness and growth, woven brilliantly and spectacularly with triumphs and celebrations. Now it is complete. Lexi and I are filled with gratitude that we had these past months to be gently weaned from Paul's protectiveness. We ask you to release him to his highest good, and to remember him with all the celebration that we feel for him in our hearts.

Hundreds of people came, mostly members of The Inside Edge, plus our families and many old friends from our cooking days. Mara Getz, Paul's favorite vocalist, sang "The Wind Beneath My Wings" to his friend Zavier's guitar accompaniment. Then the minister, Dr. Peggy Bassett, invited those gathered to share stories about Paul. In the telling, we were all reminded of his kindness and nobility, how he had lived his life with courage and wisdom and heart. As friends shared their favorite memories of times spent with him, and of his endearing idiosyncrasies, we could all feel a level of joy and celebration rising within us, and in my heart I could hear Paul's familiar laughter, feel his gentle hug.

After the service, one of Paul's buddies from the men's discussion group, The Razor's Edge, told me, "We had a party, a sort of wake, for Paul last night that was wonderful. It felt like he was really there."

"Oh, *that's* where he was!" I said, delighted to have an explanation for his absence the night before.

Our friend Marilyn arrived towing a trailer filled with 500 helium balloons. After the service, everyone gathered on the lawn outside the church to release them into the sky together. As the balloons floated away, disappearing into the clouds, one lingered behind, bobbing and dancing in the breeze. We all knew it was Paul, waving goodbye.

A young woman named Andrea Bell, whom Paul and I had befriended and helped early in her career, had gone on to become one of the most successful caterers in Los Angeles. She telephoned the day before the memorial service to ask if people would be coming back to our home afterwards. I hadn't thought about it, but I liked the idea, and she offered to provide the food. More than a hundred people came through the door to find a lavish buffet of croissant sandwiches and pasta salads and desserts. I will never forget that act of kindness. (Be sure to try Andrea's Carrot Orange Bisque on page 420. It is spectacular!)

Friends and family worried that I was in a state of denial in the months that followed Paul's death, and probably I was. If so, denial is wonderful; it felt much more like a state of grace.

With the support of our daughter Lexi, and Lauren, my office manager, I continued to run our business.

Dr. Barbara DeAngelis, who had become a close friend in the days before Paul died, told me, "Diana, Paul awakened you to your potential. He spent his life encouraging you and nurturing you. But his mission will not be complete until you can walk alone as an independent human being."

Paul and I married when I was only 22. Walking alone was a completely new adventure for me, and I was frightened, though intrigued, by the challenge. If only I could ease the grief that overwhelmed me at times. Well, maybe I could!

Paul and I had both been impressed with results achieved by Tim Piering, one of our most popular morning speakers and the author of *Breaking Free to Mental and Financial Independence*, in helping people overcome their fears by doing what they were most afraid of. I decided to make an appointment with him.

We met early one Saturday morning at his office in Sierra Madre. We talked awhile and he asked if Paul would want me to grieve. I found it hard to imagine he would have. Then Tim took me on a drive high into the mountains nearby. He parked and led me out onto a bridge which spanned a dry river bed 300 feet below. I watched as he attached ropes and a pulley to himself, then climbed over the railing and rapelled to the bottom of the canyon. Climbing back up the hill, he called, "Want to try it?"

"No way!"

He went over the side once again, showing me how he could maneuver up and down with the pulley, and how a safety rope was in place just in case. It did seem very safe, and I began to feel that maybe I could do it, and said that I might try it some day. With that small bit of encouragement, Tim wasted no time strapping me in gear and attaching a rope to my rapelling ring. He showed me how to gradually roll the pulley and how to come to a complete stop during the descent. He attached the safety rope to himself, and said, "Okay. Now just step over the railing."

"HA! Easy for you to say."

"It's a metaphor, Diana, for how willing you are to really go for the gold in your life."

I can't remember ever being more physically terrified. I, who had recurring nightmares about teetering on a window ledge, trembled at just the thought of lifting my leg over the railing. Very, very slowly, I eased one leg over saying, "Oh, my God, I am so scared!" Tim held both of my hands against the railing as I lifted the second leg over, still leaning as far as I could back toward him.

"Let's just forget the whole thing," I said.

"You don't have to do this, Diana. It's your decision."

Once again, I resolved to try.

"Now, let go with one hand and hold the rope tightly so you won't start moving."

At this point I was so frightened I was bleating like a sheep. But then, I did as Tim said. I think that was the crucial moment, letting go of the first hand. Then the second hand, and there I was, swinging in small arcs over the canyon. So far, so good.

"Now . . . very slowly . . . inch your way down a foot or two." That worked alright. At that moment, the fear transformed into excitement. I spent a long time lowering myself to the bottom, relishing the view and my victory. Tim ran down to meet me.

"Look what you did, Diana! You *did* it!"

I had, hadn't I?

❧

Here is a recipe that I find comforting to make when the world is topsy-turvy. The batter turns all sorts of weird colors when I am mixing it, from purple to a terrible gray brown, a result of its interesting chemistry. At that point it gives no hint of the very beautiful and satisfying loaf it will become.

Plum-Crazy Bread

Makes a 9 x 5-inch loaf

❧

Recipe courtesy of Frances Pelham.

1 (1-pound, 13-ounce) can purple plums	½ teaspoon ground cinnamon
	½ teaspoon ground cloves
1 stick (¼ pound) butter	½ cup seedless raisins
2 teaspoons baking soda	¾ cup finely chopped walnuts
2 cups sifted flour	
1 cup sugar	Whipped cream cheese, for serving
½ teaspoon salt	

1. Preheat oven to 350°F. Butter and flour a 9 x 5-inch loaf pan. Drain the plums; remove the pits and purée the pulp in a blender or food processor. In a saucepan, heat the pulp with the butter, stirring until melted. Remove from the heat and place in a large mixing bowl. Stir in baking soda—the mixture will foam and take on an unappetizing charcoal brown color at this point—don't worry about it. (I told you this was crazy bread!) Let the mixture cool to lukewarm.

2. Add flour, sugar, salt, cinnamon, cloves, raisins and walnuts. Mix well, then pour into the prepared pan. Bake for 70 to 80 minutes, until the center is firm. Cool for 1 hour in the pan, then turn out onto a rack. Serve warm with whipped cream cheese. Yum!

❧

"Who am I without Paul?" I wondered in the weeks that followed. When friends called and offered me their home on a quiet beach in Kauai for a week, I eagerly accepted. There I spent time in solitude, walking, thinking, writing in my journal, following most every whim.

I explored my new-found freedom, and for the first time in over 26 years, I asked myself what was pleasing to *me*, instead of to *us*. I treasured the private, uninterrupted days of reading, searching the beach for sea shells, eating popcorn for breakfast if I wished. In that solitude, dormant sexual yearnings stirred. Gazing at myself in the mirror, I wondered if I would, in time, recycle my 48-year-old body into a new relationship. In restaurants and markets I began to watch men and study them. How could any man ever live up to the memory of the husband I'd had? Paul had been handsome, wise, poetic, kind, devoted, romantic, a perfect prince. I'd been the envy of many women over the years. I couldn't imagine being with anyone else.

Meanwhile, Ted, still on his search, was invited as a guest to our Orange County breakfast meeting. He later told his daughter that the instant he entered the restaurant, he *knew* his future wife was in the room.

It was my first morning back at work. I stood at a microphone on a stage in front of the crowded room hosting the morning meeting. I knew the audience well—they were friends and supporters who had been through the past months with me and were eager to hear about my Hawaiian sojourn and how I was faring. Knowing that people feel awkward around those who have recently lost a loved one, I decided to be light about it to put them at ease. I described how beautiful and relaxing Hawaii had been, then jokingly said, "I'm enjoying my solitude; so much, in fact, that the first man who looks at me with the idea of a live-in relationship may just become the victim of an axe murder!" Shocked laughter and applause were their responses.

After the meeting, as I was mingling with the group, a voice behind me asked, "Will you live with me?"

I spun around and looked into the bright blue eyes of a man I'd never seen before. Startled, I raised my hand as if I had an axe, and he ducked away. I grinned and moved on, giving it no more thought.

I continued to savor my solitude in the months ahead. When you are in a relationship, or even if you are caring for or raising a child, there is always an allowance for interruption. That permission is at the heart of any relationship. Now, I appreciated this time of knowing I would not be interrupted. I spent my alone time doing whatever interested me, feeling Paul still with me as the days passed, though not as intensely as in the beginning.

Each Wednesday night, to save driving time between Los Angeles and San Diego, I stayed by myself at the same apartment on the beach our friends the Probstein's had loaned us for our anniversary. Simply furnished, carpet and over-stuffed furniture the color of sand, masses of pillows in ocean blue, that peaceful spot became my cocoon. One night I was listening to music on the extraordinary sound system, and as the sun was setting, I was moved to dance. I was wearing a nightgown I loved, and I whirled, spun and drifted to the music for a long time. The phone rang. It was Lexi. "What are you doing?"

"I'm dancing in my nightgown to Barbra Streisand and watching the sun go down."

"I'm glad *I'm* not there."

"Me, too," I said, "Because I couldn't do this if there were anybody here."

I was alone, but because I still felt Paul's protective presence, I was not lonely. I had many men friends in my business, and often had lunch with different ones, yet after a few months I began to wonder what it would be like to go out on a date. If Paul were going to send somebody, how would I know?

One morning, the speaker at the San Diego breakfast addressed the subject of flirting. It was a concept I hadn't given any thought to in a very long time. She explained that flirting was simply being friendly and making oneself available. I found myself embarrassed even to be thinking of it.

She said, "Now, everybody, please stand up and look around. Pick someone of the opposite sex and walk up to them. Your assignment is to say something as outrageous as possible."

I glanced around to see if I could escape quietly from the room, but I could hear people in the room laughing and having a good time, so I made myself participate.

I spotted an old friend nearby, a very attractive man, who was safely in a relationship.

Blushing madly, I blurted, "Hey, Bill! I think you're hot!"

He hugged me and tried his line out on me. "Hey, Diana! I think you have a really great body."

We laughed at our silliness, and with that simple exercise, the idea of flirting became humorous and much, much easier.

The following Saturday was The Inside Edge annual picnic, with 400 people in attendance. The night before, on impulse, I went to a toy store and bought a silly squirt gun that looked like a hot dog in a bun. At the picnic I playfully squirted different people, mostly men, who chased me rather politely. Everyone was respectful; no one was playful. I was, after all, a sort of mother superior type who ran the organization.

When I saw Ted Wentworth (who was looking very cute that day— a bit like Robin Williams in shorts and a baseball cap) I squirted him, too. But his reaction was much different than the others. He took off after me with a vengeance. And caught me! Before I knew it, he wrestled the gun out of my hand and squirted me back, right in the face! So much for unflappable—I was in shock.

He grinned at the look on my face and said, "Aw, I'm sorry, pretty lady! Here, come with me."

He led me to a nearby water fountain to refill my gun. As he handed it back to me, he asked, "So, are you going to have dinner with me?"

Our first date was an early dinner—before a meeting we were both attending. I enjoyed it, so the following week when I was in Orange County again, we made a date for dinner at Ted's house. I was impressed that he would offer to cook for me, knowing my background. (Over the years, few people ever volunteered to do that, thinking Paul and I dined only on the most sophisticated and elegantly presented dishes—such as quail eggs and miniature hot-house vegetables.) As I followed his telephone directions to his home, I felt very shy and a bit frightened of feeling trapped in some sort of strange bachelor pad.

But his home atop Spyglass Hill was beautiful. He was especially proud of his garden, built during his late wife's illness, and of a pink sandstone he had selected and quarried in Sedona, Arizona. He showed me around the house, then served grilled fish and a baked potato for dinner on the patio. He forgot to serve the rolls he'd put in the oven and I found that endearing.

For dessert, Ted suggested we go for an ice cream cone and a walk around nearby Balboa Island. He confessed to me later that I was a few years older than his ideal future wife specifications, so he put me to a little test. "Do you want to go in the car or on my motorcycle?"

"Oh, let's go on the motorcycle." I said. Whew! I passed!

After a mile or so of walking, Ted took my hand to help me aboard the ferry, then again to help me off, but the second time he didn't let go. We walked and talked for hours. It was the first time I had held another man's hand in 26 years and it felt strange . . . exciting . . . a little bit dangerous.

From the beginning Ted made me laugh. He simply looks at the world through a different slat in the fence than most people do. I liked his aliveness, intelligence and rapid-fire wit.

I didn't think of him romantically at first, but I did enjoy talking with him. We had so much in common: losing our spouses to cancer, daughters the same age (my 21-year-old Lexi was born right in the middle of his Christy and Kathy, making them all eight months apart), and our passion for similar subjects. Ted said he didn't want to alarm me by calling me too much. He encouraged me to be the one to make the moves when I wanted to see him or talk to him or advance our relationship in any way. Because I lived in Los Angeles and he lived 50 miles away in Newport Beach we spent hours talking on the phone. Our developing friendship felt comfortable and safe. I loved the way I felt around him—warm, respected, protected.

We were talking on the phone one day when I mentioned the possibility of getting together the following Saturday. Ted suggested we go to Catalina Island for the weekend on his boat. I was startled and wanted to be very clear with him that I was not suggesting spending a whole weekend together and that the thought of doing that was a bit terrifying to me. He reassured me that he would continue to let me make the moves when I was ready. Before hanging up, he asked how I was feeling about our conversation. I said, "Warm and fuzzy."

Two hours later, eighteen long-stemmed American Beauty roses arrived. The card read:

Dear Warm:
Watch the buds—like a friendship, each opens a petal at a time.

Fuzzy

The following Saturday we had lunch together on his patio. When he gave me a choice of a boat ride or a flight in his Cessna 210, I chose flying. Ted drove me to John Wayne airport right up to the plane, parking under the wing. Before we got out, he leaned close to me, and looked into my eyes.

"Diana, I will open my heart to you completely and at the most profound levels. And, if you need to leave, I'll understand."

I leaned closer and kissed him. His lips felt wonderful. It was then I realized I was in love.

I learned early on that Ted was extraordinarily intuitive. One evening, sitting at my computer, I had a very sharp stomach pain. It made me gasp, but it didn't last long and I chalked it up to eating too much popcorn. (I had become quite a popcorn addict and ate it several times a day.)

Moments later, the telephone rang and Ted asked, "What was that pain?"

I'd already forgotten and said, "What pain?"

"The one in your abdomen, just to the left of your navel."

"How did you know about that?"

He told me he had been out for a walk, felt the pain, and realized it wasn't his own, "so I figured it was yours."

Not long after that, I thought it might be fun to test that intuitive ability, so I mentally sent him a message to call me. The phone rang within minutes. *"What?"* Ted asked.

One Thursday, as a further test, I mentally sent him a message to send me flowers again. Nothing happened, and I didn't give it any more thought. Late Friday afternoon he drove me to Temecula to visit his ranch for the first time. As he showed me around the hilltop ranch house I saw two arrangements of flowers with cards that had my name on them.

"How sweet of you!"

"Well, one is because you wanted them yesterday," he said. "There was no point in sending them to your house because you were going to be here with me. The other one is for today, to say, 'I'm happy you're here.' "

That evening we dined at Ted's favorite restaurant, where he was eager to have me taste the chicken in red wine that he calls the best Coq au Vin in the world. A puzzled look came over his face. "Was Paul very square-shouldered, and did he eat like this?" Ted lifted his fork in a special way Paul had and I said, "Yes."

"He's *in* me, Diana." And later, leaving the restaurant, he said, "I have a strange desire to throw money on the sidewalk." I told him Paul would always drop change from his pockets for children to find.

Ferrari Bistro Coq au Vin
Makes 8 servings

ɘ

The Ferraris serve this with homemade noodles with a light cream sauce and a sprinkling of fresh Parmesan cheese. (Recipe courtesy of Josette and Giuseppe Ferrari.)

2 (3- to 4-pound) chickens,
   cut up
½ cup vegetable oil
4 tablespoons (¼ cup) flour
¼ cup cognac or brandy
3 onions, quartered
2 cloves minced garlic
1 bottle (750 ml) red Burgundy
   (about 3 cups)
1 tablespoon tomato paste
⅛ teaspoon crumbled dried
   thyme

1 tablespoon sugar
1 teaspoon salt
Freshly-ground pepper
4 sprigs celery and 4 celery
   tops tied with string
2 whole bay leaves
1 pint mushrooms
1 tablespoon butter
1 tablespoon or so Madeira
   (and perhaps a little
   more cognac)
Chopped fresh parsley

BROWN COLORING *(a classic French technique):*
¼ cup sugar   1 teaspoon vegetable oil
¼ cup water   A few drops red food coloring
2 tablespoons boiling water

1. Rinse and dry the chicken pieces well. In a large skillet, heat H cup vegetable oil and brown the chicken pieces. When brown, pour off the oil, leaving any brown and crusty pieces in the bottom of the pan. Remove the skin from the chicken and return to the pan. Sprinkle flour over the chicken pieces and stir with a wooden spoon until the flour is absorbed. Heat cognac or brandy in a ladle over a flame, ignite it with a match, and pour it over the chicken; shake the pan until the flame dies. Add the quartered onions to the pan and sauté until soft.

2. Stir in garlic, Burgundy, tomato paste, thyme, sugar, salt and freshly ground pepper to your liking. Stir often until the mixture starts to boil. Meanwhile, tie together the celery sprigs and tops with string; add to the pot with bay leaves. When the liquid begins to boil, reduce the heat, cover and simmer slowly for about an hour.

3. Rinse the mushrooms briefly. If the mushroom caps are small, leave them whole; if large, cut into quarters through the stem. Melt 1 tablespoon butter in a medium skillet, sauté the mushrooms for 2 minutes and set aside.

4. Make the brown coloring—any extra may be stored in the refrigerator for other uses. In a small skillet, boil the sugar and water until the sugar caramelizes and turns a very dark, burnt brown (sugar loses its sweetness when it is burnt). Add boiling water, oil and red food coloring. Stir, cool and then store until ready to use.

5. When ready to serve the chicken, discard the parsley/celery bundle and bay leaves. Color the sauce to a rich red-brown with a bit of the brown food coloring. Stir in a tablespoon or so of Madeira, a little more cognac, if desired, then taste and adjust seasonings.

6. Place chicken on serving plates. If sauce needs to be a little thicker, cook it, stirring, over high heat for a minute or two to evaporate some of the liquid. Top the chicken with sauce and sprinkle with fresh parsley.

෴

Once a week or so, Ted would tell me he could feel Paul come into him. It would be when we were dancing or doing something Paul enjoyed. Ted said he didn't mind, that he was willing to share me.

Ted's marriage proposal was very romantic and absolutely perfect. On Friday morning I packed for what I thought was to be a weekend in Carmel, just north of Big Sur on the Central Coast of California. We had spent several weekends there and it seemed an ideal spot, in my mind, for what I suspected would happen. I should have known that Ted is never predictable.

Ted picked me up at Santa Monica Airport and I hopped aboard his plane with the special dress he told me to bring to wear to dinner. We flew far enough north to be out of the high-traffic zones, and I served us a lunch of sandwiches and fresh fruit.

Before long, I noticed that we were not flying along the coastline, like we usually did, but farther inland. I watched curiously as he circled and landed in the tiny airport in Mariposa. Within minutes, a rental car drove up to the plane, we transferred the luggage, and we were off for an hour's drive to Yosemite National Park and the historic Ahwahnee Hotel.

Ted had reserved the most romantic table in the immense, vaulted-ceiling dining room, next to a 20-foot-high arched window that looked out over the grounds and the forest beyond. Of course, I knew what was coming along with dinner, but I marveled at how sweet both the setting and his words were.

Ted reached for my hand and said, "Diana, what I love about our relationship is . . ." and then he spent the first three courses of our dinner telling me all the things he loved about who we are together.

Over dessert, he took both my hands, looked at me shyly and asked, "So, will you marry me?" I was flooded with a sense that this was absolutely right, just as I'd known that marrying Paul was right.

"I would love to marry you!"

Tears in his eyes, he smiled broadly and said, "Start shopping for a ring. You may have any ring you want!"

When I telephoned my best friend, Mary Kelly, in Hawaii with news that Ted and I would marry, she said, "Wow! You certainly have a *short shelf-life!*"

Since Mary has a ministerial license, she performed our marriage service in front of a few close friends and both of our families, when Mary and her husband Don came to visit us on their own honeymoon. At our request, she invited the spirits of Sharon and Paul to participate in the ceremony. No one present doubted that they were there, silently applauding, wishing us joy.

We have been married five years now. It is easy living with a man who shares with me the experience of being widowed. We cherish being able to talk, without editing, about our previous spouses whenever a memory or a new level of grief rises to the surface. We know we don't feel less love for each other because we still feel so much love for them. And neither of us minds being called by our predecessors' names. (Good thing! It happens often.)

People sometimes ask how my first marriage compared with this one. I tell them that though I certainly had never expected a double feature, I would say that my first marriage was poignant like *Love Story*, and this one is more along the lines of *Romancing the Stone*—a romantic comedy-adventure full of surprises.

And, yes, Paul still shows up. The eeriest proof of Paul's presence so far was the result of the wide personality difference between my two men. Paul was an artist and very visual. If I changed my nail polish, bought a new lipstick or curled my hair a different way, Paul noticed and commented immediately.

But often I've wondered if Ted sees me at all. I go to special effort to look nice and he just doesn't notice. Once, I even tried on some green contact lenses over my dark brown eyes and when Ted got home, I asked if he noticed anything different.

"No."

"Look in my eyes. Now, do you notice anything different?"

"Gee, Diana, I'm sorry but I don't. You look very pretty."

Ted does feel me, though. There is no question about that, and over time, his seeing me has lost importance. (Good thing, too. I'm a bit vain and not getting any younger.)

Imagine my surprise not long ago when we walked into a department store and Ted stopped suddenly and said, "Diana! *Those earrings!*"

"*What* earrings?"

"Those *daisy* earrings!"

I saw a large display of single and double daisy earrings on the counter.

"What *about* them?"

"*Paul* wants you to have those daisy earrings!"

"Which ones?"

"The single daisies with the yellow centers."

I felt a chill as I approached the display for a closer look. They were nearly identical to a pair I wore for years—Paul's favorite earrings that he repaired for me year after year.

When these things happen I know that Paul is telling me, "This is the *someone*, Kitten. Isn't it great? You can have us both!"

11
For the Fun of It!

I wish I'd drunk more champagne.
—Last words of Maynard Keynes, economist

An English Prayer

Give me a good digestion, Lord,
and also something to digest;
Give me a healthy body, Lord,
and a sense to keep it at its best;
Give me a healthy mind, good Lord,
to keep the good and pure in sight,
Which, seeing sin, is not appalled,
But finds a way to set it right.

Give me a mind that is not bound,
that does not whimper, whine, or sigh.
Don't let me worry over much
about the fussy thing called I.
Give me a sense of humor, Lord;
Give me the grace to see a joke,
To get some happiness from life
and pass it on to other folk.

—Found on the wall of England's Chester Cathedral

Sweet Revenge

Diana von Welanetz Wentworth

Seldom have I seen such calculating mirth. She is a nun on a spiritual mission as she lifts her left leg, leans back and takes aim with a softball. Her target is a small round board that will drop the brown-robed cleric into the vat of cold water. Yes, there is more going on here at the Friary of San Lorenzo in the hills of Santa Ynez than a simple game of Dunk the Monk. This is about revenge. I know about revenge. I lie awake at night plotting comeuppance for *my* spiritual companion.

We are in a meadow amid rolling hills, surrounded by booths selling crafts, homemade jams and pies, and on-the-spot haircuts, enveloped by smoke from juicy barbecued Italian sausages. We were led here through centipeding green meadows by following road signs that promised a country fair. I'm a sucker for such folksy rural events and have promised Ted a rewarding stop.

Blue tarps stretch from pole to pole to protect the booths from too much springtime sun. People lounge on haystacks watching the milk-bottle throw, the beanbag toss and the meadow-muffin drop. A young boy and girl battle it out with pillows atop two sawhorses. Their eyes are alight with the goal of getting even!

Ted has taught me that there is a principle of good-natured revenge between couples that adds a little pepper to the marriage pot! When you know you've been had, the soul jumps out to play!

Occasionally, Ted has something delectable on his plate and makes a pretense of preparing the most perfect bite for me. After arranging it just so, he brings the fork toward my waiting mouth. Just as I am ready to bite down, I watch it move away and disappear into his mouth. He smiles, and I pretend I am annoyed. Once more he carefully prepares a special taste and offers it to me. In my determination to eat it this time, I nearly bite the plastic fork in half.

"Tastes twice as good now, doesn't it?" he says.

We visit the pastry booth for dessert.

"My doctor says I will never outgrow my need for chocolate," Ted murmurs as he orders a chocolate brownie for himself, peanut butter pie for me. He wolfs his down as I slowly savor every bite of mine. Bam! He's finished his and stolen an edge of the perfect section of pie I pushed aside to savor last.

"Slow tax!" he yells as he dashes away. Slow tax is Ted's shrewd rationalization for stealing a piece of what is left on the plate of a slow eater after he has cleaned his own plate. I begin to laugh at memories of all the taxes he has collected from me.

Toward the parking lot, we see that the nun is back for a second try. The wind-up, the toss and splash! The soaking-wet friar gets up slowly in the tub of cold water, grinning sheepishly.

"You're very quiet," Ted remarks as we drive away.

I give him a sideways look and a sly smile. *Ah, yes*, I think to myself, *revenge will be sweet.* (To be continued . . .)

Sweet Revenge Brownies

Makes 48 brownies

Ted likes these warm from the oven, topped with vanilla bean ice cream.

6 ounces unsweetened baking chocolate
2 sticks (½ pound) butter
2 cups white sugar
4 large eggs
1 cup all-purpose flour
1 tablespoon pure vanilla extract
2 cups mini-marshmallows
1½ cups semi-sweet chocolate chips, divided

1. Preheat oven to 300°F. (Do not attempt to bake at a higher temperature, or the brownies will burn.) Generously grease an 8×12-inch baking pan, or use a foil pan from the supermarket which is great for freezing or presenting the brownies as a gift.

2. Combine chocolate and butter in a medium saucepan. Melt over medium-low heat, stirring constantly, until the chocolate is nearly melted. Remove from heat and stir until smooth.

3. Whisk in the white sugar until blended, followed by the eggs, one at a time, the flour and the vanilla.

4. Fold in the mini-marshmallows and 1 cup of chocolate chips.

5. Pour into the prepared baking pan and smooth evenly. Sprinkle the remaining ½ cup chocolate chips on top.

6. Bake for about 53 to 55 minutes, or until a toothpick inserted in the center comes out clean. Do not overbake. Cool to room temperature. Wrap in foil and store at room temperature or freeze. Cut into 48 squares for serving.

Somebody Slept in My Hair!

Diana von Welanetz Wentworth

"Somebody slept in my hair," Ted is likely to mumble as he looks from the bed into the mirror across the room.

"Yep, it's called bed-head," I say. "Now get back in here and hug me."

Is there anything more delicious than snuggling under the covers with the person you love? Especially on a Saturday morning when there is no need to hurry, when you can just enjoy the warmth and doze awhile?

Sometimes to Ted there is. It might be birding. (He can identify most every bird and loves to take early walks in the sanctuaries nearby, binoculars around his neck.) Or boating. (We go back and forth across the 26-mile channel to Catalina whenever the weekend weather is nice enough.) Or an early stroll around Balboa Island doling out scraps of bread to the ducks on the beach.

I usually have a warning that he is feeling adventurous and my languor is to be short-lived because he kicks his feet in the air and says, "FEEET," which, I've learned, means that his feet are ready to get up, get out and get going.

But one morning, there was no warning. Ted got up and crept around the end of the bed. Suddenly two strong hands on my ankles pulled my legs to the floor from the bottom of the bed. This left me in an awkward backbend, nightie askew, with my head still under the covers. It never happened again—some things are only funny once.

Now, he has a new strategy. If he hears me slip out of bed to visit the bathroom, he's up in a flash and makes the bed in a hurry before I return. Outfoxes me every time!

I am good-naturedly resigned to Ted's early Saturday schedule because he adds so much adventure and fun to what would otherwise be a rather sedentary writer's life. Let's be honest—if I insisted on dawdling in bed, I'd miss the flight of the black-capped night herons of Balboa Island heading for bed in Huntington Beach, or the sight of acorn woodpeckers filling up a thousand holes in a telephone pole near our ranch, or the first bite of a warm Chocolate Cinnamon Roll, which just wouldn't taste right any other time of day.

This recipe was shared with me by my first mother-in-law. They are easy to make. I keep them individually wrapped in foil in the freezer, then just pop them in a 300°F oven for 20 to 30 minutes while we dress. In no time, they are ready to nibble in the car or on Ted's motorcycle.

Gram's Chocolate Cinnamon Rolls

Makes 10 rolls

∾

(*Recipe reprinted from* Celebrations, A Menu Cookbook for Informal Entertaining, *by Diana and Paul von Welanetz [J.P. Tarcher].*)

DOUGH:

1 package active dry yeast	*1 egg*
½ stick (¾ cup) butter	*½ teaspoon salt*
¼ cup cocoa	*2¼ cups flour*
¼ cup sugar	

FILLING:

3 tablespoons softened butter	*½ cup miniature chocolate*
2 heaping tablespoons	*chips*
crumbled brown sugar	*⅓ cup finely chopped walnuts*
1½ teaspoons cinnamon	*or pecans*

GLAZE:

2 tablespoons soft butter   *Cream or milk*
¾ cup powdered sugar

1. Butter a 9-inch round cake pan. Stir the yeast into ¾ cup warm water and set aside.

2. In the large bowl of an electric mixer, beat together butter, cocoa, sugar, egg, salt and 1 cup of the flour. Stir in the yeast mixture and continue beating 2 minutes at medium speed. Remove the beaters and mix in 1¼ cups more flour with a wooden spoon or your hands. Turn out onto a floured surface and knead for a few minutes until smooth. Return to the bowl, cover with a damp towel and let rise in a warm spot for 1 hour or until doubled.

3. Punch the air out of the dough and place on buttered foil. Roll into a 12 × 9-inch rectangle. Spread softened butter over the dough, sprinkle with brown sugar, cinnamon, chocolate chips and walnuts or pecans. Roll up lengthwise. Cut into 10 equal slices and arrange, cut-side down and sides touching, in prepared pan. Again, cover with a damp towel and allow to rise in a warm place for about 30 minutes until doubled in size. Meanwhile, preheat oven to 375°F.

4. Bake rolls for 25 minutes, or until lightly browned. Remove from oven and spread tops with 2 tablespoons soft butter. Combine powdered sugar and enough cream or milk to make a glaze; spread over the rolls. Serve warm.

Calories That Don't Count

Author Unknown—submitted by Bobbie Lippman

1. FOOD ON FOOT. All food eaten while standing has no calories. Exactly why is not clear, but the current theory relates to gravity. The calories apparently bypass the stomach, flowing directly down the legs and through the soles of the feet into the floor, like electricity. Walking appears to accelerate this process, so that an ice cream bar or hot dog eaten at the state fair actually has a calorie deficit.

2. TV FOOD. Anything eaten in front of the TV has no calories. This may have something to do with radiation leakage, which negates not only the calories in the food but all recollections of having eaten it.

3. UNEVEN EDGES. Pies and cakes should be cut neatly in even wedges or slices. If not, the responsibility falls on the person putting them away to "straighten up the edges" by slicing away the offending irregularities, which have no calories when eaten.

4. BALANCE FOOD. If you drink a diet soda with a candy bar, they cancel each other out.

5. LEFT-HANDED FOOD. If you have a glass of punch in your right hand, anything eaten with the other hand has no calories. Several principles are at work here. First of all, you're probably standing up at a wedding reception (see FOOD ON FOOT). Then there's the electronic field. A wet glass in one hand forms a negative charge to reverse the polarity of the

calories attracted to the other hand. It's not quite known how it works, but it's reversible if you're left-handed.

6. FOOD FOR MEDICINAL PURPOSES. Food used for medicinal purposes *never* counts. This includes hot chocolate, malted milk, toast and Sara Lee cheesecake.

7. WHIPPED CREAM, SOUR CREAM, BUTTER. These all act as a poultice that actually "draws out" the calories when placed on any food, leaving them calorie-free. Afterward, you can eat the poultice, too, as all calories are neutralized by it.

8. FOOD ON TOOTHPICKS. Sausage, mini-franks, cheese and crackers are all fattening *unless* impaled on frilled toothpicks. The insertion of a sharp object allows the calories to leak out the bottom.

9. CHILDREN'S FOOD. Anything produced, purchased or intended for minors is calorie-free when eaten by adults. This category covers a wide range, beginning with a spoonful of baby-food custard, consumed for demonstration purposes, up to and including cookies baked to send to college.

10. CHARITABLE FOODS. Girl Scout Cookies, bake-sale cakes, ice cream socials and church strawberry festivals all have a religious dispensation from calories.

11. CUSTOM-MADE FOOD. Anything somebody makes "just for you" must be eaten regardless of calories because to do otherwise would be uncaring and insensitive. Our kind intentions will not go unrewarded.

Guide to Calorie Burning

Author Unknown—submitted by Bobbie Lippman

Beating around the bush 75
Jumping to conclusions...100
Climbing the walls..150
Swallowing your pride...50
Passing the buck...25
Throwing your weight around
    (depending on your weight) 50–300
Dragging your heels..100
Pushing your luck 250
Making mountains out of molehills 500
Hitting the nail on the head 50
Wading through paperwork......................................300
Bending over backwards 75
Jumping on the bandwagon 200
Balancing the books..25
Running around in circles...350
Eating crow 225
Tooting your own horn 25
Climbing the ladder of success...............................750
Pulling out the stops 75
Adding fuel to the fire...150
Wrapping it up at the day's end..............................12

Where Do You Buy "Scratch"?

Author Unknown

My mother never let me help much in the kitchen. As a result, my cooking ability was practically nonexistent when I got married. But I did remember Mother mentioning to her friends that she'd made cakes, pies and other things from scratch. So my first priority after the honeymoon was to locate some scratch. With Mother's delicious cakes in mind, my first trip to the supermarket was to buy some scratch. I found the aisle that read "baking items." I spent a good 15 minutes looking at everything from vegetable oil, sugar, flour and chocolate, without seeing a sign of scratch. I was sure it wouldn't be with the pickles or the meat. I asked the clerk if they carried scratch. He looked at me funny and finally said, "You'll have to go to the store on the corner." When I got there, it turned out to be a feed store. I thought it rather strange, but I decided cakes were feed. "Do you have scratch?" I asked the clerk. He asked me how much I wanted. I suggested a pound or two. His reply was, "How many chickens do you have? It only comes in 20-pound bags." I really didn't understand why he mentioned chickens, but I had heard Mother say she made chicken casserole from scratch so I bought 20 pounds and hurried home.

My next problem was to find a recipe calling for scratch. I went through every single page of my lovely *Better Homes and Gardens Cookbook,* given as a wedding present, looking for a recipe calling for scratch. There I was with 20 pounds of scratch and no recipe.

When I opened the scratch I had doubts that a beautiful fluffy cake would ever result from such a hard-looking ingredient. I hoped with the addition of liquids and heat, the result would be successful. I had no need to mention my problem to my husband as he suggested very early in our marriage he liked to cook and would gladly take over anytime. One day he made a pie and when I told him how good it was, he said he made it from scratch. That assured me it could be done.

Being a new bride is scary and when I found out he made pies, cakes and even lemon pudding from scratch . . . well, if he made all those things from scratch I was sure he had bought a 20-pound bag also. But I couldn't find where he stored it and I checked my supply . . . it was still full.

At this point I was ready to give up because all the people knew about scratch except me.

I decided to try a different approach. One day when my husband was not doing anything, I said, "Honey, I wish you'd bake a cake." He got out the flour, sugar, eggs, milk and shortening, but not a sign of scratch. I watched him blend it together, pour it into a pan and slide it into the oven to bake. An hour later as we were eating the cake, I looked at him and smiled and said, "Honey, why don't we raise a few chickens?"

The Great Horseradish Caper

Theodore S. Wentworth

Life is too serious to be taken seriously.

—Oscar Wilde

Serve the dinner backward, do anything—but for goodness sake, do something weird.

—Elsa Maxwell

Diana has written numerous essays about me in this book, so you probably know by now that I have a rather unusual, conceptual sense of humor. Diana wonders where it comes from, so I asked my mother Alice. She said it definitely comes from the Althisar side of her family. She then went into a long tale about her childhood, and about her grandfather, Charles Althisar, whom I particularly resemble.

Charlie had red hair and a mustache, was rather round (I'm not), and he loved to sing Irish love songs to his Mame and play tricks on his daughter Alice, who was my mother Alice's mother, Alice. Charlie and all these Alices lived together in a large white, three-story house on East 24th Street between Farragut and Glenwood in the Flatbush section of Brooklyn.

There was always lots of laughter in the house and never a mean word. Charlie seldom got mad; when he did he would go down the stairs stomping like an elephant—but (like me) he got over it fast and never held a grudge.

It was a merry household where everyone ate together in the dining room promptly at 6:00 P.M. On warm summer evenings, while the women did the dishes, someone would go to Flatbush Avenue to buy some hand-packed ice cream to eat out on the porch. On special occasions, they would walk to the corner drugstore for a Glenwood Special—a huge chocolate sundae that cost 25 cents and had scoops of vanilla, strawberry and chocolate ice creams, chocolate sauce, whipped cream and a cherry.

On Sundays, Grandfather liked a huge breakfast to tide him over until Sunday dinner: six big pancakes, two pork chops with lots of pan gravy and a very big cup of coffee. (He said a second cup never tasted as good.) Sometimes, he would steal some of the dough from the fresh bread Mame was kneading, drop it in oil or butter in a skillet and fry it to serve like a hot doughnut with butter and maple syrup from the little Log Cabin can. How differently families ate in those days!

Sunday dinner would be served at 1 or 2, and afterward the whole family piled into the car for a Sunday drive. Mame would spend the morning baking vanilla cake with chocolate pudding icing or her famous pound cake, while the six-rib prime rib or ham was roasting. A favorite accompaniment was macaroni and cheese made with sharp New York cheddar. Some Sundays, roast ham and a cheese soufflé would bring the family to the table faster than anything else. The main course was always some sort of huge roast, the remains of which were made into hash the next night and sandwiches in the days that followed.

Grandfather Althisar loved fresh, strong horseradish with his Sunday roast. It had to be served in the special crystal horseradish jar trimmed in silver with a wooden spoon attached to the lid. As in most households of the day, Mame would buy her horseradish, either white or red that had been colored with beet juice, from the cart of a neighborhood vendor. On the Sundays when Mame forgot, Charles had a good-humored way of dealing with the horseradish that hadn't been freshened in a timely fashion. He would say, "Mame, this horseradish is weak! Look, I can eat it right off the spoon!" Charlie would load up a heaping portion and pop it in his mouth to demonstrate.

One Sunday, Mame decided to test Grandfather's sense of humor. She had noticed that if the horseradish was fresh it had a smooth quality to it, but if it was old it looked more chunky. She had purchased freshly grated horseradish the day before. She put only a little of it in the crystal holder to look exactly like what had been there before. She pushed it around to make it look old, and she didn't polish up the crystal like she usually did. Everyone at the table was in on the joke, having been giggling over the idea since doing the breakfast dishes together.

Charlie was dressed in his Sunday best, seated at the head of the large rectangular table covered with a starched tablecloth and linen napkins. Predictably, he reached for the crystal holder and, sensing it was old, he gathered some of the weak condiment barely covering the bottom into a heaping spoonful that he popped righteously into his mouth.

There was no breath in him to say, "Mame . . ." His eyes watered and twinkled at the same time. He loved it. He knew in a moment that he was the deserving target of a caper that would become famous within the family. He had sprung a trap on himself.

The super-fresh horseradish prevented him from breathing in or breathing out. His sinuses became crystal clear, clearer than ever before. He confided later that "funny . . . no smoke!" was the thought in his head as he headed for the nearest bathroom, depositing as much as he could into his napkin as he ran.

When he returned to the table a few minutes later, he was ribbed by everyone there, tears of laughter on everyone's cheeks, including Charlie's.

Everyone in the family was a little more wary during the following months, waiting for Charlie's revenge. Whatever form it took, he must have had a lot of fun plotting it. Surely, it was hearing stories about Charlie that introduced me to the concept of sweet revenge in a marriage, and how sweet, how *very* sweet it is.

Fresh Horseradish

Makes 2 cups

❧

1 root fresh horseradish   *2 teaspoons salt*
½ cup white vinegar

1. Using a vegetable peeler, scrape any discolored spots from a root of fresh horseradish. Cut it into cubes approximately 1 inch in size. Use a blender to chop a few cubes at a time, or a food processor to chop the whole amount, until it is chopped very fine. Mix with the white vinegar and salt.

2. Pack into clean, well-scrubbed jars, cover tightly and allow to ripen in the refrigerator for a week before serving. Once the container is opened, the horseradish loses its strength quickly.

Grandma's Three-Meal Macaroni and Cheese

Makes 6 servings

❧

Alice says it is traditional to serve this hot the first day, cold and cut in squares with a salad the next day, and then sliced and fried in butter to serve hot for a third meal. The recipe is easily doubled. Unfortunately, Nabisco has stopped making the Uneeda biscuits that she used instead of bread crumbs—there are lots of old-fashioned recipes that call for them.

8 ounces elbow macaroni
½ stick (4 tablespoons) butter
3 tablespoons flour
1 teaspoon powdered dry
  mustard
2½ cups milk
¼ cup minced green or
  white onion
1 tablespoon Worcestershire
  sauce

Salt and pepper to taste
Freshly grated nutmeg to taste
Tabasco (hot pepper) sauce
  to taste
12 ounces sharp New York
  Cheddar cheese, grated
1 cup fresh white bread
  crumbs
2 to 3 tablespoons grated
  Parmesan cheese

1. Preheat oven to 350°F. Butter a 2-quart casserole dish, such as an 8-inch square Pyrex dish.

2. Cook macaroni in boiling salted water until just tender. Drain off almost all the water and leave the macaroni in the bottom of the pot to keep warm. Meanwhile, melt the butter in a skillet, stir in the flour and dry mustard and cook this roux for 3 or 4 minutes. Slowly add the milk, minced onion and Worcestershire sauce, and cook over medium heat, stirring constantly until the cream sauce has thickened. Season to taste with salt, white pepper, nutmeg and a few shakes of Tabasco. Add all but 1 cup of the grated cheese and stir over low heat until the cheese has melted.

3. Pour out the water from the macaroni and stir in the cheese sauce along with the bread crumbs. Sprinkle the top with the remaining cheddar and a light sprinkling of grated Parmesan. Bake for 30 minutes or until browned on top.

Tooty Toots

Diana von Welanetz Wentworth

The cardboard tubes from inside rolls of paper towels have a name at our house: tooty toots. When you hold the hollow tube to your lips and say something, it comes out sounding like "tooty toot."

We have established a policy that whoever uses the last piece of paper toweling must unwrap and install a new one, ready for the next user. The reward for this is a harmless little tube we save for sneaking up on and bopping each other unexpectedly on the head. The noise the tooty toot makes during a perfectly delivered bop is addictive.

Whenever I am lucky enough to have a perfect, new tooty toot, I conceal it somewhere that I will be most likely to want it, like under my pillow or in a kitchen drawer. I use my stash of tooty toots often. When Ted gets frisky under the covers after we've turned off the lights, I bop him one. Sometimes he just says, "Awww, you got me!," but sometimes it leads to a highly competitive wrestling match that can be a lot of fun, too.

Because I work at home and he goes to the office every day, I have access to the lion's share of our tooty toots. But, when it comes to other familial mischief, he outdoes me by far.

When Ted's daughters were small they became resigned to Ted awakening them by throwing himself bodily across them with a cry of "ARRRGH." It is a sight to behold—he springs airborne from the bedroom door like a 200-pound flying squirrel. His payoff is their groan of "DAAAAD . . ."

Now, when any of our three girls comes for an overnight visit, he likes to revive the tradition, even for my daughter, Lexi, who has learned quickly and good naturedly to put just the right amount of resignation in her "TEDDDD . . . Y." He has brought it to my attention that all three seem to wait in bed until he gets them up this way and, should he forget, they let him know about it.

One of his favorite antics (and our least favorite by far), is surprising any of the four of us by tossing water and ice cubes over the shower door while we are relishing our privacy under the hot water. The first time he did this to me, I was so stunned that I burst into tears. Seeing my reaction, he jumped in the shower with me, fully dressed, to hug me until I calmed down. (That saved his rotten life!) And it must have made a lasting impression because now, fortunately, he lets me shower in peace.

Once, when Lexi was with us as a first visit as a brand-new stepdaughter, he was surprisingly considerate. Instead of barging in on her shower, Ted disappeared out the front door and around the side of the house. Suddenly, from the bathroom, came "TEDDDD . . .Y!" He'd turned off the hot water at the source.

On a recent family weekend, as the three girls and I were in the kitchen making breakfast, our moment for revenge came at last. Christy said, "Dad's in the shower," and our eyes lit up all at once. With hardly a word exchanged, we filled pitchers and other containers with ice cubes and water, and crept stealthily into the bathroom. Ted's intuition was in its usual fine form and, without peeking from behind the shower curtain, he knew he was doomed. The anguished "AWWWWWW" we heard was music to our ears.

Tooty-Toot
Texas Barbecued Beans

Makes about 1 gallon

❧

It might be fun to create a centerpiece of tooty-toots for some good-natured bopping when you serve these.

1 (55-ounce) can Brick Oven
  beans
2 (16-ounce) cans pork and beans
1 (15-ounce) can drained
  black beans
4 medium onions
¾ cup firmly packed dark
  brown sugar

½ cup Dijon-style mustard
½ cup dark (unsulfured)
  molasses
3 tablespoons Worcestershire
  sauce
6 to 8 shakes Tabasco sauce

1. Place all the beans in a 5- to 6-quart oven-proof casserole, bean pot or Crockpot. Cut off the root and stem ends of the onions, then cut each in eighths through the center. Add the onion sections to the beans along with the brown sugar, mustard, molasses, Worcestershire sauce and Tabasco sauce. Stir to blend.

2. Bake in oven or Crockpot at 350°F for 2 hours (high on Crockpot), then reduce heat to between 200°F and 250°F (low on Crockpot), and continue cooking for 4 to 5 hours until thickened to your taste. Stir mixture from time to time.

The only really good vegetable is Tabasco sauce. Put Tabasco sauce in everything.

—P.J. O'Rourke

A Favorite Rum Cake Recipe

Author Unknown—submitted by Bobbie Lippman

∾

1 or 2 quarts rum (1.5 1iters)	Baking powder
1 cup butter	1 teaspoon baking soda
1 teaspoon sugar	Lemon juice
3 large eggs	Brown sugar
1 cup dried fruit	Nuts

Before you start, sample the rum and check for quality. Good, isn't it? Now go ahead. Select a large mixing bowl, measuring cup, etc., and check the rum again for quality. It must be just right. Try it again. With an electric mixer, beat 1 cup butter in a large fluffy bowl. Add 1 teaspoon sugar and beat again. Meanwhile, make certain the rum is of the finest quality. Add 2 large eggs and 2 cups of fried fruit . . . and beat until very high. If the fruit gets stuck in the beaters, just pry it loose with a screwdriver. Sample the rum again, checking for consistency. Nest, sift in 3 cups baking powder and a pinch of rum, 1 teaspoon toda and 1 cup tepper or salt. Anyway, don't fret. Just tample the tum again and fist in H pint jemon luice, fold in chopped buttermilk and the strained nuts. Tample rum again. Now, 1 bablespoon swrown bugar, or whatever color is abailable. Mix well. Grease oven and curn on take pan to 350°F. Pour the whole mess in oven. Cake tum rake out after mifty finutes . . .

¿Hay Huevos?

Diana von Welanetz Wentworth

One crisp morning we drove our two-seater John Deere trans-porter to our oldest avocado grove, 20 acres at the bottom of the hill far below the ranch house, to check on how the tree thinning was coming along. Every other tree had to be removed because they had become too crowded and lofty, making them less pro-ductive and hard to reach for picking.

Two of the Mexican men we'd hired to do the job were busy sawing the felled trees into firewood as we drove up. Ted waved and exchanged pleasantries with them and I noticed that, as usual, these new workers were amused at Ted's fractured Spanish.

As we continued along, further up the hill, I noticed a large jar of mayonnaise sitting on a table in the sun. "Uh oh," I said, "maybe they don't know mayonnaise has to be refrigerated. The eggs in it can spoil and make them sick."

Ted shouted at them, "*¡Tiene huevos en la mayonesa!*"

"Honey . . . I think you just told him he had testicles in his mayonnaise."

Now, the reason I worried about this is because long ago I lived in a small town high in the mountains north of Mexico City, where one morning I was reminded the hard way that the word for eggs can be a slang term for testicles. I made the mistake of asking a shopkeeper "*¿Tiene huevos?*" (Do you have eggs [or testicles in this usage]?) rather than "*¿Hay huevos?*" (Are there any eggs?).

He replied, "*¡Cómo no!*" (Of course!) as he and two other men collapsed against the shelves with laughter. Realizing my mistake, I fled the store red-faced with embarrassment.

Our new workers were now looking at Ted quizzically, so he jerked our vehicle to a stop, set the emergency brake (forgetting to put the gear in neutral) and hopped out. The transporter, with me—still a passenger—rolled slowly down the road, over a ledge and into a grapefruit tree, with Ted pulling on the back all the while, trying to reduce the effects of the pending encounter with the tree's branches.

By now the workers were thinking we were *muy loco* for sure. Stretching our inadequate vocabulary to the limits, we finally made them understand about the mayonnaise. We took the offending jar to dispose of it and, chuckling loudly, drove off with a grapefruit impaled on the front bumper.

On the way back to the ranch house we made plans to rustle up two servings of our favorite Mexican egg dish for breakfast—the very dish that got me in so much trouble in the market years ago. The recipe comes from our friend Betty Kempe who served it every morning for years at her hotel, the Villa Santa Monica in San Miguel de Allende, Guanajuato. I keep the sauce for making it on hand in the freezer at all times—it's so handy for weekend mornings.

Huevos Diablos

Makes 6 servings

2 tablespoons olive oil
1 medium onion, minced
1 clove garlic, minced
1 (1-pound 14-ounce) can
  crushed tomatoes in
  tomato purée
1 teaspoon Worcestershire sauce
A good dash of cayenne
  (ground red pepper)

¾ cup grated Parmesan
6 large eggs
Butter
Paprika
Warm corn or flour tortillas,
  or toasted French rolls
  (bolillos) for mopping up the
  delicious sauce

1. In a heavy saucepan, heat the olive oil and sauté the onion until transparent and just beginning to brown. Add garlic and cook

briefly. Stir in the tomatoes, Worcestershire sauce and cayenne. Bring to a simmer, lower the heat and cook for about 10 minutes. (This sauce may be refrigerated or frozen at this point if making ahead.)

2. About 20 minutes before serving, preheat oven to 350°F. Set out 6 individual casserole dishes or oven-proof soup bowls with about a 2-cup capacity for baking and serving the eggs. Stir grated Parmesan into the sauce (2 tablespoons per serving, if not using all the sauce at once) and divide the mixture evenly between baking dishes. Break 1 large egg into each dish, dot each egg with butter, and sprinkle the tops with a bit of Parmesan and a dash of paprika for color. Bake, uncovered, for 10 to 20 minutes, depending on the size of the containers, just until the egg whites are set, but yolks still soft.

3. Serve with warm corn or flour tortillas, or with toasted *bolillos*.

12
Parties with a Purpose

The purpose of life is a life of purpose.
—Robert Byrne

$\mathcal{A}$ Group Grace

Let's join hands in a circle, please.
Now look around the circle, recognizing and
acknowledging each of God's beautiful creations
with us this day.
Let's close our eyes for a moment and think back
over the day just past, the good parts of the day,
and the not so good parts. (pause)
And now, take a deep breath and become aware
of the godliness which you and each one of us
expresses in our lives.
We thank God for that awareness of that love
and power at work in our lives. We accept it in
love. We bless this food of which we are about to
partake, and the loving souls which have pre-
pared it. For this world, this love and this aware-
ness, we say,
"Thank you, Father-Mother God." Amen.

—Rev. Bob Biddick

Happy New Year!

Chick Moorman

New Year's Eve is an ideal time to celebrate connectedness, reflect on the past year and look ahead to the future. In the past, we saw it as an occasion to get away from our children to celebrate in private or with friends. But a few years ago, we decided to spend New Year's Eve as a family. Now it has become a tradition, and the ritual has become an eagerly anticipated opportunity for our family to grow closer.

Deciding what treats to purchase (my children usually pick junk food, I buy ingredients for my favorite Taco Dip), shopping together, and decorating with confetti and streamers occupy much of the day. Dinner followed by card or board games fill the early evening. When interest in the games dies down, we gather in the living room, sit in a circle and begin the most meaningful part of our New Year's Eve together: "Topic Talk." One family member suggests a subject like "A new friend I made this year," or "My favorite song this year" to structure our conversation. We each take a turn, responding orally to the question, telling as much as we choose, while the rest of the family listens and munches on the snacks until everyone has responded. When we've all had an opportunity to respond, we ask questions and elaborate on our remarks.

We enjoy topics that help us to reflect on the previous year:

- My favorite book this year
- Something I did that I am proud of
- Something I wish I could do over
- My favorite place I visited this year
- Something I bought for myself
- Something I did for others

Around 11:00 P.M. we complete our discussion and get out our "goals" list—which we shared and recorded the year before. We take turns reading our goals from the preceding year and telling whether or not we reached them. Past goals have included:

- Go to horseback-riding camp
- Get a medal in wrestling
- Make the high school baseball team
- Do a workshop in a foreign country

After reviewing the goals and how we achieved or didn't achieve them, we enthusiastically set new ones for the coming New Year, with my daughter Jenny recording it all. The goals are then put away until our next New Year's Eve celebration.

It is now close to midnight. We turn on the TV and count down the minutes and seconds. The traditional hugs, kisses and noise-making are a special part of our celebration, and we end our evening with a big group hug. Here is a family recipe that is a big hit, year after year.

Taco Dip

Makes 8 or more servings

❧

1 (16-ounce) can refried beans
1 (10-ounce) carton sour cream
1 (1.25-ounce) package taco
  seasoning mix
1 (8-ounce) package shredded
  Cheddar cheese
3 to 4 cups chopped lettuce

Diced or sliced vegetables of
  your choice for the topping:
  tomato, green pepper (or
  pickled jalapeños), black
  olives, mushrooms
Nacho chips, for serving

1. On a large platter, arrange a layer of the refried beans.

2. Combine the sour cream and taco seasoning; mix thoroughly and spread in a layer over the beans.

3. Cover the top with chopped lettuce, and top with the vegetable toppings of your choice. Serve with nacho chips.

A Party Idea
That Could Change
Your Life

Susan Jeffers

Nothing happens unless first a dream.

—Carl Sandburg

The best party I ever attended was in 1986. It was called the 1991 Party! Let me explain. The party was proposed by The Inside Edge, a very forward-looking group that I belonged to in Los Angeles. The premise was that everyone coming to the party had to envision what they would like to have happen in their lives five years into the future, which in our case was 1991. After we created our vision, we were then to stretch our imaginations, that is make our vision more than we actually thought we could accomplish.

When we came to the party, we were to act as if it really were 1991 and our vision had come true. That means we were to dress the part, talk the part and come with any props demonstrating our amazing journey to the completion of our dream. In addition to applauding our own success, we were to applaud the success of everyone else as well: a perfect scenario for an evening of congratulations, excitement, creativity, laughter and fun!

I remember that one man's vision was to be a multimillionaire giving away money to others, by the year 1991. He was dressed as a "beach bum"—his dream of retirement—and he was handing out lottery tickets to everyone at the party. One woman brought a mock *Time Magazine* with her face emblazoned on the cover. Her vision was winning an international award for making advances in the peace movement. My husband, who produced *I, Claudius*, came in evening clothes, having envisioned the premier of his first co-production with the Russians. One woman came with a large sandwich board on which were painted the images of her new husband and two children, all of which she envisioned having by the year 1991.

What did I envision? In 1986, I was embarking on a career as a writer. As yet, I had not succeeded in getting anything accepted by a publisher. My stretch for the party was that *three* book contracts would be signed by the year 1991. (Mind you, I would have been happy if one book contract had been signed.) In the spirit of the party, I showed up with three mock books that I could show everyone, and throughout the evening I talked about the incredible success of all three books. I even told my remarkable story of success to a video camera that recorded it for all posterity.

It was an evening of people supporting each other in pursuit of their dreams. Someone congratulated me on my bestseller, telling me that she had seen me on four television shows. Another congratulated me for winning the Pulitzer Prize. And so it went.

By the end of the evening I believed that creating three books by the year 1991 was a definite possibility. It was no longer a stretch. And what did happen by the year 1991? You guessed it. I actually did write three successful books—with a fourth one on the way. It's amazing what one party will do.

The menu for this party was simple. The buffett featured as the entree two types of lasagna—one with meat-sauce and one with vegetables and cream sauce. (These are made by Stouffer's and are available frozen in large foil pans at places like Costco and Price Club or Smart and Final.) Accompanying the lasagnas was a huge salad with several kinds of lettuces, mushrooms and artichokes, and hot garlic bread.

The frozen lasagnas were lifted from their pans while still frozen and transfered to attractive oven-to-table baking dishes, making them as attractive as homemade. Extra sauces for topping the lasagnas—creamy alfredo and spicy marinara—were served in bowls on the side.

Desserts were bite-size squares of brownies and single-layer carrot cake, also available frozen in large sheets at the same sources.

Of course, not everyone's vision was realized in the same way they created it . . . they were meant to travel a different path. But one thing is for sure . . . everyone had a great time and they really got to know each other. And after all is said and done, isn't that what parties are all about?

Come as You Will Be . . . in 2003!

Join us for a celebration that will stretch your imagination and catapult you into your own future.

When: _____

Where: _____

Given by: _____

RSVP to: _____

Arrive as who you will be five years hence. Dress in your very best. Speak only in present or past tense the entire evening, as if all your goals have been achieved and all your dreams have already come true.

You will be videotaped as you arrive. Bring props to show everyone what you have achieved in the years between, such as bestselling books you've written, magazine covers you've been on, awards you've won. Throughout the evening you will have the opportunity to applaud others in their achievements and to receive their congratulations.

WARNING:
You will never be the same!

The Trim-the-Tree Vision Party

Diana von Welanetz Wentworth

Ten years ago, we invited 60 or so people to a holiday tree-trimming party. Each of them was asked to select a holiday ornament that had special meaning to them or represented their heart's desire and bring it to the party prepared to tell the group about it. This seemed like a good way for the members of a new organization to get to know each other.

The afternoon of the party, we decorated the tree with sparkling white lights, but no ornaments. Because we didn't have enough seating space for such a crowd, we set out dishes of finger food—dips, bite-sized appetizers and sandwich makings. Our daughter, Lexi, put plates of appetizers and cookies around the house so people would have cause to move about and mingle. Drinks were self-serve on the patio from an ice tub.

Once our guests arrived and had a chance to mingle for awhile, we gathered them in a large circle around the living room and began the tree-trimming. Choosing one of our more extroverted guests to begin, we asked him to "show and tell." He had us all laughing about the quirky ornament he'd made out of paper money, representing his goal of being more playful with money. A man then showed a miniature frame holding a picture of his mother who had recently been diagnosed with Alzheimer's disease. He was planning to take the next few months off to care for her himself and to write a little book about the experience to share with others.

Jack Canfield brought a white crystalline spider on a web ornament that represented his desire to reach out and create a wider and deeper web of relationships. "I've been focusing too much on my work and not enough on my family and friendships," he said.

The storytelling continued around the room. Some people made or purchased ornaments that represented their goals, dreams and wishes for the next year, ranging from miniature bestsellers to a man and woman holding hands. Several brought ornaments they'd found in their travels to Asia, the Middle East and Latin America. I especially remember a star made of olive wood from Bethlehem.

A woman held a tiny child in a cradle, which symbolized her yearning to have a baby the following year. One perfect crystal heart represented a desire to be more transparent. We hadn't anticipated how revealing the process would be, or the depth of vulnerability that would be revealed. Moving from laughter to tears over and over again, we celebrated our diversity only to become filled with our oneness.

After waving goodbye to our guests, we turned out the lights, put another log on the fire and sat next to the twinkling tree. The ornaments were all bunched together in the middle branches. We left them nestled just as they were and never finished the tree with our traditional ornaments that year because we knew we had been visited by the true Spirit of Christmas.

The Best Birthday

Mary Olsen Kelly

I come from a family of great cooks. My grandmother is famous for her Texas Fudge Cake and pies of all kinds. My mother is an excellent cook who can make something from nothing, and whose Doomsday Cookies (see page 20) are a gift from the gods. My sister is a true culinary artist who delights in mastering the most challenging recipes she can find.

Somehow, the great cooking gene was mutated in me, but I nonetheless appreciate the talents of the rest of my family. Food is really just an excuse to spend time together, in my mutant opinion. One of the best gatherings we have had in the name of food was my brother's 26th birthday. For me, it changed forever the meaning of the annual celebration; it was The Best Birthday.

All the family gathered at my sister's beautiful Southwestern-style home in northern California for an evening of gourmet food and birthday cake. The meal was sumptuous—Barbara had outdone herself—and as we all reached for seconds, we suddenly realized that this meal, no matter how exquisite, was not going to be complete without hearing from the birthday boy.

Bob started to give a little speech, then said, "I feel like I am pretty confused at this age. What I'd really like is to hear what each of you were doing when you were 26."

We all settled more deeply into our chairs, and there was silence as each person thought back to an earlier time: 26 . . . not yet 30. Still so young, yet truly an adult. One by one, we spoke of our thoughts and dreams at 26.

I told of graduating with a master's degree in theater, eschewing a comfortable teaching position in favor of moving to New York

City and struggling to become an actress. Ah, the terrifying yet soulful life of a starving artist with so many dreams at 26.

My sister spoke of hitchhiking around Europe for years, then coming home and turning her life around at that exact age. We all nodded, remembering what a dramatic change she had made in herself then.

My dad talked softly and with great difficulty about the death of his first child. The baby boy was just six weeks old when he died of heart complications. My father was only 26 when he lost the son who would have been our older brother.

One by one, we spoke. We celebrated birth, confusion, change and loss as the wheel of my brother's life turned. Another birthday, the passing of yet another year.

And yes, we ate the famous Texas Fudge Cake since it is my brother's favorite. It tasted especially wonderful that night.

Grandmother Whitehead's Famous Texas Fudge Cake

Makes about 12 servings

⅓ cup cocoa
2 sticks (1 cup) butter or
   margarine
2 cups flour
2 cups sugar
1 teaspoon baking soda

½ teaspoon salt
2 large eggs
½ cup sour cream
   or buttermilk (sour
   cream is richer)
1 teaspoon vanilla

ICING:
¾ stick (⅜ cup) butter or
   margarine
¼ cup milk
3 tablespoons cocoa

¾ box powdered sugar
¾ cup finely chopped nuts
   of your choice
1 teaspoon vanilla

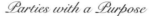

1. Preheat the oven to 350°F. Butter an 11 x 15-inch pan. Put cocoa in a medium saucepan; gradually stir in 1 cup water and bring to a boil. Add butter or margarine and let melt. Set aside.

2. Sift together onto wax paper the flour, sugar, baking soda and salt; add to the hot mixture. Lightly beat the eggs and add them to the mixture along with sour cream and vanilla. Pour the mixture into the prepared pan. Bake for 30 minutes, or until it feels firm in the center.

3. While the cake is baking, prepare the icing. In a saucepan, combine butter or margarine, milk, and cocoa; bring to a boil. Add powdered sugar and beat until smooth. Add chopped nuts and vanilla. Spread over the *hot* cake. Cool before cutting.

The Ultimate Birthday Party

Mark Victor Hansen

Patty, my wife, suddenly sat up in bed at 3:49 A.M. and told me the 19 people she would like to have invited to her ultimate birthday party. She told me exactly where she wanted it. She did this all while being in deep sleep. She then reentered la la land, not knowing she ever told me her deepest party desires.

I sneaked out of bed, bypassed the bathroom and went upstairs to capture her party of parties on paper so it could be manifested in elegance, panache and savoir faire.

Patty and I work together in our office. Fortunately, she was away from the office enough that I could telephone her deeply loved, respected, appreciated and well-thought-of friends and invite them to join us at her party to celebrate absolute birthday bliss. I scheduled it two days before her actual birthday so she wouldn't suspect.

I told her we were going to a black-tie Prudential Insurance meeting, and that my client virtually insisted she attend. (I had been a professional speaker for over a decade at that time and Patty had attended more than her share of awards nights.)

At 6:00 P.M. we rolled up in front of Antonello's Italian Ristorante, a magnificent four-star restaurant.

Astonished, she asked, "Prudential is having their meeting here?"

"Yes," I said.

As we entered the portals of Antonello's, the owner, Antonio, gave her two dozen red roses and kissed her on the cheek. Her eyes were wide open in shock and disbelief as she stuttered,

"Thank you." Antonio, an elegant, handsome and articulate man, offered Patty his arm and graciously led us to the table.

Nineteen friends burst into "Happy Birthday to You" along with the ending of the Hallelujah Chorus. Patty received a standing ovation for being born. Dumbfounded, she asked again, "Prudential invited you all here?" Everyone smiled and burst into laughter, tears, cheers and loving hugs.

Patty literally had her dreams come true at her ultimate birthday bash. Everyone she loved and wanted there was in attendance.

We feasted on Fusilli Pasta and had a wonderful time. As Bob Hope would say, "Thanks for the memories . . ."

Fusilli con Spinaci e Ricotta

(from *Antonello's Ristorante, Newport Beach, California*)
Makes 6 or more servings

1 pound dried fusilli
  (corkscrew-shaped pasta)
1½ cups extra-virgin olive oil
2 tablespoons minced garlic
6 cups chopped fresh spinach

2 cups ricotta cheese
Salt and pepper to taste
½ cup freshly grated
  Parmesan cheese

1. Cook the pasta in rapidly boiling water with 1 tablespoon salt for 8 to 10 minutes until almost tender—it should be *al dente*. Meanwhile, make the sauce.

2. Heat olive oil in a large skillet. Add the garlic and sauté until it just starts to turn golden. Add the spinach, sauté a minute or two, then add the ricotta cheese and seasonings to taste. Set aside.

3. When the pasta is done, drain off the water and toss the *fusilli* with the sauce. Serve in a bowl-topped with Parmesan.

Thanksgiving at Eagle's Ridge Ranch

Diana von Welanetz Wentworth

Small cheer and great welcome makes a merry feast.

—William Shakespeare

Thanksgiving has always been my favorite holiday. As food writers and cooking teachers, my late husband and I loved to taste others' traditional family recipes. We even created an extra Thanksgiving celebration every year by inviting our extended family of friends to bring leftovers to our home on the day after Thanksgiving.

Yearly, on that Friday evening, we shared not only food, but what we called "The Thankful Process," in which we would invite each guest to tell in turn everyone assembled what they were feeling particularly thankful for that year. It became another wonderful way for our guests to really get to know each other.

After Paul died, I met and fell in love with Ted. Our first Thanksgiving together, a few weeks before our wedding, was the first time our parents and our three daughters had the opportunity to explore what this new family might become. Because we wanted to make our time together last as long as possible we decided to host the feast at Ted's weekend house on his ranch in Temecula, a hilltop avocado and citrus ranch with a distant ocean view.

Ted had a huge round tabletop made to fit over the dining table so we could seat all 16 attendees. The girls decorated the house with peach-hued persimmon leaves, Jack-Be-Little mini-pumpkins and colorful ears of Indian corn we found at a produce stand. I made a feast of every traditional Thanksgiving dish I knew plus Alice Wentworth's Yummy Yams (see page 186).

We spontaneously began what would become a family tradition that year. Rather than saying what we felt thankful for, Ted and I took turns welcoming each family member to the table and telling them specifically how we love and appreciate them.

Without prompting, the others followed suit. When each person had done the same acknowledging and welcoming, there was such a high energy of joy and open-heartedness in the room that we wondered why we hadn't thought to get our marriage license and be married in the midst of such a meaningful family celebration.

Being at the ranch for Thanksgiving has become a special time for all of us during the past five years. Looking back, our Thanksgivings never have quite the same texture two years running. At the second one, Ted and I were close to celebrating our first anniversary: I'd sold my house in Los Angeles, moved to my new home in Corona del Mar and the family really *felt* like a family.

The third year was a comedy of errors—the winds blew fiercely Thanksgiving morning and we found ourselves with no electricity. I was worried about how I'd do the cooking, but my daughter Lexi, who had years of experience as an assistant in my cooking classes, took over. She led the team that loaded the uncooked food into two cars along with a portable oven and an electric skillet, then she and I spent the next four hours at her hotel room in town, which had a microwave oven, and prepared the turkey, gravy and yams right there. On the way back, we bought a large container of freshly mashed potatoes from the hotel restaurant, and when we arrived at the ranch we found the electricity had just been restored. We heated everything up and the feast was miraculously almost as good as usual. (Our thankful process was especially triumphant that year!)

This past Thanksgiving was heartwarming because the family grew by two. My older brother and I had recently reunited after being estranged for almost 30 years. Gene and his wife Marilyn flew in from Seattle for our Thanksgiving feast for the first time. This coming year, there are hints we'll be celebrating the engagement of one of our daughters.

If I am blessed to live long enough to sit in the proverbial rocking chair and savor my memories, I imagine I will measure my life by the Thanksgivings.

I occasionally try out new recipes on the group, but only one or two each year, and only for the side dishes. Certain things must stay the same: Herb Stuffing made from wild sage growing on our hillsides, and our easy and delicious Foil-Cooked Turkey—probably like no other you've seen. Try it, please! I promise you a moist bird and lots of lovely juices for gravy (with or without giblets). It is a method Paul and I taught in our classes for years, and people tell me all the time that it is still their favorite—not just for Thanksgiving, but all year long.

Foil-Cooked Turkey with Herb Stuffing and Giblet Gravy

Makes 16 servings, with leftovers

1 turkey (at least 14 pounds)
Salt and pepper
1 tablespoon vegetable oil

½ cup Kitchen Bouquet
  (brown gravy seasoning)
Extra-heavy aluminum foil

STUFFING:
1 pound (4 sticks) butter
  or margarine
4 cups chicken broth
4 stalks celery, finely chopped
2 large onions, finely chopped
2 cups chopped parsley

Chopped fresh sage to taste or
  a fresh (2-ounce) jar of
  dried sage
2 (16-ounce) packages
  Pepperidge Farm herb-
  stuffing mix
Salt and pepper to taste

GRAVY (some with giblets, some without):

Turkey giblets and neck
1 onion, cut up
10 peppercorns
1 stalk celery or celery leaves,
 cut up
Parsley stems (optional)

2 teaspoons salt
Cold water to cover
Drippings from the cooked
 turkey
1 cup flour

TIMETABLE	
For Foil-Roasted Turkey at 450°	
WEIGHT	TIME
	Stuffed or Unstuffed
14 to 17 pounds	*2¼ to 2½ hours*
18 to 21 pounds	*3¼ to 3½ hours*
22 to 25 pounds	*3½ to 3¾ hours*

1. The stuffing may be made the day before the party, but for health reasons the turkey should be stuffed just before going in the oven. In a large pot, melt the butter in the water; remove from heat. Stir in the celery, onion and parsley, followed by the stuffing mix, tossing it lightly with a fork to moisten evenly. Season to taste with sage, salt and pepper—it will need a lot. Refrigerate until ready to stuff the bird.

2. About an hour before the turkey is to go in the oven, clean and dry the turkey with paper towels. Set aside giblets and neck to use in making the broth for the gravy. Take care that both turkey and stuffing are *cold* so bacteria will not grow. Stuff both cavities of the turkey very loosely (stuffing swells while cooking). Put the rest of the stuffing in an oven-proof casserole dish and set it aside. Later you will sprinkle this extra stuffing with broth and bake it at 325°F for an hour or so. If you won't be needing all this stuffing the first day, refrigerate this part and bake when needed. It is a good idea to offer both stuffings to your guests, as there are some people who like wet stuffing and others who prefer it dry. The stuffing from inside the turkey will be *very* moist!

3. Preheat the oven to 450°F. Set the turkey on a long, wide piece of extra-heavy aluminum foil that will reach around the bird easily with some to spare. You will have to connect two pieces together, sealing them with several folds. Mix the vegetable oil with the brown gravy seasoning in a small bowl. Using a pastry brush, brush the turkey all over, even under the wings, until it is completely covered with a brown glaze. This will give the finished turkey a rich, oven-browned color. Wrap the foil up around the turkey, taking care not to tear a hole in the foil. Seal the foil on top of the bird to form a *loose* package. Poke a small hole on top near the large cavity with a sharp knife, to let some steam escape during the cooking. Put the wrapped turkey on the rack of a roasting pan and place in the oven. Bake for the time specified in the chart on the previous page.

4. Now put all the giblets except the liver into a large saucepan along with the neck, onion, peppercorns, celery, parsley stems, salt and cold water to cover. Bring to a boil, turn down the heat to medium, cover the pot and simmer gently until the giblets can be pierced easily with a fork—this will take 1 to 1½ hours for a large bird. Add the liver and simmer 10 to 15 more minutes. Strain the broth into a bowl, skim off the fat, taste for seasoning and set aside. When the neck is cool enough to handle, remove the meat with your fingers. Chop the giblets coarsely and put them with the neck meat into a small bowl with just enough broth to cover and keep it moist; then set aside. Now, sit down and put your feet up until the turkey is done!

5. When the turkey is done, remove it from the oven and prick several holes in the bottom side of the foil with a knife, so that the juices will come spurting out into the roasting pan. Place the extra baking dish of stuffing (sprinkled lightly with the a bit of the strained giblet broth) into the oven at 325°F so it will be done when you are ready to serve.

6. When the juices from the turkey have finished running into the roasting pan, open the foil—be very careful that the steam that emerges doesn't burn you. Remove the turkey to a platter in a warm spot to rest while you make the gravy. Place a tent of foil over the bird to hold in the heat.

7. Pour the juices from the roasting pan into a very large heat-proof glass measuring cup if you have one, or into a mixing bowl. Let the fat rise to the top for a few minutes, then spoon the fat off the top and reserve 1 cup. Throw out the rest of the fat. Put the 1 cup of fat into a large heavy saucepan with the 1 cup of flour and let this mixture cook for 2 or 3 minutes. Meanwhile, measure the skimmed turkey drippings and add enough of the reserved broth to make 10 cups of liquid. Stir this into the flour mixture and bring to a simmer. Let simmer for 2 to 3 minutes. If the gravy is too thin, shake a little flour and water together in a sealed jar and stir it immediately into the simmering gravy—this will prevent lumps. Taste for seasoning. Pour the gravy into two separate serving bowls, adding the reserved giblets to one of them.

8. If possible, ask someone else to carve the turkey while you put the rest of the dinner on the table.

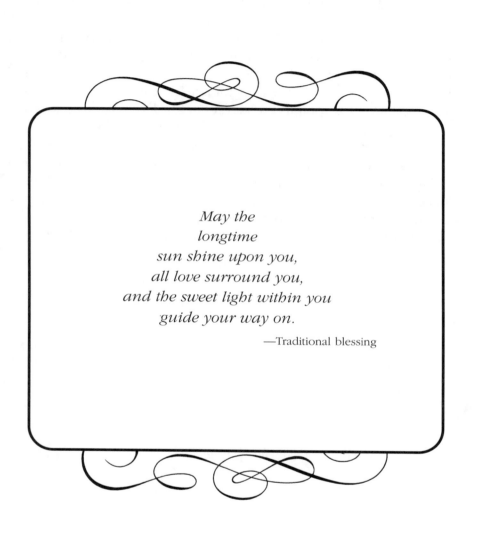

*May the
longtime
sun shine upon you,
all love surround you,
and the sweet light within you
guide your way on.*

—Traditional blessing

More Chicken Soup Anyone?

Many of the stories and recipes you have just read were submitted by readers such as yourself. We invite you, too, to share a story and recipe that you feel belongs in a future volume of the *Chicken Soup for the Soul Cookbook*.

We plan to publish a new cookbook, as well as a special collection of *Chicken Soup for the Soul Parties with a Purpose,* in the next two years. Send your stories and recipes to:

Diana Wentworth
Chicken Soup for the Soul Cookbook
4631 Teller Avenue, Suite 101
Newport Beach, CA 92660
FAX: 714-720-9356

We will ensure that you (and the source, if previously published) are credited for your submission. Thank you for your contributions.

Soup Kitchens for the Soul

∾

One of the most exciting developments with the *Chicken Soup for the Soul* book series is the impact it has had on readers who are welfare recipients, homeless, living in shelters and halfway houses, or incarcerated in state prisons. Here is just one excerpt from a letter we received from a prisoner in the Billerica House of Corrections in Massachusetts:

> *I received a copy of* Chicken Soup *when I attended a ten-week course on alternatives to violence. Since reading this book, my whole perspective as an inmate dealing with other inmates has dramatically changed. I no longer feel violent or hatred toward anyone. My soul has been blessed with these wonderful stories. I simply can't thank you enough.*
>
> Sincerely, Phil S.

A teenage girl writes:

> *I have just finished reading your book* Chicken Soup for the Soul. *I feel that I have the power to do anything after reading it.*
> *You see I had given up on a lot of my dreams—to travel around the world, to go to college, to marry and to have children—but after reading this book, I feel I have the power to do everything and anything. Thanks!!*
>
> Erica Lynn P., age 14

As a result we have established the Soup Kitchens for the Soul Project. We are donating thousands of copies of *Chicken Soup for the Soul* and *A 2nd Helping of Chicken Soup for the Soul* to men and women in prisons, halfway houses, homeless shelters, battered women shelters, literacy programs, inner-city schools and other programs for at-risk adults and teenagers.

We welcome and invite your participation in this project in the following way. For every $12.95 you contribute, we will send a copy of both *Chicken Soup* books to a prison, county jail, shelter or other nonprofit agency. We also invite you to submit the names of worthy programs that you think should receive copies of the books.

The program will be administered by The Foundation for Self-Esteem in Culver City, California. Please make your check payable to The Foundation for Self-Esteem and send it to:

Soup Kitchens for the Soul
The Foundation for Self-Esteem
6035 Bristol Parkway
Culver City, CA 90230

or

Call 310-568-1505 and make your contribution by credit card.

We will acknowledge receipt of your contribution and let you know where the books you paid for were sent.

For the Hungry
and the Homeless

∾

While writing this book, we became especially aware of how fortunate we all are to have homes where we are surrounded by family and food that nourish us whenever we wish. Many in this world are not so fortunate.

Our publishers at Health Communications are joining us in donating 20 cents from each cookbook sold to organizations that support the hungry and the homeless. By purchasing this book, you have contributed 20 cents to worthy causes across the country. Thank you for participating in this work.

Who Is Jack Canfield?

Jack Canfield is one of America's leading experts in the development of human potential and personal effectiveness. He is both a dynamic and entertaining speaker and a highly sought-after trainer with a wonderful ability to inform and inspire audiences toward increased levels of self-esteem and peak performance.

He is the author and narrator of several bestselling audiocassette and videocassette programs, including *Self-Esteem and Peak Performance, How to Build High Self-Esteem* and *Self-Esteem in the Classroom*. He is regularly seen on television shows such as *Good Morning America, 20/20* and *NBC Nightly News*. He has published eight books, including *Chicken Soup for the Soul, A 2nd Helping of Chicken Soup for the Soul, 100 Ways to Build Self-Concept in the Classroom* (with Harold C. Wells) and *Dare to Win* (with Mark Victor Hansen).

Jack addresses more than 100 groups each year. His clients include professional associations, school districts, government agencies, churches, sales organizations and corporations. His corporate clients have included the American Management Association, AT&T, Campbell Soup, Clairol, Domino's Pizza, G.E., ITT Hartford Insurance, Johnson & Johnson, NCR, New England Telephone, Re/Max, Scott Paper, Sunkist, Supercuts, TRW and Virgin Records. Jack is also on the faculties of two schools for entrepreneurs—Income Builders International and the Street-Smart Business School.

Jack conducts an annual eight-day Training of Trainers program in the areas of self-esteem and peak performance. It attracts educators, counselors, parenting trainers, corporate trainers, professional speakers, ministers and others interested in developing their speaking and seminar-leading skills.

To contact Jack for further information about his books, tapes and trainings, or to schedule him for a presentation, please write to:

The Canfield Training Group
6035 Bristol Parkway
Culver City, CA 90230

Call toll-free 1-800-237-8336 or fax 310-337-7465.

Who Is Mark Victor Hansen?

Mark Victor Hansen has been called a human activator—a man who ignites individuals to recognize their full potential. During his 20-plus years as a professional speaker, he has shared his expertise in sales excellence and strategies and in personal empowerment and development with more than 1 million people in 32 countries. In more than 4,000 presentations, he has inspired hundreds of thousands of people to create a more powerful and purposeful future for themselves while stimulating the sale of millions of dollars worth of goods and services.

A *New York Times* bestselling author, Mark has written several books, including *Future Diary, How to Achieve Total Prosperity* and *The Miracle of Tithing*. With his best friend, Jack Canfield, Mark has written *Chicken Soup for the Soul, A 2nd Helping of Chicken Soup for the Soul* and *Dare to Win*.

Mark believes strongly in the teaching power of audiocassettes and videocassettes. He has produced a complete library of programs that have enabled his audience members to utilize their innate abilities within their business and personal lives. His message has made him a popular radio and television personality, and he starred in his own PBS special "Build a Better You."

Mark presents an annual Hawaiian retreat, "Wake Up Hawaii," designed for leaders, entrepreneurs and achievers who want to break through spiritual, mental, physical and financial blocks and unlock their highest potential. Because Mark is a strong believer in family values this retreat includes a children's program that parallels the adult program.

Mark has dedicated his life to making a profound and positive difference in people's lives. He is a big man with a big heart and a big spirit—an inspiration to all who seek to better themselves.

For more information on Mark Victor Hansen's seminars, books and tapes, or to schedule him for a presentation to your company or organization, contact:

M.V. Hansen and Associates, Inc.
P.O. Box 7665
Newport Beach, CA 92658-7665

Call 1-800-433-2314 or in California 714-759-9304

Who Is Diana von Welanetz Wentworth?

❧

Diana von Welanetz Wentworth has enjoyed a celebrated career as an award-winning cookbook author, public speaker and television host.

The six books she authored with her late husband, Paul von Welanetz, include *The Pleasure of Your Company* (Atheneum), for which they received the coveted French Tastemaker "Cookbook of the Year" award in the category of entertaining. Others were: *With Love from Your Kitchen* and *The Art of Buffet Entertaining* (both of which were main selections of the Better Homes and Gardens Book Club), *The von Welanetz Guide to Ethnic Ingredients, LA Cuisine* and *Celebrations* (all published by J.P. Tarcher). *The von Welanetz Guide to Ethnic Ingredients* is still considered the classic reference book of international ingredients. *Bon Appétit* magazine called it "A splendid work! . . . Just about every exotic, unusual and rare ingredient used in dishes in all corners of the world is covered."

Diana and Paul's long-running daily television series, *The New Way Gourmet,* appeared nationally, first on the Cable Health Network, then on the Lifetime Network.

In 1985, after their return from the First International Peace Congress in the Soviet Union, Diana and Paul founded an organization called The Inside Edge. It is a humanitarian forum and supportive community dedicated to inspiring its members to live lives of boldness, integrity, sharing and cooperation. The Inside Edge meets weekly for breakfast in Southern California, and it was at one morning meeting that Jack Canfield and Mark Victor Hansen decided to do a book of stories together that became *Chicken Soup for the Soul.*

Paul was diagnosed with cancer shortly after the couples' 25th wedding anniversary. Before his death, Paul promised to send someone who would treasure Diana as he had. He did, and Diana is now married to medical and human-rights attorney, Theodore S. Wentworth, who credits Paul with leading him into the arms of his love.

Diana has appeared on national and local television shows, and has spoken to women's organizations and at culinary events and food fairs throughout the United States. To schedule her for a presentation to your organization or company (without pots and pans!), please write to:

Diana Wentworth
4631 Teller Avenue, Suite 101
Newport Beach, CA 92660

or fax 714-720-9356

The Inside Edge may be reached at:
714-730-5050

Contributors

Thea Alexander's book, *2150AD*, has changed millions of lives, as has her seven-title *Macro Study Series*. She has lectured internationally, authored a newspaper column and conducted two TV interview series. Educated (Phi Beta Kappa) as a counselor, she invented a new succinct (2 to 6 hours) technique of assisting people toward their potential, called Personal Evolution Tutoring, which she both uses and teaches others to use. She may be reached at PO Box 26880, Tempe, AZ 85285-6880, 602-991-7077 or fax 602-991-0766.

Antoineta Baldwin was raised in the small beach town of Redondo Beach, California, the youngest of 8 children. She has retired from a management position as an inventory specialist and is now juggling her time between excercising, producing wearable art, boating with her husband Wayne and working as a volunteer for the needy in the South Bay area.

Joe Batten, C.P.A.E., is a professional speaker and a successful businessperson who knows how to inspire confidence in organizations in good economic times and bad. His 35 years as an author, consultant and speaker have earned him the title of Corporate Mentor. Joe wrote the best-selling book *Tough-Minded Management* and 15 other books. Joe is a man who loves life and laughter and translates that warmth and passion to every audience. You can reach Joe by writing to 912 Walnut Street, Des Moines, IA 50309-3502 or call 515-244-3176.

Andrea Bell was called "the Creme de la Creme of Caterers" by *Los Angeles Magazine*. Her L.A. Celebrations! has created party extravaganzas for presidents and princes, as well as the Hollywood elite. Ms. Bell is an internationally trained chef who not only attended LeNôtre, la Varenne and The Cordon Bleu in France, but also trained in India and with Madeleine Kamman and James Beard. Andrea Bell can be contacted at L.A. Celebrations! Catering and Event Coordination, 1716 South Robertson Boulevard, Los Angeles, CA 90035 or call 310-837-8900.

Rhonda Rima Nielsen-Bisnar is a personal injury and workers' compensation attorney in private practice in Newport Beach, California. She is happily married to her law partner and soulmate John Paul Bisnar. Rhonda and John have a combined family of five children. Rhonda's current passions are peace studies, mediation and conflict resolution. Rhonda hopes to move her career into the arena of international conflict resolution and contribute whatever she can in this lifetime to the furtherance and maintenance of world peace.

Jean Brady teaches two weekly cooking series in Rustic Canyon in addition to private groups and is partner in Santa Monica's Seasonal Table Cooking School. She is a party planner with a top Los Angeles catering company, co-author of *The Ultimate L.A. Food Guide* and obviously the mother of two incredible wonderful grown boys. Watercress sales have been discontinued indefinitely. Contact her at 680 Brooktree Road, Santa Monica, CA 90402 or call 310-454-4220.

Helice Bridges is a renowned keynote speaker, trainer, author and consultant. Known for her compassion, humor, integrity and personal power, she teaches corporations, organizations and schools worldwide how to build positive relationships and raise self-esteem in *one minute or less*. Helice is founder of Difference Makers International. To contact Helice or order Blue Ribbons, school curriculum or other products write DMI, PO Box 2115, Del Mar, CA 92014 or call 619-634-1851.

Linda Bruce is a wife and mother of two from Petaluma, California. She is the owner of The B&C Balloon Company, a full-scale balloon delivery and decorating service. Linda is an award-winning, certified balloon artist and a popular speaker/instructor at national and international balloon conventions.

Mike Buettell is a highly respected junior high school counselor in Irvine, California. Partially disabled, he is a living inspiration to his students that courage, perseverance and a sense of humor can overcome any obstacle. He can be reached in care of Rancho Middle School, 4861 Michelson, Irvine, CA 92715.

Martha A. Burich is an Adjunct Professor of Psychology at St. Louis Community College and President of Successful Solutions, a training and consulting firm providing in-house training to companies and school districts. She is the author of several books and audio tapes, including *Good Parent Sense, Discipline and Counseling Skills in the Classroom* and *How to Drive Yourself Sane*. She lives with her husband of 15 years, Tony, and their 12-year-old son, Anthony. She can be reached at Successful Solutions, 1704 McCready, St. Louis, MO 63117-2106 or call 314-645-0431.

Elaine Cannon was born, reared and enriched in Salt Lake City, Utah. She graduated from the University of Utah, Institute of Children's Literature. She has been working since the age of 17 and is busier than ever since retiring. She has been involved in the whole gamut of the media world—creating, hosting, ghosting, taping, editing, executing, authoring, lecturing, directing, producing and publishing—world-wide awarded and rewarded. She has been married to D.J. Cannon for 52 years and has 6 grown children, 25 grandchildren and 4 great-grandbabies. Greatly blessed and having lots of fun.

John Catenacci, a chemical engineer by training and practice, works pretty much full time as a safety and environmental manager for an established chemical company while enjoying, with his employer's support, a successful consulting business based on his extensive experiences in team building and improving organizational performance. He is also a published writer of both short fiction and non-fiction articles.

Chris "Mr. C" Cavert is a nationally known presenter and trainer in the area of "Experiential Play and Games" for pro-social learning and self-esteem. He has written the full spectrum E.A.G.E.R. Curriculum, which he uses to train child care professionals. Chris can be reached through the Experiential Specialists, 121 East Lake Road, Colgate, WI 53017.

Charles "Chuck Champlin" is the retired arts editor and columnist of the *Los Angeles Times*. He is a television host, a teacher at USC and the author of several books, including *George Lucas: The Creative Impulse* and *Back There Where the Past Was*, a memoir of his boyhood in Upstate New York, where three generations of his family were champagne-makers.

Rita Chopra was born and educated in New Delhi, India. She now spends her time between Lincoln, Massachusetts, and La Jolla, California. **Mallika Chopra** recently graduated from Brown University and currently lives and works in New York City. They can be reached at Quantum Publications, PO Box 1088, Sudbury, MA 01776 or call 508-440-8400.

Sharon Civalleri is a clinical hypnotherapist, counselor, speaker and writer. She also produces a line of dynamic self-help audio tapes on a variety of subjects. You may contact her at 5855 Naples Plaza, Suite 304, Naples Island, Long Beach, CA 90803 or call 310-434-6565.

Rosemarie Cortez is a professional speaker on personal and professional topics for schools, organizations and businesses. Founder of her own consulting business known as Open Door Presentations, she is author of the forthcoming book *Freeing the Woman Within* and inventor of the Temper-Mentor Anger product. She can be reached at Open Door Presentations, 3352 Calvin Avenue, San Jose, CA 95124-2543 or call 408-377-3616.

Bonnie Cox is a part-time writer and full-time realtor who lives in Newport Beach, California, with her husband Michael and cat "Bud." Because of her work schedule, she enjoys dishes that can be quickly prepared ahead of time. She loves animals and shares a love for fruit with her "new friend" Bogie. You can contact Bonnie at 184 Westport, Newport Beach, CA 92660 or call 714-644-0352.

Barbara Curtis is a sales management consultant to the publishing industry and the owner of Books Beyond Borders, Int'l.—a company whose purpose is to market and distribute selected small- to medium-sized U.S.-based publishers' products internationally. She can be reached at 1670 Loma Verde Drive, El Dorado Hills, CA 95762 or call/fax 916-933-5091.

Barbara DeAngelis, Ph.D., is one of America's foremost experts on relationships and personal growth. She is the author of four best-selling books including *How to Make Love All the Time, Secrets About Men Every Woman Should Know, Are You the One for Me?* and her most recent *New York Times* best-seller, *Real Moments*. Through her work as one of the nation's most sought-after motivational speakers, Barbara has inspired millions of people to experience more love and meaning in their lives. Barbara's award-winning television infomercial, *Making Love Work*, appears each day on hundreds of channels throughout the United States. For a free schedule of seminars, or more information about ordering Barbara's books or tapes, please call 800-682-LOVE.

Jamie Sparling Drew is an educator, psychometrist, devoted mother of ten through attrition and transition (death of spouses) and grandmother of twelve. She has been the president of three real estate corporations for nearly 30 years, a poet, painter, potter, Church of Religious Science Practitioner in Training, Director of the Science of Mind Board, writer, Prescott Art docent and delighted wife of Robert Kenneth Drew.

Burt Dubin is the developer of the *Speaking Success System*, a powerful instrument for helping aspiring and professional speakers position, package, promote and present themselves. "You are a master—an absolute master—I recommend your system wihtout reservation," says Joseph J. Charbonneau, CSP, CPAE. Burt may be reached at Personal Achievement Institute, 1 Speaking Success Road, Kingman, AZ 86402 or call 800-321-1225.

John Enright was born in Yakima, Washington, in 1927. He received his undergraduate degree from Yale and his graduate degree from UC Berkeley Graduate School in Psychology. He escaped the deadening effect of mindless behaviorism by meeting and studying with Fritz Perls. John created some of the "human potential" movement and took it around the world. Now he is learning to love while trying to write some poetry and protect the earth.

Kyoko Enright was born Kyoko Hosho in Tokyo, Japan, in July of 1964. She was an American exchange student for a year in Massachusetts. She graduated form Dokkyo University with a major in German. Kyoko was an international guide in Mexico, India and various parts of Africa. Her goal is to break the bonds of culture and habit, and become a free woman—as well as a cross-cultural cook!

Warren Farrell, Ph.D., is the author of the award-winning bestsellers *Why Men Are the Way They Are* and *The Myth of Male Power*. He is the only man in the U.S. ever elected three times to the board of directors of the National Organization for Women (NOW) in New York City. He conducts workshops for corporations, colleges and government agencies focused on getting the sexes and races to "walk a mile in each other's moccasins." (He figures that if he tries to get the sexes to understand each other, he'll always be employed!) All of Dr. Farrell's books are available in paperback from Putnam-Berkeley; information about his speaking and audio tapes can be obtained by calling 619-753-5000 or faxing him at 619-753-2436. Dr. Farrell lives in Encinitas, California.

Kathy O'Grady Fellows is happily teaching kindergarten in Newport-Mesa Unified School District. She's been cookin' up lessons for elementary grades in the Southern California area since 1965. She is the mother of 3 daughters and currently resides in Laguna Beach, California.

Pam Finger is a workshop facilitator and consultant who specializes in self-esteem and values-clarification issues. She is president and co-founder of Inner Trek, a training and consulting organization. She is also president of the Rochester chapter of the National Council on Self-Esteem. She may be contacted through Inner Trek, PO Box 32, Fairport, NY 14450 or by calling 716-223-0153 or by fax 716-223-0147.

Joan Fountain is a powerful and engaging trainer, speaker and writer with the ability to simultaneously captivate, motivate and educate audiences. She communicates from the heart and takes a hands-on approach to her subject matter, tackling sensitive and complex issues in thought-provoking workshops and presentations. Offering expert training in cultural diversity, sensitivity and awareness, she also addresses issues ranging from conflict resolution and burnout to case management, sexual harassment, team building and self-esteem. In addition to state, county, federal and other public sector clients, Joan Fountain has provided innovative consultation and training to The Westinghouse

Corporation, American Airlines, GTE and other Fortune 500 corporations. A sought-after keynote speaker, Joan Fountain has appeared as the guest of nationally syndicated television talk show hosts Oprah Winfrey, Phil Donahue, Sally Jesse Rafael, Montel Williams and Faith Daniels. Her inspirational new book, *Don't Get Me Started*, will be released in the Fall of 1995. Joan can be reached at 3104 O Street #220, Sacramento, CA 95816 or call 916-454-5412.

Norma Brandel Gibbs is a former mayor of Seal Beach and of Huntington Beach, California. She is Professor Emeritus of California State University, Long Beach where she specialized in mental hygiene and home, school and community studies. Norma founded Interval House, a home for victims of domestic violence. Much of her time is currently devoted to volunteer roles in civic endeavors. She enjoys giving workshops on how to live with yourself and like it! In demand as a speaker and facilitator, she may be reached at 17087 Westport Drive, Huntington Beach, CA or call 714-846-3247.

Caroline Goering is President of Turning Points, located in Blue Hill, Maine. She leads workshops in parent education and does child-care provider training. She also leads "Beauty from the Inside Out" workshops for individuals and small businesses. She can be reached at PO Box 355, Blue Hill, ME 04614 or call 207-374-2175.

Cyndi James Gossett is an accomplished actress/singer. Ms. Gossett has more than 30 television and film roles to her credit. Her original one-woman show, *The Hand of God,* is gaining acclaim as a fund-raiser for abuse centers nationwide. As an international nightclub performer she has been the opening act for both Rich Little and Jay Leno, and her versatility inspired Cristina Ferrare to select her as co-host of a daily talk show in Los Angeles.

Vaughn Greditzer has been a singer, model, teacher, painter, designer (her hand-painted silk fashions have been featured by Bergdorf Goodman, *Women's Wear Daily* and Princess Cruise Lines), mother (5 children—3 adopted), animal lover (at one point had more than 100) and has always been an avid cook. She lives two hours from Paris and may be reached at Bercheres, 28260 France.

Susie Gross is a native Californian who has filled her life with her love of art and beauty. She is a professional *trompe lóeil* artist, with works in homes and buildings throughout the United States, Canada and Mexico. She can be reached at her family compound at Willow Creek Farm in Templeton, California, where she and her family are developing a working vacation art school, by calling 805-237-0626.

Patty Hansen has her priorities straight—being Mom is number one. As the other half of the "Mark/Patty Team," she devotes her time between being Chief Financial Officer and trouble-shooter at M.V. Hansen & Associates, Inc., and full-time driver, caretaker and homework assistant to their two daughters, Elisabeth and Melanie. She also loves to squeeze in some time to garden, raise chickens and play on the beach. She is currently at work on her first book. She can be reached at PO Box 7665, Newport Beach, CA 92658 or by calling 714-759-9304.

Floren Harper modeled, sang and acted in her twenties. She grew up and discovered books, acquired degrees from Columbia University, taught speech and drama for 15 years, wrote on teaching theatre and helped create an English language arts curriculum,

Interaction with James Moffett. Now she is a painter and nascent activist. She can be reached at 21801 Ocean Vista Drive, Laguna Beach, CA 92677.

Natalie Hartanov Haughton is the author of four nationally distributed cookbooks: *The 5 in 10 Dessert Cookbook* (Hearst Books), *365 Great Chocolate Desserts* (HarperCollins), *365 Easy One Dish Meals* (Harper & Row) and *Cookies* (HP Books). Natalie has been food editor at the *Los Angeles Daily News* since 1976. She has judged numerous cooking competitions, including the National Chicken Cooking Contest, the 1982 Pillsbury Bake-Off, Gilroy Great Garlic Recipe Contest and Cook-off and International Chili Cook-off. Over the years, Natalie has won several awards for her food writing, including the Vesta Awards, General Foods Awards for Excellence in Nutrition Communications and the Newspaper Food Editors and Writers Food Writing Contest.

Kirby Howard has spent the last 20 years working in the travel industry in both the hotel and airline fields. She studies metaphysics and lives in an enchanted cottage near Dallas with five of her dear animal companions. She is a collector of rare people and stories. Kirby may be reached at 3806 Olympia, Irving, TX 75062 or call 214-252-6374.

Sharon Huffman is the founder of the Center for Enlightened Leadership, where she teaches inspired leadership and true empowerment. She coaches individuals to reach their full potential and live in balance while making a noble contribution to our world. Speaker, consultant and author, her work appears in *Women of Vision and Gratitude* by Louise Hay and Friends. She can be reached at PO Box 2194, Del Mar, CA 92014 or call 619-481-4181.

D. Trinidad Hunt is an international author, educator, speaker, corporate trainer and consultant. Her award-winning book, *Learning to Learn: Maximizing Your Performance Potential,* and audiocassette series have propelled numerous companies to organizational excellence. Trin speaks to that special place in each of us, inspiring us to direct our rare and unique energies in a significant way. Her message is straightforward and compelling. For further information call 800-707-ELAN or fax 808-239-2482, or write to Elan Enterprises at 47-430 Hui Nene Street, Kaneohe, HI 96744.

Ann Hyatt is a professional inspirational speaker, and co-author and author of seminars offering life skills in relationships and reaching life's purpose and dreams. Her teaching has been applauded for its delightful humor coupled with its down-to-earth method of making things simple, which reaches right into the heart. She can be reached at PO Box 1062, Maple Valley, WA 98038 or call 206-886-0159.

Cheewa James is a sought-after motivational speaker and expert in the field of communication, working with businesses and organizations to improve communication networks and to enhance client contact. Cheewa's professional speaking applies the age-old wisdom of the Native American to help meet the challenges of the 21st century. Her presentations center on the power of communication to build leadership and enhance business and personal relationships. She can be reached at 3330 Union Springs Way, Sacramento, CA 95827 or call 916-369-6616.

Susan Jeffers, Ph.D., has helped millions of people overcome their fears and move forward in life with confidence and love. She is the author of *Feel the Fear and Do It Anyway, Dare* to Connect, Opening Our Hearts to Men, The Journey from Lost to Found, Thoughts of Power and Love plus her *Fear-Less Series* of affirmation books and tapes *(Inner Talk for Peace of Mind, Inner Talk for a Confident Day* and *Inner Talk for a Love That Works)*. As well as being a best-selling author, she is a popular workshop leader and public speaker and has been a guest on many radio and television shows including numerous appearances on *Oprah!* She has also created many audiotapes on fear, relationships and personal growth.

Avril Johannes, born in England, lived 20 years in Alaska. A professional aviculturist, she has published short stories in *Bird Breeder, Alaska Magazine* and various newspapers. She has three grown children and is presently working on a book about Alaska. She can be reached at 8070 New Hope Road, Grants Pass, OR 97527.

Jeanne Jones is an internationally respected food consultant living in La Jolla, California, who specializes in recipe, menu and product development. She is the author of 25 cookbooks, including *Cook It Light Classics* (Macmillan, 1992), *Light and Hearty* (Crown, 1994) and *Cook It Light Desserts* (Macmillan, 1994). Known as the "Dear Abby" of the food world, she writes "Cook It Light," a syndicated column that reaches 30 million readers each week. As the acknowledged pioneer in spa cuisine, she has created menus for Canyon Ranch Fitness Resorts and Four Seasons Hotels. Jeanne is a frequent speaker on food and lifestyle topics for audiences ranging from chefs to physicians.

Ronald W. Jue, Ph.D., is a clinical psychologist with a private practice in Newport Beach, California, and is internationally known for his dynamic and powerful workshops in personal transformation, intuition and imagery. His work focuses on helping individuals integrate mind/body/spirit in their lives and work. He can be reached at PO Box 5805, Fullerton, CA 92635 or call 714-738-8889.

Oswald F. "Ozzie" Jurock, formerly President, Chairman and CEO of National Real Estate Service in Vancouver, had a distinguished 26-year career in the Canadian real estate industry. A native of Cologne, Germany, Mr. Jurock has addressed audiences throughout Canada, the U.S.A. and the Republic of China. He captured first place in the Practicing Industry Lay Writers Category of the annual Morguard Literary Awards Competition each time he entered the competition (1982 and 1992). As one of the most highly regarded authorities on real estate in Canada today, Mr. Jurock has been a member of almost every real estate association, council and board in British Columbia. Mr. Jurock now owns Jurock Publishing Ltd. and acts as publisher and chief editor of the monthly *Jurock's Real Estate Investor* newsletter and its companion weekly real estate fax service and hotline.

Irene Kassorla, Ph.D. is a best-selling author, lecturer and well-known media personality. In her international psychology practice, she treats patients by phone in Europe, Asia, Australia and throughout the United States. Her daily activities include frequent TV and radio appearances, lecturing and conducting in-person sessions with patients in Los Angeles. She can be reached by calling 310-205-0226.

Zoie Kaye is an independent training consultant and keynote speaker. Since 1993, Ms. Kaye's primary client has been SkillPath, whose independent consultants are rated the best in the field of training business people. Ms. Kaye specializes in presenting such programs as *Managing Skills for Women, Assertive Communication Skills* and *Coaching and*

Team Building. Her keynote speeches cover similar topics, with an emphasis on women's issues. Ms. Kaye can be reached at Instar Communications, 20 Sunnyside Avenue, Suite A-199, Mill Valley, CA 94941 or call 415-389-8841.

Sam Keen was overeducated at Harvard and Princeton and was a professor of philosophy and religion at various legitimate institutions before becoming a free-lance thinker, lecturer, seminar leader and consultant. He is the author of a dozen books, including *Fire in the Belly* and *Hymns to an Unknown God.* He was a contributing editor to *Psychology Today,* a co-producer of the award-winning *Faces of the Enemy* and the subject of a Bill Moyers PBS Special, *Your Mythic Journey with Sam Keen.* He has a marked disrespect for accepted boundaries, tired answers, uncritical ideologies and the sacred jargon of various professions. When not writing or traveling around the world lecturing and doing seminars on a wide range of topics on which he is not necessarily an expert but a skilled explorer, he fiddles with horses and growing things on his farm in the hills above Sonoma. Sam can be reached at 16331 Norrbom Road, Sonoma, CA 95476 or call 707-996-9010.

Mary Olsen Kelly is the co-owner (with her husband Don) of The Black Pearl Galleries, a chain of fine jewelry stores in Hawaii specializing in rare, exotic black pearls from Tahiti. She is also the co-author (again with Don) of *Finding Each Other, How to Attract Your Ideal Mate,* published by Simon and Schuster. She can be reached at 1142 Auahi Street, Suite 1714, Honolulu, HI 96814.

Kimberly Kirberger is a well-known jewelry designer currently living in Pacific Palisades, California. Her pieces sell in the finest stores in the country and are used in feature films and television shows such as *Melrose Place* and *Models, Inc.* For a list of stores that carry her jewelry or for further information, call 310-454-2197.

Art Linkletter has been a television and radio star for more than 60 years. He has won two Emmy Awards and received four Emmy nominations, a Grammy Award and ten honorary doctorate degrees. He has written 23 books. Art has served on President Nixon's National Advisory Council for Drug Abuse Prevention and on the Presidential Commission to Improve Reading in the United States. He can be reached at 8484 Wilshire Boulevard, Suite 205, Beverly Hills, CA 90211, call 213-658-7603 or fax 213-655-5173.

Bobbie Jensen Lippman is a prolific human-interest writer whose work has appeared in national and international publications. She hosts a daily radio program called "Bobbie's Beat on the Air," which is broadcast locally, plus statewide on Oregon Public Broadcasting and over-the-radio talking-book network in the midwest. Bobbie is involved with the visually impaired and is also very active in hospice work. She may be reached at 13650 South Coast Highway, South Beach, OR 97366 or call 503-867-3805.

Florence Littauer, C.S.P., C.P.A.E., is the president of CLASS Speakers, Inc., an international organization that trains, promotes and books speakers. She is a popular and inspirational speaker for both church and business groups and is the author of more than 20 books including her best-sellers, *Silver Boxes, Personality Plus* and *Dare to Dream.* She can be reached at CLASS, 1645 S. Rancho Santa Fe, #102, San Marcos, CA 92069 or call 800-433-6633.

Tony Luna is founder of Tony Luna Creative Services, a representation and consultation service for commercial artists. He is also an instructor at the Art Center College of Design in the field of creativity and business. Mr. Luna is a member of the Board of Directors of U.P. Inc., a non-profit organization dedicated to empowering young people through the arts by promoting talented youth into education and employment in the creative industries. Together with his wife Paula, Mr. Luna has co-authored *The Disaster Recovery Handbook* and instituted Disaster Recovery Services to assist survivors of disasters in their emotional and physical recovery. If you are interested in learning more about any of these areas of interest you may reach him at 819 North Bel Aire Drive, Burbank, CA 91501-1205 or call 818-842-5490 or online: Tonyluna@aol.com.

Dennis E. Mannering, CSP, has provided more than 2,500 presentations positively influencing the lives of thousands of people through his simple but direct method of getting to the heart of quality living and working. He incorporates stories of both family and business experiences to make his talks memorable and thought-provoking. Contact Dennis at 1-800-236-3445 for more information on his motivational, customer service, sales or teamwork programs.

Dick Martin's career in show business is much like cooking—you need the right ingredients. He had the desire, a great partner, Dan Rowan, a good agent and a lot of hard work. Rowan and Martin worked in night clubs for many years. Their first television break was hosting *The Dean Martin Summer Show*. This led to their own show called *Rowan and Martin's Laugh In*. When Martin's partner retired in 1975, he turned to directing. Directing is really like cooking: It's all in the prep—the better you do your preparation, the better the picture.

Betty Fobair McDermott, an internationally recognized leadership trainer in the fields of management, human relations and communications, facilitates innovative, positive changes within corporations and individuals. She works with American, European and Asian firms to develop creative teams to research and market consumer products. She co-authored *California Cooks!*, published by Ward-Ritchie Press and a Doubleday Book of the Month selection. You can reach her at 10303 Whipple Street, North Hollywood, CA 91602.

Linda McNamar is a writer and workshop facilitator. She holds a Bachelor's Degree in Education from Eastern Michigan University.

Carol Miller, president of Posh Parties and its corporate meal division, the Commissary, is renowned for creative event and party planning in Southern California. The Posh Parties' staff pride themselves on providing extraordinary culinary experiences, having served more than five million meals since 1979. Carol's world travels have given her a broad background, enabling her to adapt unusual cuisine's into contemporary menus. She can be reached at Posh Parties, 3500 W. Moore Street, Suite B, Santa Ana, CA 92704 or call 714-556-6480.

Chick Moorman is the owner and director of the *Institute for Personal Power*, a consulting firm dedicated to providing high-quality professional development activities for educators and parents. Having conducted 100 workshops on cooperative learning, enhancing self-esteem and developing positive attitudes, his mission is to help people experience a greater sense of personal power in their lives, so they can in turn empower others.

Ernie Nagamatsu is from Garden Grove, California, and grew up in a truck farming community. Ernie attended the University of Southern California, School of Dentistry, and also has an art background from UCLA and Otis Art Institute. As an avocation, he has done some freelance art work and taught various cooking classes in California and Hawaii. Ernie has also served for eight years on the governor-appointed California State Board of Dental Examiners and has a private dental practice in Los Angeles. Ernie's favorite food pastime is making bread and traveling the world to learn the ethnography of food. He recently learned about the food of Bhutan. Ernie can be reached at 1245 Wilshire Boulevard, Suite 903, Los Angeles, CA 90017 or call 213-481-1420.

Udana Power has been eating for years. In love with the way foods crunch and slurp and twirl around in her mouth, she has explored everything from gourmet to health to fast food and family holiday dining. Her explorations have led her to concoct various eclectic versions of well-known phenomena in the eating and eating-related fields. Faced with a screenwriting career that demands long, sustained and focused concentration as well as a singing career that requires charismatic energy and no phlegm, plus an acting career that requires surgery . . . ahem . . . excuse me: big tits, little butt and definition in the thighs—Udana has given up acting and is excelling stupendously in writing and singing. Watch for her upcoming feature films now in various stages of development or pre-production: *Don Juan, The Fawn, Pocket Woman, Les Fantastiques du New Orleans* and *The Sneaker Genie*—all brought to you by the CEO of the Waffle Club.

Bobbie Probstein is a writer and photographer whose primary interest is the interplay of body, mind and spirit to bring forth positive changes in any human condition. Her autobiography, *Return to Center,* is in its third printing. Her second book, *Healing Now,* has been widely praised and is invaluable for anyone affected by illness or preparing for surgery. Excerpts from Bobbie's work have been included in numerous collections. She may be reached at PO Box 3654, Dana Point, CA 92629.

Anne Cooper Ready writes screenplays and executive speeches. She also coaches clients for personal appearances and media interviews at her company, *Ready for Media,* headquartered in Santa Monica, California. Anne leaves enough time for crab feasts at Santa Monica's *Maryland Crab House* on 24th and Pico.

Naomi Rhode, RDH, CSP, CPAE, is immediate past president of the National Speakers Association and is known for her inspirational, dynamic speaking to both healthcare and general audiences. She is co-owner and vice president of SmartPractice, a marketing and manufacturing company that provides products and services to the healthcare industry worldwide. Naomi is the author of two inspirational gift books, *The Gift of Family—A Legacy of Love* and *More Beautiful Than Diamonds—The Gift of Friendship.* She can be reached at 3400 East McDowell, Phoenix, AZ 85008 or call 602-225-9090.

Nancy Richard-Guilford is a professional speaker specializing in interactive workshops on self-esteem, optimum performance and creating a joyful life. Known for her humor and practical strategies, she is the author of *Yikes! Time for Plan B.* You can contact Nancy at PO Box 24220, Ventura, CA 93002-4220 or call 805-648-6590.

Patti Rypinski moved in 1947, from Louisiana to Newport Beach, California, where she saw her first mountain! She immediately fell in love with what was then a sleepy little beach town. After marrying her high school sweetheart in 1961, Pat and her husband started several companies together including Armor All, a car-care chemical corporation of which Alan is chairman emeritus and where Pat is credited for naming the product which is now a household name. They are surrounded by three dogs, two cats and singing birds. She loves to garden, paint and entertain. She jumped at the chance to write about her beloved family.

Glenna Salsbury, C.S.P., C.P.A.E., graduated from Northwestern University in Evanston, Illinois, obtained her master's degree from UCLA and, 16 years later, earned a Master's of Theology from Fuller Seminary. In 1980 Glenna founded her own company, which provides keynote presentations and personal growth seminars. In her personal life, Glenna is married to Jim Salsbury, a former Detroit Lion and Green Bay Packer, and has three daughters. Call or write to obtain her powerful six-pack tape album entitled, *Passion, Power and Purpose*. She can be reached at 9228 North 64th Place, Paradise Valley, AZ 85253 or call 602-483-7732.

Gino Sky is the author of two novels: *Appaloosa Rising, The Legend of the Cowboy Buddha* and *Coyote Silk*; a collection of stories, *Near the Postcard Beautiful*; and five books of poetry—the most recent being *Spirit Bone*, published by Limberlost Press. His two novels will soon be published in Korea. He is currently living in Boise, Idaho, working on two novels and a new collection of stories. He is also the host of a radio show, *Poetry-in-Commotion*, for Boise State University's public radio station, KBSU.

Claudia Stromberg is a former interior designer, and gourmet store and cooking school owner. She and her husband Russ are pursuing a long-term dream by opening Rewards, a gallery featuring contemporary jewelry and sculpture from the finest artists of the American Southwest. Long-time collectors, they decided to put behind them the fast-paced, high-stress life they led in the Los Angeles area and chose the more relaxed lifestyle of Austin, Texas. They find working with artists from many cultures endlessly fascinating and being surrounded by beautiful works of art a real joy—their personal recipe for "Chicken Soup for the Soul."

Barbara Swain is a cookbook author, cooking teacher and speaker. Her specialty is "cooking for singles and couples," which is the subject of her latest book, *Intimate Dining—Memorable Meals for Two* (Fisher Books). Also, as a food stylist, Barbara prepares food for still and motion picture photography. She can be reached at 512 Continental Court, Pasadena, CA 91103 or call 818-796-6582.

Hazel Court Taylor was born in Birmingham, England. She starred in many British films and London Productions. The post-war *Curse of Frankenstein*, with Peter Cushing brought her international fame, and was followed by the classic CBS TV series *Dick and the Duchess* and the *Alfred Hitchcock Presents Show*. It was Edgar Allen Poe's horror films with Vincent Price that brought lasting recognition for her as the "Scream Queen." Today her time is spent sculpting in the sun in California, where she resides with her husband, actor/director Don Taylor.

Francis Xavier Trujillo, Ed.D., is a highly acclaimed speaker, educator, and writer. Known internationally as a deeply caring individual, Frank writes passionately about children and the important sacrifices and investments each of us can make in helping build a better future. President of ProTeach Publications, Frank's provocative posters grace the walls of thousands of schools and businesses in the United States. You can direct inquiries about poster catalogs or Frank's speaking to: ProTeach Publications, PO Box 19262, Sacramento, CA 95819 or call 916-737-1840.

Rama J. Vernon, president of the Center for International Dialogue, has organized more than 200 conferences, forums and exchanges between the United States and Russia. Founder of six successful non-profit organizations, including the magazine *Yoga Journal*, she is creator of the 1st Israeli-Arab-International Conference "Yoga for Peace: In the Middle East," Jerusalem 1995; "Uniting the Americas Conference," Costa Rica, 1992; and many other leadership conferences. A mother of five, Rama's background in Asian philosophy and East-West psychology inspires her unique approach to her position as co-director of the Institute for Peace and Conflict Resolution studies.

Sirah Vettese, Ph.D., is a counselor, health educator, writer, seminar leader and author. She is a consultant and spokesperson for Enchanté, Ltd., a family multi-media company that teaches the value of emotional literacy—the ability to acknowledge, accept and appropriately express emotions. Sirah is mother to Damien (22), Michael (19) and Shazara (12), and partner to Harold H. Bloomfield, M.D. (Yale-trained psychiatrist and best-selling author). Dr. Vettese can be contacted at Enchanté, PO Box 620471, Woodside, CA 94062 or call 1-800-473-2363.

Dottie Walters is the president of the Walters International Speakers bureau in California. She is the author of *The Greatest Speakers I Have Ever Heard*, featuring Jack Canfield and Mark Victor Hansen, and *Speak and Grow Rich,* with her daughter, Lilly. She is founder of The International Group of Agents and Bureaus and is the editor/publisher of *Sharing Ideas* news magazine—the largest in the world for paid professional speakers. She can be reached at PO Box 1120, Glendora, CA 91740 or call 818-335-8069 or fax 818-335-6127.

Carlos Warter, M.D., Ph.D., is the author of *Recovery of the Sacred,* and is a medical doctor and transpersonal psychotherapist based in Sedona, Arizona. Chilean born, he is founder and President of the World Health Foundation for Development and Peace for which he was awarded the U.N. Peace Messenger, and is a member of the American and International Association of Group Psychotherapy. Dr. Warter's dedication to holistic healing and personal growth has earned him many accolades, including the Pax Mundi Award. He has developed a new approach for awakening human potential based on ethics, creativity and global awareness. He is the author of several books in Spanish and English including *The Ebb and Flow of Living, Despertar* and *Soul Remembers.*

Ralph Waterhouse, a native of England, continues to traverse both continents as an accomplished painter. Self-taught, his efforts have been recognized by the Royal Society for the Protection of Birds and the World Wildlife Fund. Published both in Britain as well as in the United States, Ralph has focused his work on environmental and endangered landscapes of California. His clients include former Prime Minister Margaret Thatcher. Ralph has had a gallery for more than ten years and represents some of the top national artists. The gallery shows work from highly rendered realism to impressionism. He may be reached at Waterhouse Gallery, 1114 State Street, Santa Barbara, CA 93101 or call 805-962-8885.

Patricia Wayne currently is president of the PTA for the Saddleback School District and is involved with working on reform in public education. She holds an M.F.A. in Performing Arts Administration and encourages schools to enhance children's self-esteem through the arts. She owns her own network distribution business and helps others achieve their personal and financial goals by creating more time and money in their lives. Pat can be reached at Pathways, Inc., 24831 Via Princesa, Lake Forest, CA 92630 or call 714-455-3357.

Theodore S. Wentworth (Ted) is, so far, a husband, father, rancher, pilot, yachtsman, bird watcher, writer and attorney. He has more than 30 years experience as a trial lawyer specializing in human rights, medical law and consumer litigation. He is featured in *Who's Who in America*. He may be reached at 4631 Teller Ave., Suite 100, Newport Beach, CA 92660.

Bettie B. Youngs, Ph.D., Ed.D., is one of the nation's most respected voices on the role of self-esteem and its effects on health and wellness, vitality, achievement and productivity in both the homeplace and workplace. She is the author of 14 books published in 27 languages, including *How to Develop Self-Esteem in Your Child: 6 Vital Ingredients, Safeguarding Your Teenager from the Dragons of Life, Stress and Your Child: Helping Kids Cope with the Strains and Pressures of Life* and *Values from the Heartland*. She can be reached at Bettie B. Youngs & Associates, 3060 Racetrack View Drive, Del Mar, CA 92014.

Susan Zolla and **Kathy Jensen** own and operate the Channel Road Inn in Santa Monica, California. The two have the pleasure of providing excellent lodging and breakfast to guests that range from celebrities to honeymooners, individuals seeking solitude to family reunions. Before operating the inn, both women served many meals to their own families and friends. They have re-created the best of their home lives to create a home at the Channel Road Inn for all who pass through its doors. They can be reached at the Channel Road Inn, 219 W. Channel Road, Santa Monica, CA 90402 or call 310-459-1920.

Thunder Cake by Patty Hansen. Reprinted by permission of Patty Hansen. ©1995 Patty Hansen.

The Pheasant by Bettie B. Youngs. Reprinted by permission of Health Communications, Inc. from *Values from the Heartland* by Bettie B. Youngs. ©1995 Bettie B. Youngs.

Arroz con Leche by Rosemarie Cortez. Reprinted by permission of Rosemarie Cortez. ©1995 Rosemarie Cortez.

Nanny's Raisin Nut Cake by Barbara DeAngelis. Reprinted by permission of Barbara DeAngelis. ©1995 Barbara DeAngelis.

Grandma's Thick "Everything" Soup by Irene C. Kassorla. Reprinted by permission of Irene C. Kassorla. ©1995 Irene C. Kassorla.

How I Learned to Love Tomatoes by Jeanne Jones. Reprinted by permission of Jeanne Jones. ©1995 Jeanne Jones.

Utah Pioneer Scones by Susie Gross. Reprinted by permission of Susie Gross. ©1995 Susie Gross.

Grammy Rufi's Country Cooking by Diana von Welanetz Wentworth. Reprinted by permission of Diana von Welanetz Wentworth. ©1995 Diana von Welanetz Wentworth.

Bukda, A Braided Bohemian Bread by Pat Wayne. Reprinted by permission of Pat Wayne. ©1995 Pat Wayne.

Gagi's Gumbo by D. Trinidad Hunt. Reprinted by permission of Trinidad Hunt. ©1995 Trinidad Hunt.

Grandma Yehle's Summer Kitchen by Pam Finger. Reprinted by permission of Pam Finger. ©1995 Pam Finger.

Almost Grandma's Apple Pie by Kirby Howard. Reprinted by permission of Kirby Howard. ©1995 Kirby Howard.

From Dancer to Cook by Patti Rypinski. Reprinted by permission of Patti Rypinski. ©1995 Patti Rypinski.

Homemade Children by Naomi Rhode. Reprinted by permission of Naomi Rhode. ©1995 Naomi Rhode.

The Sound of Snowflakes and Warm Cranberry Pie by Avril Johannes. Reprinted by permission of Avril Johannes. ©1995 Avril Johannes.

Happy Hooligan—Dog Gourmet by Floren Harper. Reprinted by permission of Floren Harper. ©1995 Floren Harper.

Our Italian-American Kitchen by Carol Miller. Reprinted by permission of Carol Miller. ©1995 Carol Miller.

Dad's Chicken Cacciatore by Sam Keen. Reprinted by permission of Sam Keen. ©1995 Sam Keen.

The Pheasant by Bettie B. Youngs. Reprinted by permission of Health Communications, Inc. from *Values from the Heartland* by Bettie B. Youngs. ©1995 Bettie B. Youngs.

A Spiced Chocolate Applesauce Cake for Dad by Claudia Stromberg. Reprinted by permission of Claudia Stromberg. ©1995 Claudia Stromberg.

My First Cooking Class by Dick Martin. Reprinted by permission of Dick Martin. ©1995 Dick Martin.

Foule and the Art of Living by John Catenacci. Reprinted by permission of John Catenacci. ©1995 John Catenacci.

Family Secret Sesame Chicken by Ronald W. Jue. Reprinted by permission of Ronald W. Jue. ©1995 Ronald W. Jue.

Health Nut Pancakes by Rama J. Vernon. Reprinted by permission of Rama J. Vernon. ©1995 Rama J. Vernon.

Beer Bread by Charles Champlin. Reprinted by permission of Charles Champlin. ©1995 Charles Champlin.

The One that Got Away by Ralph Waterhouse. Reprinted by permission of Ralph Waterhouse. ©1995 Ralph Waterhouse.

Long Beach, British Columbia, Salmon Supreme by Val van de Wall. Reprinted by permission of Val van de Wall. ©1995 Val van de Wall.

Tomato Mix-Up by Art Linkletter. Reprinted by permission of Art Linkletter. ©1995 Art Linkletter.

Things My Father Taught Me, Including "Cabin Stew" by Bobbie Jensen Lippman. Reprinted by permission of Bobbie Jensen Lippman. ©1995 Bobbie Jensen Lippman.

Elvis Pie by Diana von Welanetz Wentworth. Reprinted by permission of Diana von Welanetz Wentworth. ©1995 Diana von Welanetz Wentworth.

In Hella's Kitchen by Sharon Huffman. Reprinted by permission of Sharon Huffman. ©1995 Sharon Huffman.

Friendship Forever Fondue by Sharon Civalleri. Reprinted by permission of Sharon Civalleri. ©1995 Sharon Civalleri.

Cyndi's Quickie Quiche by Cyndi James Gossett. Reprinted by permission of Cyndi James Gossett. ©1995 Cyndi James Gossett.

The Finnish Connection by Dennis Mannering. Reprinted by permission of Dennis Mannering. ©1995 Dennis Mannering.

Cooking for a Friend Is More than Just Feeding a Friend by Barbara Swain. Reprinted

Sarson Ka Saag by Rita and Mallika Chopra. Reprinted by permission of Rita and Mallika Chopra. ©1995 Rita and Mallika Chopra.

The Wooden Spoon by Tony Luna. Reprinted by permission of Tony Luna. ©1995 Tony Luna.

What on Earth Is Shoo-Fly Pie Anyway? by Mary Helen Livingston. Reprinted with permission from *The Best of Guideposts* published by Guideposts Books.

Magical Vegetarian Moussaka by Sirah Vettese. Reprinted by permission of Sirah Vettese. ©1995 Sirah Vettese.

Reunion by Burt Dubin. Reprinted by permission of Burt Dubin. ©1995 Burt Dubin.

Salmon Wellington, Chez Jo by Ozzie Jurock. Reprinted by permission of Ozzie Jurock. ©1995 Ozzie Jurock.

The Case of the Missing Chocolate by Diana von Welanetz Wentworth. Reprinted by permission of Diana von Welanetz Wentworth. ©1995 Diana von Welanetz Wentworth.

Love from Afar by Diana von Welanetz Wentworth. Reprinted by permission of Diana von Welanetz Wentworth. ©1995 Diana von Welanetz Wentworth.

Twice in a Lifetime by Rhonda Nielsen Bisnar. Reprinted by permission of Rhonda Nielsen Bisnar. ©1995 Rhonda Nielsen Bisnar.

Working Miracles for the Judge by Andrea Bell. Reprinted by permission of Andrea Bell. ©1995 Andrea Bell.

A Love Story with Recipes by Diana von Welanetz Wentworth. Reprinted by permission of Diana von Welanetz Wentworth. ©1995 Diana von Welanetz Wentworth.

Egg Casserole Chimay. Recipe adapted from an idea by Flo Braker. It is reprinted from *Celebrations* by Diana and Paul von Welanetz (J.P. Tarcher).

Sweet Revenge by Diana von Welanetz Wentworth. Reprinted by permission of Diana von Welanetz Wentworth. ©1995 Diana von Welanetz Wentworth.

Somebody Slept in My Hair! by Diana von Welanetz Wentworth. Reprinted by permission of Diana von Welanetz Wentworth. ©1995 Diana von Welanetz Wentworth.

The Great Horseradish Caper by Theodore Wentworth. Reprinted by permission of Theodore Wentworth. ©1995 Theodore Wentworth.

Tooty Toots by Diana von Welanetz Wentworth. Reprinted by permission of Diana von Welanetz. ©1995 Diana von Welanetz Wentworth.

¿Hay Huevos? by Diana von Welanetz Wentworth. Reprinted by permission of Diana von Welanetz Wentworth. ©1995 Diana von Welanetz Wentworth.

Huevos Diablos reprinted from *The Pleasure of Your Company* by Diana and Paul von Welanetz (Atheneum).

Happy New Year by Chick Moorman. Reprinted by permission of Chick Moorman. ©1995 Chick Moorman.

A *Party Idea That Could Change Your Life* by Susan Jeffers. Reprinted by permission of Susan Jeffers. ©1995 Susan Jeffers.

Trim-the-Tree Vision Party by Diana von Welanetz Wentworth. Reprinted by permission of Diana von Welanetz Wentworth. ©1995 Diana von Welanetz Wentworth.

The Best Birthday by Mary Olsen Kelly. Reprinted by permission of Mary Olsen Kelly. ©1995 Mary Olsen Kelly.

The Ultimate Birthday Party by Mark Victor Hansen. Reprinted by permission of Mark Victor Hansen. ©1995 Mark Victor Hansen.

Thanksgiving at Eagle's Ridge Ranch by Diana von Welanetz Wentworth. Reprinted by permission of Diana von Welanetz Wentworth. ©1995 Diana von Welanetz Wentworth.

Recipe Index

455